# Abraham's God

*The Origin and History of the Beliefs of Jews, Christians, and Muslims*

# Abraham's God

*The Origin and History of the Beliefs of Jews,
Christians, and Muslims*

*John W. Dickerson*

MOUNTAIN ARBOR
PRESS
Alpharetta, Georgia

Paperback ISBN: 978-1-63183-680-0
Hardcover ISBN: 978-1-63183-681-7
ePub ISBN: 978-1-63183-682-4
Mobi ISBN: 978-1-63183-682-1

Library of Congress Control Number: 2019913103

Printed in the United States of America          0 9 5 1 9

∞This paper meets the requirements of ANSI/NISO Z39.48-1992 (Permanence of Paper)

# Contents

**Islam**

**Abraham's God after Four Thousand Years**

# Introduction

F our thousand years ago, a man named Abraham[1] was commanded by his God to g*et out of your country, From your family And from your father's house, To a land that I will show you* (Gen. 12:1).[2] Abraham's God has guided human history ever since, as Jews, Christians, and Muslims have followed his commands.

A century ago, Christianity governed over 80% of all of humanity through its domination of Western Civilization.[3] Today in synagogues, churches, and mosques, over half of humanity proclaim Abraham's God as their God.[4] By 2050, Jewish, Christian, and Islamic believers are expected to add over two billion new believers who will then be over 60% of the world's

---

[1] While there is no firm consensus, based on the account in Genesis 14 and the 1974 discovery of the Ebla tablets, a reasonable range of dates for Abraham is 2300 to 2000 BC. "The Real Story of the Ebla Tablets: Ebla and the Cities of the Plain." D.N. Freedman, *Biblical Archaeologist* 41, no. 4:143–164. (1978).

[2] Abraham is known to Muslims as Ibrahim. The story of his migration out of Ur to Egypt and Canaan in the Qur'an is similar to the Bible presentation.

[3] *Why Did Europe Conquer the World?* Philip T. Hoffman Princeton University Press 2015 p. 2

[4] "The Future of World Religions: Population Growth Projections, 2010-2050" The Pew Forum on Religion & Public Life. Pew Research Center. April 2, 2015 http://www.pewforum.org/2015/04/02/religious-projections-2010-2050/

population.[5]   The religions of Abraham's God provided the common culture foundation for much of Western Civilization and are the cultural framework for understanding the current chaos in our social, political and economic structures. The origin and history of the beliefs in Abraham's God are then an essential primer for understanding the core culture of most of humanity. Understanding the common core of beliefs may allow Jews, Christians and Muslims to find policies for a peaceful future.

*Abraham's God: The Origin and History of the Beliefs of Jews, Christians, and Muslims* is Volume One which starts at the beginning of human existence and ends in the 9th century when Christianity and Islam had become the hegemonic powers of Europe, the Middle East, and North Africa. The Second Volume, *Abraham's Devil: The History of Evil in Judaism, Christianity, and Islam and the Effects on the 21st Century*, will continue the story of how the religions of Abraham's God have led us to the cultural and political turmoil we face today.

*Abraham's God* and *Abraham's Devil* are not books on religion for the religious. They are stories of the human struggle to find meaning in life and define God's role in human existence. The result of that struggle is that the beliefs of three people—an ancient desert nomad, a peasant Jew, and an Arab trader—have evolved into the entangled faiths of Judaism, Christianity, and Islam, are now professed by half of mankind!

From the beginning of human existence, people believed that every facet of nature was determined by a god: rain for their crops, food for their families, diseases, children, death, floods, and war. Everything depended on some god: a being whose irritation or indulgence meant scarcity or abundance, suffering or sustenance, pain or pleasure. People worshipped and sacrificed to their gods, they fought and killed for their gods, they

---

[5] "The Future of World Religions: Population Growth Projections, 2010-2050" *The Pew Forum on Religion & Public Life.* Pew Research Center. April 2, 2015

committed unspeakable atrocities in the name of their gods, and they asked their gods for sanction and forgiveness. Over the earliest of human millennia, only the names of those gods changed.

Among the many was Abraham's God, believed as the One God who created the universe and formed humans with separate souls that survive death and exist forever. The One God who created humans with a free will to perform great good as well as evil, but the One God who offers forgiveness and redemption from their sins. The One God who will send an emissary to end time, resurrect the dead, and pass final judgement. The One God who will consign each human to everlasting bliss in heaven or condemn them to eternal torment in hell. Jews, Christians, and Muslims together share these fundamental elements of faith in One God—Abraham's God.

While they agree on these fundamentals of faith, they disagree on all else, from sin and salvation to ritual and redemption. Each claims the true path to paradise in the next life while creating a hell for many in this life. Each claims peace, yet none brings peace. Each extols harmony for humanity but allows hostility and hatred.

This book is not about sin and salvation, nor the rituals of redemption in Judaism, Christianity, and Islam. Very few pages will be spent on those topics. Nor is it about which path or ritual is right or wrong. *Abraham's God* is the story of how those roots of agreed fundamental faith were first formed in Judaism and how Christianity and Islam each grafted on to those roots and became fully formed, independent, yet deeply integrated religions.

The story in *Abraham's God* begins with the earliest humans in dark ages past and ends in the Dark Ages. By then, Christianity and Islam had fully separated from Judaism, developed their own theologies, and were hegemonic powers: Christianity ruling

Western Civilization from the Dardanelles to the Pyrenees and Islamic Civilization ruling from Spain and Morocco to the borders of India and China. *Abraham's God* will be best understood by those familiar with the major stories in the Bible or Qur'an, as well as a general familiarity with history.

The second book, *Abraham's Devil*, will continue the story of the struggle to define God's relationship with evil and how that has shaped today's societies. Islam and Christianity will clash in the Crusades, and Christians will fight Christians as the Reformation detonates the theology of the Roman Catholic Church. Islam will become the Ottoman Empire and devolve in the late 19th and early 20th centuries and then find a spectacular resurgence. Within all that is the theme of evil and the Devil and his demise, which is at the core of our 21st century issues and division.

*Abraham's God* and *Abraham's Devil* together are not just a history of three of the world's most important religions. History is often thought of as a sequence of names and dates and battles and wars, with today being the culmination of those things. There is a standing philosophical question as to whether history is a set of random events or if history is nudged this way or that by other larger forces. Martin Luther King is famously quoted as saying, "The arc of history is long but bends towards justice."[6] The contention of these books is that Abraham's God has nudged the long arc of history to shape our world, and that Abraham's Devil continues to nudge history and shape our future. This is not to presume that there is a God or gods plotting human fate—that is a matter of faith—but rather that the ideas of faith, once absorbed

---

[6] King first used this quote in an article "The Gospel Messenger, Out of the Long Night" in the *Official Organ of the Church of the Brethren* published February 8, 1958 by the General Brotherhood Board, Elgin, Illinois. p. 14. However, he used it in quotation marks, and is believed to have been quoting Theodore Parker a early 19th century Unitarian minister. See https://quoteinvestigator.com/2012/11/15/arc-of-universe/#note-4794-8

into the very being of a society, will continue to shape that society for many generations.

*Abraham's God* is the history of the ideas that have guided the arc of the human experience and formed Western society. Powerful ideas that have echoed across the centuries as they drove human experience. In 2010, I visited Bethlehem and saw posters and billboards of Islamic mothers celebrating the martyrdom of their sons and daughters who had died while killing Jews in the Intifada. Near Bethlehem, 2200 years earlier, a Jewish mother proclaimed her pride for her sons' deaths in another intifada. A Jewish mother and Muslim mother twenty-two centuries apart, each celebrating the horrific deaths of their children in the name of Abraham's God—tragic and violent stories of Abraham's God nudging history across the centuries.

Mohamed Atta flew his plane into the World Trade Center because of his absolute faith in the God of Abraham,[7] just as others across the centuries committed horrific violence because of their absolute faith in the God of Abraham. The 21st century clash between Islam and the West brings urgency to the understanding of the origins and history of Abraham's God and how Judaism, Christianity, and Islam have come to believe what they believe.

I am neither a politician, nor a professor, nor a preacher, so there could be a place for me in heaven. Nor am I a professional writer, so do not expect the polished professionalism of that class.[8] What I will tell you is simply what I have learned through my study over the long course of my life, about which you should know some things.

---

[7] This is made unquestionably clear in his last message the night before the attack. Copies can be found in many places, including
https://www.theguardian.com/world/2001/sep/30/terrorism.september113

[8] One sin committed in this regard is the formatting of footnotes, and horror of horrors, there is an occasional citation from a website. Although the book has been professionally edited, I apologize for any typos, punctuation, syntax errors or grammatical constructs, and hope they will not be too distracting.

Religion was always integral to my life. As a young boy, I went to church regularly with my family at Bethlehem Lutheran Church in Fort Wayne, Indiana, and attended its grade school. I learned all the usual Bible stories and participated in the services and rituals, such as being Joseph or a shepherd in the Christmas pageant or singing in the children's choir. These were not side events; rather, they were very much a part of my life.

At some point, I became vaguely aware that while almost everyone went to a church, not all churches were alike. There were Catholics, my grandparents were Methodists, and there were some other people called Jews. I'd never even heard of Islam back then. I knew about Heaven and Hell and was told that we were on the path to Heaven, but maybe some of those others were going to Hell. My repeating this to a Catholic neighbor created a loud rift, which went away after a few weeks. Similar disputes did not easily dissipate and became the source of vicious violence in centuries past.

I took religion seriously, memorizing most of the key elements of the Lutheran Catechism, and the supporting Bible passages from the King James version. As a "learned" Bible scholar, I was selected to speak to the congregation on behalf of our class at our 8th grade confirmation. My religious studies continued when I attended Concordia Lutheran High School.

There is a reason Matthew 18:3-4 says that you need to believe like a child to enter the kingdom of Heaven.[9] Children, for the most part, believe what they are told, but by high school they ask questions. I became more inquisitive, especially when I was exposed to people from other religions. Catholics seemed abundant in the neighborhood where we had moved. One of them was Bruce Patterson. He became my best friend and we had "debates" on the distinctions between Catholics and Lutherans.

---

[9] KJV: *Verily I say unto you, except ye be converted, and become as a little child, ye shall not enter the kingdom of heaven.*

Neither of us knew very much about the doctrines of our religions, but I was prompted by our discussions to learn more, if for no other reason than to better Bruce in our debates.

Dr. Armin Oldsen was my high school religion teacher. He was famous among Lutherans. In the early '50s, he was the voice of the *Lutheran Hour*, a weekly radio show that was the precursor to Billy Graham and TV Evangelism.[10] If he didn't know everything about religion, then who did? In his class, I began asking questions. Things like, "If God is all knowing, and knows I am going to Heaven or Hell, what difference does it make what I do?" or one that Bruce and I struggled with, "How do we know Lutherans are right and Catholics are wrong?" Or vice-versa. I asked a lot of questions in class, many that stemmed from the debate between those two 16-year-old Lutheran and Catholic theologians. One day I found a note taped to my high school locker that read, "Dr. Oldsen would like to see you in his office." Now that was truly a command from God.

Dr. Oldsen complimented me on my enthusiasm for wanting to understand and suggested that my questions went beyond the general level of the class and that he would appreciate if I kept them a little more to myself. He then humorously said that he had been studying religion for a very long time and that even he didn't know everything. "Someday," he advised, "you'll know and understand a great deal more, but then there may not be answers for everything; some things simply must be accepted on faith alone."[11]

---

[10] Dr. Oldsen was the principal speaker between 1951 and 1953. Some of his important sermons can be found at http://www.lutheranhour.org/history.htm

[11] Decades after the fact, I cannot be sure those were his exact words, but I am sure they were close. In the early 60s I had frequent contact with the esteemed man prior to attending Concordia. My father was an architect and was involved in several church construction projects with Dr. Oldsen. He was the Pastor for the Clear Lake Chapel where our family attended summer services. My familiarity with him may have emboldened my questions and his private admonition to tone them down.

But if we blindly accept the faith handed to us, if we do not examine faith, how can we be certain that our faith is not false? Accepting the faith handed to you brings conflict with those who are handed a different faith. Those who say we should set faith aside or keep it to ourselves and simply accept the differences between faiths are naive. History has mountains of bodies and our headlines continue to scream of conflicts in faith. Islam versus everyone, Israel and the Palestinians, Shiites' rule over Sunnis, the history of anti-Semitism, Protestant England ruling over Irish Catholics, Hindus versus Muslims, the Lebanese and Sudanese civil wars, the Thirty Years' War, the Crusades, and on back to the Israeli-Canaanite Wars. And these are but a few of the religiously fueled wars of history where violent deaths are measured in the tens of thousands. The arguments, violence, and bickering through the centuries between Judaism, Christianity, and Islam extends to today's political fights. Legalizing abortion and gay marriage or requiring insurance coverage for birth control are simply extended religious arguments. Religious strife is ubiquitous. Faith must be examined, and its origins and history explored, if ways to reconcile the divides are to be found.

I have spent over fifty years now attempting to follow the path of a philosopher—someone whose aim is to understand and explain the nature of life, existence, and even faith. Not full time, of course—there was a family with four children to nurture, a career to build, and eventually many grandchildren to enjoy. Not in scholastic manner, but through extensive reading, travel, continuous questioning, studying, discussing, and always asking myself: *Why? How? How did a religion, based on a minor peasant in rural Galilee, come to captivate the culture of Western civilization for 2000 years? Why have Jews been so vilified throughout the centuries? Why has the religion of Islam vehemently reemerged? Why does their common God of Abraham cause or allow vast human suffering?* And today we face more immediate critical questions. *How can faith alone cause people to fly planes into buildings, plant bombs in crowds, and shoot innocent children? How have the religions of Abraham's God become the hegemonic empires of human culture and politics that have dominated human existence for over thirteen centuries?*

After fifty years of thought and study, I do know and understand a great deal more than that young boy sitting in Dr. Oldsen's office. Half of the world's population may declare themselves as Jews, Christians, or Muslims, but very few have any knowledge of the origin and history of their faiths. The vast majority unquestioningly accept by faith alone the ancient beliefs and shibboleths, oblivious of their origin or history. Others cling heedlessly to their faith, with the results being conflicts, disputes, and violence between faiths. Knowing how the religions of Jews, Christians, and Muslims were formed and evolved is essential to understanding today's discord, and a potential pathway to a peaceful future, however distant.

First and foremost, I am writing book for my grandchildren. They will grow up in a very messy world with little grasp of how religions became ingrained in the society of their ancestors and begot the world in which they live. I write for those who like myself, possess a curiosity and desire to learn how these great world religions came to be and created the societies in which we live. Finally, I am writing for those who see an empty world and wish to learn how generations long-past approached the questions of life and embedded their answers into the religions of most of the world's people. Perhaps in all of that, there are ideas for a better future for humanity.

Almost all the questions of the ancient humans have been answered. You—yes you—would be praised and worshipped for having the answers to rain, and storms, earthquakes, the sun and stars, and most of the questions of life. Yet many questions remain, questions still unanswered on life and its meaning. We have bitten into the fruit and eaten of the Tree of Knowledge. For good or for evil, there is no turning back.

Not that there are answers for everything, but for me at least, many things are much clearer. The God of a desert nomad, a peasant Jew, and an Arab trader guided the arc of Western history and continues to impact the issues of today. Over half of the world's people believe that One God is the all-powerful creator of the universe and all that is in it. They all believe that humans possess a soul that survives death and will exist eternally in paradise or punishment. They all believe these things without knowing how these ideas were begotten. My hope is that this book, *Abraham's God,* will make clearer *The Origin and History of the Beliefs of Jews, Christians, and Muslims* for you as well.

# In the Beginning - Judaism

# Chapter One – Ex *Nihilo*

Have you ever wondered when religion began? Muhammad started Islam long after Paul initiated Christianity, and long before then it was Moses and Judaism, and all three of them go back to Abraham. But what came before him? Before the Egyptian and Assyrian gods and the others all around the world—Mayans, Hindus, Buddhists, Egyptians, and many others? Long before people could even write, more than 5000 years ago, what did people believe?

In the mountains of southeastern Turkey, close to the Syrian border, is Göbekli Tepe. Although the ruins have been known since the 1960s, no one knew what they were. Beginning in the late 1990s, a German archeologist, Klaus Schmidt, began to seriously study the area. Using a variety of dating techniques, Göbekli Tepe was found to be 11,000 years old. Built at the very beginning of human civilization, Göbekli Tepe is the oldest known place of worship. It is known as the First Temple,[12] the place where 7000 years before Abraham, 9000 years before Jesus, and 9600 years before Muhammad, people were

---

[12] http://www.smithsonianmag.com/history/gobekli-tepe-the-worlds-first-temple-83613665/

worshipping gods. Since the dawn of humanity, humans have been seeking a god in their lives!

At Göbekli Tepe, numerous carved images of creatures are believed to be a part of the religious rites held there.[13] In other places, even older human relics have been found. Sculptures of pregnant women carved from reindeer antlers, thought to have religious significance for fertility, have been dated to 32,000 years ago.[14] So, just who were the people of Göbekli Tepe worshipping? Who was the god behind the fertility talisman? Who were the gods of the ancient people found around the world?

Every tribe and society in every corner of the earth had a pantheon of gods.[15] In the ancient stone walls of Jericho were found skulls buried in a way that suggests ancestor worship[16]; in Australia, the spirits of the Tapu; in New Zealand, the Atau spirits of nature; in Hawaii, the war god Ku; in Africa, the star worship of the Dogon people; in North America, the Totems, the blood sacrifices of the Aztecs, and the worship of the Incan Sun god Inti, and on and on.[17] Without a written record, we can only guess the meanings of the carvings, the stones, the altars, amulets, monuments, and burial grounds that are found in every ancient civilization. In Western Europe alone there are an estimated 50,000 megaliths dating from over 5000 years ago.[18] Everywhere archeologists look, they find indications of some form of religious worship. Each one seems to signify some belief in a

---

[13] *The Social Conquest of Earth* Edward O Wilson, (Liveright; 2012) p. 103

[14] "The History of Religion" Karen Farrington, (Barnes and Noble, 2001) p. 14

[15] Except perhaps for the Indus River Civilization discovered in 1920. It consisted of over 1000 towns located along 1000 miles along the Indus River. The Indus Civilization flourished from 3500 to 1900BC. "Despite almost a century of subsequent excavation, no self-evident religious structures have been found at any Indus site...." *The Indus: Lost Civilizations* Andrew Robinson, (Reaktion Books, 2015) Kindle Edition Loc 1598

[16] *The First Cities* Dora Jane Hamblin, (Time Life Books, 1973) pp. 38-39

[17] *The History of Religion* Karen Farrington, (Barnes and Noble, 2001) pp. 12-26

[18] This number is widely quoted including in "European Prehistory: A Survey, Milisauskas", Sarunas editors, (Springer Science & Business Media, 2011) p. 226

supernatural spirit world. From the famous Stonehenge to simple altars used for cremation, "They are the places of the gods."[19] Long before God commanded Abraham to leave Ur, humans had begotten their gods.

Caves have been discovered in Hungary and China where humans used fire 400,000 years ago.[20] By 50,000 years ago, archeological records show that humans had mastered the basic skills to make tools, build shelters, and make clothes.[21] By 35,000 years ago, people were painting in caves in many corners of the world. Clearly people were communicating with language and had acquired the conscious processes that separates humanity from the animal kingdom.[22] Thousands of years later, Rene' Descartes offered, "I think, therefore I am" as the essence of the self, of being human. In that common sense of understanding, 2500 generations before Descartes, man had begun to think.[23] Man had become human.

But what does it mean to think, to be human? When you get up in the morning and are brushing your teeth or making breakfast, you go about tasks with little conscious thought, breaking eggs, pouring coffee, making the bed, opening the toothpaste tube, etc. But while you are unconsciously accomplishing those tasks, you may also be consciously thinking, *Make sure the kids have sweaters, it's cold out today* or *I need to make a dental appointment* or *call mother.* Or you might even be

---

[19] *The History of Religion* Karen Farrington, (Barnes and Noble, 2001) pp. 12-13. In which the quote is from "Gods of the Earth" by Michael Jordon.

[20] *A History of the World* Hugh Thomas, (Harper and Row) p. 6

[21] *The Ascent of Man* J. Bronowski, (Little Brown & Co, 1973) p. 46

[22] The conscious skills through which humans developed language, shelter, tools, megaliths, and eventually smart phones clearly differentiate humans from animals. This philosophical question has its own rich literature which is far beyond the scope of this book.

[23] Many have discussed this concept. Examples can be found in *The Brain* by Richard M. Restak, MD (Warner Books) pp. 234 -235 and in *How the Mind Works* by Steven Pinker (WW Norton and Company, 1997) p. 561

trying to analyze the problem of conscious thought! While doing those things, you are doing something that no other creature is known to do; you are having conscious thoughts. You are being human.[24]

Now, try, in your conscious thought, to imagine the era when human consciousness had barely risen over its rivals of the animal kingdom. Imagine you are one of those first, newly conscious humans. With consciousness comes the ability for you and your small band to communicate better; it allows you to better outwit your prey and your enemies; it helps you to make better tools for killing, cooking, and building. You have more meat and other foods; you wear clothes and build shelter to protect yourself from the weather. In short, you and your tribe lead a more robust life. You live longer, you are stronger, and you have more children who learn to do more and better things. And you have more time to think.[25]

Your conscious mind now begins to notice patterns: the rising and setting of the sun and the moon, the coming and goings of the seasons, the movement of animal herds. You notice that some things make you sick while others do not. You see relationships between events. You recognize that certain rocks, when struck together, cause sparks that will start fires, that seeds falling on the ground are where plants grow, and that chewing certain plants makes you feel different. You hear the thunder and see the rain, the lightning, the stars, the rising and setting of the sun, and

---

[24] The beginning of human consciousness, indeed its very existence is a much-debated topic in philosophy and neuropsychology. Many books have been written on it and its evolution. Steven Pinker talks extensively about it in his book *How the Mind Works*, particularly on pages 131 to 148. *From Brains to Consciousness?* is a selection of essays on the subject, edited by Steven Rose. Julian James in his famous book *The Origins of Consciousness in the Breakdown of the Bi-Cameral Mind* offers a compelling version of the rise of consciousness through the evolution of the corpus callosum. And Daniel Dennett in his *Consciousness Explained* offers his detailed "multiple drafts" model. And there are many other theories including those involving God.

[25] *The Ascent of Man* J. Bronowski, (Little Brown & Co; 1973) p. 11

everything that surrounds you. You observe life itself: fertility, disease, war, quakes, famine, and death. But what causes these things that you have now named with your nascent language?

You intuitively sense that something or someone must be causing the events of nature around you. You club a hollow tree and it makes a noise. Is someone in the sky doing the same and making thunder? Something, someone, somewhere must be making nature happen. Someone is controlling your life, determining when the seasons begin and end, when the rain comes and goes. Who lives in the fire? Who moves the sun across the sky? Who hides the moon? Who brings the rain and storms and lightening? Who causes plants to grow? Who determines who lives, who is sick, and who dies?

Who? You certainly do not know or understand these things; you are ignorant of everything. For all that you do not know, for all of which you are ignorant, there must be something, someone, somewhere, who controls everything that affects you. Someone or something controls the things that you do not and knows all the things you do not. Unseen beings arise in your imagination. They know all. They control all.

From deep inside of you, sounds and sights fill your sleep and twilight moments, speaking to you in strange sounds and appearing in dramatic dreams. You awaken with nightmares that you cannot comprehend. Forces on the winds and powers in the dark— things that can take your life—take on lives of their own. In the depths of your imagination, forms emerge from the darkness of the oblivion. All is becoming clear. Those beings of the night, those sounds from nowhere, those forces that bring life and death—from the ether of ignorance, from your imagination, spirits and gods arise to cause the rain, the seasons, every aspect of nature. They control all. You in your ignorance have imagined them. You and your consciousness have begotten them.

Humanity of a thousand generations move around the earth, from Africa to the Artic, from the Americas to the archipelagos of the oceans. Humans evolve and spread, taking with them the gods of their imaginations—gods that morph and mutate during the journey. Over the generations—the symbols of the gods, the figurines, statues, cave paintings, and megaliths—are transformed into the embodiment of the gods themselves. Gods of ether in your mind are now the wood, the clay, the paint and the stone gods of reality.

Your mystical imagination continues to be stirred by the molecules of mushrooms, toads, plants, vapors, dreams, or even transcendent rituals. And others of your tribe, your brother perhaps, sometimes seems to have the power of the gods in the magic he performs or in the events he foretells. An entire new class of humans—shamans, magicians, prophets, and priests—evolve as the intermediaries and agents of the gods and their powers. The power of the gods is now shared with the power of the priests. They foresee your fate in the incense rising from the fires, or the entrails of goats splattered on the rocks, or in a sleepless dream in the smoke of secret plants. The gods of your ignorance have now escaped from your imagination. They are now real, and you must serve them.

To assuage starvation, pain, suffering, and death, or to curry favor for fertility, success in battle, or bounteous crops and herds, homage must now be paid. Gifts and sacrifices must be delivered. The priests have now brought forth rituals, chants, and sacrifices to appease or append the power of the gods. If slaughtering and burning your best goat in a mystical ritual did not bring rain, or good crops, or end some pestilence, then perhaps the life of your virgin daughter or a fellow tribesman is required to appease a powerful god. Does a token delivered to that figure in paint or mask or placed at the base of some statue relieve the pain in your side? Perhaps you did not perform the right ritual or serve the right god. Or perhaps your sacrifice was too small? You need to contribute more to the gods. The gods you imagine have entered your subsistence economy.

Thousands of years and hundreds of generations go by. Many humans stop foraging for food and begin to grow it; others have stopped hunting meat and begin to raise it. They no longer roam as nomads but settle and build their first houses, farms, and cities. And as they gather, they tell the stories of events of times past. The stories are told and retold, embellished and retold, altered and retold, exaggerated and retold, invented and retold until actual events have morphed into myths, but myths believed as the real events of old. The stories of the ice that covered the earth and the fire that comes from within it, the floods that covered it all, the giant beings and heroes of old merge in the imagination of mortals. Unseen gods on the earth now reside as spirits in the heavens or demons in the earth and are given names: Brahma, Krishna, Shiva, Vishnu, Anshar, Ishtar, Marduk, Nintu, Pangu, Shangdi, Yu-huang, Enlil, Nanna, Utu, Isis, Osiris, Anubis, Yahweh, Mazda, Mainyu, Apollo, Zeus, El, Athena, Baal, Elhoim, and hundreds more. Which is the "real" God? How could you know?

You surrendered to these gods, gave them power over yourself and all the things you see and hear, all that you imagine. Your gods control all. You and your tribe perform rituals and sacrifice to your gods. You acknowledge their power. For homage and hope, you and your fellow humans devote generations to building mounds and monuments, still-visible testaments to your faith in the gods.

You quake in your fear before the power of the gods. You are nothing but a whim to the very gods that your ancestors first imagined. In your mind, those supernatural gods are now the cause and rulers of all, the gods that owe their existence to your imagination. When a child cries in the night, fearing a monster in the closet or under the bed, the parent turns on the light to show the child that the feared monsters are only in their imagination.

But when our ancient forebearers cried in fear of the gods and demons in their dark, there was no one to turn on the light of knowledge to show them that the beings they feared were only in their imagination.

Even today, in the full light of modern knowledge, those gods of old remain in our fantasy and humor. Movies from *Ghost* to *Ghostbusters* fuel the imagination of the supernatural. How many gods of the supernatural do your children see on their screens, small and large? Superman? Superwoman? The Incredible Hulk? Batman? Spiderman? Doom Patrol? Justice League? The Secret Six? The Avengers? Danny Phantom, Sym-Bionic Titan, Kim Possible, Elena of Avatar, Powerpuff Girls, and hundreds more imaginary creatures with mythical and supernatural powers. Yes, you say, they know better; they understand it is make-believe in the comfort of your home on Saturday morning. But to those frightened and shivering in the wilderness of old, the supernatural beings controlling all were not make believe, but totally believed. Both are humans imagining beings with powers over real events. In the name of entertainment, we evoke the concept of the supernatural in flights of fantasy. In the name of fear, our ancestors invoked the concept of the gods to assuage their ignorance.

The supernatural was neither innocent nor entertainment. Captain John Smith, the leader of the settlers at Jamestown, described the Native Americans at Quiyoughcohannock, who annually sacrificed their children to the god Okee. They believed they were bartering children to receive deer, turkeys, and corn.[26] The Indians were killing their own children to appease a god of their imagination. To which gods of imagination are today's children being sacrificed?

---

[26] *The History of the Devil and the Idea of Evil* Dr. Paul Carus, (Dover Edition, 2008) as originally published by The Open Court Publishing Company of Chicago in 1900, pp. 2-4

It does not matter if the gods of old were formed out of ignorance and fear, through the drugs of nature,[27] or through some change during the evolution of the brain or in any other way. The unassailable truth is that "Men and women started to worship gods as soon as they became recognizably human."[28] Ritual and faith brought a sense of meaning and security to the ravages of ancient life, even if that meant deliberately sacrificing lives.

*The Golden Bough* is a famous classic book on the early gods. Written in 1890 by James Frazer, it is a long and detailed study of the gods, myths, rituals, and practices of primitive human tribes. Frazer sums up his life's study by saying: When ancient man recognizes "sadly that both the order of nature" and "the control which he had believed himself to exercise over it were purely imaginary," he "throws himself humbly on the mercy of certain great invisible beings behind the veil of nature to whom he now ascribes all those far-reaching powers."[29]

That God or gods purposefully control human existence is the most powerful and significant thought in history. Those ancient gods of fear and ignorance were locked into the human mind.[30] Knowledge has set them free, but the ghosts of those gods still haunt our modern minds.

---

[27] *Food of the Gods: The Search for the Original Tree of Knowledge A Radical History of Plants, Drugs, and Human Evolution* Terrence McKenna, (Bantam New Age, 1992) pp. 41-42. The entire book is a discussion of the use of drugs by ancient humans in achieving a knowledge of a god-like "Transcendent Other."

[28] *A History of God: The 4,000-Year Quest of Judaism, Christianity and Islam* Karen Armstrong, (Alfred A. Knopf, 1994) p. xix

[29] *The Golden Bough: A Study in Magic and Religion* Sir James George Frazer (Simon and Schuster, 1996) p. 824

[30] So locked, that several books have been written positing a gene responsible for pointing humans towards god and providing a universal human sense of spirituality. For a start, see "Faith-Boosting Genes: A search for the genetic basis of spirituality" by Carl Zimmer, published in *Scientific American,* October 2004, and *The God Gene: How Faith is Hardwired into our Genes* by Dean H. Hamer (Anchor Press, 2004).

# Chapter Two – The Writings of the Gods

Centuries before God was first commanding Abraham to leave the city of Ur, the human mind was unlocking the power of the written word. Spoken words of mighty deeds, imperfect in the memory, could be perfected and passed to others. An Egyptian Pharaoh told Toth, the god of writing, the following:

> You have invented an elixir, not of memory but of reminding, and you offer your pupils the appearance of wisdom, not true wisdom, for they will read many things without instruction and will therefore seem to know many things, when they are for the most part ignorant....[31]

No longer did you need to memorize something if you had it in writing. Writing allowed humans to pass information to others and to future generations. It was the invention that made almost all else possible.

One of the oldest known examples of human writing were symbols of a foot, a hand, and two heads pressed into a two-inch

---

[31] *The Story of Writing: Alphabets, Hieroglyphs & Pictograms* Andrew Robinson, (Thames and Hudson, 2001) p. 8

by two-inch clay tablet around the year 3300 BC.[32] No one knows what it meant. Within a few hundred years, writing advanced to more practical and important things. The Sumerians kept records to account for their beer production. Where there is accounting, there will be complaining. Several centuries before Abraham, a man by the name of Nanni wanted his money back for the delivery of defective merchandise and wrote:

> You did not do what you promised me. I have sent messengers gentlemen like ourselves to reclaim my money.... From now on I will no longer accept any copper from you that is not of fine quality. I shall henceforth select the ingots individually in my own yard and will exercise my right of rejection.[33]

Some things never change.

Within a few centuries after Abraham, man had written the first set of laws, the Code of Hammurabi, and perhaps the first history book, the biography of Tiglath-Pileser I.[34] The Egyptian Book of the Dead[35] and the Epic of Gilgamesh which included a creation and flood story, were among the first religious books written. The book of Genesis would repeat their creation and flood story centuries later.[36]

Stories repeated thousands of times with a thousand changes were now the written events and myths from ages past. The gods begotten of ignorance and morphed into sacred myth were now materialized on cuts and scratches in clay or stains on the skins of animals. History from the memory of generations was now

---

[32] *The Birth of Writing* Robert Claiborne, (Time Life Books, 1974) p. 10

[33] *The Birth of Writing* Robert Claiborne, (Time Life Books, 1974) p. 9

[34] *The Story of Writing: Alphabets, Hieroglyphs & Pictograms* Andrew Robinson, (Thames and Hudson, 2001) pp. 78-79

[35] *The Story of Writing: Alphabets, Hieroglyphs & Pictograms* Andrew Robinson, (Thames and Hudson, 2001) p. 102

[36] *The Birth of Writing* Robert Claiborne, (Time Life Books, 1974) pp. 139-146

recorded, and interactions with God could now be written, disbursed, discussed, debated, preserved, and revered.

Within a few centuries of 900 BC, the foundational beliefs of all of mankind's classic religions were compiled and written. The oral ether of generations past solidified into the texts that are still revered today. First came the oldest Hindu texts: the Vedas, the Upanishads, and later the Bhagavad Gita and others. There were also the five classics works traditionally attributed to Confucius; Buddha's numerous sutras; Zoroaster's works in the Avesta and Gathas; the Greek writings of Homer, Plato, and Archimedes; and what would become the Torah of the Old Testament of the Abrahamic religions. These were first written between the 10th and 3rd centuries BC, known as the Axial Age.[37]

The gods who were created in the recesses of men's minds; the gods who had taken form in the spirits of the heavens and the monuments of earth; the gods whose priests had developed rituals of homage, worship, and sacrifice, were now "carved in stone." The beliefs of over 75% of today's population—Hindus, Buddhists, Jews, Christian, Muslims—flow directly from the religious writings of the Axial Age.[38] The words on those old stones and tablets, and the parchment versions that followed, have guided humanity ever since.

Those ancient religious texts are a confusing compendium. Each is nebulous in origin and purports some level of divine intent. Any concept of truth is thwarted by competing claims with no verifiable elements. Each is based on old oral myths

---

[37] *The Great Transformation: The Beginning of Our Religious Traditions* Karen Armstrong, (Alfred A. Knoff, 2006) p xii. The citation is for the religions, dates, and the Karl Jaspers definition of the Axial Age. However, the entire book is an exposition on the religious ideas that came into written existence during that time.

[38] "The Future of World Religions: Population Growth Projections, 2010-2050" *The Pew Forum on Religion & Public Life.* Pew Research Center, April 2, 2015. "The Global Religious Landscape" *The Pew Forum on Religion & Public Life.* Pew Research Center, December 2012. 31.4% Christian, 23.2% Muslim, 15% Hindu, 7.1% Buddhist. If the ideology of Confucianism from the Analects of Confucius written ~450BC is included, the number reaches 90%.

transferred to paper in ages past and proclaimed as the words of the gods. And each generation with absolute conviction conveys to its youth the belief and certainty in its myths of old. Each generation was convinced that their myths and faith, and only their myths and faith, written in their version of a divine book, were the real facts of all existence.

One of the writings of the Axial Age became the most influential to humanity.[39] Its stories are the foundation for all the Abrahamic religions. It is called the Hebrew Bible (also known as the Tanakh or Mikra) by the Jews, the Old Testament by Christians, and the Tawrat and Zabur by Muslims.[40] People have been revising it, reading it, quoting from it, translating it, debating it, writing about it, and arguing and fighting over it for 2,500 years. The Old Testament is integral to Judaism, Christianity, and Islam. It is considered by some to be great literature or the first work of history, but to many it is the Word of God, inspired by God, given by God, revealed by God, or the Divine Word. Regardless of how it is described, no one can deny its impact on human existence. Twenty-five centuries after it was written, President Obama offered that "Isaiah 40:31 has been a great source of encouragement in my life, and I quote from it often. Psalm 46 is also important to me."[41] Both are found in the Old Testament and were written in the Axial Age.

The history of the Old Testament is deeply clouded until sometime in the 3rd century BC, when it approached its current form. It was written in Aramaic and Hebrew and according to a popular story was translated into Greek between 285 and 246 BC during the reign of Ptolemy II. But that popular story is

---

[39] The Qur'an was written over 1000 years after the Axial Age and will be discussed in depth separately in the section on Islam.

[40] *Tawrat* is the Muslim term for the Torah and *Zabur* is the term for the Book of Psalms. Each religion and different sects of those religions have different understandings of what material constitutes the "Old Testament."

[41] "Cathedral Age" Midsummer 2012 Edition, *Washington National Cathedral* p. 21

universally understood as apocryphal. However, it is agreed that the Hebrew Bible was in existence by 132 BC. "In 400 BC there is no hint of a canon. By 200 BC it is there."[42]

The first five books of the Old Testament are called the Torah or Pentateuch. Historically, they were written by Moses over 3000 years ago. However, long ago, some began to doubt that Moses had written them. Genesis 36:31-43 is a list of Edomite Kings, who lived long after Moses[43] making it very improbable that he wrote it. But there were other issues, and theologians across the ages—Origen, the bishop of Alexandria, in the 200s; Isaac Yashush in the 1100s; Joseph Bonfils in the 1200s; Tostatus, bishop of Avila in the 1500s; Thomas Hobbes in the early 1600s, and many others—questioned the accuracy and reliability of the Torah.

But questioning the sacred writings was not healthy. Isaac La Peyrère was an influential writer and theologian of the 17th century. His books questioned the Bible and were banned and burned. He was told to recant or burn himself. He chose to recant. In the mid-1600s, Benedict Spinoza, known also for his advancement of the telescope, found the ire of Jews, Catholics, and Protestants for daring to openly say that the books of the Torah were not written by Moses.[44] The Sacred Books of the Catholics, Protestants, and Jews were not to be examined. They were not even to be questioned!

After the Catholic Church stopped burning people at the stake for being impertinent, even more people began to ask questions.[45]

---

[42] *A History of the Jews,* Paul Johnson, (Harper Perennial, 1988) pp. 95

[43] *Biblical Origins: An Adopted Legacy* Petros Koutoupis, (Virtualbookworm.com Publishing, 2008) p. 7

[44] *Who Wrote the Bible?* Richard Elliot Friedman, (Perennial Library, 1987) pp. 18-21 record all the above examples.

[45] *Giordano Bruno: Philosopher / Heretic* Ingrid D. Rowland, (University of Chicago Press, 2008) p. 7 The book tells the fascinating tale of Bruno and the Church's long running attempt to silence his outspoken questioning. He was the last person burned at the stake by the Catholic Church. As late as 1983, Pope John Paul II refused to pardon Bruno for his "obstinate and pertinacious" questions.

By the late 1800s, scholars, particularly German scholars, began openly asking brazen questions. In response, on November 18, 1893, Pope Leo XIII issued his encyclical, *Providentissimus Deus* (On the Study of Holy Scripture)

> Wherefore, it must be recognized that the Sacred Writings are wrapt in a certain religious obscurity, and that no one can enter into their interior without a guide…and that in reading and making use of His word, they must follow the Church as their guide and their teacher.[46]

This sounds pretty much like what every parent at one time told their child: "Just do what I tell you and stop asking so many questions!" At the beginning of the 20th century, the Catholic Church was saying exactly that: Do not question the Bible; it means what we say it means. A similar position is held today by Islam regarding the Qur'an: "The Holy Prophet (peace_ be_upon_him) forbade the discussion of thorny questions."[47]

Still, for the next fifty years, thorny questions about the entire Bible continued to relentlessly pile up. The issues could not be ignored. In 1943, Pope Pius XII issued *Divino afflante Spiritu* (Inspired by the Holy Spirit) which stated:

> Let the interpreter then, with all care and without neglecting any light derived from recent research, endeavor to determine the peculiar character and circumstances of the sacred writer, the age in which he

---

[46] "Biblical Exegesis." *The Online Catholic Encyclopedia,*
http://www.newadvent.org/cathen/05692b.htm

[47] Translation of Sunan Abu-Dawud, "Knowledge (Kitab Al-Ilm)", Book 25, Number 3648

lived, the sources written or oral to which he had recourse and the forms of expression he employed.[48]

Word of God or not, it was finally accepted that the Bible could be studied as a historical document and thorny questions could be asked. After World War II, the number of Catholic and Protestant theological institutions asking those thorny questions grew significantly. Scholars began to deeply research the questions of who wrote the Bible, the times in which it was written, the styles in which it was written, and why it had been written. As the 20th century went forward, the words in the Bible remained the same, but fewer and fewer words would be accepted "by faith alone."

The last stand for the Bible as the literal and inerrant Word of God, at least within Catholicism, came on November 18, 1965, at the Church Council known as Vatican II. The Catholic Church's position on the Bible was that it was "completely forbidden to admit that the sacred author could have erred, since divine inspiration of its very nature precludes and rejects all error in everything, both religious and profane." By then the prelates of the Church understood the that the Bible contained too many errors and could no longer be proclaimed the perfect Word of God. Instead, the Church's position became, "The books of Scripture must be acknowledged as teaching firmly, faithfully and without error that truth which God wanted put into the sacred writings for the sake of our salvation."[49] The new position became, that the Bible has errors, just none that affect your

---

[48] The easiest place to find the entire document is the Vatican website; http://w2.vatican.va/content/pius-xii/en/encyclicals/documents/hf_pxii_enc_ 30091943_divino-afflante-spiritu.html. The quotation will be found in section 33.

[49] The complete story is told in "Biblical Scholarship 50 years After *Divino Afflante Spiritu*" by John R. Donahue, published in *America: the Jesuit Review* September 18, 1993. The second quote is from "The Dogmatic Constitution on Divine Revelation Dei Verbum Solemnly Promulgated by His Holiness Pope Paul VI on November 18,1965 "

salvation. Deciding which biblical words were "for the sake of salvation" was left to be argued another day.

Everything in the Bible was now open to question. For the first time in history, the Bible could be studied openly and without retribution. New methods of Bible study were used. If you took sentences from Jane Austen and Danielle Steel novels and somehow edited them together with some of your own sentences into a new book, it would be easy to tell who wrote which passages and where you, the redactor, had added or deleted things. Using this technique and others, some very dedicated and talented people who know ancient languages have concluded that the Torah probably had five major authors. They have been given different letters to identify them. A letter system was used: J (German for Yahweh)  E (for Elohim)  D (Deuteronomy)  P (Priestly)  and R (Redactor).[50] This analysis, generally referred to as the Documentary Hypothesis, can explain a great deal about the history of Judaism, its changes, and where various ideas originated.[51] It also inflamed a lot of passions.[52]

With this new approach came explanations for some of the questions. For example, why were there two different stories of creation in Genesis?[53] Creation in Genesis 1 was written by E and creation in Genesis 2 was written by J, and both were later edited by P. Both stories are very similar to creation stories found in the

---

[50] Richard Elliot Friedman's book *Who Wrote the Bible?* (First Perennial Library, 1989) explains in detail how each of these writers were determined and sorts out the details of the history of the time of writing.

[51] *Biblical Origins: An Adopted Legacy* Petros Koutoupis, (Virtualbookworm.com Publishing, 2008) Appendix E, pp. 284-313 is a fascinating glimpse of a Bible scholar going about the process of identifying the writers and times that something in the Old Testament was written or redacted. In this case, it is when and who wrote Genesis 14.

[52] The Documentary Hypothesis is a long running and heated debated, because it runs counter to the idea of the Torah being the word of God as revealed to Moses.

[53] Dr. Charles Wheeler of Carson-Newman University has a thorough and excellent explanation of the two versions on his website https://web.cn.edu/kwheeler/Genesis_texts.html

Enuma Elis and the Babylonian era Epic of Atrahasis which are older Acadian myths.[54] But those creation stories are overshadowed by the voluminous scientific evidence confirming the mythical nature of all creation fables. Regardless of theme parks in Kentucky, the beginning of the stars, planets, plants, animals, and humans is well understood, often in exacting detail.[55] And with the new approach to the Bible, Christians no longer need accept the creation myths found there.

There is another famous story in the Torah of God making the sun stand still as Joshua fought the Battle of Jericho (remember they still thought that it was the Sun that went around the Earth):

*And the sun stood still, and the moon stayed, until the*
*people had avenged themselves upon their enemies. Is not*
*this written in the book of Jasher? So the sun stood still*
*in the midst of heaven, and hasted not to go down about*
*a whole day* (Josh. 10:13).

This is a spectacular event for the entire world to see, at a time when people everywhere studied the sky, and yet it is not mentioned in any other recordings anywhere in the world.

One last example is the story of camels. If you read a report of Benjamin Franklin sending emails to Thomas Jefferson, you would know the story was not true because the internet was not invented until long after both had died. In Genesis 12:16, Abraham was given camels as payment for loaning Sarah to the Pharaoh's harem. (Today we might call Abraham a pimp.) That story, or at least the camel part of it, simply cannot be true

---

[54] *The Bible In The British Museum: Interpreting The Evidence* T.C. Mitchell (The British Museum Press, 2004) p. 69

[55] This will be presented more fully in my subsequent book, *Abraham's Devil.*

because camels were not domesticated until a thousand years later, after the time of King David, around 1000 BC.[56]

There are other less spectacular examples, like the Astartu Relief of Tiglath-pileser III, describing his victory at Astaroth, which is told differently in Deuteronomy 1:14 and Joshua 9:10,[57] or that there is absolutely nothing in all of the Egyptian monuments and documents that says anything about Moses.[58] Looking at hundreds of such things, many people wondered, just where did all these Bible stories come from?

More and more questions of every aspect of the Bible kept piling up. In 2005, Cardinal Joseph Aloisius Ratzinger, a German Bible scholar, was named Pope Benedict XVI. He himself, like numerous other scholars, understood that many of the stories of the Bible did not pass historical scrutiny. He explained, "This is a dramatic situation for faith because its point of reference is being placed in doubt." Faith "is in danger of clutching at thin air," he said. Pope Benedict XVI maintained that instead of looking at the individual flaws in scriptures, "you have to attend to the content and to the unity of Scripture as a whole." He continued, stating, "A voice greater than man's echoes in Scripture's human words; the individual writings of the Bible point somehow to the living process that shapes the one

---

[56] Israeli scientists in 2014 pinpointed the introduction of camels into Palestine between 930 and 900 BC and their widespread use more than a century later. "Camels Had No Business In Genesis" John Noble Wilford, *New York Times* Feb 10 2014 p D5 and "Domesticated Camels Came to Israel in 930 B.C., Centuries Later Than Bible Says" Mairav Zonszein February 10, 2014 http://news.nationalgeographic.com/news/2014/02/140210-domesticated-camels-israel-bible-archaeology-science/

[57] *The Bible In The British Museum: Interpreting The Evidence* T.C. Mitchell, (The British Museum Press, 2004) p. 52

[58] *The Evolution of God* Robert Wright, (Little Brown and Company, 2009) p. 109

Scripture."[59] The myths of old,[60] first written in the Axial Age, were no longer words from God, but had been transformed into pious creations,[61] reflecting metaphors of a higher truth essential to salvation.[62]

Whether myths, pious creations, or echoes from God, the biblical narratives found in the Old Testament carried powerfully across the centuries. People guided their lives as whole societies and countries functioned around them. One might say that large strands in the DNA of Western civilization are based on those narratives.[63] Judaism, Christianity, and Islam are unquestionably founded on the ancient scriptural stories of Israel. With so much at stake, we need to look further and see if there is something we can learn from the non-scriptural stories of ancient Israel.

---

[59] This and the above quotes are from *Jesus of Nazareth: From the Baptism in the Jordan to the Transfiguration* by Pope Benedict XVI (Ignatius Press, 2007) pp. xviii - xix

[60] *The New Jerome Biblical Commentary* edited by Raymond Brown, Joseph Fitzmyer, and Roland Murphy. (Prentice-Hall, 1990) The word "myth" is never used, but descriptions like "the story may not be historical" p. 636 or "strains credulity" p. 681 or "is probably a Midrashic element" p. 636 make the point.

[61] *The Final Philosophy, Or, System of Perfectible Knowledge Issuing from the Harmony of Science and Religion*, Charles Woodruff Shields and DD Scribner, (Armstrong & Co, 1877) p. 244. Republished by Arkose Press in 2015.

[62] Ratzinger has written many books, and this is a simple summary that I believe reflects his view. For a more complete understanding of his view of exegesis, see the article, "Biblical Interpretation in Crisis: The 1988 Erasmus Lecture" by Benedict XVI, April 26, 2008, which can be found here:
https://www.firstthings.com/web-exclusives/2008/04/biblical-interpretation-in-crisis

[63] Some argue that the DNA was the Greco-Roman philosophy and politics, but that was totally subsumed by Christianity in the 4th and 5th centuries. This will be discussed later.

# Chapter Three – Ancient Israel in History

The biblical stories of Ancient Israel overlap the periods known as the Middle and Late Bronze Age, and the beginning of the Iron Age. They cover the period from Abraham's coming to Canaan in ~2000 BC through Moses in Egypt, then through Joshua as the Israelites returned to Canaan, followed by Kings David and Solomon, until Nebuchadnezzar destroyed Jerusalem in 587 BC.

We can study this period through the writings of the Old Testament and through the discoveries of archeologists. This chapter will look at what archeology has uncovered, while the following two chapters will look at stories of the Old Testament, and then we will look at what the Old Testament tells us of the relationship between Abraham's God and the people of Ancient Israel.

It took over two million years for humans to perfect the making of stone tools, but even with them, humans were bounded by the need for shelter and food to survive. After the last Ice Age (nearly 12,000 years ago) better strains of grain evolved that provided a surplus of food and energy, allowing humans to expand their efforts beyond daily existence. Things improved further about 7000 years ago, when tools of pure copper were first made. Centuries later in China and/or at the eastern end of the Mediterranean Sea, someone mixed tin with copper and made bronze. With its sharp, hard edge, bronze tools increased agriculture productivity so that tribes of hunter-gatherers and pastoralists could form permanent agricultural settlements. The Bronze Age was the beginning of civilization as we know it, around 3800 BC.[64]

The Nile River Valley in Egypt and the land between the Tigris and Euphrates Rivers in what is today known as Iraq are considered the "Cradles of Civilization."[65] The agricultural surplus that came with bronze tools brought forth the first cities and then the first civilizations of the Middle East: the Sumer, Akkad, Elam, and Amorites, followed by the Assyrians, the Hurrians, and others. At the same time, the Egyptians emerged and began erecting pyramids. Over the next 2000 years, writing and many other inventions and discoveries came into being, as numerous tribal entities came and went, and the Bronze Age was eclipsed by the Iron Age.

By the late Bronze Age, 1500 BC to 1175 BC, significant trade had developed throughout the eastern Mediterranean and the Middle East. Bronze required copper from Cyprus, Turkey, Palestine, and Iran as well as tin from various places, including Africa and Afghanistan.[66] Great quantities of copper and tin were hauled from Africa to Babylon through the passes in Canaan in

---

[64] *The Ascent of Man* Jacob Bronowski (Little Brown and Company 1973) p. 126

[65] Felipe Fernandez-Armesto in his book *Civilizations* pp. 182–200 points out that while these river valleys are the conventional starting point for "civilization" it does not imply that all civilizations diffused from there outward. Archeology has documented that other "civilizations" began in the same era, independently in other parts of the world.

[66] *1177 BC: The Year Civilization Collapsed* Eric H Cline (Princeton University Press 2014) On page 76 Cline discusses the inventory of a Uluburun ship containing ten tons of cooper from Cypress and one ton of tin "probably from Badakhshan region of Afghanistan one of the few places it was available during the second millennium BC."

what is now Israel and Palestine. [67] For centuries, the ores and the implements made from bronze, flowed up and down the trade routes through Canaan at the intersection of the Egyptian, Assyrian, and Hittite (Turkish) Empires. Along with tin, copper, and bronze went dates, gold, clothes, leather, and daughters sent from one king to another to seal in blood the peace and friendship of trade.[68] This is attested by the clay tablets with the earliest collections of human writing.[69] However, "goods" were not the only things that flowed on the trade routes: language, ideas, culture and myths were constantly being exchanged as well.

Megiddo, also known as Armageddon in the New Testament book of Revelations, is an ancient fortress town, now in northwest Israel. From the most ancient times until World War I, civilizations fought for this strategic land. [70] If you visit Megiddo and look out from the heights of its ruins, you instantly understand its strategic significance. To the right is the Jezreel Valley, the main road from Egypt. To the left are the passes to the coastal roads that lead to Western Turkey and Asia Minor. Straight ahead, the terrain opens East towards the Sea of Galilee, then over the gentle rise of the Golan Heights towards Damascus, the plains of Anatolia and on to Babylon and Assyria (Iraq & Iran). In front of Megiddo, the caravans of trade, the armies of

---

[67] *History of the World* Hugh Thomas (Harper and Row1979) p. 38

[68] *1177 BC: The Year Civilization Collapsed*, Eric H Cline (Princeton University Press 2014) Beginning on p 53 in the section "Greeting-Gifts and Family Relations" Cline uses the Amarna archives to detail the gifts and items exchanged along the trade routes through Canaan. Beyond daughters, there were architects, sculptors and skilled masons which explains the similarities of architectural structures in the area.

[69] *1177 BC: The Year Civilization Collapsed*, Eric H Cline (Princeton University Press 2014) pp. 51-57

[70] *1177 BC: The Year Civilization Collapsed*, Eric H Cline (Princeton University Press 2014) pp. 29 Thutmose III had captured Megiddo in 1479 BC. General Edmund Allenby read a translation of Thutmose III's tactics and copied them in World War I at the Battle of Megiddo in September 1918. That battle is considered to mark the end of the Ottoman Empire.

war, and a river of ideas flowed during the centuries of the Bronze Age.

The Egyptian Pharaoh Thutmose III captured the area in 1479 BC from the Canaanites, then for centuries fought to control Megiddo and Canaan throughout the remaining Bronze Age. [71]The battles that occurred here are carved in stone on the walls, monuments, and tablets of the great Middle East civilizations. On them is not a single mention of Israel or its people. Nor is there any mention of Abraham, Moses, or the dramatic Exodus of the Israelites from Egypt.

In the late 1800s, about 400 clay tablets dating between 1404 BC and 1340 BC were found in Amarna in Egypt which are now referred to as the Amarna letters. Seven of them are from the king of Jerusalem, Abdi-Heba, to his master, the Pharaoh of Egypt. The letters ask for help in defending against the "habiru" who have overrun the Pharaoh's cities in the area. Some apologists think that since 'Habiru' sounds like "Hebrew" the Amarna letters are proof of the Israelite invasion of Canaan under Joshua. These claims are senseless because they project modern English interpretations and pronunciations onto very ancient languages. It turns out that in the original language of which there are hundreds of examples, the term 'habiru' was a categorical term meaning outlaws, raiders, mercenaries, etc., and was not a reference to a specific tribe. [72]

The same Amarna letters have another oblique reference that *may* have some relationship to the Israelites. Sometime in the 13th century BC, the Shasu pastoralist tribe from the Sinai or Negev area were allowed by the pharaoh to enter the land of Goshen to graze their cattle during a drought. The Bible tells of a similar situation. *And thou shalt dwell in the land of Goshen, and thou*

[71] *1177 BC: The Year Civilization Collapsed*, Eric H Cline (Princeton University Press 2014) p 59
[72] "Who were the Early Israelites? Anson Rainey *Biblical Archaeologocal Review* 34:06 Nov/Dec 2008 pp51-55

*shalt be near unto me, thou, and thy children, and thy children's children, and thy flocks, and thy herds, and all that thou hast: And there will I nourish thee; for yet there are five years of famine; lest thou, and thy household, and all that thou hast, come to poverty* (Genesis 45:10-11). The Shasu are also mentioned in several other Egyptian texts.[73]

Unfortunately, Shasu and Hebrew does not connect in English as well as Habiru and Hebrew. These events are more likely the echoes of the fluid shifting of tribes in Canaan and the surrounding lands towards the end of the Bronze Age. Beyond these two allusions, there simply are no known references to the tribes of Israel or the Hebrews anywhere until the very end of the Bronze Age, long after the times of Abraham and Moses.

The Bronze Age came to an end over a brief few decades: 1210 BC to 1170 BC. Not because the Iron Age began but because of the collapse of cities and trade. According to historian Robert Drews, "Within a period of forty or fifty years at the end of the thirteenth and beginning of the twelfth century almost every significant city or palace in the eastern Mediterranean world was destroyed."[74] Some use 1177 BC as the final date for the Bronze Age, symbolized by a battle between Ramses III and the Sea People, an unknown group of immigrants and warriors who invaded the coastal areas of Egypt, Israel, Lebanon, and Syria. Historically, the Old Testament "Philistines," in the area now known as Gaza, were their descendants.[75] Whether the late

---

[73] "Who were the Early Israelites? Anson Rainey *Biblical Archaeologocal Review* 34:06 Nov/Dec 2008 pp51-55

[74] *The End of the Bronze Age: Changes in Warfare and the Catastrophe ca. 1200 B.C.* Robert Drews (Princeton University Press 1993) pp. xii,

[75] In July of 2016 the discovery of an ancient Philistine cemetery near Tel Ashkelon in Israel was announced. Initial reports indicate that the Philistines were very different than the people in Canaan at the time. Future DNA studies may confirm if the Philistines were a part of the Sea People. http://www.ancient-origins.net/news-history-archaeology/discovery-3000-year-old-philistine-cemetery-may-change-history-006270

Bronze Age ended through uprisings, war, climate change, earthquakes, the invasion of Sea Peoples, or some combination of them all, we may never know. But we do know that the Ancient Empires of Iraq, Iran, Turkey, Cyprus, Upper Egypt, and Mycenae suffered destruction, serious decline, or total collapse in those few short decades. And with that destruction came the decline of trade through Canaan which had flourished for centuries prior in the Bronze Age.[76] The decline of trade diminished the imperative to control the land of Canaan. And in that void in the 12th century BC the first Israelites appear.[77]

Obelisk-shaped stones, called Steles, were often used in ancient history to commemorate battles and actions of rulers. The granite Merneptah Stele, discovered in 1896 and now in the British Museum in London, describes the battles and victories of the Egyptian Pharaoh Merneptah around the year 1208 BC. It provides the very first mention of "Israel" anywhere. The Israelites are referred to as a people, or a tribe, not a place. In a single line, the Merneptah Stele mentions destroying the Israelites in Canaan: *Israel is laid waste and his seed is not.* Even then, this single line is an otherwise unimportant detail on a large 10.5-foot-high stone covering several Egyptian battles. It is the first mention anywhere of Israel or the Israelites, and it will be the last mention of Israel for another 350 years.[78] Merneptah's report of destroying the seed of Israel rang true.

The next historical records of Israel are on three stone monuments in the 9th century BC. The events they record are

---

[76] The end of the Bronze Age is extensively covered in *1177 B.C. The Year Civilization Collapsed* Eric H. Cline (Princeton University Press 2014) The references in the previous two paragraphs are from that book.

[77] "Israelite Life Before the Kings," *Biblical Archaeology Review*, Robert D. Miller, March/April 2013.

[78] The Merneptah Stele is discussed in *A History of the Jews* Paul Johnson p .25; *The Bible in the British Museum* T.C. Mitchell p 41 and *The Evolution of God* Robert Wright pp. 114-115

also mentioned in the Bible. The first is the Kurkh Stele,[79] which describes battles in 879 BC and 853 BC, in which the Assyrian King Shalmaneser and his son defeated a coalition that included King Ahab of the Israelites (1 Kings 16:30–33; 1 Kings 21:17–29). The second is the Tel Dan Stele,[80] which mentions the defeat of the "House of David," probably by Hazael, king of Aram, or his son Ben-Hadad sometime after 843 BC (2 Kings 13:1-3; 2 Kings 13:24). The third is the Moabite Stone,[81] also called the Mesha Stele, which tells of the Moabites overthrowing the rule of Israel around 840 BC (2 Kings 3). That is the entire historical record of Israel in ancient times.[82]

And there is no archeological evidence to be found of the Kingdoms of David and Solomon in Jerusalem itself. "Over a century of archaeological explorations...(has)failed to reveal evidence for any meaningful 10th-century building activity."[83] The history book of ancient Israel from Abraham to Solomon's Temple is nothing but blank pages.

---

[79] *"The Bible in the British Museum: Interpreting the Evidence" T.C. Mitchell* (The British Museum Press, 2004) pp. 44-45

[80] The Tel Dan Stele was only discovered in 1993 and is now on display in the Israel Museum in Jerusalem. It is the only non-biblical reference to King David. However even the accuracy and authenticity of this mention have been intensely debated. See the *New York Times Review of Books*, June 14th, 2000 "A Sling and a Prayer" the review of *King David* Steven L. McKenzie (Oxford University Press 2000)

[81] *"The Bible in the British Museum: Interpreting the Evidence" T.C. Mitchell (The* British Museum Press, 2004) p. 51

[82] After these three references, the number of monuments and archeological mentions of Israel increase. The next famous monument is the Black Obelisk of Shalmaneser III describing ~841 – 838 BC and the King of Israel Jehu bringing tribute to Shalmaneser, an event not described in the Bible. *"The Bible in the British Museum"* T.C. Mitchell pp 46-47

[83] "A Great United Monarchy? Israel Finkelstein *Archaeological and Historical Perspectives* as found in "One God – One Cult – One Nation," *Archaeological and Biblical Perspectives* Ed. by Kratz, Reinhard G. / Spieckermann, Hermann De Gruyter Publishers 2010.

# Chapter Four – From the Arabs to Egypt

The Old Testament fills the blank pages of Israel's history with a rich and glorious narrative. Moses himself was said to have written the story from Creation until the Jews entered the Promised Land (Canaan) in the books of Genesis, Exodus, Leviticus, Numbers, and Deuteronomy. It is a detailed story of the people of Israel told from the beginning of time through the times of Abraham and Moses.

The books of Joshua, Judges, Samuel, Kings, and Chronicles then continue the history of Israel until it was a great and thriving society under Kings David and Solomon. The biblical books of the prophets, such as Jeremiah, Amos, Hosea, Isaiah, and others, then focus on the relationship of the nation of Israel with Abraham's God. Others, such as Psalms, Song of Solomon, and Ruth, provide songs, poetry, and personal stories of the times. The stories found in these books have merged into a seamless narrative taught as historical fact. It is a story that has long endured. Simon Schama of the PBS documentary *The Story of Jews*, says the following in his book of the same name:

> All these fables of origination continued to be embellished, enriched, varied and repeated over many generations to

give the Israelites a strong sense of a divinely ordained history and an imagined collective ancestry....[84]

As the caravans of trade crisscrossed the Middle East through the land of Canaan, the myths and stories of old, morphed and changed. The biblical books of Israel's history blended myths and stories borrowed from the neighboring tribes, which were then edited and redacted centuries later into the form we know today.[85] We can see this same process in our own story telling today.

The Lapps and Finns had ancient stories of snow and ice gods and goddesses, which Hans Christian Anderson crafted into his Christian morality tale in the 1845 story, "The Snow Queen."[86] The story of an evil devil with a mirror that would not reflect good is eventually overcome when the heroine reads the Christian "Lord's Prayer" and breaks the spell. "The Snow Queen" then went on to be adapted into dozens of versions, with different plot twists and characters. In 2014, Disney turned Anderson's "The Snow Queen" into the movie *Frozen*. Little girls everywhere now sing the songs, dress up in costumes, and play act their own plots of ancient Norse gods and their mythical sidekicks.

And what if stories like that were repeated over the centuries and given the imprimatur of God? The origin of everything is told in Genesis 1, and again with a different twist in Genesis 2. The

---

[84] *The Story of the Jews: Finding the Words 1000BC to 1492AD* Simon Schama (Harper Collins 2013) p. 46

[85] *The Chaldean Account of Genesis: Containing the description of Creation, The Fall of Man, The Deluge, The Tower of Babel, The Times of the Patricians, and Nimrod*, George Smith (Scribner, Armstrong and Co. 1876. republished 2018.) While an old book it gives a very thorough description and comparison between the Genesis and the written Babylonian legends found on tablets at the buried Royal Assyrian Library in the 1870's.

[86] Stephanie Castellano writes an excellent overview of the Norse gods, the Snow Queen and Frozen in her blog found here: https://antiquitynow.org/2014/06/03/the-ancient-roots-of-disneys-blockbuster-film-frozen/

biblical creation stories are repetitions of the creation myths of other ancient societies.[87] Perhaps the oldest of these is the Atrahasis Epic, written around 1900 to 1800 BC. Humanity is wiped out, except for one man and his family, as is retold in the Epic of Gilgamesh around 1700 BC,[88] and centuries later repeated in the flood story found in Genesis chapters 6-9. The Book of Genesis was not even a glimmer in the eyes of history when the stories of the creation and the flood were first composed.

Like these other stories, Genesis tells us the story of Abraham as the founder of Israel, and of the Arab peoples. Moses tells us that Abraham (originally named Abram) was taken by his father from his home in Ur to Harran, an area in modern-day southern Turkey. After his father died, Abraham was told by God to leave Turkey and settle in Canaan.

*Now the Lord said to Abram, "Go out from your country, your relatives, and your father's household to the land that I will show you. Then I will make you into a great nation, and I will bless you, and I will make your name great, so that you will exemplify divine blessing. I will bless those who bless you, but the one who treats you lightly I must curse, and all the families of the earth will bless one another by your name.*[89] (Gen. 12:1-3)

Later, the promise to Abraham is made more specific.

*On that day the Lord made a covenant with Abram and said, "To your descendants I give this land, from the*

---

[87] *The History of God* Karen Armstrong (Alfred A Knopf 1994) p. 7

[88] "*The Bible in the British Museum: Interpreting The Evidence*" T.C. Mitchell (The British Museum Press, 2004) pp 26-27 and p 70.

[89] This is also an important verse for Christianity in that Paul will later use this verse to justify to the Galatians that the 'blessings promised to Abraham would come to the gentiles' and hence Paul's mission to the Gentiles [Gal. 3:14].

*Wadi[e] of Egypt to the great river, the Euphrates—the
land of the Kenites, Kenizzites, Kadmonites, Hittites,
Perizzites, Rephaites, Amorites, Canaanites, Girgashites
and Jebusites.* (Gen. 15:18-21)

Abraham and his nephew Lot followed his God's words and
settled in Canaan. They remained until a famine forced them to
leave for Egypt. There, the pharaoh spotted Abraham's wife
Sarah. The pharaoh, thinking Sarah was Abraham's sister,
wanted her as a hot new addition to his harem. Abraham played
along and took money (and camels) from Pharaoh for Sarah.
When the Pharaoh learned that Sarah was Abraham's wife, he
threw them both out of the country. Abraham, now a successful
pimp, returned to Canaan a rich man (Gen. 12:14-20). Side note:
The Old Testament is where Jerry Springer gets his best show
ideas!

Abraham and his maid Hagar had a son, Ishmael, after which
Abraham and his now quite old wife Sarah miraculously had a
son, Isaac. A jealous conflict was unleashed between the two
women. Sarah demanded that Hagar and her son Ishmael be
thrown out of the house and be banished to the desert (Gen.
21:10). Side note: Another reality TV show!

Isaac grew up and married his cousin, Rebekah. They had
twins: Esau, born first, and then Jacob. The first born, Esau was
to inherit everything, but Rebekah favored Jacob and
masterminded a plot to deceive Isaac and swindle Esau out of his
inheritance. When Esau discovered the deceit, he *hated Jacob
because of the blessing wherewith his father blessed him: and
Esau said in his heart, "The days of mourning for my father are
at hand; then will I slay my brother Jacob"* (Gen. 27:41).

Jacob departed from the wrath of his brother and married his
cousins: two sisters, Leah and Rachel. Between them and other
women, Jacob had twelve sons. Abraham's God then appeared to
Jacob and said, *Your name is Jacob, but you will no longer be*

*called Jacob; your name will be Israel* (Gen. 35:10). Jacob's twelve sons then become the fathers of the twelve tribes of Israel. The word 'Israel" means "fought with El" or "wrestled with God." This is the biblical birth of the nation of Israel.

Esau also departed Canaan for the land of his uncle Ishmael. Ishmael married his cousins: two sisters, Mahalath and Basemath.[90] Between them and other women, Ishmael also had twelve sons. Esau also had twelve sons, who were princes of their nations (yes, it is confusing). "And they settled from Havilah to Shur, which is east of Egypt as one goes toward Assyria" (Gen. 25:18). This is the broad area of desert east of Egypt in Northern Arabia. Ishmael means "may El hear."[91] This is the biblical birth of the Arab nations.

Abraham therefore is the father of all the Arabs *and* the Israelites. Hagar is the mother of all the Arab tribes and Sarah is the mother of all the tribes of Israel. The conflict between Sarah and Hagar continues into the struggle between Jacob and Esau. Whether myth or fact, this genealogy from four thousand years ago is the beginning of a feud between the Arabs and the Israelites, between Islam and Judaism, that has lasted until our time. And Abraham's God is the God to them all. (A later chapter on Islam will tell this same story from the Islamic viewpoint as found in the Qur'an).

When the Jews reclaimed their "birthright" with the founding of the modern State of Israel in 1948, "half of Palestine's…Arabs were uprooted from their homes and became refugees"[92] as

---

[90] The Bible is not clear on this point as Genesis 26, 28 and 36 can be read with different interpretations.

[91] *The Invention of God* Thomas Rome as translated by Raymond Geuss (Harvard University Press 2013) p 72 The complete etymology of Israel and Ishmael and alternative meanings are provided. El is the creator God of the Ugarit tribes from area of Lebanon. El is the name for God of Israel used most frequently in the Hebrew text of the Old Testament. The names Ishmael and Israel then are derivatives of the name of a god commonly worshipped in the areas of today's Lebanon and Canaan.

[92] *Palestinian Identity: the construction of modern national consciousness* Rashid Khalidi (Columbia University Press 1998) p 21

several hundred thousand Arab descendants of Esau/Ishmael were displaced. Thus, from a certain perspective, Jacob's descendants took Esau's inheritance for the second time. So, the fight today in Palestine is a vicious family grudge match over the spiritual inheritance of Abraham's God and the 4000-year-old estate of Abraham's son, Isaac—a biblical Hatfield–McCoy feud on an epic scale that continues to haunt us all. Let Disney try and make that into a movie with a fairy tale ending!

Back in the 1970s, it wasn't Disney but Andrew Lloyd Weber and Tim Rice who were retelling Bible stories. Donny Osmond and David Cassidy played Jacob's son, Joseph, in the movie and stage play *Joseph and the Amazing Technicolor Dreamcoat*. Joseph was sold into slavery and probably could not sing like Donny and David; however, he was very talented and rose to the top of the Egyptian government. Joseph his father and his eleven brothers then came to Egypt, where the families grew and prospered until generations later, they somehow were converted into the slaves of the Egyptian empire.

The story was then repeated, as Moses escaped slavery and rose to govern as an Egyptian prince. Moses, played by Charlton Heston in the movie *The Ten Commandments*, then brings stunning plagues on Egypt, and heroically leads the Israelites out of their bondage. The original script for the movie can be found in Genesis 42 and the Book of Exodus.

The epic plagues and the destruction of the Egyptian army made for spectacular scenes in the movie, yet *none* of this—even the existence of the Israelites in Egypt—is mentioned in any of the considerable histories of Egypt.[93]

None the less, in the Bible, Moses led the escaped Israelites as they roamed the Arab desert for forty years. They carried their

---

[93] *The Story of the Jews: Finding the Words 1000BC to 1492AD* Simon Schama (Harper Collins 2013) p. 72

God with them in the Ark of the Covenant, "a kind of large, elaborate dog-kennel, or was present in the tabernacle in a tent."[94] Along the way the Israelites found a God with a different name: Yahweh. Yahweh is the God of the Ten Commandments, the God who orders though shalt not kill and then orders the killing and genocide of the Midianites (Num 31). [95]

So, did somebody just make this all up? While there is no mention of Moses nor of the events of the Israelites found in Egyptian historical records, there are bits and pieces of the story scattered across times, places, and peoples. For example, the story in Exodus of Moses intervening to save the Egyptian slave might have come from an Egyptian story of one Ben-Ozen, the meat carver for the Pharaoh Ramses II, who saved some slaves from their Egyptian overseers. Thomas Romer in *The Invention of God* tells in great detail these bits and pieces to reach his conclusion that Moses "must rather be understood as a construct in which memory traces of various different historical events and figures are combined."[96] Just as Broadway and Hollywood change and embellish stories in our times, the stories that traveled the caravan roads in Canaan by day and were told around the campfires by night were combined and embellished over time, into the script of Israelite history.

When the Israelites returned to Canaan, the land Abraham's grandsons had left centuries earlier, the pages of their history were no longer blank.

---

[94] *A History of the Jews,* Paul Johnson (Harper Perennial 1988) p. 41

[95] The Midianites are found in the Bible and the Qur'an. Numbers 31 is one of the more perplexing passages of the Old Testament. Abrahams God orders Moses and the Israelites to slaughter all the Midianites, except for virgin girls. It is a sick story of genocide. There is a theory that Yahweh was the God of the Midianites, and only later was "adopted" the Israelites. Karen Armstrong discusses the story of Moses, Yahweh and the Midianites in *The History of God* Karen Armstrong (Alfred A Knopf 1994) pp. 19-22

[96] *The Invention of God* Thomas Romer translated by Raymond Geuss, (Harvard University Press 2015) p 53 In a broader sense Romer shows how the Israelites God Yahweh is the composite of other gods found in the Middle East.

# Chapter Five – Returning to Canaan

When Moses and the Israelites arrived in the land of Isaac and Esau, they found it was now populated by other tribes. On Moses death, his assistant Joshua was tasked with conquering the land that...*your God is giving you* (Deut. 11:31) for the second time. God may have given it, but it took a bloody ruthless war over the life of Joshua to wrest control from the native tribes who occupied Canaan.

At the direction of Abraham's God, Joshua killed every man, woman, and child of the various tribes of Canaan: the Gibeonites, the people of Makkedah, the Libnahites, Lachish, Eglonites, Hebronites, Debirites (Josh. 10:27-39) and many others.[97] Is this the same God who, just a few years before, gave the Ten Commandments to Moses and said, "Thou shalt not kill?" Did he actually mean, *Thou shalt not kill some people but killing others is allowed*? Maybe God just could not fit all the exceptions on those stone tablets? But then, how are people to know who Abraham's God says to kill or not kill? Are people in New York,

---

[97] This same story is told in DE 20:16-18 naming some other peoples to be massacred and setting conditions under which the women and children do not have to be massacred but can be taken as "booty."

Paris, and Orlando now on the God of Abraham's kill list? Certainly, some of Ishmael's descendants think so.

The Holocaust of WWII is considered the depth of evil. Yet if you were, say, a Gibeonite, the holocaust for you occurred over 3000 years earlier. And that first holocaust was not commanded by Hitler, but by God himself. *In the cities of the nations the Lord is giving you as an inheritance, do not leave alive anything that breathes* (Deut. 10-16). And the Jews followed God's command. And how does this loving and just God say one should feel about this kind of killing? *Happy shall he be, that taketh and dasheth thy little ones against the stones* (Ps. 137:8-9).

"Yes, but..." you might say. Yes, but what? Can Abraham's God justify the many, many examples of killing, genocide, rape, and plunder of entire peoples, women, children, infants, and suckling babies? Or even human sacrifice, *Take now your son, your only son, whom you love, Isaac, and go to the land of Moriah, and offer him there as a burnt offering on one of the mountains of which I will tell you* (Gen. 22:1-13).[98] Or cannibalism, *And I will cause them to eat the flesh of their sons and the flesh of their daughters, and they shall eat every one the flesh of his friend* (Jer. 19:9).[99] As the common table prayer says, "God is great, God is good, and we thank him for our food."[100]

And after all the destruction, conquering, and bloodshed, "painstaking excavation of various cities supposedly conquered by the Israelites, have failed to turn up the hallmarks of violent conquest."[101] Moreover, "The excavations of Israeli archeologist

---

[98] God gives Isaac a last second reprieve, none the less God commanded a human sacrifice. There are a dozen other examples, including 2 Chronicles 28:1-3 where King David's son, Ahaz also the King of Israel sacrificed his son and burned him on the alter.

[99] Also found in [Lev. 26:29], [Deut. 28:53], [Ezek. 5:8-10].

[100] Yes, these examples are not in the same context, but they do show that the God of Abraham is not a kind, loving and peaceful God with flowing grey hair. Maybe having a son will temper his anger.

[101] *The Evolution of God* Robert Wright (Little Brown and Company 2009) p. 107

since 1967…have found no trace of the mass destruction described in the book of Joshua, no signs of foreign invasion, and no Egyptian artifacts…."[102] And still, the Israelites had yet to conquer Canaan: *When Joshua had grown old, having lived many years, the Lord told him, "You are old and have lived many years, but much of the land still remains to be possessed"* (Josh. 13:1-3). And despite all these promises and enmity from the God of Abraham, the Canaanites have survived as the Lebanese people of today.[103]

Over three thousand years later, Israel still does not possess all of Canaan, while the Islamic "Philistines" from Gaza continue to attack using the war ethics of Israel's God of Abraham to make almost daily news. So much for the God of loving your enemies.

Before "Genocide" Joshua died, he distributed the land of Canaan to the tribes representing the twelve sons of Jacob/Israel. Sometime thereafter, the Bible tells us, in the book of Kings,[104] that Israel became two separate "nations": The northern area of Canaan was called Israel, and the area to the south and east surrounding Jerusalem was called Judea. During that time, the Israelites depended on Judges for wisdom and an occasional council for war. Deborah, Gideon, Samson (of Delilah fame) and Samuel being the more recognized names.

For the next two centuries, the tribes lived in a form of anarchy. *In those days, there was no king in Israel, everyone did what was right in his eyes* (Judg. 21:25) as the tribes of Israel

---

[102] *The Great Transformation* Karen Armstrong (Alford A Knopf 1994) p, 39

[103] "Continuity and Admixture in the Last Five Millennia of Levantine History from Ancient Canaanite and Present-Day Lebanese Genome Sequences" Marc Haber, Claude Doumet-Serhal, Christiana Scheib , Yali Xue, Petr Danecek, Massimo Mezzavilla, Sonia Youhanna, Rui Martiniano, Javier Prado-Martinez, Michał Szpak, Elizabeth Matisoo-Smith, Holger Schutkowski, Richard Mikulski, Pierre Zalloua, Toomas Kivisild, Chris Tyler-Smith 'The American Journal of Human Genetics', Volume 101, Issue 2, pp. 274–282, Published Online: July 27, 2017

[104] 1 Kings 11 tells the beginning of the split into the two kingdoms.

were often at war with one another in a "succession of intrigue, treachery, usurpation, assassination and regicide."[105]

While God denies telling the Israelites to participate in human sacrifice,[106] the fact is the Israelites did.[107] The book of Judges tells us clearly of a specific case of the Israelites sacrificing a child. It is a story your Sunday school probably failed to mention.

One of the Judges, Jephthah, swore that if Abraham's God helped him win a battle, he would sacrifice one of his family members. Jephthah's daughter came out of the house dancing with timbrels to happily meet her victorious returning father, only to meet her death as a human sacrifice to Abraham's God (Judg. 11:30-40). What kind of twisted faith could allow that father to kill his own daughter in some evil ritual? What kind of ruler of the universe could allow it? While this period in the Bible is "full of fascinating information about Canaan in the Late Bronze Age (it) is flavored with mythical material and fantasy presented in a confused fashion...."[108] One can only hope that the story of that little girl being sacrificed was the product of biblical myth and fantasy.

There is another worldwide famous story of the period of the Judges that is taught in Sunday school and used in innumerable pep talks and analogies. When the Philistines attacked Samaria, the Israelites found their hero in a young boy from Judea. David

---

[105] "Jews God and History" Max I Dimond Kindle loc 762
[106] The KJV translated this in the sense "I commanded them not to do it" while it is widely recognized and translated in most other versions that the wording was "I did not command them to do it." However, the story in Jerimiah 7 19-32 gives an example of God kindling the fire for the sacrifices.
[107] "The Aniconic Tradition" Brian B Schmidt in *The Triumph of Elohim* edited by Diana V. Edelman Kok (Pharos Publishing 1995) pp 88-89 lays out all the examples of human sacrifice in early Israel, including 2 Kings 16:3, 17:17, 17:31 and 21:6, 2 Chron 28:3, Lev 18:21 Jer 7:3, 32:35 and Ex 22:29,
[108] *A History of the Jews,* Paul Johnson (Harper Perennial 1988) p. 45.

killed the Philistines' Goliath[109] with his slingshot and created one of the best-known legends in history (1 Sam. 17). David went on to become king and unite the twelve tribes into the nation of Israel, making Jerusalem its capital. Also not taught in Sunday school is that David enjoyed dancing naked in front of the servant girls[110]—or that it was his bastard son Solomon[111] who went on to build a magnificent temple (1 Kings 6) making Israel into a strong country and controlling the land Canaan, which today we call Palestine. Or so the Bible says.

*King Solomon was wiser and richer than all the kings of the earth—he surpassed them all. People came from all over the world to be with Solomon and drink in the wisdom God had given him. And everyone who came brought gifts—artifacts of gold and silver, fashionable robes and gowns, the latest in weapons, exotic spices, and horses and mules—parades of visitors, year after year.* (1 Kings 10:23-25, MSG)

---

[109] Recently a strong case has been made that Goliath was a pitiable defenseless sufferer of a hereditary pituitary disorder. "Hereditary Gigantism-the biblical giant Goliath and his brothers"
Deirdre E Donnelly1 and Patrick J Morrison *Ulster Med Journal* 2014 May; 83(2): 86–88.

[110] The KJV is, "How glorious was the king of Israel today, who uncovered himself in the eyes of the handmaids of his servants, as one of the vain fellows shamelessly uncovereth himself (2 Sam. 6:14, 16, 20) Or if you prefer the Living Bible translation, it is "He exposed himself to the girls along the street . . . like a common pervert!"

[111] Solomon's mother was Bathsheba the wife of Uriah, with whom David had a child. After David has Uriah killed, Bathsheba and David have a second son, Solomon. 2 Samuel 12. Jewish law prohibits David from marrying Bathsheba. "One who is suspected of having committed adultery with another man's wife is not permitted to marry her after she has been divorced or after she has become a widow (Sotah 25a; Yeb. 24b) (Jewish Encyclopedia; Marriage Laws by Solomon Schechter and Julius H. Greenstone) http://www.jewishencyclopedia.com/articles/10435-marriage -laws

But the archeological records within Israel and the surrounding nations contain no mention of Solomon's visitors, his wisdom, nor his wealth. The tribes of Israel were of no consequence to anyone else. In his *History of the Jews* Paul Johnson relates the fabulous wealth of the temple objects and then says, "one must doubt whether they were ever there in the first place."[112] And the same can be said of all the stories of ancient Israel.

---

[112] *A History of the Jews,* Paul Johnson (Harper Perennial 1988) p. 63

# Chapter Six – Judaism before the Captivity

Contrary to everything you think you learned about Judaism; the fact is that ancient Judaism was not a monotheistic religion. "It is very difficult to find a single monotheistic statement in the whole of the Pentateuch"[113] (the biblical books of Genesis, Exodus, Leviticus, Numbers, and Deuteronomy).

The very first sentence of the Bible is *In the Beginning God created the heavens and the earth* (Gen. 1:1). Yet that sentence in Hebrew uses the plural term *Elohim,* and the passage would then read, "In the beginning the Gods created the heaven and the earth."[114] The Bible often uses plural pronouns for God. *And God said, "Let us make man in our image"* (Gen. 1:26). *Behold, the man has become like one of us* (Gen. 3:22). *Come, let us go down and there confuse their language* (Gen. 11:7). Who were "us"? Were they the giants who were the sons of Nephilim and good-looking human women? (Gen. 6:4) Were they the sea monsters God would later slay (Isaiah 27:1; Ps. 74:13-14)? Was God

---

[113] *A History of God the 4,000 – Year Quest of Judaism, Christianity and Islam* Karen Armstrong (Knopf 1994) p. 23

[114] *The Invention of God* Thomas Romer as translated by Raymond Geuss (Harvard University Press 2013) p 24

speaking to his wife Asherah?[115] Or maybe the Divine Council, *God has taken his place in the divine council; in the midst of the gods he holds judgment* (Ps. 82:1).[116] *For the LORD is the great God, the great King above all gods* (Ps. 95:3).

But just who is this God? Moses has this same question when he first meets God in Exodus 3. Moses asks, Who are you? And God replies, *The* Lord *God of your fathers, the God of Abraham, the God of Isaac, and the God of Jacob.* Fine, says Moses, but what is your name? And God blows Moses off with his famous reply, *"I am who I am"* (Exod. 3:14).[117] The Bible uses several different names for God which is confusing for everyone. God tries then to clear up the confusion three chapters later. *I am Yahweh, I appeared to Abraham, to Isaac and to Jacob, as El Shaddai, but by my name Yahweh I did not make myself known to them* (Exod. 6:2-3).[118]

Regardless of his name, in ancient Judaism, God was worshipped as one among many gods, *not* as the only divine being in existence. Abraham's God himself confirms this in his first commandment when he does not say that he is the one and only God, but instead chooses to say, *Thou shalt have no other Gods before me* (Exod. 20:3).

---

[115] Some of the Israelites worshipped Asherah and Yahweh at the same time, treating Asherah as Yahweh's consort. Not only is Asherah mentioned several times in the Old Testament, but archeologist have found corroborating evidence. "Yahweh of Samaria and his Asherah" and "Yahweh of Teman and his Asherah." Are inscriptions on the Kuntillet Ajrud stele and at a tomb at Khirbat El-Qôm. Asherah worship was a common practice for the Israelites causing conflict until Hoshea removed the Asherah symbols and idols from Yahweh's temple. 2 Kings 18:4

[116] The phrase in Hebrew is "adat El," which literally means the "Council of El" the exact title of El in the Canaanite Ugaritic texts. *The Evolution of God* Robert Wright (Little Brown and Company 2009) p. 111

[117] *The Invention of God* Thomas Romer as translated by Raymond Geuss (Harvard University Press 2013) p 28 Romer explains this translation and its history.

[118] This interpretation is from *Canaanite Myth and the Hebrew Epic* Frank Moore Cross (Harvard University Press 1973) p 44 as quoted in *The Evolution of God* Robert Wright (Little Brown and Company 2009) p. 112

The first commandment was clear to the ancient Israelites because they were polytheistic and pagan. The "Early Israelite religion grew out of earlier religions, 'pagan' religions."[119] The Israelites worshipped their many gods and made sacrifices and practiced rituals to all of them in various temples, from Dan to Jerusalem. "They implicitly accepted, if not worshiped, the gods of the Canaanites, including Baal."[120] There are even indications of "ancestor worship" and "home idols"[121] to fill out the panoply of their deities. Even pagan superstition was a part of Israelite culture. Their first King, Saul, hired the witch at Endor for a séance with a dead prophet (1 Sam. 28).

The Bible consistently confirms that the people of Israel followed many gods, as their kings set up altars to Baal, Ashureh, Dagon, and others. Even King Solomon erected altars to the gods Chemosh, Ashtoreh, and Milcon just outside of Jerusalem (2 Kings 23:12-13). The Bible makes it clear that the people of Israel and Judah followed their local gods, with pagan rituals and sacrifices. Comparisons of those gods with the myths and legends of the surrounding area provide strong evidence to support the Bible on this point.[122] Until the 6th century BC, "There is overwhelming testimony to the boundless polytheism of the mass of people, even in Jerusalem, the special seat of Yahweh."[123]

While this is acknowledged by every Bible scholar, apologists paint it as the Israelites being the monotheistic followers of Abraham's God, who leave Egypt and return to

[119] *The Evolution of God* Robert Wright (Little Brown and Company 2009) The quote is from p. 129 but all of chapter five "Polytheism, the Religion of Ancient Israel" is devoted to the topic.

[120] *The Great Transformation* Karen Armstrong (Alford A Knopf 2006) p. 46

[121] *Social History of Western Civilization* Vol 1 Richard M. Golden 3rd Edition (St. Martins Press 1996) pp. 26-27, p. 30

[122] *The Invention of God* by Thomas Romer, translated by Raymond Geuss (Harvard University Press 2015) uses extensive evidence from the Bible, the narratives from other tribes in Canaan and archeological evidence to show of the origins and evolution of the gods of ancient Israel within the historical context of the period.

[123] *Pagan Christs* J.M. Robertson (University Books Inc 1966) pp 17-18

Canaan where they are corrupted into the polytheistic ways of the Canaanites. Later reforms of Hezekiah and Josiah fail, but eventually, sometime after Isaiah and the exile, Judaism returns to the one true God of monotheism. It's a nice story, but not even supported by the Bible itself, as Lowell K Handy shows in his *The Appearance of a Pantheon in Judah.* That there were a "myriad of deities with individual volition under the control of an even higher divine authority is clear from the Biblical narratives themselves."[124]

Think of today and how, to maintain peace, everyone is socially encouraged to "accept" everyone else's God. That was the basic religion of the ancient Israelites, they accepted many gods, and over time came to believe that there was one god more powerful than all the others. Scholars call it henotheism. Yahweh became the most powerful God, but not the only god of the ancient Israelites.[125]

Polytheistic ancient Judaism was missing another critical element of current Abrahamic theology. In ancient Judaism, man did not have a soul that would survive death and live in the hereafter.

*But mortals die, and are laid low; humans expire, and where are they? As waters fall from a lake, and a river wastes away and dries up, so mortals lie down and do not rise again; until the heavens are no more, they will not awake or be roused out of their sleep.* (Job 14:10-12)

---

[124] "The Appearance of a Pantheon in Judah" by Lowell K Handy *The Triumph of Elohim From Yahwisms to Judahisms* Diana V Edelman (ed) (Pharos Publishing 1995) p. 42.

[125] *The Evolution of God* Robert Wright (Little Brown and Company 2009) This is discussed in detail in Chapter 6.

All of Psalm 90 speaks to the wisdom gained from understanding the limit of your life. The entire book of Ecclesiastes speaks to having one life, including this:

> *For that which befalleth the sons of men befalleth beasts; even one thing befalleth them: as the one dieth, so dieth the other; yea, they have all one breath; so that a man hath no preeminence above a beast: for all is vanity. All go unto one place; all are of the dust, and all turn to dust again.* (Eccles. 3:19-20)

Something beyond this life was not a part of ancient Judaism. "Sheol" was in the earth, the place where everyone went when they died, but it was not a metaphysical place. Rather, it was a factual place of neither punishment nor reward: when you die, you go into the ground. That's the end of you. The Bible made the point clear. *The Dead do not praise the Lord, nor do any that go down in silence* (Ps 115:17). Ancient Jews simply did not believe in life after death.[126]

Ancient Judaism also had a very different view of evil. The existence of evil in the world is seldom considered in the books of the Bible written prior to the Captivity. There was no evil being, a Satan or devil, leading people or tribes to evil actions. Yes, a Satan is mentioned in the books of Numbers and Job, but only as one of the heavenly beings, angels, not as a God of evil.[127] There is another mention of "Satan" in Chronicles, but there is considerable debate in the translation over whether that Satan is a supernatural being or a human advisor to King David.[128] There simply is no "evil god," no Satan, no devil. It is always the "people of Israel" or Judah who are evil, not that they were

---

[126] *Life After Death a History of the Afterlife in Western Religion* Alan F Segal (Doubleday 2004) p 121

[127] *The Origen of Satan* Elaine Pagels (Vintage Books, 1996)p. 39

[128] *Interpretation A Bible Commentary for Teaching and Preaching First and Second Chronicles* Steven S Tuell (John Knox Press 2001) pp 85-86

corrupted by an evil spirit or being. Even God did not claim that the devil had made people evil before he drowned them all. For the ancient Israelites, individual existence, and good and evil actions, did not really matter.

Before the Captivity, Judaism was not monotheist, did not believe that humans had a soul; there was neither any resurrection of the dead, nor mention of a heavenly reward or hellish punishment. "There are not any notions of hell and heaven that we can identify in the Hebrew Bible."[129] The core beliefs of all Abrahamic religions—one God, of a human soul that survived death, of a resurrection and life after death, a judgement to heaven or hell—are simply not to be found in ancient Israel. Prior to the 8th century BC, the theology of Judaism had a plain and simple message: *For you are dust, and to dust you shall return* (Gen. 3:19).

---

[129] *Life After Death- A History of the Afterlife in Western Religion* Alan F Segal (Double Day 2004) p.135

# Chapter Seven – The End of Ancient Judaism: The Captivity

---

The twelve tribes of ancient Judaism were united into a single kingdom under the reigns of Saul, David, and Solomon. The destruction of this kingdom and the forced exile of its population is known as the Captivity. It is often perceived as a single event, beginning when Jerusalem was destroyed 587 BC and ending in 539 BC, when Cyrus declared that the Jews could return to Jerusalem. Oh, that history could be that simple! The Captivity really began with the first Assyrian incursions around 870—850 BC, progressed through the destruction of the ten Northern Tribes in 722 BC, then continued until the destruction of Jerusalem in 587 BC, and concluded when Ezra and Nehemiah finally rebuilt Jerusalem around 440 BC. The Captivity then was an historical process that lasted 400 plus years and was the formation of Judaism.

In the late 10th century BC, King Solomon ruled all the twelve tribes of Israel. The king had a harem of a thousand women (1 Kings 11:3). One or two women are costly, but a thousand? High maintenance costs meant high taxes on the people of Israel. When Solomon died, his son Rehoboam wanted to continue his father's high-spending ways and refused to lower the taxes. Ten of the tribes located north of Jerusalem revolted and formed the Kingdom of Israel, leaving Rehoboam as king of Judah with just two tribes (1 Kings 11:29-18:45). The Northern area became known as Samaria. Both kingdoms continued with their polytheism, including the worship of gods named Baal and Yahweh. [130]

Around 50 years later, a prophet of great legend and lore appeared among the Ten Tribes of Israel. Elijah was a desert wander who only wore animal skins and a belt. Elijah arranged a smackdown on Mt. Carmel to see which of the two gods, Baal or Yahweh, had the power to end a draught (1 Kings 18:20-40). Yahweh won, and this incident is considered the first milestone towards putting "the Israelite religion on the path to modern monotheism."[131] However, in describing the stories of Elijah, the Jewish Encyclopedia says, "it cannot be denied that the miraculous incidents of the prophet's career may have been magnified as they passed on from generation to generation."[132]

Elijah's miraculous career continued, as he returned to make appearances to Jesus and the apostles (Matt. 17:1–8; Mark 9:2–8; Luke 9:28–36) as well as an appearance in the Qur'an (37:123-126) and popped up again in the 19th century with an appearance to Joseph Smith, the founder of the Mormon Church.[133] One of Elijah's stories even carries forward to our times. It is from Elijah

---

[130] *The Invention of God* by Thomas Romer, translated by Raymond Geuss (Harvard University Press 2015) In pages 47 through 141 Romer provides in great detail the presence of Baal, Yahweh and other gods in Kingdoms of Judah and Israel during the Kingships of Saul, David, Solomon Rehoboam and Jeroboam through the time of Elijah.

[131] *The Evolution of God* Robert Wright (Little Brown and Company 2009) The story and importance of Elijah is told in chapter 6.

[132] "The Jewish Encyclopedia" Emil G. Hirsch, Eduard König, Solomon Schechter, Louis Ginzberg, M. Seligsohn, Kaufmann Kohler (1906) V:5 P:121Which can be seen here : http://www.jewishencyclopedia.com/articles/5634-elijah

[133] *Teachings of Presidents of the Church* Joseph Smith (The Church of Latter Day Saints of Jesus Christ 2007) Chapter 26

that the name Jezebel obtained its connotation of a wicked, shameless woman. The Jezebel brand of women's lingerie can now be purchased in stores everywhere.

Elijah lived at the time of the first Assyrian incursions into Israel during the reigns of Ashurnasirpal II and his son Shalmaneser III.[134] The Assyrians became the dominant force in the Fertile Crescent, because they were the "very first iron armies: iron swords, iron spear blades, iron helmets and even iron scales sewn as armor onto their tunics." The bronze weaponry of their enemies "offered no real contest" to the iron weapons of the Assyrians.[135] As they expanded east, the land of Palestine was in their path.

Between 870 and 850 BC, as described on the Kurkh Stele, the Assyrians defeated King Ahab of Israel and required an annual tribute from the ten northern tribes. A century later, around 745 BC, Israel was still paying the tribute of gold, silver, and other items to Assyrians, now under Tiglath-pileser III. That tribute wasn't enough, and around 740 BC, Tiglath began to forcibly move the elite, the artisans, merchants, and craftsmen of the ten northern tribes to Assyria (1 Chron. 5:26; 2 Kings 15:29).[136] This policy of removal, captivity, continued for another two decades.

Then, in 722 BC, the biblical accounts in 2 Kings 17:5-6, and the records of Sargon II, tell us that the Assyrian army destroyed the remainder of the ten northern tribes of Israel. The archeological record in places like Hazor and Megiddo confirm this destruction.[137] The ten northern tribes of Israel were never

---

[134] *The Bible in the British Museum: Interpreting The Evidence* T.C. Mitchell (The British Museum Press, 2004) pp. 44-45
[135] *Babylon: Mesopotamia and the Birth of Civilization* Paul Kriwaczek (Thomas Dunne Books 2012) p. 236
[136] *A History of the Jews,* Paul Johnson (Harper Perennial 1988) p. 69
[137] *A History of the Jews,* Paul Johnson (Harper Perennial 1988) p. 70

heard of again.[138] They did, however, live on in Jewish legend, "but in reality, they were simply assimilated into the surrounding Aramaean population, losing their faith and their language…as the Israelite artisans and peasants intermarried with the new settlers."[139]

History then serves up a curve ball. The ten northern tribes of the Kingdom of Israel had been swept into the dustbin of history. The tribes of Judah and Benjamin of the Kingdom of Judea living in and around Jerusalem, were unscathed and remnants of the northern tribes migrated there to safety.[140] Yet history carried forward the name of Israel as if it had been the survivor of the Assyrian invasion. And ever after, history will refer to the people and place as Israel. Sometimes it pays to be the loser.

About a decade after the destruction of the northern tribes, Hezekiah, the King of Judea,[141] began a religious transformation. He started by destroying the temples of worship outside of Jerusalem.[142] He attempted to regain some political control in Israel, and in the Philistine cities (2 Kings 18:4) and he aligned Judea with Egypt to avoid paying further Assyrian taxes. Not paying your taxes is seldom a good idea! King Sennacherib and his Assyrian army of tax collectors arrived in 701 BC and destroyed the cities of Judea and laid siege to Jerusalem. It survived because of a water supply tunnel that King Hezekiah had built.[143] That tunnel, along with inscriptions from the siege, can still be seen in Jerusalem today.

---

[138] *Jews God and History 50th Anniversary, 2nd Edition* Max I Dimont edited by Ethel Dimont (Signet Classics 1994) Kindle location 886

[139] *A History of the Jews,* Paul Johnson (Harper Perennial 1988) p. 68

[140] 2 Chronicles 15:9 states that people from Ephraim, Manasseh, and Simeon came to Judea. Probably some others did as well.

[141] Hereafter Israel will be used to mean Judea, unless otherwise noted.

[142] *The Great Transformation* Karen Armstrong (Alford A Knopf 2006) p. 100

[143] A *History of the Jews* Paul Johnson (Harper Perennial 1988) p. 73

The Bible reports that an angel came and slayed the Assyrians (2 Kings 19:35). Centuries later, the Greek historian Herodotus explained that typhus, spread by mice, had infected the Assyrian army.[144] The Bible reports that Hezekiah did in fact pay a heavy ransom (2 Kings 18-14) while The Annals of Sennacherib (The Taylor Prism) reports that Hezekiah made a deal with the Assyrians to pay their back taxes as a ransom[145] and to send some 200,000 people to Assyria as slaves.[146] Either way, the city of Jerusalem had survived the power of mighty Assyria.

While King Hezekiah was successful in fending off the Assyrians, he was unsuccessful in his religious reforms. After the typhus-laden mice had sent the gold- and silver-laden Assyrian army scurrying home, Manasseh became the king, and the Israelites went back to their practice of worshipping their many gods with their old ways of sacrifice.

*For he built up again the high places which Hezekiah his father had destroyed; and he reared up altars for Baal, and made a grove, as did Ahab king of Israel; and worshipped all the host of heaven and served them. (2 Kings 21:3)*

The Bible tells us that Abraham's God was angry at Manasseh for doing this. But then the all-powerful creator of the universe did absolutely nothing about it. Manasseh reigned for 55 years as Jerusalem became a large, thriving city and the people

---

[144] "Jews God and History" Max I Dimond Kindle loc 854

[145] *"The Bible in the British Museum: Interpreting the Evidence""* T.C. Mitchell (The British Museum Press, 2004) p 59 Also a translation of the relevant portions of the Prism in "Who Wrote the Bible" Richard Elliot Friedman (Perennial Library 1987) pp. 94

[146] *Jerusalem a Biography* Simon Sebag (Montefiore Knopf 2011) p. 44

of Israel continued to worship their many gods (2 Kings 21; 2 Chron. 33).[147]

After Manasseh, his son Amon became King of Israel and continued the popular polytheistic pagan policies of his father. Around 636 BC, Amon was assassinated, and eight-year-old Josiah became the King of Israel.

When Josiah was 26, he embarked on a program to repair the temple in Jerusalem. During the work, High Priest Hilkiah and his scribe Shaphan made an astounding discovery! Hidden in a closet, or behind a cabinet, or somewhere stuck between the rafters, they found a 600-year-old *book of the law of the Lord given by Moses* (2 Chron. 34:14, also in 2 Kings 22:8).[148,149]

It is here that question marks hang over the writing of the Old Testament. When the remnants of the northern tribes of Israel migrated to safety in Judea, they brought with them their gods, history, stories, oral myths, and writings.[150] The emigrants from the northern tribes brought stories of El, the High God of Canaanite tribes,[151] while the tribes in the south had stories of the god Yahweh.[152] These were fused together over the following centuries to form a single set of narratives that became the Old

---

[147] The long reign of Manasseh has bothered many Bible scholars perhaps including the writer of the book of Chronicles who rewrote the life of Manasseh and added a punishment in 2 Chronicles 33:10-13.
*The New Oxford Annotated Bible with Apocrypha: New Revised Standard Version* (Page 315). (Oxford University Press.) Kindle Edition.

[148] The date range for the Exodus under Moses is 1250 – 1225 BC *A History of the Jews* Paul Johnson (Harper Perennial 1988) pp. 24-26

[149] A very similar event occurred in 1972 when a very old version of the Qur'an was found during repairs of the Great Mosque of Sana'a in Yemen. This will be covered later during the discussion of Islam.

[150] *A History of the Jews* Paul Johnson (Harper Perennial 1988) p. 71

[151] *The Invention of God* Thomas Romer as translated by Raymond Geuss (Harvard University Press 2013(p 72

[152] *Who Wrote the Bible* Richard Elliot Friedman Perennial Library 1987 pp. 87-88 This is also discussed in *The Great Transformation*" Karen Armstrong (Alford A Knopf 2006) pp 64-65 and *The Evolution of God* Robert Wright (Little Brown and Co. 2009) pp. 150-159

Testament.[153] Scholars today sort out the stories from the histories of Israel and Judea using a sophisticated versions of the Jane Austen and Danielle Steele method explained earlier.

After receiving the document from Hilkiah, Josiah gathered:

*All the inhabitants of Jerusalem with him, and the priests, and the prophets, and all the people, both small and great: and he read in their ears all the words of the book of the covenant which was found in the house of the Lord.* (2 Kings 23:2)

"Religious truth sounded very different when presented in this way. Everything was clear, cut-and-dried, very different from the more elusive 'knowledge' imparted by oral transmission."[154]

King Josiah commanded that the newly discovered laws be obeyed: *And the inhabitants of Jerusalem did according to the covenant of God, the God of their fathers* (2 Kings 23:4). He then ordered an extravagant feast: a Passover. It was the first Passover observed by Judaism in 275 years (2 Chron. 35; 2 Kings 23:22).[155]

Just as his great grandfather Hezekiah, Josiah tried to reform the religion of the people of Israel.[156] Josiah wanted the people to worship one of their gods, Yahweh, exclusively.[157] While the inhabitants of Jerusalem went along with Josiah's reforms, the Israelites of the countryside continued to believe in their many gods (2 Chron. 34:32).[158] And so Josiah ruthlessly imposed his

---

[153] *Who Wrote the Bible?* Richard Elliot Friedman (Perennial Library 1987) p. 90

[154] *The Great Transformation* Karen Armstrong (Alford A Knopf 2006) p.160

[155] *"And there was no Passover like to that kept in Israel from the days of Samuel the prophet"* [2 Chron. 35:18] Samuel was believed to have lived around 900 or 275 years prior.

[156] While this story is told in Chronicles, The Book of Jeremiah supposedly written in the days of Josiah makes no mention of any of Josiah 's reforms.

[157] *The Great Transformation* Karen Armstrong (Alford A Knopf 2006) p. 161

[158] *The Triumph of Elohim From Yahwisms to Judahisms* Diana V Edelman (ed) (Kok Pharos Publishing 1995) contains five scholarly papers on the evolution of Judaism

reforms on the Israelites of the countryside, "destroying once and for all the suspect cultic practices of the old high places and provincial temples…all images were destroyed, the high places closed down, pagan heterodox and heretical priests were massacred."[159] In other words, their policy was "Believe as I do, or die!" Under the threat of the sword, Israel was forced to convert to the worship of Yahweh alone.[160]

Josiah also removed the symbol of God's wife, the Asherah pole, from Solomon's temple and prohibited the worship and rituals honoring her, the wife or consort of Yahweh (2 Kings 23:6-7).

"Josiah's theology – worship of Yahweh and Yahweh alone – would not only survive and prevail but prevail in grander intensified form. Judaism first, then Christianity and then Islam, would come to believe that the god Josiah proclaimed, Abraham's God, was not just the only god worth worshipping, but the only God in existence."[161]

While Elijah may have pointed the way, Josiah turned Israel off the road of henotheism and put it on the road to monotheism.

Israel was also literally on the road between the Assyrians and the Egyptians. It was on that road at Megiddo, where Josiah was killed in a battle with the Egyptians (2 Kings 22:29; 2 Chron. 35:20–25). [162] Josiah had forced monotheism on the people of Israel, but after his death, they returned to the worship of their many familiar gods (2 Kings 23:32). The road of Josiah's

---

from 960 BC to 587 BC. One of them "The Appearance of a Pantheon in Judah" by Lowell K Handy explores the archeological and linguistic evidence that ties the Judahistic cult of Yahweh into the more ancient Ugarit gods of El and Asherah and their melding into the Assyrian Pantheon structure.

[159] *A History of the Jews* Paul Johnson (Harper Perennial 1988) p. 73
[160] *The Great Transformation*" Karen Armstrong Alford A Knopf p. 160
[161] "The Evolution of God Robert Wright (Little Brown and Company 2009) pp. 165-166
[162] The battle is generally believed to have occurred in 609 BC, but the details of the account in Chronicles are disputed.

monotheism was a short dead end.[163] After Josiah polytheistic paganism reigned again as the religion of the Israelites.

A few years later, in 605 BC, the Egyptians and the Assyrians fought at Carchemish. This battle earned three mentions in the Bible (Jeremiah 46:2; 2 Chron. 35:20; Isaiah 10:9) and whole books in the Egyptian and Assyrian texts. Nebuchadnezzar and the Assyrians defeated Egypt and went on to conquer all of Palestine. This time with no typhus-laden mice or angels to defend it, Nebuchadnezzar took Jerusalem on March 16th, 597 BC. He repeated what had been done a century prior in the Northern Kingdom, taking all the leaders of Israel—the elite, the artisans, and the rich—to Babylon as captives.[164] Israel itself was made a province, and Josiah's son, Zedekiah, was left to govern those who remained.

Zedekiah chaffed at being a vassal of Babylon, and like his grandfather, made an alliance with Pharaoh Hophra, of Egypt, and hoped for support from the Jews of the Nile.[165] The Babylonians had had enough of Jewish revolt and returned with a vengeance. In 587 BC, Nebuchadnezzar leveled Jerusalem, tore down Solomon's temple, and destroyed the surrounding area of Judea. Zedekiah's children were killed in front of him, and then his eyes were put out.[166] All of the remaining leaders were taken to Babylon and only peasants were left behind. Some did escape and scattered to Egypt and throughout the Middle East. And the "Book"? That miracle find of Hilkiah? Who knows?

However, scholars believe that the "Book" may have been seven books in total: Deuteronomy, Joshua, Judges, 1 & 2 Samuel and 1 & 2 Kings. But the important part is that they were all compiled from other sources, and edited, perhaps by a single

---

[163] *The Great Transformation* Karen Armstrong (Alford A Knopf 2006) p. 166
[164] *A History of the Jews* Paul Johnson (Harper Perennial 1988) p. 78
[165] *The Story of the Jews: Finding the Words 1000BC to 1492AD* Simon Schama (Harper Collins 2013) pp. 43-44
[166] *A History of the Jews* Paul Johnson (Harper Perennial 1988) p. 78

person— "the Deuteronomist" who then compiled and formed them into a continuous history of the Israelites.[167]

Some scholars believe the Deuteronomist to be Jeremiah, while others believe it was a committee or series of people working over the course of the next century or more. Jeremiah does suggest that it might have been him. He says that God told him to *Take a scroll and write on it all the words that I have spoken to you against Israel and Judah and all the nations, from the day I spoke to you, from the days of Josiah until today* (Jer. 36:2-4). To commemorate the end of ancient Judaism, and the beginning of a new era for Israel, Jeremiah will be accorded the honorary title of being the "First Jew."[168]

As the Israelites crawled from under the rubble of Solomon's Temple, ancient Judaism had come to an end. All that was left were memories of their ancient stories and myths, and perhaps scraps of writings of their gods and rituals. Those memes in future centuries would become the Hebrew Bible. The Israelites were still a pagan and polytheistic people, and in their writings there were "no notions of hell and heaven, no obvious judgement and punishment for sinners nor beatific reward for the virtuous."[169] As God's chosen people trudged out of Canaan, they had no hope for a better life beyond death.

For Judaism to become the rootstock of Christianity and Islam, new beliefs were needed. Monotheism, humans with a soul that survives death, a resurrection of the body, and heavenly rewards or punishments in hell all needed to be developed, framed, and accepted. As the Israelites trundled into Babylon, those beliefs were not a part of their religion.

---

[167] *Who Wrote the Bible* Richard Elliot Friedman (Perennial Library 1987) Chapters 3 through 7 tell this story and its supporting evidence in detail.

[168] *A History of the Jews* Paul Johnson (Harper Perennial 1988) p. 79

[169] *Life After Death: a history of the afterlife in the religions of the West* A. F Segal (Doubleday 2004) p 121

# Chapter Eight – Monotheism

When Sargon II completed the annihilation of the ten northern tribes in 722 BC, he removed many of the Israelites and scattered them. He also colonized Israel: *And the King of Assyria brought down men from Babylon and from Cuthat, and from Ava and Hamath and from Sepharvin and they possessed Samaria and dwelt in the cities thereof* (2 Kings 17:24).

And when they came and settled, is there any doubt that they brought with them their own gods and their own religion? Two thousand years later the "invaders" of the Americas brought with them their religion of Christianity and colonized the New World. Just as Christianity was transported to and proselytized in the Americas, the Assyrians brought their religion to their conquered territories.

The religion of the Assyrian Empire marked a major change in the worship of God. Prior to the Assyrian Empire, as discussed earlier, the gods were a part of nature and worshipped in local temples. When the Assyrians expanded their borders, they prayed to their god Ashur wherever they were. Not only did this spread the worship of Ashur, but it brought about the idea of a transcendent god, a god who is above all. The Assyrians bragged that their god Ashur was bigger than the captured gods of the Israelites as they counted them as part of their spoils.[170] Our god Ashur is bigger than your gods El or Yahweh. It is known as monolatry, the worship of one god without denying the existence of other gods, just a short step from monotheism, the belief in only one God[171]

The Assyrian Empire had conquered Israel, but the Assyrians were in turn conquered in 612 BC by a group known as Neo-Babylonians. Under Nebuchadnezzar, they sacked Jerusalem and brought with them their god Marduk. Marduk "absorbed the functions of other gods" and "became Mesopotamia's closest approach yet to a universalist monotheism."[172] Whether Ashur or Marduk, the Israelites were in intimate contact with societies whose religions bordered on monotheism, even before they were immersed in Persian culture and its religion.

Israel was a conglomeration of polytheistic tribes whose lands, temples, and homes had been annihilated. The leadership of those tribes, and many of their people, were now enslaved in Nineveh, while others were scattered throughout the Eastern Mediterranean. The destruction of ten of those tribes had begun 250 years before, but now Jerusalem—the capital and the cultural center of Judaism—was also destroyed. Why had this happened? What had caused this evil to befall the Israelites?

For polytheism, good and evil is simple: some gods are good, and some are evil. For monotheism, good and evil are more complex, either God is not all good, or he is not all powerful. One of the biblical Prophets framed the issue this way: *Shall there be evil in a city, and God has not done it?* (Amos 3:6). Certainly, the Gibeonites, Libnahites, Eglonites, Hebronites, etc., whom the

---

[170] *The Evolution of God* Robert Wright (Little Brown and Company 2009) p. 176

[171] *Babylon: Mesopotamia and the Birth of Civilization*, Paul Kriwaczek (Thomas Dunne Books 2012) p. 231

[172] *The Evolution of God* Robert Wright (Little Brown and Company 2009) pp 88-89

Israelites had viscously and wantonly destroyed at "God's command," would agree that he was an evil God.

The search for a just God of Israel during the Captivity was then hypocritical. How could the Israelites find moral justice in their situation when they had done much worse to others? Why had Abraham's God permitted the Captivity? Did he cause the destruction of his own temple? Was there spiritual morality or just secular might? Was Abraham's God not powerful enough to protect his chosen people? If he could not protect them, how could he be the all-powerful creator of the Universe? Maybe God's press secretaries, the prophets, had the answers!

The Bible is full of "prophets." There are over 70 prophets mentioned by name, and hundreds more are mentioned in general.[173] There were prophets, oracles, seers, diviners or mediums—whatever word you prefer to use. From time to time, they showed up and explained to the Israelites that God was unhappy and was punishing the nation for some form of community sin. Prophets never showed up and offered gold stars: "Hey great job on doing your temple sacrifices. You've been good—keep it up." No, it was always *You have plowed evil; you have reaped unrighteousness; you have eaten the fruit of hypocrisy; because you trusted in your own direction* (Hosea 10:13) or *You only have I known of all the families of the earth: therefore I will punish you for all your iniquities* (Amos 3:2). The prophets always say the entire nation of Israel is being held accountable, not the person. They never say, "You, Mr. Jacob Zachariah, are being punished for your sin." It was almost the opposite; Manasseh reigned for 55 years as he returned Israel to its polytheistic pagan ways. Not only did God do absolutely

---

[173] For example, 1 Kings 18:13 (KJV 1900) "Was it not told my lord what I did when Jezebel slew the prophets of the Lord, how I hid an hundred men of the Lord's prophets by fifty in a cave, and fed them with bread and water?"

nothing, Israel grew and prospered! It was as if Manasseh was being rewarded for Israel's polytheistic and pagan ways.

In the centuries following the first Assyrian incursions, many prophets appeared, saying they had messages from Abraham's God.[174] The most remarkable Prophet of the Old Testament walked around Jerusalem naked, explaining the old and pointing the way to a new form of Judaism (Isaiah 20:2). He was Isaiah, son of Amoz (Isaiah 1:1). Always shown fully clothed in the stained-glass windows and paintings found in churches, people like him can be found on the streets of San Francisco almost every day. Tradition says that Isaiah was neither accepted into the priesthood nor welcomed in the temple,[175] which makes obvious sense. Naked people never showed up in my church either.

We cannot even be sure that Isaiah wrote anything, but a book in his name would change Judaism and set the stage for the future of Christianity. "The Great Isaiah Scroll" was discovered in Qumran along the Dead Sea in 1947. This copy of the book of Isaiah was written around 125 BC and is 1000 years older than any known copy of any book of the Hebrew Bible.[176] Aside from many deviations from later copies, it is the same 66-chapter version familiar to Christians and Jews everywhere.

The Book of Isaiah was not all written by Isaiah, much less the one man running around naked in the streets of Jerusalem. Scholars agree that the Book of Isaiah had at least three different authors. Chapters 1-39, called Proto Isaiah, was written around 700 BC at the time of Hezekiah[177] and the destruction of the

---

[174] Nahum, Micah, Habakuk, Zephaniah, Jeremiah, Obadiah, Ezekiel, Amos, Hosea to name a few.

[175] *A History of the Jews* Paul Johnson (Harper Perennial 1988) p. 75

[176] "The Digital Dead Sea Scrolls: The Great Isaiah Scroll", http://dss.collections.imj.org.il/isaiah

[177] In May of 2018 officials in Israel and at the Armstrong International Cultural Foundation in Oklahoma announced the discovery in Jerusalem of clay seals

northern tribes of Israel. Deutero-Isaiah, chapters 40-55, was written around 587 BC at the time of the destruction of Jerusalem, and Trito-Isaiah, chapters 56-66, was written after the Captivity but before the rebuilding of Jerusalem, in the late 400s BC.[178]

At some point, the three different writings, written centuries apart, were edited and compiled into a single "Book of Isaiah,"[179] thus giving it continuity and editorial voice. The literary skills of Hebrew poetry in the book of Isaiah surpass all the other prophets. Its "sparkling prose with its brilliant images…has since passed into the literature of all civilized nations."[180]

The Book of Isaiah covers the Assyrian wars, the Captivity, and the beginning of the Jewish return to Jerusalem from Babylon. During that time, Israel was in danger of disappearing by assimilation. To avoid this, the Israelites had to be given a new understanding that explained the events of old and pointed to a hopeful way forward. The Book of Isaiah does precisely that.

Isaiah begins with God saying to abandon the old:

*I hate your new moon festivals and your appointed feasts; they have become a burden to Me. So when you spread out your hands in prayer, I will hide My eyes from you; yes, even though you multiply prayers, I will not listen. Your hands are covered with blood. Wash yourselves, make yourselves clean; remove the evil of your deeds*

---

"believed to have been used by the biblical prophet Isaiah and King Hezekiah." The Jerusalem Post May 27th, 2018

[178] While shelves of books have been written on this topic the fundamental evidence is that Isaiah 1 says that he was a prophet beginning in the reign of Uzziah's who ruled from 783 – 742 BC beginning in chapter 40 are the events of King Cyrus of Babylon who ruled between 576 – 530 BC over 200 years later. The writing of chapters 56-66 fits into the saga of Ezra and Nehemiah in the 400s.

[179] From here forward I will use the word Isaiah, to refer collectively to the three authors.

[180] *A History of the Jews* Paul Johnson (Harper Perennial 1988) p. 74

*from My sight. Cease to do evil, learn to do good; seek justice, reprove the ruthless; defend the orphan, plead for the widow.* (Isaiah 1:13-17)

Life in God's universe was not about the feasts, the sacrifices and the superficial rituals in a beautiful temple but about how you live your life outside that temple.[181, 182] Yes, the Israelites were obeying the commands of God, but they were only going through the motions. They were going to temple, doing sacrifices, praying, and using incense in a meaningless way, while ignoring the poor, the orphans and widows.[183] Isaiah said loudly to every Jew, and the nation of Israel, that every individual was responsible for social justice and had an individual relationship with God.[184] This was a revolutionary difference from the national God of Ancient Israel in the Torah.[185]

Isaiah reaffirmed that the Israelites are God's people: *I have formed thee; thou art my servant: O Israel, thou shalt not be forgotten of me* (Isaiah 44:21). But then Isaiah took the final step; there is only one God: *Thus saith the Lord the King of Israel, and his redeemer the Lord of hosts; I am the first, and I am the last; and beside me there is no God* (Isaiah 44:6). *I am the Lord, and there is none else, there is no God beside me* (*Isaiah 45:5-6*). Chapters 44 and 45 repeat the theme of one God and one God

---

[181] *A History of God: The 4,000 Year Old Quest of Judaism, Christianity and Islam* Karen Armstrong (Albert A Knopf 1994) p. 44

[182] Jesus would repeat this message, and it should resonant with people today comfortably sitting in multi-million-dollar air-conditioned theaters of religion.

[183] Isaiah was not the only Prophet writing on this topic. Ezekiel who was among the first deported to Babylon was writing on the theme of one God and the individuals' responsibility to God and his fellow men. This topic is covered in *The Great Transformation* Karen Armstrong (Alfred A Knoff 2006) pp. 167-175 *A History of the Jews* Paul Johnson (Harper Perennial 1988) p. 81-83

[184] Believed to have been written earlier, the Book of Hosea may have foreshadowed Isaiah's message.

[185] As an aside, this echoes todays situation. Where is today's Isaiah saying people need to care for people and not lawyers and bigger and more government!

only. The author of Second Isaiah is the first known monotheist.[186] Abraham's God, the God of Israel, is no longer one amongst the many gods, nor is he the Henotheistic Chairman of the Board of gods; he is now the one, the only: GOD.

Isaiah's Jews are universally credited with being the world's first monotheistic religion. However, it must be kept in mind that Isaiah's proclamation came from within the Assyrian/Persian captivity,[187] and has its roots in the culture of his captives. "The foundations of the monotheism that the Hebrew tribes were to make the world's patrimony were being laid here in Assyria in the last part of the second millennium BCE."[188] But how could this one, all-powerful God of Abraham, the creator of the universe, be so weak and ineffective against the Assyrians? Ah-ha! Isaiah has the answer: yes, the Assyrians destroyed Israel, but it was an action instituted by God:

> *Woe to Assyria, the rod of My anger And the staff in whose hands is My indignation, I will send him against an hypocritical nation, and against the people of my wrath will I give him a charge, to take the spoil, and to take the prey, and to tread them down like the mire of the streets.* (Isaiah 10:5-6)

Yahweh used the Assyrians to cause the destruction of Israel, to show both the Assyrians and the Israelites who is in charge.[189]

But who wants to worship a God that has just destroyed the places where you live and shipped you off into slavery? Isaiah introduces another radical idea: *I have wiped out your transgressions like a thick cloud, and your sins like a heavy mist.*

---

[186] *Cosmos and Chaos and the World to Come* Norman Cohn (Yale University Press 1993) p. 152

[187] Since it is agreed that chapters 39-54 were written after the destruction of Jerusalem.

[188] *Babylon: Mesopotamia and the Birth of Civilization*, Paul Kriwaczek (Thomas Dunne Books 2012) p. 231

[189] *The Evolution of God* Robert Wright (Little Brown and Company 2009) p. 176-181

*Return to Me, for I have redeemed you* (Isaiah 44:22). Redemption: forget the past, let's start again! You can worship me again, because I have forgiven you, but always remember I am the guy in charge. Isaiah is spouting the psychology of battered wife syndrome with Israel as the battered wife of God!

Isaiah continues with his radical thoughts, Abraham's God is the source of both good *and* evil: *I form the light, and create darkness: I make peace, and create evil: I the Lord do all these things* (Isaiah 45:7). Abraham's God of Isaiah, of Jews, Christians, and Muslims…creates evil! He is the Jekyll and Hyde of the Universe.[190]

God's plan is completed by sending the Babylonian King Cyrus to avenge the Assyrians and do good by the Israelites.

> *Cyrus, whose right hand I have holden, to subdue nations before him, and to loose the loins of kings; to open the doors before him, and that the gates may not be shut: I will go before thee, and make the crooked places straight; I will break in pieces the doors of brass, and cut in sunder the bars of iron; And I will give thee the treasures of darkness, and hidden riches of secret places, that thou mayest know that I am the LORD, who call thee by thy name, even the God of Israel.* (Isaiah 45:1-3)

Isaiah provides Israel with a complete explanation of three centuries of horrible events. God needed to punish the nation of Israel once again for disobeying God's Laws or only following them by going through the motions. Simply attending services and rituals without following God's wishes needed to be punished. His slap upside the head to get the attention of the

---

[190] This one passage strikes at the heart of the Abrahamic religions. How can there be moral certainty with an immoral or amoral deity who has demonstrated capricious behavior? This issue will be debated by theologians for centuries. The verse is a confusing thought that we will discuss in depth in the book Abraham's Devil.

Israelites was having the Assyrians wipe out the ten tribes, exiling the rest. But then God forgives the Israelites and has the Persian Cyrus defeat the Assyrians and come to the rescue of Israel. "You see, this proves I am the one God of all," or so said the three "Isaiah's" as they wrote their story over the course of three centuries as the facts on the ground unfolded. The Jews had left Jerusalem as just another beaten tribe of pagan polytheists. Now in Babylon, the final editor of the book of Isaiah stitched together a rationale for their past and gave them monotheism.

Generations long past had formed their gods from ignorance and fear; they were the many gods of ancient Israel, the lessor gods of Elijah, the gods that Hezekiah and Josiah had tried to banish from Israel. All were now stricken from existence by the words of Isaiah. Monotheism, the idea that there was but one God, the creator of all existence, was now the theology of Israel. Now Abraham's God had become the one God of Judaism. Still missing were other doctrines needed for a future Judaism, Christianity, and Islam.

# Chapter Nine – Thus Spoke Zarathustra

In 540 BC, Cyrus the Great conquered the Neo-Babylonians creating Persian Empire.[191] Long before Cyrus, a man named Zarathustra began preaching a new religion which became the Persian religion known as Zoroastrianism.[192] Around 1200 BC, Zoroastrianism may have begun among the Aryan raiders in northeastern Iran.[193] It was a complex set of myths and rituals that had spread and morphed for hundreds of years.[194] While its origination and spread are beyond the scope of this book, *Zoroastrians, Their Beliefs and Practices* by Mary Boyce, *The Great Transformation* by Karen Armstrong, and *In Search of Zarathustra, the First Prophet and the Ideas that Changed the*

---

[191] The terms Babylonian Empire and Persian Empire are used by different sources. I will go with Persian.

[192] Whether or not Zoroastrianism had earlier roots entangled with a god called Mithra or whether Mithra came after Zoroastrianism is a chicken and egg debate for scholars. However, if you want to read more on this topic, I suggest *The Mysteries of Mithras: The Pagan Belief That Shaped the Christian World* Payam Nabarz (Inner Traditions 2005)

[193] *The Great Transformation* Karen Armstrong (Alfred A Knoff 2006) p. 8

[194] *World Religions from Ancient History to the Present* Geoffery Parrinder (Hamlyn Publishing Ltd 1971) Chapter 12, *The Great Transformation* Karen Armstrong (Alfred A Knoff 2006) Chapter 1, and *In Search of Zarathustra, the First Prophet and the Ideas that Changed the World* Paul Kriwaczek (Alfred A Knopf 2003) each tell the story in interesting detail

*World* by Paul Kriwaczek provide the evidence and tell the story in considerable detail.

Rituals and myth are not theology. Rituals are the cover to the book of theology. Just as you cannot judge a book by its cover, you cannot judge a theology by its rituals. Baptism, the dress of priests, the chanting in Latin, the stories of the saints, the wafer and the wine, or the incense ball are symbols and aspects of ritual, not Christian theology. The same is true for the cleansing, fire, chants, and other practices that are Zoroastrian rituals, not Zoroastrian theology.

Strip away the rituals and the myths and the most important aspects of Zoroastrian theology are its belief in one god, a messiah, a resurrection, a final judgment, a hell, and an everlasting life in paradise.[195] These are the Zoroastrian beliefs from centuries before their inclusion into Judaism, Christianity, and Islam.

Ahura Mazda is the god of Zoroastrianism who created the universe and is the source of all that is good. There is also a "devil," an evil spirit[196] named Angra Mainyu, who is the source of all evil. Zoroastrianism is the first known religion based on the principal of non-violence. Its ethical values are personified in the Holy Immortals, something like the Christian Holy Ghost, except there were five of them. They were of one mind, voice, and action which parallels with the Zoroastrian motto, "Good thoughts, good words, good deeds."[197]

Zarathustra (or sometimes called Zoroaster) is the chief prophet of Zoroastrianism. Zarathustra has many parallels with

---

[195] *Life After Death - A History of the Afterlife in Western Religion* Alan F Segal (Double Day 2004) p. 250 Interestingly the word paradise is Persian, which along with other loan words date the writing of the Book of Ecclesiastes to the end of the captivity or after Alexander the Great.

[196] *Biblical Origins: An Adapted Legacy* Petros Koutoupis (Virtualbookworm Publishing Inc 2008) p. 36

[197] *Zoroastrians Their Beliefs and Practices* Mary Boyce (Routledge 2001) p. 23

Jesus. He was sent from God and born of a virgin, he began preaching at the age of 30, and was purified by a "baptism," after which God was present when Zarathustra came out of the river.[198] Long before Jesus, Zarathustra was proclaiming one of the earliest formulations of the Golden Rule: *Whatever is disagreeable to yourself, do not do unto others* (Shayast-na-Shayast 13:29).

Isaiah proclaims Cyrus as God's right hand man, yet "Cyrus put himself forward as a champion of Zoroastrianism"[199] which was the major religion of the Persians.[200] Decades before Ezra and Nehemiah reestablished Judaism in Jerusalem, Darius, who followed Cyrus as king in the Persian Achaemenid Dynasty, proclaimed this on a "billboard" which he prominently carved on a cliff beside a main Persian Royal road: *Ahura Mazda bestowed this Kingdom upon me; Ahura Mazda bore me aid until I took possession of the Kingdom; by favor of Ahura Mazda I hold the Kingdom.*[201] Zoroastrianism would remain the major Persian religion until the Arab Islamic invasion over a thousand years in the future.[202]

For generations, Jews worked for their Persian Zoroastrian masters as "scribes or business agents, or household workers, or

---

[198] These parallels and others are discussed in *Cosmos, Chaos and the World to Come* Norman Cohn (Yale University Press 1993) pp. 99-102 and *The Great Transformation* Karen Armstrong (Alfred A Knopf 2006) pp. 8-9

[199] *A History of Zoroastrianism: Volume II: Under the Achaemenians* Mary Boyce (E.J. Brill 1982) p. 43

[200] While there is debate on Cyrus, it is clear Darius (ruled 522-486BC) and Xerxes (ruled 486-465BC) were devoted to Zoroastrianism. Artaxerxes I (ruled 465–425 BC) maintained Zoroastrianism but was tolerant of other religions sending Ezra and Nehemiah to Jerusalem to reestablish Judaism.
https://www.britannica.com/biography/Artaxerxes-II

[201] *In Search of Zarathustra* Paul Kriwaczek (Andrew A. Knopf 2003) p. 186

[202] Zorastrianism remained the dominate religion of Persia until Yazdegard II who was the last Emperor of Persia prior to the Islamic Arab invasion. In an effort to unite his kingdom he declared Zoroastrianism as the exclusive religion of the Empire. *The History of the Medieval World* Susan Wise Bauer (W.W. Norton 2010) p 123

outdoor workers," where they "came to know as much about Zoroastrianism as the Jewish faith."[203]

Cyrus ended the Captivity in 539 BC and ordered freedom to the conquered peoples, the return of their gods, and the rebuilding of their temples.[204] For the Jews, the prophet Ezra recorded:

*Thus says Cyrus king of Persia: All the kingdoms of the earth the Lord God of heaven has given me. And He has commanded me to build Him a house at Jerusalem which is in Judah...let the men of his place help him with silver and gold, with goods and livestock, besides the freewill offerings for the house of God which is in Jerusalem.* (Ezra 1:2-4)

The Jews were one among the many peoples covered by the order, with a sort of form letter replacing the names of the god and the people being sent back to their homeland.[205]

Isaiah reports that Abraham's God is very high on Cyrus.[206] *That saith of Cyrus, He is my shepherd, and shall perform all my pleasure: even saying to Jerusalem, Thou shalt be built; and to the temple, Thy foundation shall be laid* (Isaiah 44:28). Cyrus had decreed the Jews could return to Palestine but did not restore the independent nation of Israel; it would remain a territory of the Persians for another 200 years until the arrival of Alexander the Great.

---

[203] *Cosmos, Chaos and the World to Come* Norman Cohn (Yale University Press 1993) p. 223

[204] From the Cyrus Cylinder in the British Museum *The Bible in the British Museum"* T.C. Mitchell p. 83. But it seems that same wording was sent to every religion that had been held captive in Babylon by Nebuchadnezzar.

[205] *A History of Zoroastrianism: Volume II: Under the Achaemenians* Mary Boyce (E.J. Brill 1982) p. 64

[206] Abraham's God seems high on Zoroastrianism as well. In Qur'an 22:17 Zoroastrians are specifically named as eligible for salvation.

The first Jews who returned found hostility from those who had remained in Judea, and the re-settlement was a failure.[207] The Bible reports that twenty years later, in 520 BC, 42,360 exiles returned under Zerubbabel, the governor the Persians appointed over Judea. But the people living in Judea did not want the Israelites to return and rebuild the temple and city (Ezra 2:2; 2:64). They wrote a letter saying so:

*To King Artaxerxes: Your servants, the men in the region beyond the River, and now let it be known to the King that the Jews who came up from you have come to us at Jerusalem; they are rebuilding the rebellious and evil city and are finishing the walls and repairing the foundations.* (Ezra 4:11-12)

That rebuilding program also failed (Ezra 3-6). For another 75 years, the people held out against the rebuilding of Jerusalem. Ezra was a scribe in the Persian court who claimed to be a descendant of Moses' brother some 40 to 50 generations earlier. The Emperor tasked Ezra with rebuilding Jerusalem. He gave Ezra a supply of gold and silver to grease palms and finance the expedition, and a letter of instruction and authority:

*Artaxerxes, [a] king of kings, To Ezra the priest, a scribe of the Law of the God of heaven: Perfect peace, and so forth [b].I issue a decree that all those of the people of Israel and the priests and Levites in my realm, who volunteer to go up to Jerusalem, may go with you. And whereas you are being sent by the king and his seven counselors to inquire concerning Judah and Jerusalem, with regard to the Law of your God which is in your hand.* (Ezra 7:12-14)

---

[207] *A History of the Jews* Paul Johnson (Harper Perennial 1988) p. 86

With his pedigree and the financial and political backing of the emperor, Ezra left to make yet another attempt at rebuilding Jerusalem and a Jewish nation in Palestine.[208] Yet again, the people of Palestine refused to go along with the plan.

The problem was the inter-marriage among the Jews, Arabs, Persians and others which had gone on for centuries. After seven to ten generations, those who had remained behind had assimilated with the surrounding peoples and established an essentially new culture and country. Palestinians of the 5th century BC were asking the returning Jews, "Why should we turn over control of our country to you, the returnee interlopers?" Palestinians 2,500 years later were asking the same question of the Jews who returned to Palestine after World War II.

Jerusalem was still not getting rebuilt. In the 20th year of King Artaxerxes' reign, or 445 BC, the emperor appointed his trusted sommelier[209]Nehemiah, to go to Jerusalem and join Ezra in the rebuilding project (Neh. 2:1). Over continuing local opposition, Nehemiah rebuilt Jerusalem and made an agreement to repopulate the city (Neh. 11:1-4).

After all the struggle and resistance, there was a need to unify the people. Like Josiah centuries before, Ezra called the people together and read from books. Not ones miraculously found, but ones he brought from Babylon (Neh. 8:1-8). It was 400 years after the first Assyrian incursion, 280 years after the elimination of the ten tribes, 180 years after Josiah's attempts at monotheism, and 143 years after the destruction of Jerusalem. Judaism was

---

[208] The Biblical timeline of this period is not fully agreed on by scholars. The central question is whether Ezra is referring to Artaxerxes I or Artaxerxes II which would mean his arrival date was either 458 BC or 397 BC. The same dating problem arises for Nehemiah. The earlier date is the one used in this chronology. The later date would imply that the Palestinian area was more strongly intertwined with the Persian Zoroastrian culture for another 50 years.

[209] The actual title was translated as "cup-bearer," The duties at the time included the tasting and serving of wine, hence a sommelier. *The Kings Cup-Bearer* O.F. Walton (Google Books originally published in 1892) p. 8 p. 21

officially re-inaugurated in Jerusalem,[210] and the term "Jews" is now applied to the people of Israel, the followers of Abraham's God.[211]

Ezra read something that was an "official authorized accurate version. And that in turn meant sorting through and selecting and editing the vast literature of history, politics and religion" available in Babylon.[212] Over the centuries, these books "fuse(d) the most important documents of the divergent Mosaic documents, including the Deuteronomy of Josiah into the five books of the Pentateuch, namely Genesis, Exodus, Leviticus, Numbers, and Deuteronomy."[213] It is doubtful that Ezra read all of that to the people, but whatever he read is believed to be the foundation of the Old Testament of the Bible which would still see considerable future redaction and editing. [214]

It is precisely this fusion of documents that gives us two different creation stories, two peoples (Hebrews and Israelites) two Moses (Levite Moses and Midianite Moses) two kingdoms (Judah and Israel) two temples (Bethel and Jerusalem) and even two Gods (Yahweh and El) as well as duplications of many stories that are clearly merged. Muhammad will claim 1000 years later that Ezra's fusion had created errors that he and God corrected with the Qur'an.[215, 216]

---

[210] *A History of the Jews* Paul Johnson (Harper Perennial 1988) p. 87

[211] *Josephus The Essential Writings* Paul L Maier (Kregel Publications 1988) p. 191

[212] *A History of the Jews* Paul Johnson (Harper Perennial 1988) p. 87

[213] *Jews God and History 50th Anniversary, 2nd Edition* Max I Dimont edited by Ethel Dimont (Signet Classics 1994) Kindle location 886

[214] *The Triumph of Elohim From Yahwisms to Judaisms* Edited by Diana V. Edelman (Kok Pharos Publishing 1995) p110 Essay by Thomas L Thompson

[215] Islam believes that God had originally given Moses the Torah, Qur'an 2:87 But that the Torah had been corrupted. Qur'an 2:75-79 Islamic tradition says that Ezra, who is mentioned in Qur'an 9:30 was the one who corrupted it. Which is intriguing as modern scholarship shows that Ezra was almost certainly one of the writers, editors, or redactors.

[216] Both state that no changes are to be made to the documents. "Ye shall not add unto the word which I command you, neither shall ye diminish ought from it, that ye may keep the commandments of the Lord your God." Deuteronomy 4:2 Muhammad writes essentially the same thing in Qur'an 2:106 and 10:64

Ezra and his fellow scribes in Babylon may not have been the authors, but they were the editors of the heart of the readings brought back to Jerusalem. It is that editing, that compilation, that rewording, that scholars today study in order to sort out the origins, theologies, duplications, and contradictions that are found throughout the Old Testament. And 2,500 years later, Bible scholars again using the "Jane Austen and Danielle Steele" and other techniques unsort the fused text into the J, E, P, D, and R text.

We can only make an educated guess at which documents and which stories left with the Israelites from Jerusalem, and which returned with the Jews. But the words Ezra read formulated a nation of Israel, provided it with a culture, and unified its history of divine origination.[217] That story of divine origination would be the footpath on which Jesus and Muhammad would walk many centuries later.

Modern Judaism, Christianity, and Islam would be built on the stories compiled by Hilkiah or Shaphan, then edited and redacted by scribes and scholars like Jeremiah or Baruch and many others in Babylon. That is what Ezra read. The oral stories of old, written in the Axial Age, were now probably in recognizable written form.

But Ezra and Nehemiah and other returnees brought more than just books of the Old Testament. They brought new ideas— Zoroastrian ideas that had been infused into the Judaist community. Indeed, the Jews during the Captivity "absorbed Zoroastrian beliefs and adapted them to their own aspirations."[218] The people of Israel had lived together with the Persians and their Zoroastrian religion for centuries. Ezra, a scribe raised and trained in the court of the King, and Nehemiah, a functionary in

---

[217] *The Story of the Jews: Finding the Words 1000BC to 1492AD* Simon Schama (Harper Collins 2013) p. 46

[218] *Social History of Western Civilization* Richard M Golden (St Martin Press 1996 p. 34

his court, were just two of many thousands of scribes and scholars who worked closely in the Zoroastrian environment, while others in Palestine lived under Zoroastrian colonial rule.

Here is a passage on the Zoroastrian view of death and the afterlife:

> At death, one's actions are weighed in the balance. If the good outweigh the bad, one passes to heaven, but if not, to hell where the punishment is made to fit the crime. But this is still not the end. Eternal hell is an immoral teaching in Zoroastrian eyes. A good God would never allow his creatures to suffer eternally. The purpose of the punishment is to reform so that on the day of resurrection all maybe raised by the Savior to face the final judgement. Then when all are pure, the devil and all his works are finally destroyed, and the distinction between heaven and earth is overcome so that all may worship and live with God in the full glory of his creation.[219]

During the Captivity, Judaism inherited the genes of Zoroastrianism and later passed them on to Christianity and Islam. Accepting that the critical theologies were not initiated by the Jews is difficult for Jews, Christians, and Muslims. Writing on this topic, the historian Bernard Lewis said, "Those who believe themselves to be in unique possession of the truth are easily convinced that the discovery of this truth was their achievement."[220]

---

[219] *World Religions from Ancient History to the Present* Geoffrey Parrinder (Hamlyn Publishing Ltd 1971) p. 181 In addition Daryush Mehta the Zoroastrian Chaplain at Harvard, has personally confirmed that this does reflect the general concepts of Zoroastrianism.

[220] *The Middle East a Brief History of the last 2000 Years* Bernard Lewis, (Scribner 1995) p. 26

Ideas of social justice, taking care of the poor, a God of reason who offers repentance, a savior figure for Israel who brings a period of peace—all these ideas, thought of today as exclusively Jewish–Christian-Islamic, were present in Persian Zoroastrianism prior to the Captivity.[221]

Whether the writers and editors, from Isaiah and Jeremiah to Ezra and Daniel, creatively advanced new ideas or absorbed, embraced, and embellished the ideas of their Zoroastrian masters, we will never know. "It is possible to trace," however, the central ideas of Zoroastrianism "to all the current monotheistic world religions."[222] Zoroastrianism "has probably had more influence on mankind, directly and indirectly, than any other single faith."[223] One way or the other, the core ideas of Zoroastrianism were present in Judaism only after the Babylonian captivity.[224]

The Zoroastrian "idea of an anointed savior, born of a holy seed, who will come at the end of time and ensure the final triumph of good over evil"[225] was put into the words of Isaiah[226] and then made into a beautiful Christmas carol:

O come, O come, Emmanuel
And ransom captive Israel
That mourns in lonely exile here
Until the Son of God appear
Rejoice! Rejoice! Emmanuel
Shall come to thee, O Israel.

[221] *An Introduction to the New Testament and the Origins of Christianity* Delbert Burkett (Cambridge Press 2002) Chapter "Conceptions of the afterlife"

[222] *The Mysteries of Mithras: The Pagan Belief That Shaped the Christian World* by Payam Nabarz (Inner Traditions 2005) Loc 166

[223] *Zoroastrians: Their Religious Beliefs and Practices* Mary Boyce, (Routledge 1979) p 1

[224] *The Triumph of Elohim From Yahwisms to Judaisms* Edited by Diana V. Edelman (Kok Pharos Publishing 1995) p23

[225] *The Middle East a Brief History of the last 2000 Years* Bernard Lewis, (Scribner 1995) p. 28

[226] Isa. 7:14 and Isa. 35:10

O come, O come, Thou Lord of might,
Who to Thy tribes, on Sinai's height,
In ancient times didst give the Law,
In cloud, and majesty and awe.
Rejoice! Rejoice! Emmanuel
Shall come to thee, O Israel.

After the destruction of Jerusalem in 587 BC, when the Israelites looked at the total desolation around them and contemplated their faith in Abraham's God, they could not help but ask: *What went wrong? What did we do to deserve this?* Almost 150 years later, Ezra read the answers found in the libraries of Babylon. The Jews then waited for the coming of Emmanuel.

# Chapter Ten – The Return to Everlasting Life

The Captivity is portrayed as a tragedy, "mourned in lonely exile," as *By the waters of Babylon, there we sat down and wept...*(Ps. 137:1-6). The real story is that "Jews fell in love with the country, [and] prospered," as they accessed the world's greatest library, learned international trade, and "acquired manners, grace and refinement."[227] Two thirds of the Jews living in Babylon decided not to return, which may explain the decades of difficulty in resettling Jerusalem. Jerusalem would again become the political center of Judaism, but for a thousand years, Babylon would be the Jewish center of study, scholarship, and thought.[228]

After Ezra and Nehemiah rebuilt Jerusalem, it remained as a small province of the Persian Empire for two centuries. While few details are known of Jewish history during that period, we do know that under Persian rule there was peace and stability, and

---

[227] *Jews God and History 50th Anniversary, 2nd Edition* Max I Dimont edited by Ethel Dimont (Signet Classics 1994) offers a full discussion in the middle of Chapter 4 Kindle locations 989-1003

[228] *Jews, God, and History, 50th Anniversary, 2nd Edition*, Max I Dimont edited by Ethel Dimont (Signet Classics 1994) Kindle 1080-1092

the Jews prospered as the population grew from 70,000 for the entire region to an estimated 120,000 in Jerusalem by the end of the 3rd century.[229] Centuries of rule from the east was about to radically change.

In 333 BC, an immense new power arrived from the West: Alexander the Great. "He changed the world more than any conqueror in history by spreading his vision of the Hellenikon— Greek culture, language, poetry, religion, sport, and Homeric kingship—from the deserts of Libya to the foothills of Afghanistan."[230] In the Hellenistic Age of the next three centuries, the world would be viewed through Greek eyes.

When Alexander first invaded Palestine, the Persians asked Israel for help in defending against the Greeks. Reflecting their ancient rivalries, Samaria and Judea had different ideas. Judea agreed to help the Persians, while Samaria sided with Alexander in exchange for the building of a temple on Mt. Gerizim. Alexander won, the Samaritans got their temple, and Jerusalem submitted to Alexander. Perhaps to salvage Israel's dignity, a myth developed that Alexander bowed to the high priest of the Jerusalem temple as he marched through.[231]

Alexander was a pupil of Aristotle. Legend has it that the two of them made a great discovery when Alexander was a young boy sitting in class while Aristotle was making tea. The boiling water condensed on the ceiling and dripped back down. *Eureka!* Rain was not caused by the gods, but by the sun evaporating the lakes and ponds, rising to the cold heavens, condensing and falling as rain! Aristotle taught Alexander that, just like the example of the rain, man could understand all of reality through reason and

---

[229] *A History of the Jews* Paul Johnson (Harper Perennial 1988) pp. 96-97 However he is quoting Pseudo-Hecataeus which Strabo claimed to be inaccurate.

[230] *Jerusalem a Biography* Simon Sebag Montefiore (Knopf 2011) p. 59

[231] *Jerusalem a Biography* Simon Sebag Montefiore (Knopf 2011) p. 58

experience.[232] Alexander's mission was to spread this Hellenistic message to all known mankind.

The Hellenistic Age brought about a profound new approach to life: "the cultivation and perfection of the individual." The goal of life was "moral freedom and dignity" through the "absence of pain by eliminating bad habits and false desires" and the "application of rational thought and self-scrutiny."[233] These ideas in the Hellenistic culture exalted man in everything, from the Olympics, to science, art, and architecture—all of which guided the development of Western philosophy and culture.

Wherever Alexander conquered, he did not destroy the cultures but infused them with Hellenistic schools, libraries, and the teachings of Aristotle, Plato, and dozens of other Greek Philosophers which have been taught ever since. Plato offers this summary of his views on the soul and life after death:

> People are, "on the termination of their first life, brought to trial and, according to their sentence, some go to the prison-houses beneath the earth, to suffer for their sins, while others, by virtue of their trial, are borne lightly upwards to some celestial spot, where they pass their days in a manner worthy of the life they have lived in their mortal form." (Phaedrus 249)

This view of the soul, death, and the afterlife meshed well and re-enforced to the Jews the ideas they had heard and studied in the Persian Zoroastrian culture. Judaism would continue to absorb these ideas over the coming centuries.

When Alexander died at the age of 30, his generals divided Alexander's Empire and established themselves as kings. One of them, Antiochus, started the Seleucid Dynasty, which ruled most of the Middle East, while another, Ptolemy, began a dynasty that

---

[232] *Josephus The Essential Writings* Paul L Maier (Kregel Publications 1988) p. 199
[233] *The Hellenistic Age* Peter Thonemann (Oxford University Press 2016) p. 87.

ruled Egypt and Libya. Two new cities were built and named after their founders: Alexander built Alexandria, and Antiochus built Antioch. Samaria and Judea were again situated between the reigning powers and were swept up in the disputes and political intrigues between the Ptolemys of Egypt and the Seleucids of Syria, Iraq, and Iran.

Alexander's Hellenism became the accepted culture, and the wave of the future. The situation was not significantly different than Americanism at the end of the 20th century. American culture and economic domination led to the fall of the Berlin Wall, the break-up of the Soviet Union, the first Iraq War, and the events in Tiananmen Square; Americanism was the accepted culture and the wave of the future.[234] In his time, Alexander's policies were as successful, and Greek culture and business reigned across the conquered lands. Like everyone else, the Jews in Palestine jumped on the bandwagon of Greek culture.

By 175 BC, when Antiochus IV took the throne of the Seleucid Empire, most of the Jews had assimilated into the Greek culture.[235] They adopted the new Greek ways and rejected the old ways of Judaism to the point that the Jewish Temple in Jerusalem was turned into a gymnasium for Greek exercise. *The craze for Hellenism and the adoption of foreign customs reached such a pitch...that the priests no longer cared about the service of the altar* (2 Macc. 4:13-14, NAB). Antiochus IV then over-reached and banned Judaism completely.[236]

*At the suggestion of Ptolemy, a decree was issued to the neighboring Greek cities, that they should adopt the same policy toward the Jews and make them partake of the sacrifices and should slay those who did not choose to*

---

[234] Francis Fukuyama's widely read 1992 book, *The End of History and the Last Man* proclaimed that history as a clash of political ideologies, was at an end.

[235] 1 Maccabees 2

[236] *A History of the Jews,* Paul Johnson (Harper Perennial 1988) p. 103

*change over to Greek customs. One could see, therefore, the misery that had come upon them.* (2 Macc. 6:8-9)

Judaism was almost at an end. For the Jews who tried to practice their faith, there were vicious reprisals: *Two women were arrested for having their babies circumcised. They were paraded around the city with their babies hung from their breasts; then they were thrown down from the city wall* (2 Macc. 6:10).

Judaism was in a quandary. When their first temple had been destroyed, and the Jews exiled, the Prophet Isaiah said this was because the Jews had *not followed* God's Law. Now the Jews who remained faithful were being destroyed because they *were* following God's Law. Which was it? The Book of Isaiah had the answer then; who would have the answer now? And what would it be?

Many books attempted to answer. The Book of the Watchers, Jubilees, the First Book of Enoch and Daniel, and others conjured complex mythologies of beings, including angels, devils, and Satans, symbolic of the dilemma of the Jews as God's chosen people and the evil occurring around them. The general theme that gained acceptance was this:

> the foreign occupation of Palestine—and the accommodation of the majority of Jews to that occupation—(was) evidence that the forces of evil had overtaken the world; in the form of Satan…[these forces had] infiltrated and had taken over God's own people, turning into allies of the Evil One.[237]

Long, long before Darth Vader, the dark side had come to Palestine. Now Judaism also had an evil god, a devil who had invaded the hearts and minds of fellow Jews and was attacking the world. Faith also grew in Isaiah's messiah, who would be sent

---

[237] *The Origen of Satan* Elaine Pagels (Vintage Books, 1996) p. 57

from God to save the Jews. But when would that messiah arrive? Where was the Rebel Alliance needed in order to keep hope alive?

There are parallels with our time as well. In 1948, Sayyid Qutb, came to the United States for his master's degree at University of Northern Colorado. He saw in 20th century American culture precisely what Jews saw in 2nd century BC Greek culture: The forces of evil were overtaking the world in the form of a Satan.[238] And the United States was the Great Satan. Qutb wrote his thoughts in a book named *Milestones*. While not filled with the exotic mythologies, the theme was like the literature of the apocalypse and would have a similar impact on Islam.

At the beginning of the 2nd century BC, Judaism was being overcome by the forces of Hellenism. But a few radical Jews said no! Abraham's God was on their side and they were willing to die to earn the reward of eternal paradise. With their total trust in Abraham's God, they changed their world with an audacious attack on Hellenism. The orthodox Jews revolted, led by a member of the Hasmonean family, Judas "the Hammer" Maccabee.[239] The violence escalated, and ruthless practices of slaughter began a bitter multi-faceted civil war.

At the end of the 20th century AD, Islam was being overcome by the forces of Americanism. But a few radical Muslims said no! Abraham's God was on their side and they were willing to die to earn the reward of eternal paradise.[240] With their total trust in Abraham's God, they changed our world by flying planes into the World Trade Center. The radical Muslims attacked, led by a member of the bin Laden family, Osama bin Laden. The violence

---

[238] *Milestones* Sayyid Qutb Edited by A.B. al-Mehri (Maktabah Book Sellers and Publishers 2006) p. 191

[239] *A History of the Jews,* Paul Johnson (Harper Perennial 1988) p. 104

[240] Qutb encourages martyrdom and promises the reward to Islamic fighters. *Milestones* Sayyid Qutb Edited by A.B. al-Mehri (Maktabah Book Sellers and Publishers 2006) p. 191

escalated, and ruthless practices of slaughter began a bitter multi-faceted war.

Back in 175 BC, the Bible reports how Antiochus IV brought about what we now call martyrdom. A pious Jew, Eleazer was commanded to eat pork at a public ritual. He refused and said, *I will show myself worthy of my old age and set a noble example for the young of how to die a good death willingly and nobly for the revered and holy laws* (2 Macc. 6:27-28). But the idea of an old man dying for a principle would not achieve the level of martyrdom seen then and now.

A second, more horrific story accomplished that. A mother and her seven sons were also being forced to violate their belief by eating pork. Antiochus tortured each son in public before the eyes of their mother and a large crowd. The sons each proclaimed that, *the King of the universe will raise us up to an everlasting renewal of life, because we have died for his laws* (2 Macc. 7:9).

After 500 years of affiliation with Zoroastrianism, now reinforced by Platonism, Judaism had accepted that life did not end at death. This was a revolutionary concept and the second most important and influential idea in all human history![241] Abraham's God would reward you with a resurrection and eternal life if you died to obey his law! The religion of Abraham's God now had another key element of faith at the beginning of the 2nd century BC.

The idea of a personal resurrection and reward in eternal life would grow and spread for centuries, manifesting itself as the defining concept of Judaism, Christianity, and Islam. Billions of humans would guide the entirety of their human existence believing that the purpose of this life existed beyond death in another life.

---

[241] The single most important and influential idea in all human history is that god, God, or gods purposefully created and control existence. The idea of life after death is a corollary, a secondary consequence

The most dramatic manifestation of the idea of a blissful life in a hereafter is martyrdom; taking your own life, or allowing it to be taken, to advance to that next life. Martyrdom would present itself in the Jewish–Roman Wars, with Christians in the Roman arenas, in the Crusades, in New York City in 2001, in Iraq and Afghanistan, in Paris and Nice, in Orlando and San Bernardino. People died then and now because of fervent faith in the poisonous promise of martyrdom. The tragedy of martyrdom will continue so long as people believe in the promise of rewards in another life. You may not agree, but that does not matter. The only thing that matters is what the potential martyrs believe as they place their finger on the trigger. The scary part is a growing number of Muslims who believe or promote the belief that they will achieve a reward if they die and kill others with them. It is the supreme act of love to die so that others might live. It is the supreme act of hatred to willingly and happily die so that others will die as well!

On May 14, 2018 in Gaza, a senior Hamas leader, Ismail Radwan, gave a speech inciting rioters to breach the border and attack the Israelis. "When we are brave, we are getting closer toward martyrdom, martyrdom, martyrdom." He urged his rioters "not to fear death but to welcome martyrdom."[242] It was a speech no different than a speech Judas "the Hammer" Maccabee might have given his troops 2200 years earlier.

A few years ago, I was in Israel and traveled to Bethlehem, which is in the Islamic West Bank. After going through the heavy security checks to pass from Israel into Palestinian territory, we drove down the main street of Bethlehem. On the lampposts in the meridian were banners in English, with mothers proclaiming their pride in the men, women, and children who had martyred themselves with suicide bombs for Abraham's God. How could mothers have such fervent faith in God that they would joyfully

---

[242] "The Gaza Protests" Rich Lowry *National Review* May 14th, 2018.

proclaim the sickening destruction and death of their own children? But then the Bible tells the same story with the same glorious pride.

As her seven Jewish sons were brutally tortured to death in front of her, the Bible says:

*The mother was the most amazing one of them all, and she deserves a special place in our memory. Although she saw her seven sons die in a single day, she endured it with great courage because she trusted in the Lord. She combined womanly emotion with manly courage and spoke words of encouragement to each of her sons in their native language. I do not know how your life began in my womb, she would say, I was not the one who gave you life and breath and put together each part of your body. It was God who did it, God who created the universe, the human race, and all that exists. He is merciful and he will give you back life and breath again, because you love his laws more than you love yourself.* (2 Macc. 7:20-23)

The foundational existence of Judaism, Christianity, and Islam is expressed by those two mothers, in the same place, 2200 years apart. Both in agony, attempting to bring hope and meaning to the death of their children. A Jewish mother watching the sickening sight of the tortuous deaths of her sons embeds them with a soul and breathes life into Christianity and Islam. Without the belief in an everlasting soul that will live forever, all of Christianity and Islam dissolves in the definity of death.

But the definity of death was all that the Old Testament offered. Right from the beginning, Abraham's God says to Adam, *for dust thou art, and unto dust shalt thou return* (Gen. 3:19). King David repeats it, *For in death there is no remembrance of You; in the grave who will give You thanks* (Ps. 6:5)? Or later, *His breath goeth forth, he returneth to his earth;*

*in that very day his thoughts perish* (Ps. 146:4). And also, *All go unto one place; all are of the dust, and all turn to dust again* (Eccles. 3:20). And in the same book,

> *For the living know that they shall die: but the dead know not any thing, neither have they any more a reward; for the memory of them is forgotten. Also their love, and their hatred, and their envy, is now perished; neither have they any more a portion forever in anything that is done under the sun.* (Eccles. 9:5-6)

And most succinctly of all, *The Dead do not praise the Lord, nor do any that go down into silence* (Ps. 115:17). Yet, he everlasting soul, the a priori of Christianity and Islam, is explicitly denied in the Jewish scriptures, the Old Testament, the Bible.

All of the texts of the Old Testament, written before Alexander the Great, say that you have but one life to live; they offer only vague hints that this life is but a foretaste of eternal life.[243] Even the Sadducees, the upper hierarchy of Jewish society, who maintained the temple and its religious rituals, agreed with the ancient scriptures: there was no life after death.[244]

For almost three centuries, Judaism was immersed in the Persian and now Greek idea of life after death. Now they emerged, empowered with those ideas, and used them in the fight for the very survival of Judaism. No longer would they go down in the silence of King David; they would battle with the absolute faith that their God, Abraham's God, *is merciful and he will give you back life and breath again, because you love his laws more than you love yourself* (2 Macc. 7:23).

---

[243] *Christianity, The First Three Thousand Years* Diarmaid McClulloch (Viking 2010) p. 70

[244] *A History of the Jews* Paul Johnson (Harper Perennial 1988) p.95 *A History of the Jewish People in the Time of Jesus Christ"* Emil Schurer (T& T Clark 1890) Kindle Loc 10006

After 25 years of brutal slaughter, the "Orthodox" Jews won the war against their Greek rulers. Their victory bolstered their new belief that they were doing God's work and would be rewarded in everlasting life. The Hasmoneans restored sacrificial practice to the temple, and on December 25th of 164 BC,[245] they created a new Jewish feast to mark the occasion: Hanukkah.[246] Out of this deadly, brutal war came a reason for Jews to go Christmas shopping, or perhaps Christians should go Hanukkah shopping.

In 142 BC, Simon Maccabee agreed to a peace with the Seleucids, which made Israel an independent kingdom for the first time in over 440 years. Simon's Hasmonean family ruled Israel for the next 115 years, and they were as zealous in re-establishing Mosaic law as the Seleucids had been in banning it. Violence and killing spread in the persecution of those who lacked ritual zeal and to the non-Jews. Mobs ruled by religious extremists ended the intellectual freedom in the Greek academies and replaced it with study of the Torah and Jewish law.[247] Twenty-two centuries later, in our times, Islam has done precisely the same thing, with their thousands of Madrassa schools teaching the Qur'an and Sharia law.[248] Is that any different than today's intellectual mobs trying to impose their view and end freedom of thought on American campuses?[249]

---

[245] *A Commentary on Daniel* Leon J. Wood, (Wipf and Stock 1998) p. 217-218.

[246] An eight-day Jewish festival that began on the 25th day of Kislev (December) and commemorated the rededication to Judaism of the temple in Jerusalem

[247] *A History of the Jews* Paul Johnson (Harper Perennial 1988) p. 106

[248] Madrassa's are Islamic religious schools teaching "Wahhabism, a particularly austere and rigid form of Islam" the ideological foundation of the clash and violence between Islam and the West. "Saudi Time Bomb." PBS Frontline which can be seen here http://www.pbs.org/wgbh/pages/frontline/shows/saudi/

[249] Three examples Amy Wax a Law School Professor was censored for her comment that "not all cultures are equal" at the University of Pennsylvania Law School. Wall Street Journal March 18, 2018 Larry Summers was forced out as the President of Harvard for suggesting that women are under-represented in math science and engineering because they might have less innate mathematical capabilities. Boston Globe January 17, 2005 and Judith Curry was forced out as a top climate scientist at the Georgia Institute of Technology for questioning if $CO_2$ contributions to

Jewish society was split. The Pharisees were a class of scribes and teachers who accepted Daniel, Enoch, and the apocalyptic literature. They believed souls survived death and those that obeyed Mosaic Law would be rewarded in the kingdom to come. The Pharisees preached these ideas to the receptive poor, who grasped at the straw of hope for a happier life after death. The Essenes saw the Jewish nation as having succumbed to the Prince of Darkness, along with the rest of the world, and were confident that God would imminently be sending the Messiah to destroy the dark side and establish a permanent Kingdom of Light on Earth. They believed in life after death, withdrew from society, and lived strict ascetic lives in the barren deserts of places like Qumran, near the Dead Sea. Others formed gangs of terrorists like the Sicarii, who preyed on all and became collectively known as the Zealots. The Sadducees did not believe in life after death because, while Greek and Zoroastrian teaching and the literature of the day may have popularized the idea, the Hebrew Bible offered no supporting text. With no confirmation of an afterlife, the Sadducees were willing to make compromises to avoid persecution.[250]

The seed of Abraham now populated Canaan, as promised by his God. Throughout the eight centuries of subjugation by the Persians and Greeks, the ancient foundation stories of Judaism percolated with Persian Zoroastrianism and Greek Platonism. New canonical and non-canonical Jewish writing collectively buoyed ideas of one creator God, of humans with a soul, of a resurrection from the dead, of a coming messiah, of a last judgement to an eternity of punishment or paradise. By the beginning of the last century BC, Judaism had assimilated the doctrines needed for Christianity and a future Islam as the Jews watched and waited for the coming of a messiah.

---

Climate Change are as large as many climate scientists hypothesize. The Spectator November 28th, 2015

[250] The summaries are from *Josephus The Essential Writings* Paul L Maier (Kregel Publications 1988) p 260 and from *A History of the Jews* Paul Johnson (Harper Perennial 1988) pp. 121 – 123.

# Chapter Eleven – The Coming of a Messiah

Simon Maccabee's grandson, Alexander Jannaeus, ruled as the fourth Hasmonean King of Israel from 103BC to 76 BC. Like Kim Jong-Il in North Korea today, absolute power made Jannaeus a corrupted tyrant. History will prove that the religions of Abraham's God protect no one from the disease of power. Jannaeus reigned for twenty-seven years because he would not tolerate dissent. Tens of thousands lost their lives questioning his regime. As he feasted with his concubines, he had 800 Jewish enemies crucified. While they are suffering on the brink of death, he had their children killed in front of them, and then slit the throats of their wives.[251]

The palace rivalry and political fighting increased as the Roman Empire pressed into the area. and brought two decades of intrigue and rebellion., In 63 BC Antipater the Idumean made a deal with the Roman General Pompey that brought Antipater to power and allowed him to rule rebellious Palestine and set up his son Herod to follow him.[252]

---

[251] *Josephus The Essential Writings* Paul L. Maier (Kregel Publications 1988) p. 224
[252] *A History of the Jews,* Paul Johnson (Harper Perennial 1988) pp 107-109

In 37 BC, Herod convinced Caesar Augustus, Mark Antony, and the Roman Senate to make him the King of Judea under the title "Rex socius et amicus populi Romani," allied king and friend of the Roman people.[253] Mark Antony told the Senate that Herod would be an advantage in the Parthian war[254,255] and that Herod should be king. So, they all voted in favor,

> And when the Senate was separated, Antony and Caesar went out, with Herod between them; while the consul and the rest of the magistrates went before them, in order to offer sacrifices [to the Roman gods], and to lay the decree in the Capitol. Antony also made a feast for Herod on the first day of his reign.[256]

They also gave him 36,000 Roman troops to bring "peace" to the Jewish conflicts.[257]

Herod had emerged from the Roman upheavals of Julius Caesar, Cleopatra, Mark Anthony, and Octavius. The son of Antipater had survived the sexual intrigues among Mark Anthony, Herod's future wife Marianne, her mother Alexandra, Cleopatra, and Herod's Uncle Joseph.[258] Herod was born a Jew, raised as a Jew, and was now the King of the Jews.[259]

Herod thrived within the Roman Empire using the ruthless tactics he had learned as the Romans clashed over who would be emperor. His first act was to execute the entire Jewish leadership, the Sanhedrin, and separate the church and state functions. His second act was to exterminate all the remaining Hasmoneans to

---

[253] *A History of the Jews,* Paul Johnson (Harper Perennial 1988) p. 110

[254] The Parthians were from the area today called Turkistan and northeast Iran who had overtaken the Seleucid Empire and threatening Rome.

[255] *The Wars of the Jews* Josephus 1.14.4

[256] *Josephus The Essential Writings* Paul L. Maier Kregel Publications 1988 p. 234

[257] *A History of the Jews,* Paul Johnson (Harper Perennial 1988) pp. 110

[258] *Josephus the Essential Writings* Paul L Maier (Kregel Publications 1988) pp. 239-241

[259] *A History of Christianity* Paul Johnson (Simon & Schuster a Touchstone Book, 1995) pp. 10-11 Johnson discusses here and in the *History of the Jews* that many did not think of Herod as Jewish.

insure there would be no challengers to his throne. He selfishly killed family, friends, and enemies. To many, Herod was a violent maniac. Matthew 2:1-23 tells of "The Slaughter of the Innocents," the killing of all male children in Bethlehem under the age of two. While clearly within the scope of Herod's numerous slayings, there are no other records confirming this crime.

For all his despotic actions, Herod did much to advance the Jewish cause. The diaspora Jews scattered throughout the ancient world had greatly increased in population after the Babylonian dispersion. During Herod's reign, there were 7 to 8 million Jews in the world, roughly 10% of the Roman population,[260] with about 2 million living in Palestine. All benefitted from the relationship that Herod had with Julius Caesar and Caesar Augustus. During Herod's reign, Jews were granted tax concessions and were given other special privileges, including exemption from Roman military service.[261] With Herod as their powerful patron with Rome, Jews thrived with "equality of economic opportunity and freedom of goods and persons. They formed wealthy communities wherever the Romans had imposed stability."[262] Herod used his influence and money to fund synagogues, libraries, and charitable organizations for the poor, widows, and orphans throughout the diaspora community.[263]

Herod was a very successful king. He used his military force to expand the kingdom beyond the size of David's, he personally revitalized the Olympic Games, and he launched a vast building program that included theaters, forums, aqueducts, schools,

---

[260] *A History of the Jews* Paul Johnson (Harper Perennial 1988) p. 112. Because other authors cite different numbers these should be viewed only as indicative.

[261] Josephus: The Essential Writings, Paul L. Maier, editor, (Kregel Publications, 1988) p. 231

[262] *A History of Christianity* Paul Johnson (Simon & Schuster a Touchstone Book, 1995) pp. 10-11

[263] *A History of the Jews,* Paul Johnson (Harper Perennial 1988) p. 113

ports, roads, and temples. But Herod's major impact on Judaism was in Jerusalem, where he converted the Jewish temple into a tourist attraction. Herod assembled 10,000 workers and 1000 supervising priests to rebuild the Temple Mount, doubling its size and raising it higher.[264] Herod's Temple was now on a scale grander than Solomon's Temple. He "spent profusely on the exterior gates, fittings and decorations being covered in gold and silver plate." The stone was "exceptionally white and the glitter of the stone and the gleam of the gold reflected many miles away in the bright sun—that was what made the Temple so striking to travelers seeing it from afar."[265]

Herod did not do this because he was a pious Jew. He did it for the same reason that tourist attractions are created today: money and jobs. Pilgrims in the hundreds of thousands converged on Jerusalem. Pious Jewish males were required to sacrifice three times a year, but others, diaspora Jews and foreign pagans, came as much for Herod's grand spectacles as to sacrifice to the Jewish God. The tourists bought sacrificial animals, paid temple fees, exchanged foreign currency into 'Holy Shekels,' and burned expensive incense. Moreover, the choirs, the orchestras, sleeping, eating and luxurious inns provided thousands of jobs as wealth poured into the Jewish temple. Caesar Augustus himself sent huge quantities of golden vessels to the diaspora Jews who, much like today, contributed to Israel. And most of the wealth, as always, went to those in charge. The temple, while a spectacle of worship, became the "Federal Reserve Bank" of Israel. Herod

---

[264] The Temple Mount in the time of Herod stood twice as high as viewed today with the Dome of the Rock at its peak. This would have allowed the temple to be seen at a much greater distance. *The Quest: Revealing the Temple Mount in Jerusalem* Leen Ritmeyer (Hendrikson Publishing 2006) is probably the definitive book on the subject.

[265] *A History of the Jews,* Paul Johnson (Harper Perennial 1988) pp. 115

installed the more trusted Pharisees and downgraded the Sadducee high priests to keep an eye on his share of the wealth.[266]

Jerusalem was not Disney by the Dead Sea. It was slaughter on a colossal scale. Each pilgrim had to sacrifice one animal, but with thousands of Pilgrims and some trying to out-sacrifice the others, the flow of blood during "spring break" was enormous. Marcus Agrippa once offered up 100 cattle for his friend Herod. The temple had 34 cisterns, with the largest containing over 2 million gallons, and an aqueduct from the Pool of Siloam to wash away the constant flow of blood from hundreds of animals. "The Temple was an awesome place with the bellows of terrified cattle blending with the ritual cries and chants and tremendous blasts of the horn and trumpet, and blood everywhere."[267]

Herod's cronyism with the Roman emperors brought expansion, prosperity, and relative peace to Israel and the Jewish people everywhere. For this, he was named Herod the Great. At the age of 70, after surviving several Roman emperors, ten wives, and many schemes against him, Herod died in agony with a final despotic act of executing one of his sons just five days before he died.[268] It was late March, 4 BC.[269]

Judaism was no longer a religion of the rural tribes of Canaan, no longer the religion of Moses, and their God, Abraham's God, was no longer the Chairman of the Board of Gods. The Jews were a strong, significant, and respected part of the Roman Empire.[270] Jewish adherents congregated in every major city and town. Jewish Palestine was a churning intrigue of political, social, and

---

[266] All of this section is from the *A History of the Jews*, Paul Johnson (Harper and Row 1987) pp. 110 - 119

[267] "*A History of the Jews,*" *Paul Johnson* (Harper Perennial 1988) pp. 116-117

[268] *Josephus the Essential Writings* Paul L Maier (Kregel Publications 1988) pp. 252 - 254

[269] *Josephus the Essential Writings* Paul L Maier (Kregel Publications 1988) pp. 252 There was a documented lunar eclipse just a few days prior to his death which astronomers have calculated to have been on March 13th 4 BC.

[270] *Jews God and History 50th Anniversary, 2nd Edition* Max I Dimont edited by Ethel Dimont (Signet Classics 1994) Kindle location 1755

religious calculation. There was extreme wealth for some and subsistence poverty for the majority. The Jewish religion conducted its rituals of sacrifice and worship on a grand, majestic, and luxurious scale. The Jewish sects, though, were deeply divided along political and religious lines.

Jewish literature was rich with Apocalyptic writings. A messiah from God would return to end the suffering of Israel, reward the Jews, and vanquish their enemies. The books of Isaiah, Daniel, Esdras, Enoch, Tobit, Ecclesiasticus, Baruch, Maccabees, and Jubilee, as well as the Assumption of Moses, the Psalms of Solomon, the Wisdom of Solomon, and others, told of the arrival of an earthly messiah who was expected to "defeat the oppressive enemies of Israel" and "establish justice on earth."[271]

The entire Jordan valley was alive with holy eccentrics. Everyone was on the lookout. "The Roman government, the Jewish Sanhedrin, the Sadducees, and even the Pharisees assumed that a messiah would make changes to the existing order."[272] There were:

> "many prophets, preachers, and holy men, representing most of the twenty-four religious sects in the country at the time, [who] went about proclaiming the coming of a messiah who would deliver the Jews from the evil of the Roman Empire."[273]

The poor rural people of Galilee and Judea believed the Messiah would be talking in terms of "the realities of power – government, taxes, justice."[274] However, "there was such a

---

[271] *The Jews in the Time of Jesus an Introduction* Stephen M Wylen, (Paulist Press 1996) pp 170-171

[272] *A History of the Jews* Paul Johnson, Harper and Row 1988 p. 125

[273] "Jews, God and History" *50th Anniversary, 2nd Edition* Max I Dimont edited by Ethel Dimont (Signet Classics 1994) Kindle location 2085

[274] *A History of the Jews,* Paul Johnson, (Harper Perennial 1988) p. 125

variety of views about the Messiah in Judaism it was almost impossible"[275] to be wrong.

Judaism's ancient vague theories of God[276] had mixed with those of the Greeks and Persians. Abraham's God was now the one all-powerful God of the universe. On that, the Jews agreed. But what was his plan for them? Many ideas abounded: human souls and life after death; martyrdom and an approaching end time; resurrection of the dead and the banishment of evil; a messiah whose kingdom would come with a final judgement; a vindicated peace on Earth and life everlasting. All these ideas swirled uncongealed in the cauldron of Jewish politics, brought to a boil by Roman subjugation.

Into that chaos, a baby would soon be born. A baby whose name and religious followers would change the world: Jesus.

---

[275] *A History of the Jews,* Paul Johnson, (Harper Perennial 1988) p. 219
[276] *A History of Christianity* Paul Johnson (Simon and Schuster a Touchstone Book, 1995) pp 14

# Christianity

# Introduction

F or over nineteen hundred years, the stories of Jesus have been ceaselessly retold, inspiring prodigious amounts of literature, art, and architecture that are bound in the traditions, holidays, and cultures of societies around the world. Just how did a peasant preaching Jewish beliefs in the 1$^{st}$ century in rural Galilee become the God of the most influential religion in human history? How did Jesus of Nazareth and Christianity become the religion of a third of the world's population in the 21$^{st}$ century? These are the questions I hope to begin answering in this section.

Almost everyone has heard the stories of Jesus of Nazareth. All that we know comes from four short books written 70 to 100 years after Jesus' birth by people who never knew or met him. For the first four centuries after Jesus, people debated and often had violent struggles over who he was and the meaning of his life. Eventually, a consensus was reached that enabled Christianity to become the dominate religion of Western Civilization. An immense repertoire of literature and art was created in his name, and yet we know next to nothing of Jesus. It is a long and complex story, full of ideas, religions, people, and wars.

You might know the story of Jesus and the development of Christianity from church or Sunday school. The story you are about to read is perhaps a little different. An analogy with John

Kennedy, the 35th President of the United States, might help to explain that difference. Kennedy faced down the Russians in the Cuban Missile Crisis and said, "Ask not what your country can do for you, but what you can do for your country." He had a pretty wife and two children. He fought heroically in WWII, stood up to the Russians, fell victim to assassination in 1963, and is esteemed as a great president. That is pretty much the standard narrative that everyone knows. When stories are told of his sexual exploits, drug habits, participation in getting the United States involved in the Vietnam War, as an accomplice in President Diem's assassination, and his permitting the Berlin Wall to be built, most people just dismiss those things and retreat to the comfort of the safe familiar narrative.[277]

The story of Jesus has been told millions of times over the centuries. Jesus was born in Bethlehem to the Virgin Mary, and was heralded by shepherds, angels, and kings as the son of God. He was the messiah who would be crucified for the redemption of human sin. In the most basic version of the narrative, if you believe in him, then when you die, you go to Heaven; if not, you go to Hell. That story is deeply embedded in people's minds and in the fabric of Western civilization. Almost everyone has heard the Jesus story, perhaps in a Sunday school, and then heard it repeated again and again from the Sunday pulpit: it is the Gospel Truth. If anything other than that story is told, people dismiss it and retreat to the comfort of the safe and beautiful age-old narrative.

To research the story of Kennedy, you can go online, to your local library, or the Kennedy Library and find a mountain of details, including pictures and stories of things that were little reported at the time. Pictures and stories of exactly what Kennedy

---

[277] While there are many books that document Kennedy's sexual behavior, drug habits and other peccadillos Seymour M Hersh's *The Dark Side of Camelot* (Little, Brown and Company 1997) is a good well documented overview of Kennedy's failings.

did and who he did it with. That mountain of detail can paint a very exact picture of the life and death of Kennedy. And all of that occurred a mere 55 to 90 years ago.

Now imagine that you are tasked with writing on Kennedy, but you may not go to the library or the Internet or use anything other than what you have already been told by others. Come on, it's only been 55-plus years since he died, and 100-plus years since he was born! Where was he born? What did he say in the famous speech he gave in the 1956 Democratic Convention? Did the CIA plot to shoot him? How many shots were fired from the grassy knoll? None, you say? But I'll bet there are many who would write fascinating stories of things that we now know did not happen that fateful day in Dallas. In fact, many, many books have been written telling tall tales of JFK's life and death, even though there is a mountain of pictures and documents showing evidence of a less idealistic version of what had really happened.

Now imagine people writing about Jesus 50 to 90 years after his life and death. Writers then had no library or Internet, no newspapers, pictures, or TV reports, Facebook postings, or Twitter comments. Not even a single Roman record! Between the events of Jesus' life and the writing of his story, not only had many decades passed, but there had been a horrific war. Nothing remained documenting the events of Jesus' life—only second- and third-hand stories told by others. Certainly, there were a few exaggerations, tall tales, and things from people's imagination. They were like the Kennedy stories of a second shooter on the "the grassy knoll" or "Russian conspiracies" or "how the CIA and Cuba were involved." Imagine how these stories might have become the accepted truth, had there been no pictures or documents of Kennedy's life? How then do we know which tales of Jesus' life were exaggerations, tall tales, or things of imagination?

It took ten months for the Warren Commission to provide the official report on Kennedy's death. That report was supported by a mountain of first-hand evidence, pictures, and documents, yet its results continue to be questioned. It took three hundred years for the Romans to provide the official report on Jesus death. That report was supported by no first-hand evidence, only second or third hand reports, yet it would go unquestioned for centuries.

The short version of the Jesus Report was the Nicene Creed, written by or at the direction of the Roman emperor. That Creed states the beliefs of most Christians today. The Nicene Creed, or words very similar to it, have been repeated in Christian churches around the world for centuries. They are still repeated at most Christian worship services today.

The Roman emperor was Constantine. He asked a Christian bishop named Eusebius to compile the evidence for the Nicene Creed into what might be called the Nicaea Report. Eusebius was ordered to produce 50 copies to be read in the churches,[278] none of which survived except as a list of books.

After the Warren Report, all the evidence was safely locked away so that future historians could review it.[279] After the Nicaea Council, only the evidence supporting the report was kept. Any other evidence was outlawed and ordered to be destroyed.[280] Those who did not follow the emperor's words were subject to persecution, or worse.[281] That evidence would be the only stories of Jesus retold in Christian churches for centuries. It would become what we today call, the New Testament.

---

[278] *Eusebius: Life of Constantine (Clarendon Ancient History Series) translated* by Averil Cameron and Stuart G. Hall (Clarendon Press 1999) p. 166

[279] Almost all of records in the Kennedy Collection were opened October 26, 2017. https://www.archives.gov/research/jfk/faqs.html

[280] Not all of the evidence was destroyed, some even on pain of death, was hidden away, The Nag Nammadi books discovered in the 1940's in Egypt are a great example of the other writing on Jesus hidden a few decades after the Council of Nicaea.

[281] *Caesar and Christ (The Story of Civilization, vol. III)* Will and Ariel Durant (MJF Books, 1944) p. 660

For the last two centuries, scholars have been re-examining and questioning the evidence of the Nicaea Report. They have been helped because some of the evidence Constantine ordered destroyed has recently turned up. It is now very clear that the New Testament is not a factual reporting of what was said and done in the years of Jesus' life and death. It is also clear that the New Testament contains some tall tales and things of someone's imagination. How can that be possible? After all, we swear to tell the truth with one hand on the Bible.

The newly discovered old evidence, and the re-examination of the New Testament does not mean that the Nicene Creed and the Nicaea Report came to the wrong conclusions. It only means that Christianity's long-fought battles over the meaning of Jesus' life and death can be reexamined, and Christians can decide for themselves, without a Roman emperor decreeing the results.

The emperor's Christianity was embodied into law as Christianity became the central institution of Western civilization. In the 21$^{st}$ century, Christianity remains a powerful force in societies around the world. Understanding Christianity requires an understanding of the long process of writing and editing the stories of Jesus, and of course, that Nicaea Report, the New Testament.

At Church or in Sunday school, they tell you the story from the New Testament: Jesus was born, lived, preached, was crucified, and posthumously made appearances to the apostles. Some who knew Jesus then wrote about what they had seen and heard. The apostles and Paul then went out and preached the gospel.

We now know that it was more like this: Jesus was born, lived, preached, and died. Over the next two decades, a man named Paul preached and wrote stories based on his dreams and visions of Jesus. A massive war then destroyed Palestine and probably killed everyone remaining who might have known or heard Jesus firsthand, or even secondhand. After that war, 80 to 100 years after Jesus' birth, some people wrote down stories of Jesus. Many decades later, those stories were attributed to evangelists, Matthew, Mark, Luke, and John. A couple of centuries later, those titles, as well as those believed to have been written by Paul and a handful of others, comprised Eusebius' Nicaea Report, the New Testament.

The New Testament story of Jesus has been the exclusive story of Jesus. You have probably read and heard that story. I'll tell it to you again, adding what we now know from the historical record and other "evidence" once ordered destroyed by the Roman emperor. You might find a few things that will surprise you.

# Chapter One – Expecting a Messiah: Jesus the Jew

Sometime before Herod died in 4 BC, a Jewish baby named Jesus was born. At the time, his birth went unheralded and unremarked, and it certainly was not recorded. Accounts of Jesus' birth would only be written many decades in the future from secondhand memories and imagination that had been fermenting in people's minds for 80 years. The authors were "educated Greeks... outsiders to Judea,"[282] people who had no firsthand knowledge; they were writing theological tracts on the meaning of Jesus' life and not biographies. Each wrote with a different point of view, but they all were motivated by the Jewish-Roman War to shift the blame for Jesus' death from the Romans onto the Jews.[283] Many different epistles and 20 or so Gospels[284] were written which would divide the followers of

---

[282] *A New History of Early Christianity,* Charles Freeman (Yale University Press 2009) p. 20

[283] *The Origin of Satan: How Christians Demonized Jews, Pagans, and Heretics,* Elaine Pagels (Vintage Books, 1996) p. 10

[284] *A New History of Early Christianity,* Charles Freeman (Yale University Press 2009) p. 20

Jesus for many centuries. Given all of that, and the fog of time and war, what do we know about Jesus?

Jesus was a rural peasant Jew. His disciples and followers were all Jewish. He preached in the area around the Sea of Galilee.[285] While we do not know much more about Jesus, the archeological records, together with Roman and Jewish writings, provide a fair sketch of rural peasant Jewish life in Galilee around the time Jesus lived and preached.

Galilee, the land of Jesus, is quite small, about the size of a typical county in the United States. It is roughly forty miles north to south, and thirty miles east to west. Its defining feature is the Sea of Galilee, a shallow spring-fed lake that is the lowest freshwater lake in the world. It is 700 feet below sea level, about 8 by 12 miles and 140 feet deep. From the southern shores, it is a few miles to Mt. Tabor, which rises to 2600 feet above the lake. The Gospels would record this as the spot where Jesus had his "transfiguration." A few miles further in the Nazareth Range is the village of Nazareth. Several parallel east-west ripples of hills work their way 25 miles north to the higher mountains at today's Lebanese border. The hills and valleys of Galilee are fertile, and the mild climate made the area very productive for growing fruits, figs, olives, grapes, nuts, and palms.[286] The rural farming class of Galilee were "peasants, small farmers, handworkers and day laborers living in small villages and medium-sized towns."[287] They struggled every day to eat and to pay their taxes. Only 3% were literate.[288]

---

[285] *Jesus: A Life*, A. N. Wilson (W. W. Norton & Company, 2004) p. 6

[286] *The Historical Figure of Jesus*, E. P. Sanders (Penguin Books, 1993) p. 102

[287] *The Lost Gospel: The Book of Q and Christian Origins*, Burton L. Mack, (Harper Collins, 1993) p. 56

[288] *The Birth of Christianity: Discovering What Happened in the Years Immediately After the Execution of Jesus*, John Dominic Crossan (Harper San Francisco, 1999) p. 234

The village of Nazareth is where Jesus lived for 30 years before beginning his ministry. It was "a hundred or so impoverished families of a modest and utterly forgettable village," most of whom "lived barely above subsistence level."[289] The Nazarenes would have lived in simple stacked-brick houses and shared a single public bath.[290] Nazareth was so small and insignificant that outside the New Testament, there is not a single record of its existence until the 4th century.

Less than an hour's walk down the hill from Nazareth was Sepphoris, the capital of Galilee, nicknamed "The Ornament of Galilee."[291] Sepphoris had everything to earn that nickname: opulent homes, theaters, and baths that made life a pleasure for its estimated 20,000 inhabitants.[292] Jesus and his family would certainly have made much of their living from Sepphoris, working there or trading goods in its market. The expense and their lowly peasant status meant they would never have visited it for pleasure.[293]

Nazareth was also a rugged three-day trek across valleys and up and down slopes, eventually climbing to Jerusalem at over 3000 feet. It was 100 miles[294] of twisting paths from the valley floors below Nazareth to Jerusalem. Visits to Jerusalem for Jewish feast days were a relief from the misery, sweat, and drudgery of work, sunup to sundown, six days a week.

---

[289] *Zealot: The Life and Times of Jesus of Nazareth*, Reza Aslan (Random House, 2014) Kindle Location 863-865

[290] *Zealot: The Life and Times of Jesus of Nazareth*, Reza Aslan (Random House, 2014) Kindle Location 858

[291] *Zealot: The Life and Times of Jesus of Nazareth*, Reza Aslan (Random House, 2014) Location 853

[292] *The Birth of Christianity: Discovering What Happened in the Years Immediately After the Execution of Jesus*, John Dominic Crossan (Harper San Francisco, 1999) p. 221

[293] *The Historical Figure of Jesus*, E. P. Sanders (Penguin Books, 1993) p. 104

[294] Google maps shows a straight-line distance of 65 miles, but the twisting roads through the hills add significantly.

Jesus' life was certainly no different. According to the lore, Jesus was a carpenter, but in the original Greek Gospels, the word used was "tekton," which might be better interpreted as "construction worker" and even "day laborer," perhaps with derogatory connotations.[295]

After Alexander the Great swept the area in 332 BC, Galilee joined the movement to Greek culture and abandoned Judaism. In 152 BC, the Maccabees returned the area to Jewish control. Under John Hyrcanus and his son Alexander Jannaeus, Galilee was forced[296] "to convert to Judaism—the only forcible mass conversion in the history of Judaism."[297]

This forced conversion did not mean that the Jews of Galilee were lukewarm. Quite the opposite. In Jesus' lifetime, Galilee "was overwhelmingly Jewish" and an "area of fierce orthodoxy and diverse heterodoxy, and of religious and political ferment."[298]

"The Galileans were fiercely loyal to Judaism,"[299] as were the Pharisees. But in a different sense. The Pharisees looked to the minute details of the law,[300] while the Jews of Galilee took a fervent, passionate view. The sense of the difference in our age might be the difference between, say, St. Patrick's Cathedral of New York and a rural Southern Baptist church. Both are solidly of the faith, but the former is reserved, formal, and ritualized, while the latter is ardent, unceremonious, and clamorous. The former is of the elite makers and shakers of society, while the latter is of a rural farming class.

---

[295] *Zealot: The Life and Times of Jesus of Nazareth*, Reza Aslan (Random House, 2014) Kindle Location 800. Conversely, A.N. Wilson in *Jesus: A Life (*Random House) page 29 suggested that *tekton* implies wisdom.

[296] *A History of the Jews,* Paul Johnson (Harper Perennial 1988) pp. 107-109

[297] *The Jews in the Time of Jesus: An Introduction*, Stephen M. Wylen (Paulist Press, 1996) p. 64. However, this neglects the forced conversion under Hedikiah.

[298] *A History of the Jews,* Paul Johnson (Harper Perennial 1988) p. 123

[299] *The Jews in the Time of Jesus: An Introduction*, Stephen M. Wylen (Paulist Press, 1996) p. 64

[300] Matthew 23 provides a good overview of the Pharisees views

While Sepphoris was its capital, Galilee had another large sophisticated urban setting at the city of Scythopolis[301] (Beit She'an). In 20 AD, when Jesus would have been in his mid-20s, King Antipas built Tiberius a new capital city on the shore of the Sea of Galilee. Having a third major city within 20 miles radically changed "the picture of the numerous self-sufficient farms or hamlets in Galilee."[302] These three major cities, together with Magdala,[303] were the centers of power, trade, and society in Galilee—and all within a day's walk!

Sepphoris, Scythopolis, Magdala, and Tiberius could not be avoided while traveling in Galilee, yet they are all missing in the Gospel stories of the life of Jesus. Perhaps his gospel wasn't for people of the cities, or maybe he just didn't like the food. Or maybe his powers there were as in his hometown, *And he could there do no mighty work, save that he laid his hands upon a few sick folk, and healed them. And he marvelled because of their unbelief. And he went 'round about the villages, teaching* (Mark 6:5-6). In Nazareth, Matthew says, *And they were offended in him.... And he did not many mighty works there because of their unbelief* (Matt. 13:57-58). Like Nazareth, perhaps the crowds in the city were a tough sell.

We can reasonably conclude that Jesus of Nazareth was a poor struggling Jewish construction worker, who preached in the minor villages of Galilee. The Gospel of John alludes to the same conclusion when one of Jesus' disciples, Philip, attempts to recruit another, Nathanael, who comments, *Nazareth! Can anything good come from there?* (John 1:46). Jesus left his family in Nazareth and moved about 30 miles away, to another small

---

[301] Technically Scythopolis was not in Galilee but just across its Southern Border but was a major city and cultural center at the time of Jesus.

[302] Johnathan Reed as quoted in *The Birth of Christianity: Discovering What Happened in the Years Immediately After the Execution of Jesus*, John Dominic Crossan (Harper San Francisco, 1999) p. 221

[303] *Jesus: A Life*, A. N. Wilson (W. W. Norton & Company, 2004)

town, Capernaum, where he continued his preaching to the rural people of Galilee.

The common understanding is that the Romans were in control of Galilee when Jesus was preaching. But that is not true. They were ruling in Judea and Samaria, but at the time of Jesus, "In Galilee there was no official Roman presence at all."[304] Galilee was ruled throughout Jesus' life by Antipas, Herod's son. It was only in 37 AD that the Roman emperor put Galilee under a Roman procurator.

All four gospels state Jesus' preaching was critical of the Second Temple Judaism that was thriving in Judea.[305] And all four gospels tell us that Jesus disrupted the routine activities in the temple during the Jewish Passover festival.[306] Neither the Jews nor the Romans were going to tolerate such behavior. "Once he began to operate openly in the Temple area, he became a marked man for both the Roman and Jewish authorities."[307]

Imagine how long you would last in Disney World, creating a disturbance and busting up the shops. The difference is that, in Roman times, such activities carried the death penalty. And busting up the shops in the temple is what got Jesus killed by the Romans with the concurrence of the Jewish elite. All of this probably occurred in 30 CE.[308] We do not know for sure because, much like his birth, his death was unheralded and unrecorded until many years later.

---

[304] *The Historical Figure of Jesus*, E. P. Sanders (Penguin Books, 1993) p. 27

[305] *Jesus of Nazareth. Holy Week: From the Entrance into Jerusalem to the Resurrection*, Pope Benedict XVI/Joseph Ratzinger, Translated by Philip J. Whitmore (Ignatius Press, 2011). Section 1 pp. 1-23 provides the flavor and context of Jesus' disputes with the Jewish temple practices.

[306] Matthew 21:12-17, Mark 11:15-19, Luke 19:45-48, John 2:13-22

[307] *A History of Christianity*, Paul Johnson (Simon and Schuster a Touchstone Book, 1995) p. 29

[308] Historians have endlessly debated this date. The descriptions in the Gospels are conflicting. Reconstructions of the Jewish Lunar Calendar and those descriptions lend weight to 30 CE, although any year between 27 AD and 35 AD is possible.

Jesus had a group of followers, mostly men and a few women. The most often named were Peter, James, and John, who were members of a group of twelve,[309] called the apostles. There were other followers, disciples that numbered 72.[310] Reports and rumors circulated verbally among his followers after his death. Those oral stories were written in the first gospel 40 years later, and it would be 60 to 70 years before they were written into the last gospel in the Bible.[311]

After his death, his members gathered in Jerusalem, into something we might call the First Jewish Jesus Church of Jerusalem. It never officially existed, but its members, the apostles, disciples, and followers of Jesus were devout Jews who continued to practice and preach the Judaism taught by Jesus.[312] All known writings point to James, listed as a brother of Jesus, as its leader.[313] They followed Jewish ritual and practice, *kept up their daily attendance at the Temple* (Acts 2:46) and were "most fair minded and were strict in their observance of the law.*" [314] They practiced Temple Judaism, expecting Jesus to return at any moment and bring the promised justice from Roman oppression.

The disciples of Jesus were doing what he had told them: be Jewish followers of the Torah. "The only thing that distinguished Jesus' followers from any other Jews was their belief that, in Jesus, the long-awaited Messiah of Israel had been found."[315]

---

[309] Mark 6:7

[310] Luke 10:1

[311] This timing will be discussed in later chapters.

[312] *Jesus: A Life*, A. N. Wilson (W. W. Norton & Company, 2004) p. 6

[313] *Christianity: The First Three Thousand Years*, Diarmaid MacClulloch (Viking, 2010) p. 98

[314] *The Antiquities of the Jews,* Flavius Josephus 20.9.1

[315] *The Brother of Jesus and the Lost Teachings of Christianity,* Jeff J Butz, (Inner Traditions/Bear and Company 2005) p. 67

Except for Jesus being the Messiah, everything else in the Jesus Church aligned with mainstream Jewish thought.[316]

But the mainstream Jewish leaders, the elite at the temple, were not in agreement with the members of the Jesus Church, *We strictly charged you not to teach in this name (Jesus) yet here you have filled Jerusalem with your teaching, and you intend to bring this man's blood upon us* (Acts 5:28). In this tension, the founders of the Jesus Church were being persecuted, even killed,[317] by the Jewish elite of Jerusalem. James, Jesus' brother and the head of the Jesus Church, was executed by the Jewish hierarchy in 62 BC.[318]

We can be certain that Jesus was a poor Jewish peasant construction worker who lived in the suburban hovels of Galilee and became one of the many iterant holy men of the time.[319] He preached messianic and apocalyptic ideas that resonated with the widespread beliefs of the times. Around the year 30 AD, he and his entourage traveled to Jerusalem for a Passover festival. While there, Jesus disrupted the peace in the temple, for which he was executed. After his death, his followers scrupulously practiced Judaism in the temple, anticipating his return as the Messiah. It never happened. Not a likely resume for a leader of millions in the millennia to come.

---

[316] *A History of Christianity*, Paul Johnson (Simon & Schuster a Touchstone Book, 1995) pp. 31-33

[317] *A History of Christianity*, Paul Johnson (Simon & Schuster a Touchstone Book, 1995) p. 35. Johnson discuss the killing of Stephen and the persecution of the Jerusalem Church.

[318] *Paul and Jesus: How the Apostle Transformed Christianity,* James T. Tabor (Simon and Schuster, 2012) p. 37

[319] *The Historical Figure of Jesus*, E. P. Sanders (Penguin Books, 1993) pp. 132-168 Sanders discusses this at length in Chapter 10 Miracles

# Chapter Two – The Visions of Paul

A fter Jesus' crucifixion, his apostles stayed in Jerusalem waiting for his return. The book of Acts is our only account of very early Christianity. All other writers, from Josephus to Clement to Eusebius, as well as the church fathers and historians of the times, follow and elaborate its story line. They all agree with the statement in Acts that the Apostles "kept up their daily attendance at the Temple" (Acts 2:46) and were led by Jesus' brother James, along with Peter and John.[320] All of the Apostles were Jews who continued in the Jewish faith. "The followers of Jesus thus formed a separate group, but by no means a church; religiously, it was an integral part of Jewry."[321] There is nothing supporting the idea they were trying to establish a new religion of Christianity. Neither Jesus nor the Apostles and his first disciples ever thought they were starting or were a part of a new religion. They were all born Jewish, practiced Judaism, and continued as pious Jews after Jesus' death.

---

[320] *Paul and Jesus: How the Apostle Transformed Christianity,* James T. Tabor (Simon and Schuster, 2012) p. 29

[321] *Myth Maker: Paul and The Invention of Christianity*, Hyam Maccoby (Barnes and Noble, 1987) p.120

Like the Essenes of Qumran, they lived in a form of socialism, sharing their resources (Acts 4:32-37).[322] They met *"daily with one accord in the temple, and breaking bread from house to house, did eat their meat with gladness and singleness of heart."* (Acts 2:46). Even in this Christian form of socialism, a dispute over the fair distribution broke out between the ethnic Hebrew Jews and those of other Jewish backgrounds, Greek Jews. Seven men were selected to resolve the matter, including one named Stephen. Somehow in this process, Stephen caught the ire of the Jewish Sanhedrin who accused him of blasphemy and stoned him to death, probably in the winter of 36-37AD (Acts 5-7).[323] Present at the stoning of Stephen was a pious Jewish Pharisee named Saul of Tarsus, *But Saul, who was also called Paul* (Acts 13:9) carried that name to fame. Paul was *Circumcised the eighth day, of the stock of Israel, of the tribe of Benjamin, a Hebrew of the Hebrews; concerning the law, a Pharisee* (Phil. 3:5). This point is repeated in his letters (Rom. 11:1; 2 Cor. 11:22; Gal. 1:14) [324] and in Acts (21:39; 22:3; 23:6; 26:5). Paul was also a "deputy sheriff" of the Jewish elite that carried out the persecution of Jesus' followers in the surrounding area: *entering house after house, he dragged off men and women and committed them to prison* (Acts 8:3).

But then Paul had "the transformative event of his life"[325] and became a mystic[326] who had trances and visions and heard the

---

[322] *Jewish History of Early Christianity,* Juan Marcos Bejarano Qutierrez (Yaron Publishing 2017) Kindle Loc 3686

[323] *Jewish History of Early Christianity,* Juan Marcos Bejarano Qutierrez (Yaron Publishing 2017) Kindle Loc. 3726

[324] Not all of the letters attributed to Paul in the New Testament were actually written by him. This will be discussed later, but references to "his letters" or "by him" should be taken to mean all of the Pauline books of the Bible unless otherwise noted.

[325] *The First Paul: Reclaiming the Radical Visionary Behind the Church's Conservative Icon,* Marcus J. Borg and John Dominic Crossan, (Harper One, 2009) p. 22

[326] *St. Paul: The Apostle We Love to Hate, Karen Armstrong (Icons Series)* (New Harvest, 2015) p. 28

voice of Jesus. Paul had never seen nor met nor heard the human Jesus. Paul's experience with Jesus was an out-of-body apparition. He described it in the third person as follows:

> *I knew a man in Christ about fourteen years ago, (whether in the body, I cannot tell; or whether out of the body, I cannot tell: God knoweth;) such as one caught up to the third heaven. And I knew such a man, (whether in the body, or out of the body, I cannot tell: God knoweth;) How that he was caught up into paradise, and heard unspeakable words, which it is not lawful for a man to utter. (2 Cor. 12:2-5)*

This was not a one-time event. Paul tells us he had many *visions and revelations of the Lord* (2 Cor. 12:1). He perhaps expresses false modesty about their number. *And to keep me from being too elated by the abundance of revelations* (2 Cor. 12:6-7).

Throughout history, there are many people who have hallucinated, heard voices, seen visions, or floated out of their body and attributed their experiences to messages from God. It is called theophany, meaning the appearance of a deity to a human. The Old Testament is full of such stories, including Isaiah 6, Psalm 18, and Ezekiel 20.

In our age, there are many who claim theophany as well, from the likes of Joseph Smith, Jim Jones, David Koresh, Rachael Armstrong, and many more that can be found in the parks and on the street corners of every major city.[327] One of them was a well-known colorful character in the 1960s and 70s: Bhagwan Shree Rajneesh. He managed to combine his messages from a god with

---

[327] "Spirituality and Hearing Voices" Simon McCarthy Jones, Amanda Waegeli and John Watkins; *Psychosis* October 5, 2013 Published online 2013 Oct 23. doi: 10.1080/17522439.2013.831945

free love, in an apparent in-body situation.[328] The one most affecting our current time is Muhammad, the founder of the Islamic faith. His visions began in 610 AD on Mt. Hira near Mecca and continued until his death.[329]

All of those mentioned freely admit to having trances, hallucinations, hearing voices, seeing visions, or floating out of their bodies. To believe in someone else's hallucinations does not change the fact that they are hallucinations. From that perspective, Muhammad and Jim Jones are no different. Depending on your faith, Paul, Joseph Smith, Muhammad, or someone else, is a true messenger from God, while the others are simply psychotic. Is faith alone how you are to distinguish who is the psychotic or who is the messenger from God? Which is which? The one your parents told you about? The biggest celebrity with the most followers? The one your nation obligates you to believe? The most famous of history? Or all the above? Continue reading: your faith is certainly based on the true messenger from God.

Paul tells us that after his transformative vision, he *went away to Arabia* (Gal. 1:17). *Then after three years, I went up to Jerusalem to visit Cephas* (Aramaic for Peter) *and remained with him fifteen days. But I saw none of the other apostles except James the Lord's brother* (Gal. 1:18-19). After that, Paul *went into the regions of Syria and Cilicia* (Gal. 1:21). Paul was a tent maker,[330] doing hard work for long hours and for many years (1 Cor. 4:12). And then Paul said, *after fourteen years I went up again to Jerusalem with Barnabas, taking Titus along with me* (Gal. 2:1).

When he arrived in Jerusalem, Paul had clear disagreements with the apostles. Paul added that he *did not yield in submission*

---

[328] *Feet of Clay: Saints, Sinners and Madmen: A Study of Gurus,* Anthony Storr (The Free Press 1996) p. 47

[329] *Islam: A Short History,* Karen Armstrong (Modern Library, 2000) pp. 3-5

[330] Acts 18:3

*for even a moment* (Gal. 2:5). He then reported that an agreement was reached and that James, Peter, and John *who seemed to be pillars, perceived the grace that was given to me, they gave the right hand of fellowship to Barnabas and me, that we should go to the Gentiles and they to the circumcised. Only, they asked us to remember the poor, the very thing I was eager to do* (Gal. 2:9-10). Problem solved?

Not at all. Peter and representatives of Jesus' brother James came to Antioch, where Paul was preaching. Paul reported that, *their conduct was not in step with the truth of the gospel* (Gal. 2:11-14). Paul meant his gospel. Here was Peter, the very Peter whom Jesus called *the rock on which I will build my church* (Matt. 16:18). And here was Paul to Peter, *I opposed him to his face, because he was clearly wrong* (Gal. 2:11). Peter, who had been by Jesus' side throughout his ministry was wrong? Paul's hallucinations of Jesus were right?

Paul says those sent by James are all wrong and a bunch of hypocrites:

> *The other Jews also joined him in this hypocritical behavior, to the extent that even Barnabas was caught up in their hypocrisy. But when I saw that they were not acting consistently with the truth of the gospel, I told Cephas [Peter] in front of everyone, "Though you are a Jew, you have been living like a gentile and not like a Jew. So how can you insist that the gentiles must live like Jews?"* (Gal. 2:13-14 ISV)

If Jesus had a clear message of his life and its meaning, then certainly it was given to James, and especially Peter who had been by Jesus' side throughout his ministry. How could Paul disagree with them? Because of his mystical trances and dreams during fourteen years in Syria? Paul not only disagrees but shows distain:

*And from those who seemed to be influential—what they were makes no difference to me; God shows no partiality—those, I say, who seemed influential added nothing to me* (Gal. 2:6). Or, even more emphatically, *With us therefore worldly standards have ceased to count in our estimate of any man; even if once they counted in our understanding of Christ, they do so no longer* (2 Cor. 5:16). In other words, pay no attention to Peter, James, and John only listen to me, Paul.

If Jesus' teaching to the Apostles was so wrong, as Paul loudly claims, what could be the purpose of Jesus' preaching to his apostles in the first place? If what Paul saw and heard in his dreams or trances was true, why was Jesus' life on earth even needed? How can the meaning of Jesus' life and death be anything other than what Jesus himself said and preached? And who would know better than the disciples, led by Jesus' own brother, James! To say Paul had trances or dreams or visions of a higher truth is to say that the dreams of anybody could be true. How could you ever know?

Joseph Smith, Jim Jones, David Koresh, Rachael Armstrong, Paul, Muhammad, or the person speaking in tongues in the park—take your pick. You have no way of knowing the truth of any of their dreams and visions. Welcome to the world of religious relativity. Let's all hold hands and sing Kumbaya! Until it is you who must die for someone else's truth. And millions upon millions have.

# Chapter Three – Paul's Truth?

That Nicaea Report, the accounting of the "truth" of Jesus would be sanctioned and "published" more than 260 years after Paul's death. Eusebius included fourteen books attributed to Paul, which were included in the New Testament.[331] Eusebius notes that one of them, the Gospel of the Hebrews, may not have been written by Paul.[332] Since then, the list of books in the New Testament written by Paul has shortened. "Virtually all scholars agree that seven of the Pauline letters are authentic: Romans, 1 and 2 Corinthians, Galatians, Philippians, 1 Thessalonians, and Philemon."[333] Of the remaining six, 1-2 Timothy and Titus were certainly not written by Paul, and there is substantial doubt on Ephesians, Colossians, and 2 Thessalonians.

---

[331] Constantine ordered Eusebius to compile a list of books which I call the Nicaea Report. Eusebius compiled his list and had fifty copies printed of which none survive. Several later Church Councils would refine Eusebius list and eventually formally approve the New Testament at the fourth session of the Council of Trent in 1546.

[332] "Ecclesiastical History" Book 3, Chapter 3, The Epistles of the Apostles.

[333] *Forged: Writing in the Name of God--Why the Bible's Authors Are Not Who We Think They Are,* Bart D. Ehrman, (Harper Collins, 2012) p. 92 Ephesians, Colossians, 2 Thessalonians might possibly have been written by him, while 1 and 2 Timothy, Titus were not.

But for all that writing, "Paul is highly allusive in what he says. He does not spell out in systematic detail his views of Jesus, Paul's Christ."[334] In fact, for Paul, it's all a mystery! Paul says that he is among the select few predestined to know the plan: *But when he* (God) *who had set me apart before I was born, and who called me by his grace (*Gal. 1:15*)* and that he is preaching the answer to the mystery. *And for me, that utterance may be given unto me, that I may open my mouth boldly, to make known the mystery of the gospel* (Eph. 6:19).

Paul might have opened his mouth boldly, but his cryptic allusions throughout his writings gave rise to innumerable interpretations that would create divisions in the Jesus movements. This could be why others wrote later in his name to try and clarify what the real Paul had said. Scholars agree that the books of 1 and 2 Timothy, Titus, 2 Thessalonians, Ephesians, Colossians were bot written by Paul, but later by other authors.[335] Those books even made it into the Nicaea Report. Paul says in Ephesians 3:3, *God revealed his secret plan and made it known to me.* If God had given his secret plan to Paul, it was others writing in Paul's name who tried to reveal it.

From the time of Jesus' execution until Paul's contentious meeting in Jerusalem, over 20 years had gone by. For 17 of those years, Paul had visions and dreams while traveling in Syria where Zoroastrianism was present.[336]

---

[334] *How Jesus Became God: The Exaltation of a Jewish Preacher from Galilee,* Bart D. Ehrman, (Harper One, 2014) p. 251

[335] *Forged: Writing in the Name of God--Why the Bible's Authors Are Not Who We Think They Are,* Bart D. Ehrman, (Harper Collins, 2012) pp. 93-115. Ehrman discusses in detail why these were not written by Paul.

[336] The extent of Zoroastrianism in the Parthenian Empire is debated. However, in the original Greek Matthew uses the term μάγοι or Magi, and "The religion of the Magi was fundamentally that of Zoroaster" *Catholic Encyclopedia* http://www.newadvent.org/cathen/09527a.htm. Paul traveled in areas of Matthew's Magi.

Zarathustra had preached centuries earlier that a messiah would defeat the forces of evil. Humans who had died would be resurrected – raised from the dead with their bodies restored. The good God would hold a final judgement, rewarding some in paradise and punishing others in hell. Afterwards, all would be purified in fire and ultimately saved. God would then create a new world without death in which all would live happily ever after.[337]

Paul then preached and wrote precisely these ideas, which would become the basic beliefs of his Christianity. These were ideas already assimilated into Judaist thought in the centuries of the Babylonian Captivity, and could have been easily reinforced in Paul's visions, during his travels in areas where they were prevalent.

Paul had one vision that would become the symbolizing ritual of his movement and the most sacred rite of Christianity: the Eucharist. Paul, in one of his few direct quotes of Jesus, says:

> *For I have received of the Lord that which also I delivered unto you, that the Lord Jesus the same night in which he was betrayed took bread: And when he had given thanks, he broke it, and said, "Take, eat: this is my body, which is broken for you: this do in remembrance of me." After the same manner also he took the cup, when he had supped, saying, "This cup is the new testament in my blood: this do ye, as oft as ye drink it, in remembrance of me.* (1 Cor. 11:23-25)

Paul clearly states that he got the idea for the Last Supper in a vision directly from Jesus. He is clear that he did not get the tradition from James, or Peter, or John or any of the apostles, but from another vision, apparition, dream, or hallucination of Jesus.

---

[337] *An Introduction to the New Testament,* Raymond E. Brown, First edition (Yale University Press, 2010) p 54

It is seldom mentioned that the Eucharist, the Last Supper, and communion would have been a shocking outrage to the apostles or any Jew. In fact, "At any period in the history of the Jewish people the notion of Jews drinking blood would be inconceivable even to those with only the barest acquaintance with Jewish dietary requirements and with the Jewish blood taboo."[338]

The strongest reactions to this rite would have been from those who *kept up their daily attendance at the Temple* (Acts 2:46) and were strict in their observance of the law.[339] James, and Jesus' disciples of the First Jewish Jesus Church of Jerusalem, were those people, and *They devoted themselves to the apostles' teaching and to the fellowship, to the breaking of bread and to prayer . . . . Every day they continued to meet together in the temple courts. They broke bread in their homes and ate together with glad and sincere hearts* (Acts 2:42 – 46). The apostles participated in traditional communal meals with the ceremonial breaking of the bread, which they certainly had done with Jesus, even on the night which he was betrayed. If the apostles had continued to participate in the abhorrent anti-Jewish blood ritual recorded by Paul, none of them would have lived out their lives in Jerusalem to be known as pious Jews and strict observers of the law. They would have, at a minimum, been prohibited from the temple, ostracized, and persecuted, and perhaps even executed.

In the 21st century, Muslims kill over the prohibition of depictions of Muhammad.[340] The Eucharist's allusion to human

---

[338] *Drinking Blood at a Kosher Eucharist? The Sound of Scholarly Silence,* Michael J. Cahill *Biblical Theology Bulletin: Journal of Bible and Culture* November 2002 vol. 32 no. 4, p. 168

[339] *The Antiquities of the Jews,* Flavius Josephus 20.9.1

[340] Some examples: in 2004, Dutch filmmaker Theo van Gogh was assassinated for his film that portrayed Muhammad; in 2012, a portrayal of Muhammad in the film the "Innocence of Muslims" was blamed by the Obama administration for attacks on

sacrifice and cannibalism would have provoked similar reactions in 1$^{st}$ century Jews: *Moreover, you shall eat no blood whatever, whether of fowl or of animal, in any of your dwelling places* (Lev. 7:26). Removing the blood is the basis of Kosher ritual slaughter. Leviticus 17 spells out, in no uncertain terms, that not only eating blood is forbidden, but contact with blood makes a person "unclean." The rite of the Last Supper is profoundly anti-Jewish and, as a learned Jew, Paul knew it. The idea that Jesus, *the* most pious Jew, would have spent his last evening on earth asking his disciples to drink a cup of his blood, even symbolically, is unthinkable.[341] Somebody needs to inform Leonardo da Vinci.[342]

How is this even possible, you ask? In all my readings and research over the years, the idea that Paul originated the Last Supper was the most unorthodox idea I came across. It is difficult to understand how few Christian critics and apologists have overlooked or failed to comment on this massive discrepancy. The Eucharist is such a scandalous violation of Jewish law that it cannot be reconciled with Jesus, preaching. The most plausible explanation is to accept what Paul tells us. He received the Eucharist in his dreams and then preached it to his Gentile followers. They in turn practiced the ritual, especially after the war, either unaware of its anti-Jewish implications, or aware of them and wanting to further separate themselves from the Jews. Mark then copied Paul, who was later copied by Matthew, all finding that it fit with their anti-Jewish agenda after the Roman War. This centerpiece of Christianity, the Eucharist ritual, is

---

the U.S. in Libya resulted in the death of the U.S. ambassador and others; in 2015, twelve people, were killed because the magazine "Charlie Hebdo" depicted Muhammad on its cover. In the same year in Garland, Texas, two men opened fire on police who were guarding a contest for Muhammad cartoons.

[341] *Paul: The Mind of the Apostle,* A. N. Wilson (W. W. Norton & Co., 1997) p. 165

[342] "The Last Supper" by Leonardo da Vinci is the iconic painting of Jesus and his apostles celebrating the eucharist. It is a fresco in the refectory of the Convent of Santa Maria delle Grazie, Milan.]

barely mentioned in any Jesus movement writing outside the Gospels for another 40 to 50 years.[343] There may have been a Last Supper, but almost certainly not the one Paul preached from his dreams.

Paul and the apostles did agree that Jesus was to return while they were all alive: *by the word of the Lord, that we who are alive and remain until the coming of the Lord* (1 Thess. 4:15) and *we who are alive and remain will be caught up together with them in the clouds to meet the Lord in the air* (1 Thess. 4:17) and *we will not all die, but we will all be changed* (1 Cor. 15:51) and *for now is our salvation nearer than when we believed* (Rom. 13:11). Paul even councils not marrying or buying anything because the end is near, *But this I say, brethren, the time is short: it remaineth, that both they that have wives be as though they had none;* (1 Cor. 7:29)…*and they that buy, as though they possessed not* (1 Cor. 7:30).

Beyond the agreement that Jesus would return in their lifetimes, Paul understood that his preaching was not in agreement with that of the apostles and other followers of Jesus. He knew he was opposed by them:

> *I am astonished that you are so quickly deserting him who called you in the grace of Christ and are turning to a different gospel*—not that there is another one [my emphasis], *but there are some who trouble you and want to distort the gospel of Christ. But even if we or an angel from heaven should preach to you a gospel contrary to the one we preached to you, let him be accursed. As we have said before, so now I say again: If anyone is preaching to you a gospel contrary to the one you received, (from Paul) let him be accursed* [my emphasis]. (Gal. 1:6-9)

---

[343] It is included in the Didache and mentioned by Ignatius around the year 100, and thereafter. *Christianity: The First Three Thousand Years,* Diarmaid MacClulloch (Viking, 2010) p. 159

Paul again strongly says he is right: there is no other gospel; the apostles and his opponents are wrong. This is the common tactic of all dreamers: Paul, Joseph Smith, Jim Jones, David Koresh, Muhammad, and the guy in the park. The myriads of seers and dreamers always contend that what they conjure in their minds is right. The others are always wrong.[344]

But then Paul does have some doubts about what he is preaching:

*I went up because of a revelation and set before them (though privately before those who seemed influential) the gospel that I proclaim among the Gentiles, in order to make sure I was not running or had not run my race in vain.* (Gal. 2:2-3)

Paul preached and wrote that Jewish law, rites, and rituals were gone: *For sin shall not have dominion over you: for ye are not under the law, but under grace* (Rom. 6:14). Paul was preaching that the Judaism of Jesus was now dead. And the apostles who had directly heard the Judaism that Jesus preached were becoming deadly against Paul. *And now, compelled by the Spirit, I am going to Jerusalem, not knowing what will happen to me there. I only know that in every city the Holy Spirit warns me that prison and hardships are facing me* (Acts 20:22-23). Sometime, in the mid to late 50s, Paul travelled to Jerusalem to meet again with the apostles. He was confronted by James and other apostles:

*You see, brother, how many tens of thousands of believers there are among the Jews, and all of them are zealous for the Law. But they have been told about you—that you teach all the Jews living among the Gentiles to forsake the Law of Moses, and that you tell them not to circumcise*

---

[344] *Feet of Clay: Saints, Sinners and Madmen: A Study of Gurus,* Anthony Storr (The Free Press 1996) p. xiii

*their children or observe the customs. What is to be done?*
(Acts 21:20-22)

For James, Jesus' brother who lived and traveled with Jesus all his life, unequivocally the Jewish Law must be observed! Can this be anything other than the message Jesus preached? Paul is told to confirm his allegiance to Judaism and submit to Jewish purity rituals.[345] Paul agrees! This may have been enough to satisfy James and the other apostles of the Jesus Movement, but there were other Jews, leaders of the temple, who knew of Paul's anti-Jewish Gospel: *Men of Israel, help! This is the man who teaches everyone everywhere to turn against our people, the Law, and this place* (Acts 21:28). *And all the city was disturbed; and the people ran together, seized Paul, and dragged him out of the temple* (Acts 21:30).

The Romans *wanted to know for certain why he was accused by the Jews,* and they *commanded the chief priests and all their council to appear* (Acts 22:30). Yet neither Peter, nor James, nor John nor any of the apostles appeared and lifted a finger or spoke a single word to help Paul! Had any of them done so, Paul might have been freed.

The men who had been by Jesus' side, those who had heard his voice as he preached, offered no help, no support, no testimony for Paul. Peter, James, and John and the others had heard Jesus say, *For truly, I say to you, until heaven and earth pass away, not an iota, not a dot, will pass from the Law until all is accomplished* (Matt. 5:18). The silence of Jesus' apostles at Paul's trial is a deafening roar: "Paul, you are wrong!"

Paul was sent to Rome, where he was executed.[346]

---

[345] Other aspects of this episode are covered in *Myth Maker: Paul and The Invention of Christianity*, Hyam Maccoby (Barnes and Noble, 1987) pp. 150-155

[346] *Paul and Jesus: How the Apostle Transformed Christianity,* James T. Tabor (Simon and Schuster, 2012)
Chapter 9 discusses the facts of the eventual ends of Paul and Peter.

# Chapter Four – The Jewish–Roman War

The Jewish–Roman War is not included in the Christian narrative. If mentioned at all, it is just an historical sidebar.[347] Imagine being told a 20th century history of Japan or Germany that left out World War II. That would be outrageous! How can one know anything about modern Germany or Japan without WWII? It is equally outrageous to attempt to learn about Christian history without the Jewish–Roman War. The future of Judaism and Christianity were totally affected by that war.

Just as Germany and Japan were totally devastated and their populations decimated in WWII, the land where Jesus preached, and his followers and disciples lived, was totally devastated and their populations decimated in the Jewish–Roman War.

Only the survivors of the Jewish-Roman War and those who did not participate in it were left to tell and write the story of Jesus. The followers of Jesus lived in Palestine and died in or before the Jewish–Roman War. They were no longer alive to

---

[347] For example, three major books on the history of Christianity, *A New History of Early Christianity*, Charles Freeman (Yale University Press 2009)  *A History of Christianity*, Paul Johnson (Simon & Schuster a Touchstone Book, 1995) and *Christianity The First Three Thousand Years* Diarmaid MacClulloch (Viking Press 2010) spend less than a page each on the Roman War. Probably because they saw it as a Jewish issue, forgetting that Jesus and his followers were Jews.

carry on what Jesus had preached. The followers of Paul lived outside of Palestine and were all alive after the Jewish–Roman war. They were alive to carry on Paul's visions and dreams. Even if any followers and disciples of Jesus did survive, their message of an apocalyptic Jewish Messiah would have been met with scorn: "Oh yeah? Where was your messiah when we needed him!" The spread and development of Christianity in the first century is the story of the Jewish–Roman War.

Israel won its independence and became a kingdom in 167 BC and remained independent until Herod's death in 4 BC.[348] Rome then allowed Herod's children to run Palestine, but it took them only a dozen years to mess things up. One son, Herod Antipas, continued to independently govern Galilee, but the other sons were removed, and their areas put under direct Roman rule.

And it came to pass that when Jesus was about 12, there went out a decree from Caesar Augustus that Quirinius should be the Governor of Samaria and Judea and the people thereof should be taxed. And all were registered in the city where they lived. And no one from Nazareth nor all of Galilee was registered or taxed, for they were not of Roman rule.

But not all agreed to be taxed, and Judas Gamala led the Jews in a revolt that was reported by Josephus and Luke (Acts 5:37). The revolt was not just about taxes, but over the loss of independence to a foreign power and culture, which Judas proclaimed was "tantamount to slavery."[349] Judas and the Zealots, believed that the Jews were to be ruled only by God in a theocracy. A few thousand Jews were killed in the revolt which failed. However, the idea that the Jews should be ruled by only Abraham's God prevailed. Judas Gamala was way ahead of his

---

[348] Other than a few years after Pompey's siege.

[349] *Josephus: The Essential Writings,* Paul L. Maier, editor (Kregel Publications, 1988) p. 260

time. The theocracy of Abraham's God under the Sharia Law of ISIS exists in that area of the world today.

In the 35 years from Quirinius' appointment through 41 CE, the Romans used seven different rulers, called procreators. The fifth one was Pontius Pilate, who ruled from 26 to 36 CE.[350] All the procreators were soldiers promoted to ruling in Judea under the only theory they knew: there was no problem that could not be solved by bloodshed. Blood only bolstered the theology of resurrection and reward as preached by the radical Essene parties and the many messiahs like Jesus who preached in Palestine. More and more Jews were turning to them.[351]

Ultimately, the Roman war was fought because Jews believed in an afterlife "where the good would achieve eternity and the wicked would not."[352] Jews "were so willing to lay down their lives rather than transgress the Torah," in fact, "They were not willing to forgo eternity in the World to Come for the sake of a few more years or a few creature comforts in this world."[353] Precisely the views of radical Islam today.

The Romans looked for leadership in Herod's grandson, Agrippa I. A friend of the infamous Roman emperor Caligula, he lasted three years. When he died, the Romans returned to incompetent procreators. Sometime around 50 CE, a Roman soldier "mooned" the crowd at Passover from the temple portico, and the ensuing riot brought about 20,000 deaths.[354] Josephus lists example after example of violence that continued to build

---

[350] *Josephus: The Essential Writings,* Paul L. Maier, editor (Kregel Publications, 1988) p. 391

[351] *Jews, God, and History, 50th Anniversary, 2nd Edition,* Max I Dimont edited by Ethel Dimont (Signet Classics 1994)  Kindle Location 1519 – 1521.

[352] *The Jews in the Time of Jesus: An Introduction,* Stephen M. Wylen (Paulist Press, 1996) p. 92

[353] *The Jews in the Time of Jesus: An Introduction,* Stephen M. Wylen (Paulist Press, 1996) p. 92

[354] *Josephus: The Essential Writings,* Paul L. Maier, editor (Kregel Publications, 1988) p. 273

the contempt between Jews and Romans. Under another procreator, Festus, the Jews built a high wall on the side of the temple to prevent the Romans from watching from their fortress. The Romans wanted to tear it down, but it was allowed to stand after an appeal to the Roman emperor Nero's wife. Festus died around 62 BC and before the next procreator could take charge, the high priest Ananus had Jesus' brother James stoned to death, but the ensuing revolt got Ananus fired.[355] The next procreator, Albiius, lasted two years, until the last Roman procreator, Florus, was appointed in 64 CE.[356] The Romans had tried numerous leaders, but none could keep the peace between the Jewish sects, their Greek neighbors, and their Roman rulers.

In the end, a neighborly clash between a Greek landowner and a Jewish synagogue turned constant conflict into an all-out war. Near Caesarea, the Jews had a synagogue adjacent to an "industrial park" owned by a Greek. On the way to the Synagogue, words were exchanged, a fight ensued, and the Roman police came and threw the Jews in jail. This inflamed the Jews to further fighting, which continued for several days.[357] The Jews then overran the Roman fortress in Jerusalem and killed its garrison. Word of this spread and "electrified the country.... Open rebellion broke out in every city, in every village, in every province."[358]

The capture of the Jerusalem fort, the killing of the Roman garrison, and the general uprising guaranteed a Roman reprisal. The Legate of Syria, Cestius Gallus, gathered a large force and

---

[355] *Josephus: The Essential Writings,* Paul L. Maier, editor (Kregel Publications, 1988) p. 276.

[356] *Josephus: The Essential Writings,* Paul L. Maier, editor (Kregel Publications, 1988) p. 391

[357] *Josephus: The Essential Writings,* Paul L. Maier, editor (Kregel Publications, 1988) p. 281

[358] *Jews, God, and History, 50th Anniversary, 2nd Edition,* Max I Dimont, edited by Ethel Dimont (Signet Classics 1994) Kindle Location 1541.

marched to Jerusalem. The Jews met him outside the city and forced a retreat that turned into a Roman rout.[359]

The Romans had conquered most of the known world. The majority acquiesced to Roman rule because life broadly improved, but also because defiance brought swift reprisal. From the Roman side, they simply could not allow any of their subjects to "win" a revolt. How could you then maintain Roman rule? Although there was no CNN, the whole world was watching, and the Romans knew it.

When news of the defeat reached Rome, Emperor Nero sent his battle-hardened General Vespasian and several legions to quell the insurrection. Vespasian went about his work, methodically wiping out resistance along the coast and in the countryside before marching on Jerusalem. In a battle in Galilee, Vespasian captured Josephus, the Jewish general, who then became an on the scene chronicler of this period of history. He is often cited in this book under *Josephus the Essential Writings* by Paul L Maier. The following is a summary of Josephus' reporting of the war. Please keep in mind Josephus was known to exaggerate, but nobody knows by how much.

Vespasian had barely begun his siege of Jerusalem when Nero died. Vespasian succeeded Nero as the Roman emperor and put his son Titus in charge of taking Jerusalem and defeating the Jews.[360] With 32,000 troops, Alexander the Great had conquered the known world. With 25,000 troops, Caesar had conquered Gaul and invaded Britain.[361] Titus had 60,000 troops, and the 25,000 Jewish warriors had no chance.[362]

Titus first tried to scare the Jews into surrender with a Jericho-type march around the city, but the walls did not come

---

[359] *A History of the Jews,* Paul Johnson (Harper Perennial 1988) p. 137

[360] *A History of the Jews* Paul Johnson (Harper Perennial 1988) p. 138

[361] Jews, God, and History, 50th Anniversary, 2nd Edition, Max I Dimont edited by Ethel Dimont (Signet Classics 1994) Kindle Location 1601

[362] *A History of the Jews,* Paul Johnson (Harper Perennial 1988) p. 139

tumbling down. Then, he unleashed his mighty siege engines to breach the walls of Jerusalem. Somehow, in ferocious hand-to-hand combat, the Jews drove the Romans back. Titus then decided starvation was the only weapon that would work. He built a dry moat around the city, with orders that anyone escaping would be crucified. Five hundred people a day were hung on crosses along the walls of the moat.

If the Jews had any chance at all, it was eliminated by their own internal treachery and fighting. The common enemy was the Romans, but each sect was the enemy of the other. Different Jewish sects controlled different parts of the city, and sometimes war broke out between them. Josephus recounted thousands of Jews killed by fellow Jews in the internecine warfare. In one such incident, 8,500 Jews were killed by fellow Jews in a single battle.[363] The starvation was horrible, with reports of women eating their own children to survive.[364]

On September 26, 70 CE, Jerusalem fell. The Roman soldiers poured "into the streets, they massacred everyone they found, burning houses with all who had taken shelter within them."[365] The estimate is that "600,000 civilians were killed in the aftermath of the siege."[366] Also, 97,000 were taken prisoner. Over a million died or were killed over the course of the Jewish–Roman War.[367] The city of Jerusalem was sacked and burned. Its walls, the temple, and all its buildings were leveled. All the trees, for miles around Jerusalem, had been cut down and used in the siege.

---

[363] *Josephus: The Essential Writings,* Paul L. Maier, editor (Kregel Publications, 1988) p. 319.

[364] *Josephus: The Essential Writings,* Paul L. Maier, editor (Kregel Publications, 1988) pp. 358-359

[365] *Josephus: The Essential Writings,* Paul L. Maier, editor (Kregel Publications, 1988) p. 365

[366] *Jews, God, and History, 50th Anniversary, 2nd Edition,* Max I Dimont edited by Ethel Dimont (Signet Classics 1994) Kindle Location 1621

[367] *Josephus: The Essential Writings,* Paul L. Maier, editor (Kregel Publications, 1988) p. 367

The clean-up of the balance of Judea and the remaining rebel encampments continued until it all ended on May 3, 73 AD, when the Romans finally took Masada. About 1000 of the remaining defenders and their families had committed mass suicide the day before. The Jewish leader, Eleazar, made a speech, saying, "death liberates the soul from its imprisonment in the mortal body. Why then should we fear death, and (not) welcome the calm of sleep."[368] The immortality of the soul had become deeply ingrained in Jewish faith, and in the followers of Jesus.[369]

As part of the victory celebration, Titus took 2500 prisoners to the stadium at Caesarea, where they were burned to death or savaged by wild beasts for the entertainment of the crowds.[370] Titus then moved on to Beirut, where he made an even bigger and more spectacular display of the deaths of his captives. Seven hundred other prisoners were selected for their size and looks, and after being paraded in Rome, they met similar fates. One of the principal leaders of the revolt, Simon, son of Giora, was paraded in Rome, then flogged to death in front of the Roman elite at the Jupiter Capitoline in the Roman Forum.[371] The world needed to know that the Romans were the masters of the universe.

There is speculation that some of Jesus Jewish followers escaped to the city of Pella in what is today Jordan. But that speculation is a dead-end.[372] In the following few decades after

---

[368] *Josephus: The Essential Writings,* Paul L. Maier, editor (Kregel Publications, 1988) p. 381. Going to Masada and seeing how the Romans attacked it, and the room where the suicide pact was enacted is a moving experience. Walking down the mountain is an exhausting experience.

[369] *The Story of the Jews: Finding the Words 1000 BC to 1492 AD,* Simon Schama (Harper Collins, 2013) p. 143

[370] *Josephus: The Essential Writings,* Paul L. Maier, editor (Kregel Publications, 1988) p. 371

[371] *Josephus: The Essential Writings,* Paul L. Maier, editor (Kregel Publications, 1988) p. 371

[372] Beginning with the Chapter, The Flight to Pella and continuing through the chapter The Bar Cochba Rebellion in "Forgotten Origins The Lost Jewish History of Early

the war, the embers of Jewish resistance would occasionally flare up, only to be doused by the Romans. The emperor Hadrian decided that enough was enough. His troops killed 580,000 Jews in the fighting while untold thousands more died of starvation and in the razing of 985 villages. Any remaining Jews were banned from the area of Jerusalem on pain of death.[373] Eusebius reports that there were no remaining members of the First Jewish Jesus Church of Jerusalem; "the church there was now composed of Gentiles."[374] Jewish temple sacrifice, that form of pagan worship practiced in Jerusalem by Jews for over a thousand years, had come to its end. Isaiah's hope for a messiah, a savior, a Jesus who would return to vanquish the Romans, had ended as well. Any eyewitnesses to the life of Jesus were almost certainly now dead. Only Paul's followers were now left to write about Jesus and record the beginnings of Christianity.

The Jewish nation of Israel was also ended. There would be constant trouble everywhere for Jews in the following centuries. Often despised and preyed upon, they survived and sometimes thrived as outsiders in the states of others. For over 1,800 years, Jews existed stateless, finding unity through a profound sense of shared community. The nation of Israel would not return until 1948.

In 2010, I visited Masada with a friend and my son. On the road to Masada, you can see the caves of Qumran, where its famous scrolls were hidden in desperation as the Romans advanced. At Masada, in the room where it was first delivered,

---

Christianity" Juan Marcos Bejarano Gutierrez Yaron Publishing 2017, Gutierrez reviews in detail the Christian narrative and its historical sources for the escape of some of Jesus followers to safety in Pella and the possibility of their survival from the Wars. He concludes that after the Bar Cocha Rebellion "The pages of history remain silent on the status of the Jewish Christian party for a considerable period." But that "there existence became a thorn in the side of the established church" after Nicaea.

[373] "Roman History" Casius Dio Book 69 as referenced in *A History of the Jews,* Paul Johnson (Harper Perennial 1988) p. 142

[374] *Eusebius: The Church History,* translation by Paul L. Maier (Kregel, 1999) p. 121

the emotion of Elazar's speech is overwhelming. But also overwhelming was the enormous determination of the Romans to obliterate any Jewish opposition to their rule. From the top of Masada, the view of the desert mountains of Judea to the west, and the Dead Sea to the east brings to life the hardship of the peoples of that time. After taking the tourist cable car to the top, my knees and body experienced the small hardship of the rugged walk off Masada's heights, but I cannot imagine the hardships faced by those who had only their legs and faith to take them both up and down the mountain of Masada almost 2000 years ago.

The areas of Samaria, Galilee, and Judea were laid to waste, the Jewish population slaughtered, and the favorable status of Jews in the eyes of the Romans died with them. Anti-Semitic attitudes rose and spread throughout the diaspora cities as the survivors of the war in Palestine and Jews elsewhere looked at the wreckage of their destroyed society, their destroyed religion, and their destroyed lives.

In the morass of demise and despair, stories of hope began to circulate. Many decades earlier, a peasant from Galilee had preached an apocalyptic and messianic message. The story of Jesus and his message would now be written and preached—by some to provide hope in the desolation of the Jewish–Roman War, by others to separate themselves from the Jews. From those writings, a new religion would emerge. Within a few centuries, Christianity would conquer the Roman conquerors.

# Chapter Five – The Struggle for Believers: Writing about Jesus

The hope for a messiah collapsed with the walls of the Jewish temple. The First Jewish Jesus Church of Jerusalem and the bodies of its members laid strewn in the debris. No savior, no messiah, and no Jesus had come to save anyone. Faith in Isaiah's promise of Emanuel had proven false.

Hope remained for Paul's Christ. Paul's visions had transfigured Jesus from Isaiah's messiah for the Jews into Zarathustra's messiah for all people. For Paul, Jesus was not a Jewish messiah but a heavenly spirit, who atoned for human sin—who would return and raise the dead and give everlasting life to those who had faith. Jesus' failure to return perversely confirmed that he was Paul's Christ and not the Messiah of Jewish expectations. Paul's messiah would return at the time of God's choosing, not a time chosen by the Roman invasion of Palestine. Besides, Paul's followers lived outside the war zone of Palestine, and it was among them that his gospel had gained the most acceptance.

Paul's gospel had conflicted with the teachings of James and the apostles, but Paul still saw his movement as a branch of Judaism, *Now I am speaking to you Gentiles, and...remember it is not you who support the root, but the root that supports you*

(Rom. 11:13, 11:18). After the war, any surviving Jewish followers of Jesus, and the followers of Paul's emerging Christianity, began to fully separate from Judaism. Not just for the theological issues but because some may have "been anxious to avoid association with the guilt of the Jews" for the war.[375]

There were clear monetary incentives as well: "The Roman imperial authorities unwittingly encouraged the process of separation between Jews and Christians by imposing a punitive tax."[376] The "fiscus Judaicus" was the yearly temple tax that the Jews of the diaspora paid. After the war, Vespasian diverted the two drachmas per adult male Jew to the temple of Jupiter Capitolinus in Rome,[377] "For Roman bureaucrats it became important to know who was and was not a Jew."[378] For Christians, it was now important not to be a branch on the Jewish root.

Before the war, the Jews had prospered under Herod. The Jews had been a respected part of the Roman Empire,[379] and Jesus' followers were broadly considered a sect of Judaism. Now, Jews were tainted by their rebellion, and Jesus' followers needed to dissociate from Judaism. And Paul's followers were teaching their anti-Jewish rhetoric, and anti-Jewish Eucharist. What better way to prove that you had nothing to do with Judaism than to participate in anti-Jewish blood rituals?

The survivors of Temple Judaism were also struggling with their own questions: Hey God, we've followed your diet laws and your sacrifices and your Sabbath, but "look at David and his lust,

---

[375] *Christianity: The First Three Thousand Years*, Diarmaid MacClulloch (Viking, 2010) p. 109

[376] *Christianity: The First Three Thousand Years*, Diarmaid MacClulloch (Viking, 2010) p. 109

[377] "TheJewishEncyclopedia.com" The complete full text of the 1906 *Jewish Encyclopedia*, FISCUS JUDAICUS: By: Richard Gottheil, Samuel Krauss

[378] *Christianity: The First Three Thousand Years*, Diarmaid MacClulloch (Viking, 2010) p. 109

[379] *A History of the Jews,* Paul Johnson (Harper Perennial 1988) p. 148

Solomon and his polygamous vanities. They weren't trampled in the dust, were they? Give us a break, won't you?" We break a few minor laws "and Jerusalem is destroyed, multitudes incinerated? Honestly? Again?"[380] The Jews needed to find something in which to believe. "The War changed everything, both for Jews and the Jesus people. Everything had to be thought over, explained again, and each group had to find its anchor in the past in some new way."[381]

Something new was required to replace Temple Judaism for the one million Jews remaining in Judea, and the four to six million in the diaspora.[382] In the coming century, a revised Jewish religion would be built on the foundation of Rabbis, the Torah, and Jewish Law. "Having lost the Kingdom of Israel, the Jews turned the Torah into a fortress of mind and spirit."[383] It would be called Rabbinic Judaism.

When Jesus did not return as believed by his Jewish followers and promised by Paul to his Gentile followers, the Jesus movement struggled with its beliefs. In the mix of political and theological revisioning, some began writing on the events and meaning of Jesus' life and death. Jesus himself left no record, nothing of what he did and said. Zero. Zip. None. You might think that the almighty powerful creator of all, the God who carved the Ten Commandments in stone for Moses, could at least have left a sentence or two about his son!

Absent anything from God and amid the havoc following the war, many people wrote stories about Jesus. In the Gospels, Luke

---

[380] *The Story of the Jews: Finding the Words 1000 BC to 1492 AD*, Simon Schama (Harper Collins, 2013) p. 162

[381] *Who wrote the New Testament? The Making of the Christian Myth*, Burton L. Mack (Harper Collins, 1996) p. 151

[382] *The Rise of Christianity: How the Obscure, Marginal Jesus Movement Became the Dominant Religious Force in the Western World in a Few Centuries,* Rodney Stark (Harper Collins, 1997) p. 57. This estimate agrees with the one in *A History of the Jews,* Paul Johnson (Harper Perennial 1988) p. 112.

[383] *A History of the Jews,* Paul Johnson (Harper Perennial 1988) p. 149

clearly confirms that *"many people have attempted to write an orderly account of the events that have transpired among us"* (Luke 1:1). They wrote from oral stories they heard from people who had heard it from others, perhaps from someone before the war. But stories that circulate after a war can be different.

My grandfather came from Germany at the age of 17 in 1912 and died in 1942. Because of the World Wars, nothing was known of the family in Germany and their fate. As I was growing up, I was told heroic stories of Grandfather coming alone as a teenage boy and struggling to find his way in America. Long after WWII, thanks to Ancestry.com and eventual contact with German relatives, the reality of events emerged. Two of Grandfather's uncles and an aunt had emigrated to Fort Wayne in 1870. They visited Germany in 1912 and brought back two of their nephews. My grandfather and his cousin lived comfortably with their aunt and uncle while getting established in America. The oral stories of Jesus that emerged after the Jewish–Roman War were almost certainly different than the actual events of Jesus's life.

Many of the books that were written about Judaism and Jesus in that 1$^{st}$ century have been lost to history. Some survived in the Bible, but many others did not. Then the discovery of the Dead Sea Scrolls and Nag Hammadi texts in Egypt in the late 1940s shined a light on Judaism in the times of Jesus, and on Jesus in the times after Jesus.[384]

Judaism was closer to "the dualistic battles between good and evil, light and darkness, characteristic of Persian Zoroastrianism" than previously thought. "It seems impossible for Jews to have read, still less believed, *both* (emphasis in the original) the authorized story of the covenant-led Bible and the version given

---

[384] Discovered in 1947, they will be discussed in more detail in a later chapter.

in" Jubilees, 1 Enoch, the Book of the Watchers, the Book of the Giants, and the Genesis Apocryphon.[385]

From Egypt came texts, including several on Gnosticism. Guess what? They told a story of "dualism, envisaging a cosmic struggle between matched forces of good and evil, darkness and light that might suggest acquaintance with the dualism of Zoroastrian religion in" Persia.[386]

There were many other books written in the names of Bible celebrities, but not by them. Today, we might consider them forgeries, but at the time it was a common practice.[387] We have many other books written "with impressive pedigrees—other Gospels, Acts, Epistles, and Apocalypses claiming to be written by the earthly apostles of Jesus."[388] Some documents even claimed to have been written by Jesus himself![389] Here is a list of some of the known books written about Jesus in formative years of early Christianity:

The Gospel of Mary
The Gospel of Bartholomew
The Gospel of Phillip
The Gospel of Thomas
The Shepard of Hamas
The Secret Gospel of Mark
The First Gospel of the
Infancy of Jesus Christ
The Gospel of Nicodemus
The Last Gospel of Peter
The Gospel of Pseudo-
Matthew

The Gospel of the Birth of
Mary
The Infancy Gospel of
Thomas
The Apocrypha of James
The Avenging of the Savior
The Life of Adam and Eve
The Apocalypse of Moses
The Acts of Paul and Thecla
The Apocalypse of Abraham
The Apocalypse of Adam
The Apocrypha of John

[385] *The Story of the Jews: Finding the Words 1000 BC to 1492 AD*, Simon Schama (Harper Collins, 2013) p. 163

[386] *Christianity: The First Three Thousand Years*, Diarmaid MacClulloch (Viking, 2010) p. 122

[387] *An Introduction to the New Testament*, Raymond E. Brown, First edition (Yale University Press, 2010) p. 589

[388] *Lost Christianites: The Battle for Scripture and Faiths We Never Knew*, Bart D. Ehrman (Oxford University Press, 2003) p. 3

[389] *Eusebius: The Church History,* Translation by Paul L. Maier (Kregel, 2007) pp. 45-48

The Ascension of Isaiah
The Testament of Moses
The Report of Pilate the
Procurator
The Epistle of the Apostles
The Letters of Herod and
Pilate
The Epistles of Jesus and
Agbarus King of Edessa
The Epistles of Paul the
Apostle to Seneca
The Letter of Peter to Philip
The Writings of Baruch
The Damascus Document
The History of Joseph the
Carpenter
The First Book of Hermas

The General Epistle of
Barnabas
The Book of Abraham
The Book of Adam
The Book of Jubilees
The Book of the Apocalypse
of Baruch
The Martyrdom of Isaiah
The Testament of Abraham
The Didache
The Book of John the
Evangelist
The Book of Marcion
The Report of Pilate to
Caesar
The Wisdom of Sirach
The Wisdom of Solomon

All these books were written from oral histories to fill in the gaps of knowledge for the earliest followers of Jesus. For example, the canonical books tell us nothing about Jesus as a little boy. The Infancy Gospel of Thomas is a collection of stories that fill in the gap of information about Jesus' childhood. It is a fun read and was a very popular book. It was supposedly written by Jesus' twin brother, Thomas. Imagine something like Dennis the Menace with the powers of God, or an uncontrolled Tabatha for those that remember the TV series *Bewitched*. According to this Infancy Gospel, Jesus used his powers to do some fun things as a little boy, like stretching a board that Joseph had cut too short (13) or making mud sparrows, then turning them into real birds to fly away (2).[390] Little Jesus did some good things too, like healing his brother James who had been bitten by a snake (16) and making 100 bushels of grain out of a single seed (12). And he even did some evil things, killing playmates that made him

---

[390] The story of Jesus turning clay birds into live birds is told twice in the Qur'an. 3:49 and 5:110

angry (3) and blinding kids who tattled on him (5).[391] Now you may laugh and say such stories are ridiculous. But they were popular in their day, as are Saturday cartoons among children today. One of the stories though is important, and that is the story of the mud sparrows, which will be discussed more fully in the section on Islam.

This example of Jesus' power as a child clearly shows how people's imaginations played into the writing of the stories of Jesus and the meaning of his life. Some, but not all of the non-canonical books can be glibly dismissed. Bible stories were not simply sitcoms you watched for a half hour before going on with your life. Beliefs were much more entrenched in the lives of people in the early centuries of the first millennium than they are today. But who wrote these books on Jesus' life?

In today's literary world, there is an industry of people who write books in the names of celebrities, often from an outline or a very rough draft. The practice of writing in another's name is called pseudepigrapha. Today, the practice of ghostwriting produces over half of the non-fiction books.[392] Not even John Kennedy wrote his famous book, *Profiles in Courage*.[393] Ted Sorenson wrote Kennedy's book. But the apostles were dead when the gospels were written in their names. Because of this, we have no idea who wrote many of the books of early Christianity: those that were found near the Dead Sea, or those

---

[391] The numbers behind each example refer to the standardized number of the story as found in mosttranslations. These are from *Lost Scriptures: Books that Did Not Make It into the New Testament,* Bart D. Ehrman (Oxford University Press, 2003) pp. 57-72

[392] "at least 60 percent of the books are ghostwritten" Madeleine Morel, a literary agent for ghostwriters on NPR Weekend Edition April 12, 2014 https://www.npr.org/2014/04/12/292382481/so-you-need-a-celebrity-book-who-ya-gonna-call-ghostwriters

[393] The original accusation was made in an interview of Drew Pearson by Mike Wallace and can be viewed here http://www.hrc.utexas.edu/multimedia/video/2008/wallace/pearson_drew.html The accusation was confirmed in Teddy Sorensen's autobiography.

found at Nag Hammadi, or those in the New Testament, except for some of Paul's letters.

While the author may not be known, from a very detailed analysis of the words, the writing style and the content, scholars can draw conclusions about where, when, and what sort of person did the writing. In general, the conclusion is that "The followers of Jesus, as we learn from the New Testament itself, were uneducated lower-class Aramaic speaking Jews from Palestine." The Gospels in the Bible were written by "highly educated, Greek speaking Christians of a later generation." The Gospels were written at a later time and not in Palestine.[394]

They were also written in a political context. The people who actually knew Jesus—the apostles and disciples—were Jewish, while Paul's followers were mostly Gentile. After the War, Paul's followers required separation from the Jewish community. For their safety, Christians needed to say, "The Romans are okay by us," "We are not Jews," and "We had nothing to do with the War." This is exactly what the Gospels of the Bible do. "The Gospel writers chose to dissociate themselves from the Jewish majority and to focus instead on the intra-Jewish conflict."[395] They did this by shifting the blame for Jesus' death from the Romans to the Jews, and by diverting Jesus' mission away from being the Jewish Messiah towards the cosmic war of good and evil. Hmm? Where have we heard that before? That is the theme of the Gospels: Mark, Matthew, Luke, and John.[396]

---

[394] *How Jesus Became God: The Exaltation of a Jewish Preacher from Galilee,* Bart D. Ehrman, (Harper One, 2014) p. 90

[395] *The Origin of Satan: How Christians Demonized Jews, Pagans, and Heretics,* Elaine Pagels (Vintage Books, 1996) p. 15

[396] *The Origin of Satan: How Christians Demonized Jews, Pagans, and Heretics,* Elaine Pagels (Vintage Books, 1996) Pagels reviews in depth the examples in the Gospels (as well as other canonical books) of the "vast cosmic conflict enveloping the universe" with Jesus crucifixion being "the culmination of the struggle between good and evil – God and Satan" p. 12

# Chapter Six – The Gospel According to Mark

Just because the names, Matthew, Mark, Luke, and John always roll off people's lips in that order does not mean that they were written in that order, or by people with those names. "The Gospel According to Mark" was the first Gospel written, and it acquired the name "Mark" sometime in the late 2nd century, almost 100 years after it was written.[397] It may or may not have been written by someone named Mark.[398] Earlier, it might have been known as "Peter's Memoirs."[399] The Church Father, Justin Martyr, writing between 150 and 160 AD quotes Gospels without ever naming them. Around 190 AD, Irenaeus, another Christian writer, began the tradition of applying names to the Gospels.[400]

In the 4th century, Eusebius – that writer of the Nicaea Report – established the name of the Gospel of Mark, quoting an earlier

---

[397] *An Introduction to the New Testament,* Raymond E. Brown First edition (Yale University Press 2010) p. 158-164

[398] *The Historical Figure of Jesus,* E. P. Sanders (Penguin Books, 1993) pp. 64-65. Sanders discusses the ambiguity, and reasons for the naming of the Gospels.

[399] *An Introduction to the New Testament*, Raymond E. Brown, First edition (Yale University Press, 2010) p. 158

[400] *Forged: Writing in the Name of God--Why the Bible's Authors Are Not Who We Think They Are, Bart D. Ehrman, (Harper Collins, 2012) p. 225 location 3520*

writing by Papias from the 2nd century.[401] We will never know if "Mark" was the Mark from 2 Timothy 4:11 *Only Luke is with me. Get Mark and bring him with you, because he is a great help to me in ministry,* or Peter's son (1 Pet. 5:13) or Peter's interpreter,[402] or the "John Mark" in Acts 15:39 or someone totally unknown to us. Almost certainly, it's the latter. Whomever he was, "there is wide scholarly agreement"[403] that Mark was the first to write a story of Jesus that has survived.[404]

The Gospel of Mark tells us nothing of Jesus' birth, nor anything about Jesus before he is age thirty. Mark first introduces us to Jesus through John the Baptist:[405] *And it came to pass in those days, that Jesus came from Nazareth of Galilee, and was baptized of John in the Jordan* (Mark 1:9). Mark told us that God is his proud father: *And a voice came out of the heavens, "Thou art my beloved Son, in thee I am well pleased"* (Mark 1:11).

Jesus did not begin his preaching until after John the Baptist was executed: *Now after John was delivered up, Jesus came into Galilee, preaching the gospel of God, and saying, the time is fulfilled, and the kingdom of God is at hand: repent ye, and believe in the gospel* (Mark 1:14-15). There is no explanation of what Jesus' gospel was—just believe it because the end is near.

The author of Mark was writing during the Jewish-Roman War to non-Jewish Greek speakers who believed that Jesus'

---

[401] *An Introduction to the New Testament*, Raymond E. Brown, First edition (Yale University Press, 2010) p. 158

[402] *Who wrote the New Testament? The Making of the Christian Myth,* Burton L. Mack (Harper Collins, 1996) p. 153

[403] *An Introduction to the New Testament,* Raymond E. Brown First edition (Yale University Press 2010) p. 164. The Catholic Church agrees, https://www.catholic.com/magazine/print-edition/whos-on-first-matthew-mark-or-luke as well as its head "Pope Francisco writes to *La Republica*: 'An open dialogue with non-believers,'" *La Republica*, Sept. 11, 2013; online at *republica.it*).

[404] Earlier stories might have been written of which we have no knowledge. The Q Gospel is widely speculated to have been written earlier and used by Mark, Matthew, and Luke in writing their Gospels.

[405] Luke 3:23 "Jesus, when he began his ministry, was about thirty years of age."

return was imminent.[406] The writer was telling his recipients to be patient and not to lose hope, that Jesus the Messiah would still return and save the day. Mark was not written as a biography; rather, it was a political document to answer questions that were on everyone's mind: "If the Jews were Gods chosen people, what did they do to deserve this abomination of destruction, and where was the promised Messiah?"[407]

Mark provided the answer by recycling the story in Isaiah, where God has given his sword to the Assyrians to punish Israel. "The author of the Gospel of Mark took full advantage of the situation by writing the story of Jesus' life as if the destruction of the Temple had been God's answer to the Jew's rejection and crucifixion of Jesus."[408] In fact, "Mark thought that the destruction of the Temple was exactly what the Jews deserved."[409]

Just as Josephus will later write, Mark describes the awful events of the war: *Now the brother shall betray the brother to death, and the father the son; and children shall rise up against their parents, and shall cause them to be put to death* (Mark 13:12). Mark is writing to offer hope to those who have seen these things firsthand and thus far survived this terrible war. Jesus says he will be returning at any minute: *And then shall they see the Son of man coming in the clouds with great power and glory* (Mark 13:26). Retain your faith, believe because *Verily I say unto you, that this generation shall not pass, till all these things be done* (Mark 13:30). But what were people to believe when that generation did pass?

---

[406] *An Introduction to the New Testament*, Raymond E. Brown, First edition (Yale University Press, 2010) p. 163

[407] This is my rendition of the Apocryphal book, 4 Ezra 7:111-129 which although written after Mark (around 90 AD to 100 AD) is a summation of thought amongst the Jews at the time.

[408] *Who wrote the New Testament?: The Making of the Christian Myth*, Burton L. Mack (Harper Collins, 1996) p. 151

[409] *The Lost Gospel: The Book of Q and Christian Origins*, Burton L. Mack, (Harper Collins, 1993) p. 178

By the time the Gospel of Mark was written, the promise of a messiah was well entrenched in Jewish society, where "Jesus had been preached as the Christ for several decades."[410] There were a rich variety of stories, oral traditions, and selected secondhand memories circulating among the people. Some came from people who might have known Paul, while others came from those who might have known someone who might have known the apostles. After more than 30 years of telling and retelling, those stories had been stretched, embellished, and molded to fit the situation at hand. And there were many stories at hand. Mark says, "Listen to me, I have the right story" by having Jesus say:

> *And then if any man shall say unto you, Lo, here is the Christ; or, Lo, there; believe it not: for there shall arise false Christs and false prophets, and shall show signs and wonders, that they may lead astray, if possible, the elect.* (Mark 13:21-22)

One thing is sure: Mark was very familiar with Paul, and his writings mirrored Paul's; "The gospel of Mark, our earliest narrative of the career and death of Jesus is heavily Pauline in its theological content."[411] Moreover, "The Gospel of Mark and Luke, and to a lesser extent Matthew, are written under the heavy influence of Paul's ideas."[412]

A very important example is the story of the Last Supper, originated by Paul, as covered in detail earlier. Here is Paul writing around 50 CE:

> *Jesus the same night in which he was betrayed took bread: And when he had given thanks, he broke it, and said, "Take, eat: this is my body, which is broken for you:*

---

[410] *An Introduction to the New Testament*, Raymond E. Brown, First edition (Yale University Press, 2010) p. 157

[411] *Paul and Jesus: How the Apostle Transformed Christianity,* James T. Tabor (Simon and Schuster, 2012) p. 7

[412] *Jesus: A Life*, A. N. Wilson (W. W. Norton & Company, 2004) p. 7

*this do in remembrance of me". After the same manner also he took the cup, when he had supped, saying, "this cup is the new testament in my blood: this do ye, as oft as ye drink it, in remembrance of me"* (1 Cor. 11:23-25).

And here is Mark 20 years later:

*Jesus took bread, and blessed, and broke it, and gave to them, and said, Take, eat: this is my body. And he took the cup, and when he had given thanks, he gave it to them: and they all drank of it. And he said unto them, this is my blood of the new testament, which is shed for many.* (Mark 14:22-24)

The indisputable fact is that Paul boldly states he originated the story of the ritual himself.[413] Paul did as he said; *he* instituted the Eucharist, from a trance or dream or vision. And the Gospel writers, beginning with Mark, followed right along. "We are forced to the conclusion that the source from which the Gospels derive their account of the Last Supper…is in fact Paul's…."[414]

About 20 years after Jesus' crucifixion, Paul also was the first to write a story of the resurrection,[415] but unlike the Eucharist story, Mark does not follow Paul. The Gospel of Mark has no resurrection story and ends ambiguously with three women standing at the empty tomb, *Trembling and bewildered, the women went out and fled from the tomb. They said nothing to anyone, because they were afraid* (Mark 16:8).

---

[413] The evidence of this is discussed at length in Chapter 11 of *Myth Maker: Paul and The Invention of Christianity,* Hyam Maccoby (Barnes and Noble, 1987) and on pages 144-156 of *Paul and Jesus*: *How the Apostle Transformed Christianity,* James T. Tabor (Simon and Schuster, 2012) and pages 158 to 163 of *How Jesus Became Christian*, Barrie Wilson Ph.D. (St. Martin's Press, 2008)

[414] *Myth Maker: Paul and The Invention of Christianity,* Hyam Maccoby (Barnes and Noble, 1987) p. 114

[415] In the third epistle he wrote (probably in 53 or 54 AD), Paul says that he had heard the story of Jesus' resurrection from others, differentiating this from other stories which he says he received in dreams or visions.

What? No resurrection story in Mark? And they told no one! How can we have an Easter; we need to fix that. And someone did by adding a resurrection story to Mark in verses 9-20 of chapter 16.[416] The issue that someone modified the Book of Mark is no longer even disputed. Even Pope Benedict XVI, commenting in his book *Jesus of Nazareth* agrees, "It's an enigmatic interruption we must leave unexplained"[417] And so Mark ended his Gospel with Jesus' missing body.

It's a mystery! But then Mark again agrees with Paul that the gospel is a mystery. A mystery of God's hidden plan. Mark writes that Jesus said, *The secret about the kingdom of God has been given to you. But to those on the outside, everything comes in parables* (Mark 4:11). Mark also has Jesus telling his disciples they should not tell anyone about what he does or who he is, *And he charged them that they should tell no man of him* (Mark 8:30). Mark repeats this in Mark 1:44, 3:12, 5:43, and 7:36. This idea of secret knowledge will be important among the groups later known as the Gnostics. More importantly, if you are the all-powerful creator and God of the universe, what is the big secret? Is your existence and plan a petty guessing game? Maybe in a few hundred years, Muhammed will have the answer.

Using oral traditions, and perhaps some unknown written sources, Mark tells of Jesus' ministry, some parables, a few miracles, and Jesus' death. Although there is no birth story in Mark, Jesus' family does make a cameo appearance, with some definite opinions of Jesus, their brother and son, *When his family heard about this, they went to take charge of him, for they said, 'He is out of his mind'* (Mark 3:21-22 ESV). Why would the writer of Mark so disparage Jesus? I guess it's just another mystery.

---

[416] *Misquoting Jesus: The Story Behind Who Changed the Bible and Why* Bart D Erdman Harper One 2005 pp. 65-68

[417] *Jesus of Nazareth. Holy Week: From the Entrance into Jerusalem to the Resurrection*, Pope Benedict XVI/Joseph Ratzinger, Translated by Philip J. Whitmore (Ignatius Press, 2011) p. 262

# Chapter Seven – *Jesus* the Movie, Written and Directed by Luke & Matthew

In the 2nd century, a writer named Papias named a book "The Gospel of Matthew." And the name stuck, even though we have no idea who wrote it. It was written in Greek to Greek-speaking Jewish Christians who had survived the war in Palestine and Syria.[418] Matthew bolsters Jesus' credentials as the Messiah by frequently having Jesus fulfill Jewish prophecies. But Matthew is "extremely hostile"[419] to the Jewish leaders, while stressing Jesus' strict adherence to Jewish law. By doing this, he separates the Jesus followers from the Jews, while maintaining the importance of following Jewish law.[420, 421]

---

[418] *An Introduction to the New Testament and the Origins of Christianity,* Delbert Burkett (Cambridge University Press, 2002) pp. 208-217 provide a good overview of the evidence for the authorship, dating and locale.

[419] *An Introduction to the New Testament and the Origins of Christianity,* Delbert Burkett (Cambridge University Press, 2002) p. 222

[420] *A History of Christian Theology: An Introduction,* William C. Placher (Westminster Press, 1983) p. 36

[421] There are hundreds of different lists of "fulfilled prophecies". Here are 12 in Matthew, followed by the Old Testament reference: Matthew 1:22 –Isaiah 7:14, Matthew 2:15 –Hosea 11:1, Matthew 2:17 –Jeremiah 31:15, Matthew 4:14 – Isaiah 9:1-2, Matthew 8:17 –Isaiah 53:4, Matthew 13:14 – Isaiah 6:9-10, Matthew 13:35

Matthew has Jesus say, *Therefore every scribe who has been trained for the kingdom of heaven is like a master of a house, who brings out of his treasure what is new and what is old* (Matt 13:52). And Matthew dutifully follows the advice. Matthew fundamentally copies the book of Mark, "almost as a scribe copying his source,"[422] polishing Mark's rough Greek and Mark's portrayal of Jesus in the process. Matthew makes "a few editorial changes to Mark's story," reproducing "the whole gospel very much as Mark wrote it."[423]

Matthew then adds the new stories of Jesus' birth and crucifixion and concludes with Jesus' appearances to the apostles. Probably written between 80 AD and 90 AD, about a decade after the Roman War and 85 years after Jesus' birth, the "narrative won important parts of the ancient world to faith in Christ."[424] Matthew told a very good story indeed, filling in gaps in Paul's and Mark's accounts.

Three important Jewish prophets, Micah, Samuel, and Isaiah had prophesied that a legitimate Messiah had to be a descendent of David.[425] For the Jews of the time, that was the common understanding. For Jesus to be the Jewish Messiah, he had to be of the house and lineage of David. Both Matthew and Luke start their Gospels with the Nativity narratives. There was no birth certificate, nor any record of Jesus' birth until Matthew and Luke used their imaginations to cobble together bits and pieces of secondhand memories and rumors that had fermented for more

---

    – Psalm 78:2, Matthew 21:4 – Zechariah 9:9, Matthew 27:9 – Zechariah 11:12-13 and two general references Matthew 2:23 – and Matthew 26:54, 56.

[422] *An Introduction to the New Testament and the Origins of Christianity,* Delbert Burkett (Cambridge University Press, 2002) p. 204

[423] *Who wrote the New Testament?: The Making of the Christian Myth,* Burton L. Mack (Harper Collins, 1996) p. 162

[424] *An Introduction to the New Testament,* Raymond E. Brown (First Yale University Press, 2010) p. 208

[425] Mic. 5:2, 2 Sam. 7:12-13 and Isa. 9:6-7

than 80 years. While they both wrote stories of Jesus descending from David, their birth stories vary in every other aspect.

Matthew starts his gospel with, *A record of the origin of Jesus Christ, the son of David, the son of Abraham: Abraham begot Isaac...* and continues 40 generations until *...and Jacob begot Joseph, the husband of Mary, of whom was born Jesus* (Matt. 1:1–17). In listing the genealogy of early Kings of Israel, Matthew leaves out Ahaziah, Jehoash, and Amaziah, who were recorded in 1 Kings 22:49-53, 2 Kings 13:10, Amos 7:10-17; and Jehoiakim, as recorded in 2 Kings 24, but what's a few generations from Abraham to David? Who will ever notice?

But even so, according to Matthew, Joseph was the 27th generation after King David. Do you even know your thirty-two 5th generation great-great-great-great-grandparents? I didn't think so. It is preposterous to think that rural Galilean peasants knew 27 generations. But just for fun, let's imagine they did. The theoretical number of people related to David after 27 generations is 134,217,728.[426] That's over 100 million descendants at a time when the entirety of the Roman Empire was only 50 million people. By Matthew's counting, *everyone* in the Middle East could have claimed to be of the house and lineage of David.

For Matthew, the average age of each generation was over 37 years. At least when Luke gives Jesus a different genealogy of 42 generations, it is a more realistic average of 24 years. But with those extra generations, the number of people in the house and lineage of David explodes to an even more astronomical number.[427] The theological question would not have been how many angels can sit on the head of a pin, but how many of David's descendants can fit in an inn in Bethlehem.

---

[426] Assuming separate parents for each generation, the calculation is 2 to the 27th power, or 134,217,728.
[427] Over 4 trillion to 4,398,046,511,104

And Bethlehem is the other difficulty: the future ruler of Israel needed not only to be of the house and lineage of David, but needed to be born in Bethlehem: *But thou, Bethlehem Ephrathah, though thou be little among the thousands of Judah, yet out of thee shall he come forth unto me that is to be ruler in Israel* (Mic. 5:2). That meant Matthew and Luke, after telling a story of Jesus being a descendant of David, needed to get him born in Bethlehem. But why does this matter, because God was Jesus' father, right? Joseph was only...the foster father? The answer is coming up.

Matthew simply says, *Now after Jesus was born in Bethlehem of Judea in the days of Herod the King* (Matt. 2:1). Luke doesn't take the easy way out; he spins out perhaps the most famous paragraph in the history of the world:

> *And it came to pass in those days, that there went out a decree from Caesar Augustus that all the world should be taxed. (And this taxing was first made when Cyrenius {Quirinius} was governor of Syria.) And all went to be taxed, every one into his own city. And Joseph also went up from Galilee, out of the city of Nazareth, into Judaea, unto the city of David, which is called Bethlehem; (because he was of the house and lineage of David:) To be taxed with Mary his espoused wife, being great with child. And so it was, that, while they were there, the days were accomplished that she should be delivered.* (Luke 2:1-6)

What a beautiful story—an enduring story. Luke could write movies for Hollywood where facts are always just a nuisance. Herod simply was not king when Quirinius was governor of

Syria.[428] And Caesar Augustus never sent out a decree for "all the world to be taxed."[429] And if Luke is referring to the property registration under Quirinius, that census did not even cover Mary and Joseph's home town of Nazareth.[430] Besides, the Romans never required people to return to the home of some ancient ancestor.[431] So the only agreement between Matthew and Luke is that Jesus was born in Bethlehem.[432] But even the canonical Gospels do not fully agree on that:

> *But some were saying, "The Messiah doesn't come from Galilee, does he? Doesn't the Scripture say that the Messiah is from David's family and from Bethlehem, the village where David lived?" So there was a division in the crowd because of him.* (John 7:41-44)

There is another reality to consider. Nazareth is about 100 mountainous miles from Bethlehem. I have personally driven the modern roads between the two places, and even today it is a steep up-and-down journey. One hundred miles on a donkey? Through the mountains? And over eight-months pregnant? And just to register for taxes? Now we are talking real miracles!

Luke and Matthew have each, in their own way, gotten Jesus to be of the house of David and born in Bethlehem. Now, they need to get him back to Nazareth. This time, Luke tells us they went to Jerusalem, where they met two prophets, Simeon and Anna (Luke 2:22-38). Rather than meeting two prophets,

---

[428] *Jesus: A Life*, A. N. Wilson (W. W. Norton & Company, 2004) p. 75

[429] *The Historical Jesus: The Life of a Mediterranean Jewish Peasant*, John Dominic Crossan (Harper Collins, 1992) p. 372

[430] *The Historical Jesus: The Life of a Mediterranean Jewish Peasant*, John Dominic Crossan (Harper Collins, 1992) p. 87

[431] *Jesus: A Revolutionary Biography*, John Dominic Crossan (Harper Collins, 1994) p. 20. All of the points in this paragraph are covered by Sanders and Crossan.

[432] Sources for each of the above facts can be found in each of the citations. They are all referenced to bolster the certainty of Luke's error.

Matthew wants Jesus to fulfill a prophecy of Hosea,[433] *Out of Egypt I called my Son* (Matt. 2:13). So instead of Jerusalem, Matthew has Jesus and family going for a tour of the pyramids before returning to Nazareth (Matt. 2:13-23).

The opening verses of the Gospels of Matthew and Luke attempt to bolster Jesus' messianic credentials with creative pedigrees to King David and novel plot lines to a birth in Bethlehem. They are full of holes and contradictions, which for centuries preachers passed over or ignored, like 21st century marketing agents producing delightful TV specials.

Luke has other problems with Jesus' life. For example, according to the Gospels, Jesus lived in the village of Nazareth until he was about age thirty. Luke says, *Then Jesus came to Nazareth, where He had been brought up. As was His custom, He entered the synagogue on the Sabbath* (Luke 4:16). But Nazareth was a tiny village of people living in subsistence-level poverty.[434] It could never have afforded the scrolls of the Torah, much less a synagogue in which to house them.

A friend pointed me to the book *In Defense of the Bible* by Steven B. Cowan and Terry L Wilder. They are Christian writers defending the authority of their religion and attempt to provide answers for many of the conundrums in the Bible. Their best explanation for the conflicts in the story of Jesus' birth is: "We must keep in mind that Luke was writing seventy or more years after the birth of Jesus. Resources such as textbooks, archives, encyclopedias, to say nothing of the Internet, were not available to him."[435] They had no way of getting their facts straight, so they wrote a good story! The Gospels were written many decades after Jesus lived and tell his stories from tales and rumors that had been

---

[433] *When Israel was a child, I loved him, and out of Egypt I called my son* [Hosea 11:1].

[434] *Zealot: The Life and Times of Jesus of Nazareth*, Reza Aslan (Random House, 2014) Kindle Loc. 863-865

[435] *In Defense of the Bible: A Comprehensive Apologetic for the Authority of Scripture*, Steven B. Cowan, Terry Wilder (B&H Publishing, 2013) p. 245

repeated and embellished, repeated and stretched, repeated and exaggerated. And that is the real Gospel truth.

Christian writers have been inventing schemes for centuries, trying to get around a very basic problem. Either Matthew or Luke, or both of them, are wrong. Even Pope Benedict XVI had to begrudgingly admit, "They are marked by different theological visions, just as their historical details are in some ways different."[436] Which is the politically correct way of saying that an aardvark and a zebra are in some ways different. You also might ask, "If Matthew and Luke got the facts of Jesus' birth wrong, what else did they get wrong?"

The Gospel of Luke and the Book of Acts were written by the same person. Let's call him Luke.[437] In Luke 24, he says of Easter Sunday three days after the crucifixion *"Now that same day two of them were going to a village called Emmaus* (Luke 24:13) and after some other events and dinner, *They rose up and returned to Jerusalem at once* (Luke 24:33); then, *As they were saying this, Jesus Himself stood among them and said to them, "Peace be unto you"* (Luke 24:36) and then Jesus *led them out as far as Bethany, and He lifted up His hands and blessed them. While He blessed them, He parted from them and was carried up into heaven* (Luke 24:50-51). A simple straightforward story of Jesus between the crucifixion and the ascension.

I am now getting old and often forget exactly what it was that I wrote a few days ago. Luke, obviously, had the same problem. The same Luke, writing in Acts a few years after the Book of Luke, clearly forgot what he had written and now told the story this way: *During the forty days after he suffered and died, he appeared to the apostles from time to time* (Acts 1:3) and *Once when he was eating with them* (Acts 1:4) but a little while later,

---

[436] *Jesus of Nazareth: The Infancy Narratives*, Pope Benedict the XVI / Joseph Ratzinger (Image, 2012)

[437] *An Introduction to the New Testament.* Raymond E. Brown. First edition (Yale University Press. 2010) p. 225 and 267-269

*he was taken up into a cloud while they were watching, and they could no longer see him. As they strained to see him rising into heaven* (Acts 1:9-10). After waving goodbye, *Then they returned to Jerusalem from the Mount of Olives* (Acts 1:12). Which story of the Ascension is correct? Is it, Easter Sunday, or forty days later? Bethany or the Mount of Olives?

Tradition votes for the Mount of Olives and, today, you can go to the Mount of Olives, which is in the Palestinian West Bank. It's just up the steep hill from the Garden of Gethsemane. After perhaps a lamb sandwich at one of the nearby Palestinian restaurants with great views of Jerusalem, you can walk across the street to the very small Church of the Ascension. You can't miss it. At least, on the day we were there, a young Palestinian man was hawking in the street and pointing to the entrance and letting us know that for a mere 20 Shekels (About $6) we could step behind the wall and onto the very spot where Jesus ascended to Heaven. I stood there, and I have pictures to prove it. And the very worn stone indicated that before I did it, millions of others had done the same thing.

After lunch and standing where Jesus departed to Heaven, you can walk across the Kidron Valley back to Jerusalem. It's a short walk, and you'll find it is much easier going down the steep hill than ascending. If you are lucky to be there on a day the Jews and Muslims are not fighting about something, you may get a two-for-one special. Go to the Wailing Wall and hope the entrance to Temple Mount is open. There you can see, but not stand on, the very spot where Muhammad ascended to Heaven from the Dome of the Rock. Jesus had a shorter route; his spot was 2451 feet above sea level, while the Dome of the Rock is only at 2400 feet.

I should not make humorous comments about all this. Mount Moriah is the name for the sequence of peaks that includes the Mount of Olives, Mount Zion, and the Temple Mount, where the

Dome of the Rock stands. These are Holy places, binding through time, the religions of human history: Judaism, Christianity, and Islam. It is the site where Abraham, the patriarch of all these religions, offered to sacrifice his son, Isaac (Gen. 22:1-19). It is the site of Solomon's and Herod's Temple. It is from here that the patron prophet of Islam—Ishmael, Abraham's firstborn by Hagar—was banished (Gen. 21:11-20). It is here where Jesus was sacrificed and ascended into Heaven. And it is here where Jesus is to return, *His feet shall stand in that day upon the mount of Olives* (Zec. 14:4). And it is Jerusalem where the bitterness between Judaism, Christianity, and Islam has spilled blood for 1400 years and where now more blood is spilled in the name of the God they share: Abraham's God.

The movie version of Jesus' life, which Matthew and Luke created—and which has been played over and over and over in people's minds for centuries—might be ignored, provided the critical issues of Christian theology reign true. Jesus is the center of faith for hundreds of millions of people, and Christianity is a foundation of Western civilization. But Matthew and Luke, as well as Mark and Paul, raise far more difficult and perplexing problems than who Jesus' grandparents were and where he was born. The biggest question of all: who was Jesus?

## Chapter Eight – Jesus as God: The Beginnings of the Great Debate

Jesus is God --- Father Son and Holy Ghost! That statement defines Christianity. It is the essence of everything Christian. Without Jesus as God, there simply is no such thing as Christianity, at least as we know it today. But it was not always that way. In the formative years of Christianity. Jesus divinity was the most important unanswered question for the new emerging religion of Jesus. Even with Jesus as God there were many more questions that nascent Christianity needed to answer.

I am not going to debate the issue of Jesus' divinity or question what kind of God Jesus may be. I want to simply show the beginnings of the Christian dispute over Jesus' divinity that will broadly be known as the Arian schism. It is a debate that will plague Christianity for centuries, until the Triune God is begotten. It will continue to plague Christianity as it struggled with Islam. It will linger in the background only to re-emerge in the Roman Catholic church in the 21$^{st}$ century.

We look back and presume Christianity always saw Jesus as a part of the Triune God. But that presumption overlooks the divide, debate, and often bloody struggles of early Christianity. During the 2$^{nd}$, 3$^{rd}$ and 4$^{th}$ centuries Christianity faced several challenges within Christianity and with Roman society that will be explored over the next several chapters. First, Christianity needed to define the divinity of Jesus and what that divinity meant. This chapter will explore the opening of those questions. Without agreed doctrines early Christianity, like today, devolved into dozens of 'denominations'. The following chapter, 'The Many Religions of Jesus', will look into that topic. Christianity's growth and division led to 'Conflicts with Rome' which is the subject of the following chapter. Then 'The Religions of Rome' will look at the pagan religions of Rome which Christianity was replacing, before moving on with Christianity's legalization and doctrinal development. It is a lot of territory to cover in 20 pages and after several rewrites this presentation seemed the most straight forward way to briefly explain a complex set of issues.

Three hundred years after Jesus crucifixion in the 4th century, Christianity enshrined Jesus as a preexistent God and only towards the end of that century will the Father, Son, and the Holy Ghost come together under Christianity's ultimate banner, the theology of the Trinity. Christianity has held fast to that vision of the Deity of Jesus ever since. It took that long because the questions were profound, and the pagan political environment was powerful.

Over those long centuries, the followers of Jesus evolved his role as God in an unfolding chronological pattern, from Paul's letters to the Gospels of Mark, Matthew, Luke, and then John.

> Originally Jesus was thought to have been exalted only at the resurrection; as Christians thought more about the matter, they came to think that he must have been the Son of God during the entire ministry, so that he became God at its outset, at baptism; as they thought even more about it, they came to think he must have been the Son of God for his entire life, and so he was born of a virgin and in that sense was the literal Son of God; as they thought

about it more again, they came to think he must have been the Son of God even before he came into the world, and so they said he was a preexisting divine being.[438]

And so it came to pass that Joseph was demoted from being Jesus' father to being Jesus' foster father.

According to Paul's statement in Romans, Jesus *was declared to be the Son of God in power according to the Spirit of Holiness by his resurrection from the dead* (Rom. 1:4). According to Paul, Jesus was only exalted to the level of God; that is, he was made a God at the time of his resurrection. And Peter, the "founder of the Christian Church" agrees, *God exalted him at his right hand as Leader and Savior, to give repentance to Israel and forgiveness of sins* (Acts 5:31).

If Jesus was exalted to being God, he "was not the Son of God who was sent from heaven to earth, he was a human who was exalted at the end of his earthly life to become the Son of God and was made then and there into a divine being."[439] And if Jesus could be exalted to the level of divinity, then certainly the Roman emperor could be exalted to the Divine, and if he could be divine why not many others, including that guy in the park who told you so?

The idea of exalting humans to the position of God harked back to the idea expressed in Psalms, whereby God *has taken his place in the divine council; in the midst of the gods he holds judgment* (Ps. 82:1). It also made clear again God's First Commandment, *Thou shalt have no other Gods before me* (Exod. 20:3; Deut. 5:7). Jesus was then not the only resurrection in Christianity; polytheism was resurrected with him as well. Polytheism was absolutely unacceptable for all Christians.

---

[438] *How Jesus Became God: The Exaltation of a Jewish Preacher from Galilee*, Bart D. Ehrman, (Harper One, 2014) p. 237

[439] *How Jesus Became God: The Exaltation of a Jewish Preacher from Galilee*, Bart D. Ehrman, (Harper One, 2014) p. 218

Was there anything that Jesus said that might shed light on the issue? And of course, the answer is not straightforward. Ask a beauty contestant before the event, the pageant, "Are you Miss America?" and she cannot say yes because the event that might make her Miss America has not yet taken place. In the Gospels of Mark, Matthew, and Luke (called the synoptic Gospels[440]) Jesus makes no claims to being God, to being sent from God, or being equal with God,[441] because the event, his crucifixion and resurrection, had not yet taken place. The synoptic gospels thereby lend support to the position of Paul and Peter: that Jesus only became God at the Resurrection.

Written about a century after Jesus was born, the Book of John[442] says something very different about the deity of Jesus. While Peter, Paul, Mark, Matthew, and Luke say that Jesus was exalted to being God, the Gospel of John clearly says that Jesus is, was, and always has been God. *In the Beginning was the Word, and the Word was with God and the Word was God. He came in the beginning with God* (John 1:1-2).[443] And John buttresses this position with statements from Jesus:

*I proceeded forth and came from God.* (8:42)

*I say unto you, Before Abraham was, I am.* (8:58)

---

[440] Mark, Matthew, and Luke are known as the synoptic Gospels because they are very similar, have mostly the same stories in the same order, and even sometimes use identical wording.

[441] *How Jesus Became God: The Exaltation of a Jewish Preacher from Galilee*, Bart D. Ehrman, (Harper One, 2014) p. 125.

[442] Jesus was born between 7 and 4 BC and the Book of John is generally ascribed to sometime in the 90s or early 100s. *A New History of Early Christianity*, Charles Freeman (Yale University Press 2009) p. 88

[443] In Greek, the "Word" is "Logos," which had its own meaning among the Greek philosophers in John's day. Christians take this to mean "In the beginning was Jesus" but that opens the door to many other questions beyond the scope of the current discussion.

*O Father glorify thou me with thine own self with the glory which I had with thee before the world was.* (17:5)

John also has Jesus saying that God was his Father, making himself equal with God.

*I and my Father are one.* (10:30)

*That all men should honour the Son, even as they honour the Father. He that honoureth not the Son honoureth not the Father which hath sent him.* (5:23)

John also makes clear that Jesus as a God was subordinate, that he was a lesser God than the Father. *I have come down from heaven, not to do my own will, but the will of him who sent me* (John 6:38).

John was the first biblical author to make statements like this, but he made them ten to thirty years after Mark, Matthew and Luke were written. If Jesus' divinity was so clear to John, why didn't Mark or Matthew or Luke say anything about Jesus being God or one with God and that he had existed for all of time? "Did they (all of them!) just decide not to mention the one thing that was most significant about Jesus?"[444] Only for John was Jesus the God of all time. Christians were rightfully confused by the very different messages in the Gospels about the divinity of Jesus.

And that confusion only increased with the addition of a third God. Ah…the mysterious Spirit of Truth, the Holy Ghost—or the Holy Spirit or, as John sometimes calls him—the Spirit Paraclete. Where does he fit in? John never says directly that he had a dream or revelation from the Holy Spirit, but he clearly implies that this Holy Spirit is the source of his inspiration. "Indeed the evangelist

---

[444] *How Jesus Became God: The Exaltation of a Jewish Preacher from Galilee*, Bart D. Ehrman, (Harper One, 2014) p. 125

(John) acknowledges this and defends such development as guided by the Spirit-Paraclete."[445] He then adds, *But when the Spirit of Truth comes, He will guide you into all truth* (John 16:13). In other words, you too can be guided by this third being sent from the Divinity: *the Spirit, who reveals the truth about God and who comes from the Father. I will send him to you from the Father* (John 15:26, GNT).

The Holy Spirit can be thought of in two different ways: as a state of being or as a personification. My sister is an avid fan of Purdue University, and one might say that Cheryl has the Purdue spirit. Spirit, meaning both an attitude and a behavior: going to games, wearing their symbols, singing the school song, contributing to the university, etc. Purdue also has "Boilermaker Pete" or "Purdue Pete," which is the personification of the Purdue spirit as expressed by my sister and other Purdue fans.

In that same sense, one could have a holy spirit by adopting a behavior and attitude that is Holy: following religious rituals, wearing symbolic clothing, attending religious services, singing hymns, and contributing funds to the church, etc. But just as Boilermaker Pete is the personification of the Purdue Spirit, there is also a Holy Ghost, the personification of the state of being Holy. That is a being called the Holy Spirit, the Holy Ghost, the Paraclete, and the Spirit of Truth. Unlike Boilermaker Pete, whom you can see and hear at ball games, or reach out and touch at pep rallies, The Holy Ghost is a member of the spirit world that can only communicate with you, or the writer of the Gospel of John, through dreams, visions, apparitions, or hallucinations. Indeed, if the writer of the Gospel of John and the Book of Revelations are the same person, then the writer says, *And I turned to see the voice that spoke with me. And being turned, I*

---

[445] *An Introduction to the New Testament,* Raymond E. Brown, First edition (Yale University Press, 2010) p. 370

*saw seven golden candlesticks* (Rev. 1:12). How else could you get messages from a Ghost, even a Holy one?

The Bible uses both the connotation of Holy Spirit as an attitude, and as a personified manifestation of God. The term is found in the Old Testament only three times,[446] each in the "attitude" sense. Paul uses the term 12 times,[447] and only once as a personification. Mark mentions the Holy Spirit five times, never clearly as a personification.[448] Matthew mentions the Holy Spirit six times,[449] three of them in the personification form.

Luke writes "Holy Spirit" 13 times,[450] with four personifications, including, *the Holy Spirit descended on him (Jesus) in bodily form* (Luke 3:22). John refers to him six times,[451] twice clearly as a personification, the previously cited John 16:13, and *the Holy Spirit, whom the Father will send in my name, he will teach you all things* (John 14:26). In the attendant footnotes, I have listed each verse and bolded those that refer to a personified Holy Spirit. Some of the references could be interpreted in both senses, and I leave it to some doctoral candidate to delve deeply into the Greek and refine my "first glance" analysis.

In all of the genuine books of Paul and the Gospels, there are 41 references to the Holy Spirit, eight of them to a personified "Holy Ghost." The book of Acts then doubles the number, adding 42 references,[452] with eight clear personifications. The Book of Acts should be renamed "The Book of the Holy Spirit." If the Holy Spirit is going to be a God, he should get at least one book

---

[446] Psalm 51:11, Isaiah 63:10, Isaiah 11:2. Some cite other references such as Genesis 1:2 which says "the Spirit of God moved on the face of the waters" which is generally not considered a separate manifestation or personification.

[447] Romans 5:5, 9:1, 14:17, 15:13, 15:16; 1 Cor. 6:19, 12:3; 2 Cor. 6:6, 13:14; 1 Thessalonians 1:5

[448] Mark 1:8, 3:22, 3:29, 12:36, 13:11

[449] Matthew 1:18, 1:20, 3:11, 12:22, 12:32, 28:19

[450] Luke 1:15, 1:35, 1:41, 1:67, 2:25, 2:26, 3:16, 3:22, 4:1, 10:21, 11:13, 12:10, 12:12.

[451] John 1:33, 14:15, 14:26, 16:4, 16:13, 20:22

[452] Acts 1:1, 1:2, 1:5, 1:8, 1:16, 2:1, 2:4, 2:33, 2:38, 4:8, 4:25, 4:31, 5:3, 5:32, 6:5, 7:51, 7:55, 8:15, 8:17, 8:19, 9:17, 9:31, 10:38, 10:44, 10:45, 10:47, 11:15, 11:16, 11:24, 13:2, 13:4, 13:9, 13:52, 15:8, 15:28, 16:6,19:2, 19:6, 20:23, 20:38, 21:11, 28:25

of his own. Book or no book, call him what you will, the Holy Ghost, the Holy Spirit, or the Spirit Paraclete—Christianity accepted this being as a God. The emerging branch of monotheistic Judaism was looking like polytheism with three Gods.

And if that wasn't a problem enough, the obvious fact was that Jesus had not returned "in power and glory." Jesus had been crucified by the Romans, who in turn had destroyed Israel and their Second Temple. How could Jesus still be a messiah, much less *the* Messiah? If this sounds questionable to you now, think how it might have sounded to Jews and Gentiles as potential converts in the first centuries after the war.

The story of the three Gods, of Jesus, of the rumors of his resurrection, of the certainty of his return to bring justice to the world—all these things were not the only stories of Jesus being told. There were many other teachers and preachers, books and stories written in the 1$^{st}$ and 2$^{nd}$ centuries that added to the legend and lore of Jesus, each with its own angle on Jesus and his life. There were many different beliefs about Jesus.

Matthew has Jesus say, *See to it that no one deceives you, because many will come in my name, proclaiming, 'I'm the Messiah,' and they will deceive many people* (Matt. 24:4-5). Jesus was but one of many preaching to the crowds, claiming messiahship. Paul cautions his converts, saying not to be *little children, tossed like waves and blown about by every wind of doctrine, by people's trickery, or by clever strategies that would lead us astray* (Eph. 4:14-15). And those many messiahs and their followers had different ideas from Paul: "If Jesus did not solve the most fundamental question of the Christian Mission, we may well doubt that his recorded words solve most subsequent debated problems in the church."[453] Amen! Neither God nor

---

[453] *An Introduction to the New Testament and the Origins of Christianity,* Delbert Burkett (Cambridge University Press, 2002) p. 331

Jesus made their theology of religion clear, compelling others to divine the intent from dreams or visions. And if there was no water?

And there was no church structure to guide people, and no church structure to contain them. Different messiahs and doctrines persuaded followers of Jesus, Jews, God Fearers, or Gentiles to go this way or that. Why else would the Gospels and Paul so often be warning of the new guy and new message in town? Think of how, in the modern world, the Christian Church has rapidly restructured its beliefs on divorce, abortion, homosexual relations, etc. The same thing happened to Christianity in the first centuries, as messiahs, prophets, and preachers were apparently a dime a dozen, each proclaiming the other as a false prophet. Whole species of Jesus communities evolved in line with the latest preacher in town, just as Darwin's finches evolved with the food they ate. Each species of Christianity gravitated to the writings that mirrored their beliefs and helped them survive. Darwin's theory of evolution aptly describes Christianity's "spiritual survival of the fittest."[454]

The two most obvious species of Christianity were derived from the dispute between Paul and the apostles in the First Jewish Jesus Church of Jerusalem. Paul proclaimed that belief in Jesus was sufficient to enter the Kingdom of God, while the apostles, following Jesus own words, thought that maintaining Jewish laws was essential. The Book of Acts attempts to bridge that difference and present a story justifying Jewish and Gentile Christianity.

Acts was written by the same writer as the Gospel of Luke, but 15 to 20 years later, probably in the 80's or early 0's AD.[455] Paul's God fearers and Gentiles had enjoyed the benefits of a

---

[454] *A History of Christianity*, Paul Johnson (Simon & Schuster a Touchstone Book, 1995) p. 43

[455] *An Introduction to the New Testament: History, Literature, Theology*. M. Eugene Boring, (John Knox Press. 2012) p.587

Jewish pedigree, but after the Jewish–Roman War, there were no more benefits of the affiliation. The Jews had been ostracized from Roman society.

Fifty years earlier, Paul had met with James and Peter in Jerusalem, and soon thereafter with Peter in Antioch. As we saw earlier, Paul painted a bitter picture of the situation of Jews and Christians sharing the same table, *But when Peter was come to Antioch, I withstood him to the face, because he was to be blamed* (Gal. 2:11). Fifty years later, that bitterness in Galatians is replaced with a picture of celebration in Acts 15. There, Paul returns to Antioch and gathered *the multitude together, they delivered the epistle: Which when they had read, they rejoiced for the consolation* (Acts 15:31). Division gone. Acts brushes aside the dispute between Paul and the apostles as insignificant, but it is a major example showing how Acts plays down the conflicts between early Christian communities of Jewish and Gentile affiliation. But Luke cannot make them disappear. Acts notes that Paul had an undescribed falling out in Antioch, *And the contention was so sharp between them, that they departed asunder one from the other.* Paul then departed *and went not with them to the work* (Acts 15:38-39). Thanks to the creative writing in Acts, for all the centuries to follow, this egregious point of contention between the apostles and Paul will be swept aside in the ecstasy of Pentecost. I am sure Paul felt that joyful spirit of unity and said thank you when he was arrested and sent to execution.

Acts may have been written to reconcile Paul and the apostles, but the Book of James accentuates differences. James was attributed to Jesus' brother, the leader of the Jewish Jesus Church of Jerusalem, but the book was not written by him. James was an Aramaic-speaking, rural Galilean Jew, who knew the Torah in Hebrew and was killed in 62 CE. The Book of James is written in polished eloquent Greek with quotes from the Greek

Septuagint, and it describes a church structure not in place until after the real James was dead.[456] It was clearly written to counter Paul's theology of salvation by faith: *a man is not justified by the works of the law, but by the faith of Jesus Christ* (Gal. 2:16) and *Therefore we conclude that a man is justified by faith without the deeds of the law* (Rom. 3:28). The author of James rejoins, *Ye see then how that by works a man is justified, and not by faith only* (Jas. 2:24).

James and Paul point to an underling question in Christianity: Is salvation solely through the grace, beneficence, magnanimous generosity of a God towards those who have faith in Jesus, or can man contribute to his own salvation? It is the difference between how one leads a life and what one believes. As we will see later, this is the difference between Islam and Paul's Christianity. It is also what becomes the difference between Catholicism and Protestantism in the Reformation. Luther wanted the Book of James taken out of the Bible because it was anti-Paul.[457] And, the Book of James might fit quite nicely into the Qur'an.

If the last few pages seem discombobulated and confusing, it is because that was early Christianity: groups of people struggling and divided over different versions of the life and meaning of Jesus. With no clear instructions from God, the leaders and pundits of the day tried explaining their beliefs in preaching and writing—beliefs perhaps derived from their dreams and visions of a ghost, holy or not. In the first centuries after Jesus, his followers were not a choir singing the celestial harmony portrayed in Acts but more like a chorus of recalcitrant cats. Christianity needed a maestro.

---

[456] *An Introduction to the New Testament,* Raymond E. Brown, First edition (Yale University Press, 2010) p.742

[457] *An Introduction to the New Testament,* Raymond E. Brown, First edition (Yale University Press, 2010) p. 744

# Chapter Nine – The Many Religions of Jesus

Jesus had preached a form of Jewish Apocalypticism: that a messiah would come shortly to avenge evil and bring perfect justice and provide eternal life. In this life, Jesus had added an emphasis on social justice. This is the same Jewish message that had been preached, prophesied, and written about for 200 years.[458] When he was nailed to the cross, there was no "Jesus" religion, no Christianity.

Jesus' apostles, disciples, and many of the people who heard him speak thought that Jesus was the promised Messiah. After the crucifixion, the apostles and disciples carried Jesus' message to many places. What the apostles did in those first years are reported by Paul, the Book of Acts, and Josephus. Writing a couple of centuries later, Eusebius tells us that, other than James and John, the rest of the "apostles were driven out of Judea by numerous deadly plots."[459] Eusebius goes on to say that some

---

[458] *A New History of Early Christianity*, Charles Freeman (Yale, 2009) pp. 14-16.

[459] *Eusebius: The Church History*, Translation by Paul L. Maier (Kregel, 2007) p. 82

Jewish Christians escaped the war by fleeing to Pella.[460] Many others fled to Alexandria in Egypt.[461] They were Jewish Christians who, like Jesus' brother James, "continued to think it necessary for the followers of Jesus to keep the Jewish law and Jewish customs."[462]

In those very early years, the beliefs that Jesus was the Jewish Messiah were circulated by roving "preachers." Each told their personal tales of Jesus, which brought different versions of the Jesus movement into being. Paul often spoke of "others" who were preaching a "different gospel" and the New Testament speaks extensively about false prophets.[463] In this process, many groups evolved, each with different beliefs about Jesus, somewhat like today's Christian denominations. Many of those denominations became dust on the pathways of Palestine, while others garnered a great deal of attention.

The Ebionites were one of the best known early Christian groups.[464] They tried to follow Jesus' dictum, *For truly, I say to you, until heaven and earth pass away, not an iota, not a dot, will pass from the Law until all is accomplished* (Matt. 5:18, ESV). "They were the likely successors to the original Jesus Movement led by James and the other disciples of Jesus."[465] The Ebionites

---

[460] Pella is located a few miles East of the Jordan River about 20 miles south of the Sea of Galilee. At the Time of the Roman War, it was in Roman territory, called the Decapolis.

[461] *A History of Christianity*, Paul Johnson (Simon & Schuster a Touchstone Book 1995) p. 42

[462] *How Jesus Became God: The Exaltation of a Jewish Preacher from Galilee*, Bart D. Ehrman, (Harper One, 2014) p. 290

[463] 2 Cor 11:3-15, Matt 24:4-5, Gal 2:11-15, Matt 7:15-20, Acts 20:28-30, 2 Tim 4:3-7,
Gal 5:20, Acts 18, Acts 19, 1 Cor 3, 2 Peter 2:12, Titus 1: 6-16, 2 Peter 1:12-21, 2 Peter 3:14-18, John 4:1-6, Matt 10;34-36, Matt 23:1-36, Matt 16:11-12, Rom12:1, Rom 15:30, Rom 16:17-20, Luke 6:26

[464] *Misquoting Jesus: The Story Behind Who Changed the Bible and Why,* Bart D. Erdman (Harper One, 2005) p. 155

[465] *How Jesus Became Christian*, Barrie Wilson Ph.D. (St. Martin's Press, 2008) p. 99

could be found everywhere there was a colony of Jews.[466] They used an Aramaic version of Matthew that is different from the Matthew in today's Bible and another book known as the "Hebrew Gospel."[467] All copies of these books were destroyed and are only known through the quotations made by the Pauline Christian writers who condemned and criticized the Ebionites.

The Ebionites believed that Jesus was not God but the Jewish Messiah, who was exalted to be the Son of God because he perfectly upheld the law.[468] As such, there was no miraculous virgin birth. "The Ebionites maintained that the Son of God was a mere man begotten by human pleasure from the joinder of Joseph and Mary."[469]

The Ebonite's gospels are known as the "Letter to Peter from James," and the "Reception." The Ebonite's rejected Paul's doctrines and declared him as a false prophet.[470] Over time, the Ebionites were squeezed between two forces: they were condemned as heretics by all the "church fathers," because they held firm to Jewish law, but they were also condemned by the emerging Rabbinic Jews because the Ebonite's continued to believe in Jesus as the Messiah. Caught between the Jews and Pauline Christians, the religion whose pedigree most closely

---

[466] *Early History of the Christian Church: From its Foundation to the End of the Fifth Century (Vol. 1),* Louis Duchesne (Lex de Leon Publishing, 1909) Kindle Edition loc. 1342

[467] *How Jesus Became Christian*, Barrie Wilson Ph.D. (St. Martin's Press, 2008) p. 101

[468] *Lost Christianities: The Battle for Scripture and Faiths We Never Knew,* Bart D. Ehrman (Oxford University Press, 2003) p. 101

[469] Apostolic Constitution compiled 390 AD as quoted in *A Dictionary of Early Christian Beliefs,* Edited by David W. Bercot (Hendrickson Publishing, 1998) p. 225

[470] *How Jesus Became Christian*, Barrie Wilson Ph.D. (St. Martin's Press, 2008) p. 101

resembled that of Jesus and his apostles faded away from Christian history.[471]

Jesus would no longer be about the Jewish Messiah, but "Paul's interpretation of Christian faith with its focus on the 'proclamation' (kerygma) of the death and resurrection of Jesus."[472] Paul's dreams and hallucinations, rejected by the apostles, would now be the only driver of Christian growth. The Ebonite's message was not totally lost. Similar beliefs continued to exist in southern Arabia, where it was claimed that the "Hebrew Gospel" had been brought to them by the Apostle Bartholomew.[473] Muhammad will perhaps eventually learn about Judaism and Christianity from some of their descendants.

We knew very little of those early Jesus movements because in 303 CE, the emperor Diocletian ordered the seizing and burning of all Christian books.[474] Even the possession of Christian books became a criminal offense. Copies of such books were burned and destroyed.[475] In 367 CE, Athanasius, the bishop of Alexandria, instituted the "the strictest condemnation to date of non-canonical Christian gospels and scriptures, leading many to be concealed or destroyed."[476] The destruction of Christian writings across the centuries has left little evidence of these early versions of Christianity. Until the mid-20th century, the only way

---

[471] *Myth Maker: Paul and The Invention of Christianity,* Hyam Maccoby (Barnes and Noble, 1987) pp. 179-181

[472] *The Lost Gospel: The Book of Q and Christian Origins,* Burton L. Mack, (Harper Collins, 1993) p. 23

[473] *Early History of the Christian Church: From its Foundation to the End of the Fifth Century (Vol. 1),* Louis Duchesne (Lex de Leon Publishing, 1909) Kindle Edition loc. 1353

[474] *A New History of Early Christianity*, Charles Freeman (Yale University Press 2009) p. 212

[475] *The Gnostic Gospels,* Elaine Pagels (Vintage Press, 1979) p. xvii

[476] *Jesus Wars: How Four Patriarchs, Three Queens, and Two Emperors Decided What Christians Would Believe for the Next 1,500 Years,* John Philip Jenkins (Harper One, 2010) p. 92

we even knew about many of the early Jesus religions was from the writings against them.

In the early 300s, St. Pachomius founded several monasteries in the center of Egypt. In 1945, Muhammad Ali (no, not the boxer) found 52 very old books in an earthenware jar in a cave just three miles from one of those monasteries. It is a great story, with murder and intrigue. Scraps of paper in the book bindings were receipts dated from 341, 346, and 348 AD.[477] We can only speculate that these books were buried to avoid being burned through Athanasius' order. Many of the 52 books were the very books referenced by the Christian Fathers, like Irenaeus, Clement of Alexandria, Tertullian, Hippolytus, and Origen under the banner of Gnosticism.[478]

Gnosticism was a prevalent form of early Christianity. The word means "knowledge" in Greek, but specifically sacred knowledge by which someone can experience their spiritual origins.[479] That might sound vague, but Gnosticism was never a simple, straightforward belief system. It was mysterious.

Jesus says much the same thing:

*I thank thee, O Father, Lord of heaven and earth, that thou hast hid these things from the wise and prudent, and hast revealed them unto babes: even so, Father; for so it seemed good in thy sight. All things are delivered to me of my Father: and no man knoweth who the Son is, but the Father; and who the Father is, but the Son, and he to whom the Son will reveal him. (Luke 10:21-22)*

---

[477] *Lost Christianities: The Battle for Scripture and Faiths We Never Knew,* Bart D. Ehrman (Oxford University Press, 2003) p. 54

[478] The list is from a variety of quotations found in *A Dictionary of Christian Beliefs,* edited by David W. Bercott (Henrickson, 1998) pp. 306-308

[479] *A History of Christian Theology: An Introduction,* William C. Placher (Westminster Press, 1983) p. 46

And Paul said, *But we speak the wisdom of God in a mystery, even the hidden wisdom, which God ordained before the world unto our glory* (1 Cor. 2:7).

In discovering these books in Egypt, scholars gained an exciting firsthand look into early Christianity. "We may have to recognize that early Christianity is far more diverse than anyone expected before the Nag Hammadi discoveries."[480] In fact, Gnosticism itself is far more diverse than anyone expected.

The point is not to discuss the various concepts of Gnosticism but only to show that a major branch of Christianity in those earliest years was far different than what we think of as Christianity today. Between their discovery and 1990, over 4000 books and articles were written on the newly discovered Gnostics texts.[481] As James M. Robinson, a professor, scholar and writer on early Christianity said, "The relation of Gnosticism to early Christianity is all too complex."[482] The following is my very general understanding of Gnostic Christianity.

Gnosticism starts with the premise that God is perfect and could not have created an imperfect world, full of pain, suffering, and hate. Somehow, a male great power came from nothing to manage all things and a female of great intelligence came to produce all things, including demi-gods, angels, demons, and others that inhabit the spiritual realm. The God of perfect harmony was above the spiritual realm and far removed from the material world of the human condition of evil and suffering. Jesus was sent from the spiritual realm to give humans knowledge of this mystery so they might join the peace and harmony of the spiritual realm.

---

[480] *The Gnostic Gospels,* Elaine Pagels (Vintage Press, 1979) p. xxii

[481] *The Gnostic Gospels,* Elaine Pagels (Vintage Press, 1979) p. xxxiv- xxxv

[482] *Nag Hammadi, Gnosticism, & Early Christianity: Fourteen Leading Scholars Discuss the Current Issues in Gnostic Studies,* Harold W. Attridge, Edited by Charles W. Hedrick and Robert Hodgson, Jr. (Hendrickson Publishing, 1986) p. 127

Jesus, as a part of that "Kingdom of Heaven," could have no contact with the material world, hence his body was but an illusion that could not really feel the pain and suffering of the cross. Only the illusion of his body died on the cross. His resurrection was merely the brief appearance of his spiritual entity. And what is the secret handshake that gets you this knowledge? It's still a mystery. If that doesn't blur your thought process, nothing will. Keep in mind that these conclusions have more support in the Bible than the idea of a Triune God that will be discussed later.

Jesus said, *Unto you it is given to know the mystery of the kingdom of God: but unto them that are without, all these things are done in parables* (Mark 4:11). Or, *To you it has been granted to know the mysteries of the kingdom of heaven, but to them it has not been granted* (Matt. 13:11). Or Jesus' *transfiguration into a divine being* (Matt. 17:1-13). Or perhaps Paul, *Even the mystery which hath been hid from ages and from generations, but now is made manifest to his saints* (Col. 1:26). If you like mysteries, your local bookstore will have many books on Gnostic beliefs and the Nag Hammadi writings. Everything from, *The Complete Idiot's Guide to the Gnostic Gospels* by J. Michael Matkin to *Gnosticism and the New Testament* by Pheme Perkins or *Nag Hammadi Gnosticism and Early Christianity*, edited by Charles W. Hedrick and Robert Hodgson, Jr., or two by Elaine Pagels: *The Gnostic Gospels* and *Beyond Belief*, the later focusing on the Gospel of Thomas.

The Ebionites and the Gnostics are examples of just two facets of the central questions early Christians were trying to answer: Was Jesus God? What was the relationship between Jesus, God, and humanity?

The disciples were not sure themselves and asked: *"Are you the Son of God, then?" And he said to them, "You say that I am"* (Luke 22:70). Okay, when did he become God? When he was born? When he was baptized? When he was crucified? When he ascended into Heaven? Or did he exist as God before he was born? If he was God, then there was and is more than one God; and if there is more than one, could there be many more? Was Jesus human? Was he just a teacher or prophet? If he was God and man, how did that work? Was he sometimes God and sometimes man? Was he two things or natures in one being? Was he a man that God adopted as his son? If he was God, how could a God feel the pain and suffering of crucifixion? The questions went on and on.

Several major groupings of Christian belief emerged and aligned along the lines of Jesus' divinity. That Jesus was God and had only one nature was the belief of the Apollinarians, Docetists, Gnostics, Manicheans, Miaphysites, Monophysites, Valentinians, and Basilides. That Jesus was human was the belief of the Ebionites and Montanists. That Jesus was God and man and had two natures was the theology of the Adoptionists, Cerinthians, Chalcedonians, Eutyches, Marcions, Nestorians, Sabellians, and various other Logos/Man ideologies.[483]

These divisions were only on the question of whether Jesus was God. Neither God nor Jesus had left a clear message for people to follow. And there still was no "Bible." No one could agree, because no one knew. It was all speculation.

Each of the questions, and countless others, created a horde of beliefs spread by roaming preachers of the Christian theology du jour. Who in your area was the preacher of the month? "The central and eastern Mediterranean in the 1st and 2nd centuries swarmed with an infinite multitude of religious ideas, struggling to propagate themselves."[484] There was no assumed theology, no

---

[483] *Jesus Wars: How Four Patriarchs, Three Queens, and Two Emperors Decided What Christians Would Believe for the Next 1,500 Years*, John Philip Jenkins (Harper One, 2010). Adapted from the longer list on pp. 69-73

[484] *A History of Christianity*, Paul Johnson (Simon & Schuster a Touchstone Book, 1995) p. 43

accepted orthodoxy, no "correct" belief. There were only local communities and individuals who were fiercely certain of their own beliefs. They selected and latched onto rumors and stories and writings and amplified them into more rumors and stories and writings needed to support their beliefs. "Christians" in different areas "varied in the stress they placed on Jesus' humanity or his divinity, and without exercising too much ingenuity" could find what they needed in stories, tradition, and writings to support their opinions.[485]

Some used their ingenuity to justify wife swapping. The logic was simple, *Those who believed were of one heart and soul, and no one said that any of the things that belonged to him was his own, but they had everything in common* (Acts 4:32). This was not an obscure minority. Clement, Irenaeus, and Hippolytus each expended considerable ink and paper writing against the Carpocratians as the wife-swapping Christians were called.[486] I'll bet they didn't teach you about Christian wife swapping in Sunday school. Dr. Oldsen certainly didn't teach that in my religion class back in high school.

Today, we might say that the tent of Christianity was quite large in those first centuries. There was also no structure of either worship or organization through which these theological questions could be resolved. The first steps toward a structure was taken by Clement in the 2nd century. He paraphrased Isaiah, "I will establish their bishops in righteousness and their deacons in faith."[487] He appointed a bishop vetoing the local preferences at Corinth.[488] This is the first time the bishop of Rome presumed

---

[485] *Jesus Wars: How Four Patriarchs, Three Queens, and Two Emperors Decided What Christians Would Believe for the Next 1,500 Years,* John Philip Jenkins (Harper One, 2010) p. ix

[486] *Lost Christianities: The Battle for Scripture and Faiths We Never Knew,* Bart D. Ehrman (Oxford University Press, 2003) pp. 73-74

[487] 1st Clement 44:1

[488] *Christianity: The First Three Thousand Years,* Diarmaid MacClulloch (Viking, 2010) p. 132

his authority, and it would certainly not be the last. Moral authority for this structure came from Ignatius around the year 100 AD, when he wrote to eight of his colleagues as he was awaiting death by martyrdom, "You must all follow the bishops as Jesus Christ [followed] the Father. Let no one do anything apart from the bishop that has to do with the church." But what if each bishop has a different belief?

This has been only a brief cross section of how roaming preachers, preaching roaming gospels to local communities who had with little communication and organization led to each Christian community having its own set of traditions, oral stories, and literature to support their beliefs and the jobs of their clergy. Early Christianity became a collection of disparate groups of Jesus followers who were struggling to find practices and doctrines on which they could agree.

And the disagreements between them were not quiet debates while sipping wine or weaving cloth; "What to us might seem like philosophical niceties drove ordinary people to the point of wishing to kill, torture, or expel their neighbors."[489] That is how Christianity became that chorus of recalcitrant cats.

Those struggles led to major disputes among Jesus' followers and clashes with the Roman Empire.

---

[489] *Jesus Wars: How Four Patriarchs, Three Queens, and Two Emperors Decided What Christians Would Believe for the Next 1,500 Years,* John Philip Jenkins (Harper One, 2010) p. 25

# Chapter Ten – Conflicts with Rome

The Roman Empire was very tolerant of any religion, so long as that religion was tolerant of all other religions. This had its origin in the belief that religion was local and not transcendent.

> In the days of antiquity, it was regarded as a fundamental principle that man has duties towards the Divinity, and that the citizen of any particular State has special obligations to the gods of his native land.... A Roman owed an especial reverence to the gods of Rome, an Athenian to those of Athens, and so on. On the other hand, not only was he free from obligation to the gods of other lands, but he was forbidden to worship them. Religion was essentially national.[490]

This was an ancient tradition dating back to the earliest days, when, "every city had been inspired and founded by its own particular divinity as his or her earthly home."[491] Religion was a

---

[490] *Early History of the Christian Church: From Its Foundation to the End of the Fifth Century (Vol. 1),* Louis Duchesne (Lex de Leon Publishing, 1909) Kindle Edition loc. 1081

[491] *Babylon: Mesopotamia and the Birth of Civilization,* Paul Kriwaczek (Thomas Dunne Books, 2012) p. 27

patriotic duty; it was a part of the culture. The local gods were accorded mutual respect. From the Roman perspective the God of Judaism was just another local God, in this case of the people of Palestine, and worshipping Him was therefore perfectly legal. Jews were not "disturbing the peace" by practicing Judaism and had no requirement to sacrifice to any other Roman gods. The beliefs of the Jews and the political situation between Rome and Israel was immaterial. Judaism was "religio licita."

"Now so long as Christianity was regarded as a sect of Judaism, it shared...the legal protection bestowed on that ancient national religion."[492] However, after the war, Paul's Christians began to disavow Judaism and began losing the legal protections enjoyed by Jews. Christianity became a "movement" and slipped into the chasm of "religio illicita." As such Christians were required by law to sacrifice within any other "religio licita". Anyone not doing so under Roman Law was disturbing the peace, or guilty of sedition, or treason. The theology of Jesus was immaterial.

To make matters worse, to Christians all those gods of the Roman Empire were false gods and idols. As Christians evangelized their brand of nascent illegal Christianity, they were upsetting Roman culture, disturbing the peace, and violating the laws of the Roman Empire. The Romans could not allow that. Bring on the lions! (Something very similar occurred in the 16th and early 17th centuries when preachers roamed the countryside of central and northern Europe, preaching their brand of Christianity in the aftermath of the Reformation. This greatly disturbed the peace and lead to the devastation of the Thirty Years War. [493] When the West evangelized Christianity to its

---

[492] *History of the Christian Church (The Complete Eight Volumes in One)*. Philip Schaff (2014) Kindle loc. 12660

[493] From a personal example while visiting the Lutheran Church in Buchholz Westphalia Germany I saw a monument to the preachers who brought the reformation to the area in 1529. This church is close to Westphalia where the Thirty Years War would be settled in 1648.

colonies and conquered territories in the 16th and into the 20th century there was no consideration given to the fact that they were disturbing their culture and religious balance  The Roman Empire in its own way was simply seeking to avoid the disruption of its culture of the type that  missionaries of Christianity created in  China, India, Africa, the Middle East, Central and South America.)

Trajan was emperor from 98 AD until 117 AD; Pliny was his governor in a part of what is now Turkey. Pliny wrote to Trajan requesting guidance in how he should deal with accusations of people being Christian.[494] The established policy was that Christians should not be sought out, that any accusation needed to be public, and that merely admitting to being a Christian was sufficient proof of guilt. But if the accused denied they were Christian or offered proof of worshipping any legal gods, they were to be set free; if not… they incurred the death penalty. The separation of Christians of any stripe from Judaism was now a vital issue, which accelerated their separation.[495]

Trajan's "toleration" of Christianity was the norm. But Christians were not the norm. They did not participate in the games, nor sacrifice to the usual gods. From the Roman perspective, Christians met secretly at night, men and women together, behind closed doors; additionally, through the Eucharist, they partook of blood rituals, cannibalism, and other horrors. They were accused of hatred of the human race.[496] They were easy targets for the neurotic persecutions of Nero and Domitian.

Contrary to what many have been taught, Christians were not broadly persecuted in the first centuries. They openly built

---

[494] This is the very first reference of Christians recorded be non-Christians.

[495] Pieces of this story of persecution can be found in numerous books and articles but all of it including its Roman legal basis can be found at *Early History of the Christian Church: From Its Foundation to the End of the Fifth Century (Vol. 1)*, Louis Duchesne (Lex de Leon Publishing, 1909) Kindle Edition, Chapter 8.

[496] *World Religions: From Ancient History to the Present*, Geoffrey Parrinder, editor, (Hamlyn Publishing Ltd 1971) p. 429

churches and worshipped and performed their rituals. Legally, the situation was very much like today's political correctness: I am offended that some speaker with whom I disagree is speaking on campus, or that some building is named after a Confederate general, or that someone used some word, which has, by my standards, improper connotations—sanctions must be imposed! In Roman times, all it took was for someone to say that a Christian was offending them, and the sanctions could bring death. However, until the 3rd century, the potential of persecution of Christians was strictly a local matter, and most emperors restrained their actions to keep it that way.

Still, martyrdom was a scourge on Christianity. As the Christian writer Tertullian (180 to 240 AD) put it, "If the Tiber reaches the walls, if the Nile fails to rise to the fields, if the sky doesn't move, if there is a famine or a plague, the cry is at once: 'The Christians to the Lions!'"[497] Many Christians answered the alarm bell by volunteering to be the first item on the lunch menu. Perhaps, they hoped for the glory of being among the first saints of Christianity, all of whom died an agonizing death of martyrdom.[498]

But the line for martyrdom would have been short. The total number of Christians in the year 200 AD was probably no more than a quarter million and by 250 AD, around one million. In fact, some have calculated far lower numbers, perhaps only 50,000 in the year 200 AD. Spectacular growth, yes, but a very small, nettlesome percentage of the 60 million people in the Roman Empire.[499]

---

[497] *A History of Christianity*, Paul Johnson (Simon & Schuster a Touchstone Book 1995) p. 71

[498] *Christianity: The First Three Thousand Years*, Diarmaid MacClulloch (Viking, 2010) p. 161

[499] The number of Christians at any time is the subject of the book *The Rise of Christianity: How the Obscure, Marginal Jesus Movement Became the Dominant*

Eagerness for martyrdom is inexplicable without the certainty of an afterlife in paradise. With that fervent belief, when persecutions did happen, whole groups of Christians stepped forward to volunteer for execution.[500] Cyprian, the bishop of Carthage around 250 AD, wrote, "What an honor and security it is to go gladly from this place to depart gloriously from amongst oppressions and afflictions—to shut one's eyes for a moment and to open them again and see God and Christ."[501] Perhaps these were the words of quiet assurance Jim Jones was saying as he handed out the Kool-Aid.[502] Or change those last words to 'Allah' and this could easily be describing the thoughts of Mohamed Atta at 8:46 AM on September 11, 2001 as he flew American Flight 11 into the North Tower of the World Trade Center in New York City.[503]

Stories of the bravery of Christians circulated and became legends. With no big screen theaters to satisfy the hunger for violence and gore, "Christian' mythology emerged with an emphasis on the minutiae of violence. Martyrdom became a form of spectacle itself."[504]

Before a cheering crowd, Blandina, a Christian slave girl, was first whipped, then fried on a hot griddle, then hung in a net to be gored by bulls. Somehow still alive, she was tied to a post to be

---

*Religious Force in the Western World in a Few Centuries,* Rodney Stark (Harper Collins, 1997). These estimates are on pp. 5-9

[500] *A New History of Early Christianity,* Charles Freeman (Yale University Press 2009) p. 206

[501] *Cyprian of Carthage, Treatise 11,* Chapter 13" Exhortation to Martyrdom, Addressed to Fortunatus ". An interpretation can be found here. http://www.newadvent.org/fathers/050711.htm

[502] In 1978 Jim Jones handed out cyanide laced Kool-Aid to 900 members of his Peoples Temple of the Disciples of Christ in Jonestown, Guyana. "Jim Jones— From Poverty to Power of Life and Death" Robert Lindsey *New York Times* November 30th, 1978

[503] "9-11 Commission Report" *National Commission on Terrorist Attacks* upon the United States Government Printing Office 2004 p. 7

[504] *A New History of Early Christianity,* Charles Freeman (Yale University Press 2009) p. 208

the afternoon snack for the wild beasts.[505] Laurentius, a Spanish deacon in Rome, earned his Sainthood by being slowly roasted to death:[506] "After the long-continued heat has burned his side away, Lawrence on his own part hails the judge and addresses him briefly from the gridiron: 'This part of my body has been burned long enough; turn it round and try what your hot god of fire has done.'" So, the prefect orders him to be turned about, and then, "It is done," says Lawrence, "eat it up, try whether it is nicer raw or roasted."[507] This is the stuff of gruesome rumors of legend and lore.

Martyrdom was not the favorite Sunday afternoon participation sport for all Christians. Prominent Christian writers like Clement, Origen, and others argued strongly against this form of suicide. Clement of Alexandria wrote an entire book, *Stomateis*, condemning the idea.[508] "Multitudes of nominal Christians especially at the beginning, sacrificed to the gods, or procured from the magistrate false certificate that they had done so."[509] But there was no Bible yet so that a bishop or Deacon could point believers to the words of Jesus, *But when they persecute you in this city, flee ye into another* (Matt. 10:23). Bible or no Bible, whether for Jesus or to save their own hides, "The truth is the overwhelming majority of Christians"[510] did what they had to do to avoid persecution.

---

[505] *A New History of Early Christianity*, Charles Freeman (Yale, 2009) p. 209

[506] *History of the Christian Church (The Complete Eight Volumes in One)* Philip Schaff (2014) Kindle loc. 12992

[507] As quoted from 'Hymns of Martyrdom' by Prudentius at http://thegingerbeardman.blogspot.com/2012/08/sancte-laurentius-ora-pro-nobis.html

[508] *A New History of Early Christianity*, Charles Freeman (Yale University Press 2009) p. 210

[509] *History of the Christian Church (The Complete Eight Volumes in One)* Philip Schaff (2014) Kindle loc. 12969

[510] *Christianity: The First Three Thousand Years*, Diarmaid MacClulloch (Viking, 2010) p. 161

Two emperors continued the persecutions. When Decius came to power in 249 AD, he issued a new edict requiring everyone to make a sacrifice to the Roman gods, excepting the Jews as explained above.[511] This was the first persecution of Christians that was applied across the Roman Empire. The next emperor, Valerian, continued the pressure. People stopped converting to Christianity; huge numbers rushed back to paganism, and others simply laid low. The pressure was ratcheted up when all bishops and priests were ordered to be hauled before the governors.[512] That was so effective that Christianity was on the edge of collapse.[513] But then, Valerian was captured by the Persians, and the persecutions came to an end when the new emperor, Gallienus, published an edict of toleration in 253 AD.[514] Peace then came to the Christians for the next 40 years.

Peace with the Romans, that is. Internal feuding of Christianity was going in the opposite direction. The Christians who had avoided persecution were not all welcomed back with open arms. Forgiveness was not the Christian charity of the day, and the question became, "Just who is empowered to forgive those who were not steadfast?"

Cyprian, the bishop of Carthage, was unforgiving and wanted to keep out those who had renounced Christianity. Stephen, the bishop of Rome, declared that those who escaped persecution by denying Christianity should be forgiven and reconciled with the Church. Cyprian was the "Anti-Christ," declared Stephen, and backed his authority with the words, *"Thou art Peter and upon*

---

[511] *A New History of Early Christianity*, Charles Freeman (Yale University Press 2009) pp. 210-211

[512] *A New History of Early Christianity*, Charles Freeman (Yale University Press 2009) p. 211

[513] *When Jesus Became God: The Struggle to Define Christianity during the Last Days of Rome,* Richard E. Rubenstein (Mariner Books, 2000) p. 18

[514] *Caesar and Christ (The Story of Civilization, vol. III), Will* and Ariel Durant, (MJF Books, 1944) p. 650

*this rock I will build my church"* (Matt. 16:18). This was the first step taken towards a "Papacy" by the bishop of Rome, but there was yet no "Pope" in any sense of a singular overseer of Christianity.[515]

In the 3rd century, Stephen may have thought himself the apostolic successor to Peter, but he was still only the bishop of Rome. A few decades after Stephen, the title "Pope" was used with Pope Marcellinus and was applied to other bishops as well. The exclusive title of Pope was first applied to Gregory VII in the 11th century.[516]

The bitterness and controversy of this issue were not wiped away with Stephen's words, stating that he had the authority to forgive those who denied Christianity in order to escape persecution. While the issue would return in the coming decades under the name of Donatism, relative peace ensued so that Christianity could return to fighting over its most important issue. Almost 300 years after Jesus, and there was still no consensus on the nature of Jesus' divinity.

Rome was the Imperial Capital, perhaps the first city boasting a population of one million people and was full of "immigrants" from throughout the empire. Rival sects of Christians brought their own beliefs, and each denounced the other for heresy. According to the Roman writers Celsus, Cyprian, Tertullian, and the later indications from Eusebius, the Christian groups were at war with each other.[517] But those wars within Christianity did not impede its growth. The estimates are wide, but between 250 AD and the early 300s, Christianity grew from a couple hundred thousand to perhaps a few million. However, that growth was

---

[515] *Christianity: The First Three Thousand Years*, Diarmaid MacClulloch (Viking, 2010) pp. 174-175

[516] *Lives of the Popes: Illustrated Biographies of Every Pope from St. Peter to the Present,* Michael J. Walsh (Salamander Books, 1998) p. 34

[517] *Christianity: The First Three Thousand Years*, Diarmaid MacClulloch (Viking, 2010) pp. 216-217

very patchy, with only 26 churches in all of today's France, and two in all of today's Portugal and western Spain. Carthage, or today's Tunisia, had many Christians, but Libya, Algeria, and Morocco had virtually none. Alexandria rivaled Rome in its Christian size, but the total of the Roman Empire was certainly under 10% and concentrated in the cities.[518] Although there was relative peace, Christianity was still "religio illicita."

City life in the Roman world was mostly misery. Half the children died at birth or in infancy. Those who survived lost at least one parent before maturity. The density of early Roman cities is estimated at 200 persons per acre, or 100 persons living on the typical suburban plot in modern America—double the density of the most crowded cities on earth today.[519]

But the density alone cannot describe the squalid filth and disease. The smell of "sweat, urine, feces, and decay," "the mud, open sewers, manure and the crowds," "the flies, mosquitoes and insects," "the tapeworm, whipworm and other fecal-borne bacteria and protozoal diseases" were everyday life. Add to that, the shoddy buildings collapsing, "the fires, earthquakes, famines, epidemics and devastating riots and a picture of life as misery emerges."[520]

No wonder Cyprian wrote of Christians going, "gladly from this place to depart gloriously from amongst oppressions and afflictions—to shut one's eyes for a moment and to open them again and see God and Christ."[521] Cyprian also wrote *De*

---

[518] *A New History of Early Christianity*, Charles Freeman (Yale University Press 2009) pp. 217-222

[519] https://en.wikipedia.org/wiki/List_of_cities_by_population_density Manila the densest at 168/acre and Cairo the 39th at 72/acre.

[520] Chapter Seven "Urban Chaos and Crisis" in *The Rise of Christianity: How the Obscure, Marginal Jesus Movement Became the Dominant Religious Force in the Western World in a Few Centuries,* Rodney Stark (Harper Collins, 1997) covers in detail the horrid conditions of the Roman city life for the common people.

[521] *Cyprian of Carthage Treatise 11,* Chapter 13"" Exhortation to Martyrdom, Addressed to Fortunatus. An interpretation can be found here.

*Mortalitate (On the Plague)* a book that earned him the infamy of having his name attached to a tragedy—the Plague of Cyprian. In his book, he welcomes the plague as giving many Christians a quicker path to Heaven.[522]

And in this misery, Christianity spread rapidly in the late 3rd century. Whatever the doctrines of a Church, Christian believers assumed that their membership alone would assure them a ticket out of their hell on earth, to a paradise in Heaven.[523]

But there was another perverse reason, as explained by Dionysius the bishop of Alexandria. During the plague, pagans "pushed the sufferers away and fled from their dearest, throwing them into the roads before they were dead." Christians "took charge of the sick, attending to their every need." This resulted in "substantially higher rates of survival" for Christians, and more survivors meant increasing their percentage of the population after each round of epidemic. "Their noticeable better survival rate would have seemed a 'miracle' to Christians and pagans alike," thus further increasing conversions to Christianity in the aftermath.[524] Whatever the reason, in the peace in the last decades of the 3rd century, Christianity experienced substantial growth.

And much of this growth can be attributed to a new sect in the religions of Jesus. Manicheanism appeared in the late 3rd century and experienced explosive growth. Let me allow its founder to tell his own story. This is from a letter Mani wrote to Archelaus, the bishop of Caschar, sometime around 275 AD:

---

http://www.newadvent.org/fathers/050711.htm

[522] *A New History of Early Christianity*, Charles Freeman (Yale University Press 2009) p. 221 see also *The Rise of Christianity: How the Obscure, Marginal Jesus Movement Became the Dominant Religious Force in the Western World in a Few Centuries,* Rodney Stark (Harper Collins, 1997) pp. 80-82

[523] "A New History of Early Christianity" Charles Freeman Yale University Press 2009 p. 221

[524] *The Rise of Christianity: How the Obscure, Marginal Jesus Movement Became the Dominant Religious Force in the Western World in a Few Centuries,* Rodney Stark (Harper Collins, 1997) pp. 74-75

Manichaeus, an apostle of Jesus Christ and all the saints who are with me…. I was exceedingly delighted to observe the love cherished by you, which is truly of the largest measure. But I was distressed by your faith, which is not in accordance with the right standard. I have considered it necessary to send this letter to you…to protect you against erroneous opinion, particularly against notions such as the belief that good and evil have the same origin? How can such persons be so bold as to call God the maker and inventor of Satan and his wicked deeds?[525]

Manicheanism combined Christian Gnosticism with the Zoroastrian view of good and evil.[526] Others say the recipe called for a touch of Buddha:[527] "In spite of it all, these men were Christian."[528] In the 1990s, in Egypt, ancient documents were discovered which described Manicheanism. It was a variant of Christianity with an organized religious life, officers, and a monastery.[529]

Mani spent his early years among the Elchesaites, a Jewish/Christian Gnostic sect in Iraq.[530] He wrote several books as Manicheanism spread and gained wide acceptance, with adherents from China to Spain: "The rapidity with which Manichaeism overran the Western lands seems to indicate that it

---

[525] "The disputation of Archelaus and Manes" 6.182 as quoted in *A Dictionary of Christian Beliefs: A Reference Guide to More Than 700 Topics Discussed by the Early Church Fathers,* edited by David W. Bercott (Henrickson, 1998) p. 418

[526] *Constantine the Emperor,* David Potter (Oxford University Press, 2013) p. 86

[527] *World Religions: From Ancient History to the Present,* Geoffrey Parrinder, editor, (Facts on File Publications, 1984) p. 189

[528] *Early History of the Christian Church: From Its Foundation to the End of the Fifth Century (Vol. 1),* Louis Duchesne (Lex de Leon Publishing, 1909) Kindle Edition loc 5668

[529] *Christianity: The First Three Thousand Years,* Diarmaid MacClulloch (Viking, 2010) p. 171

[530] *The Lost History of Christianity,* Philip Jenkins (Harper One, 2008) pp. 67-68

absorbed the surviving 2nd-century Gnostic heresies."[531] Or perhaps it simply "made sense" to the common people struggling with the numerous uncertain complexities of the many Christianity's. At one time, Manicheanism was the largest version of Christianity, rivaling all of the rest of Christianity combined.[532]

That made Manicheanism less than popular among its rivals. Eusebius, in addition to calling Mani maniacal and demonic, said, "At one time he proclaimed himself the Paraclete, the Holy Spirit himself – conceited crackbrain that he was."[533] None the less, St. Augustine, one of the most famous of all Christian theologians, began his Christianity as perhaps the most famous follower of Mani.[534] And in a few more centuries, Muhammad would agree with Mani—that Jesus was a prophet, not God.

As the 3rd century turned to the 4th, the Christian conflicts with Rome were leading to the Diocletian Persecutions, and Manicheanism was the shooting star among the many Jesus sects.

---

[531] *Early History of the Christian Church: From Its Foundation to the End of the Fifth Century (Vol. 1),* Louis Duchesne (Lex de Leon Publishing, 1909) Kindle Edition loc 5661

[532] *A History of Christian Theology: An Introduction,* William C. Placher (Westminster Press, 1983) p. 110

[533] *Eusebius: The Church History,* translation by Paul L. Maier (Kregel, 1999) p. 250

[534] Manicheanism was Augustine's entry point into Christianity where he stayed for nine years. *A History of Christianity,* Paul Johnson (Simon & Schuster a Touchstone Book, 1995) p. 114

# Chapter Eleven – The Roman Religions

The Romans had no idea why things happened. All classes from Caesars to soldiers were the same as their caveman ancestors. They believed there was a pantheon of unseen and unheard gods somewhere who were controlling everything. These gods could and did intervene in events on Earth.[535] When the gods were displeased, bad things happened: defeat in battle, famines, or plagues. Keeping the gods happy was the key, and that was the job description of the Roman emperor.

One of the emperor's titles was Pontifex Maximus or Chief Priest.[536] The Roman emperor was responsible for politics and religion. He was the pope and the king. When there was an official ceremony, he was not a participant; he was the chief officiate. He was responsible for keeping the gods happy and for communicating with them. There simply was no separation of church and state in Roman times.

The preamble to an edict of Diocletian from 295 AD read, "The Immortal gods themselves, favorable as always to the

---

[535] *Constantine the Emperor*, David Potter (Oxford University Press, 2013) p. 79

[536] *Caesar and Christ (*The Story of Civilization, vol. III) Will and Ariel Durant, (MJF Books, 1944)  p. 656

Roman name, will be pleased in the future if we see to it that all those who live under our rule shall be observed by us to live pious, religious, quiet and chaste lives in all matters."[537] Now imagine Congress passing laws that began "To please God, we are making the following law...." Rome had become an empire by the favor of the gods, and it was the duty of the emperors to keep the favor of the gods. Rituals that had developed for hundreds of years were maintained and followed precisely. Every prayer was read from a fixed script to avoid a word being left out or said in the wrong order.[538]

The word "sacrifice" is often misunderstood when discussed as a part of ancient rituals. Think slaughterhouse, butcher shop, outdoor barbecue, and church service combined.

Sacrifice was the common ritual of the Romans, Jews, and pagans throughout the ancient world. Sacrifices were a recognition of the gods and a spiritual understanding that human life required the sacrifice of other life. Sacrifices were offered to a deity but eaten by humans.[539] It is a connection lost when barbequing chickens processed at 10,000 per hour in a modern chicken factory. Caged versus free-range is of little meaning. We have simply eliminated the gore and ritual, and most importantly, we no longer have spiritual involvement. Not so in the ancient temples, whether of Israel or the Roman Empire. Here is a description of the process of Roman public sacrifice:

> [Sacrifices] could be as small and relatively insignificant as breadcrumbs thrown into the hearth at home in honor of Vesta, through to say, a chicken to Jupiter or indeed several animals such as cows and so on. Clearly one would

---

[537] *Constantine the Emperor*, David Potter (Oxford University Press, 2013) p. 84
Chaste meant something quite different to the Romans. The edict was against "close marriages" which included not marrying your grandparents!

[538] *Constantine the Emperor*, David Potter (Oxford University Press, 2013) p. 78

[539] *World Religions: From Ancient History to the Present*, Geoffrey Parrinder, editor, (Facts on File Publications, 1984) p. 19

sacrifice as high a price as was required for the particular favour being asked of the god in question. The minor, personal, types of sacrifice were more properly referred to as Victima or Hostia whilst the word "Sacrificium" was generally referred to the "victim" of the more important public ceremonies. Public sacrificial ceremonies were state affairs which would generally take place in a Forum according to strict liturgy and hymns called "carmina". The value of the sacrifice would be in proportion to the State's needs. We can imagine whole herds of cattle being religiously gored at the sacrificial altar. Various cuts of the meat would be reserved for the gods whilst the rest would be eaten in one huge religious feast.

Each deity had his or her own specific rites to be followed in the sacrificial ceremony, but there were also a number of common elements. The procession would be preceded by a public crier who, shouting "hoc age", would lead the public to stop working and attend the ritual. Musicians would assist the crier either by playing their instruments or doing a little shouting themselves. The procession was headed by the chief priest and possibly the individual offering/funding the actual sacrifice(s). These persons would be dressed in the purest white.

The animal to be sacrificed would also be dressed up for the occasion. Normally, this might include some gold on the horns (if it had any) a frilly collar and a crown of leaves taken from the plant or tree most sacred to the divinity in question. Once they had arrived to the altar, the actual sacrifice would commence. An officer of the procession would shout "Favete Linguis" to entice all attendants to keep silent. A piper would start to play and continue throughout the ceremony in order to drown out any unwanted and potentially negative noise.

At this point, the Priest would touch the altar with one hand and deliver a prayer to the god(s) in question. This prayer would always start with mentioning the god Janus and finish with the goddess Vesta, suggesting that these two divinities were generally regarded as a good bracket within which to summon all the others.

The ceremonial killing of the beast, or "Immolatio," would follow. This included sprinkling some cereal and scents mixed with salt over the animal. Then, the priest would take a sip of wine from a cup, which he would then offer to those around him. This was called "Libatio" and is obviously very reminiscent of the later Christian communion.

The last of the wine would be poured between the sacrificial animal's horns. Some hairs would be taken from the same area and cast into the sacred fire. This would be a sort of "hors d'oeuvres" for the gods I suppose. Then, turning to the East or South East (towards the Alban hills, I think) the priest would trace a line from head to tail on the animal and hand it over to his aids called "Victimarii" for it to be killed.

The animal was killed, skinned, opened up and washed so that the Aruspices could move in, take a good look and make their predictions. The animal would then be butchered and, those parts that weren't reserved for the gods, would be cooked and consumed by those attending the ceremony.[540]

---

[540] Used with permission.
http://www.mariamilani.com/ancient_rome/sacrifices_in_ancient_rome.htm

Jewish sacrifice was very similar, except that fortune-telling, while mentioned in the Bible, was not ritually included.[541] For the Romans, prophecy or fortune-telling was a very important part of the ritual, and Aruspices or Haruspices, in Latin, were the fortune tellers of the day. Just as astrologers look at star charts to prophesy if it will be a good day for a date or to ask for a raise, Haruspices looked at the entrails of the sacrificed animal and predicated which way the ancient stock market would be going, or if the emperor would win in battle, or whatever was the question of the day. Hey, is that any less effective than calling 1-800-FORTUNE?

Christianity had been peacefully tolerated within the Roman Empire for 40 years as the end of the 3rd century approached. It had grown and spread with only occasional local outbursts of protest. The last decade had been tense, as numerous tribes of Goths had crossed the Danube and Rhine rivers, sometimes penetrating far into Roman territory. The Roman archenemy, the Persians, had reasserted themselves and started actions in the east, and there were insurrections in the south of Egypt. Add to that economic inflation, and, even with the success of the Roman generals in stemming the attacks, everyone knew all was not well.

Two Roman writers, Lactantius and Eusebius, tell similar stories of what happened next.[542] In the autumn of 299 AD, a triumphal procession was held in Antioch to celebrate a recent victory by Galerius over the Persians. The emperors, Diocletian and Galerius, then offered a public sacrifice like the one

---

[541] The first seven chapters of the book of Leviticus describe the procedures for Jewish sacrifice. Chapter 4 "How Unique was Israelite Prophecy" by Jonathan Stokl in *World Religions: From Ancient History to the Present*, Geoffrey Parrinder, editor, (Facts on File Publications, 1984) explains that there was very little difference in the forms of prophecy in the Middle East.

[542] A literary version of "Lactantius, De Mortibus Persecutorum" 10.6 is told in *When Jesus Became God: The Struggle to Define Christianity during the Last Days of Rome,* Richard E. Rubenstein (Harcourt, 1999) pp. 24-28

described above. When it came time for the haruspices to provide their fortune-telling, they could not do so. Here are Lactantius' own words:

> While he sacrificed, some attendants of his, who were Christians, stood by and put the sign of the cross on their foreheads. At this the demons were chased away, and the holy rites interrupted. The soothsayers trembled, unable to investigate the wonted marks on the entrails of the victims. They frequently repeated the sacrifices, as if the former had been unpropitious; but when the victims were slain, they gave no tokens for divination.[543]

For Roman Emperor Diocletian, the problem was obvious: the Christians. They had been given the chance over the past 40 years to get along and go along. Instead, they not only disrespected other legal Roman gods, they branded them as evil and demonic. This "short circuit" created divisiveness in the Roman world, particularly in the army where the percentage of Christians was higher than in civilian life.[544] The Roman emperor was failing in his duty to please the gods and maintain the peace.

Diocletian's first step was to throw all Christians out of the army who would not demonstrate loyalty by offering sacrifice to the Roman gods.[545] When that proved insufficient, the emperors did decide to call 1-800-FORTUNE, which in the day meant a visit to the oracle of Apollo. Galerius and Diocletian went to Didyma, the most renowned oracle of the Hellenic world, where they were told by the oracle that Christians had interfered with

---

[543] As published by the Wisconsin Lutheran Church on the website
http://www.fourthcentury.com/index.php/persecution-sources/#299

[544] *A Study of History,* Arnold J. Toynbee (Oxford University Press, 1957) p. 66

[545] *When Jesus Became God: The Struggle to Define Christianity during the Last Days of Rome,* Richard E. Rubenstein (Harcourt, 1999) p. 28

communications with the gods.[546] On February 23, 303 AD, the Roman emperor Diocletian acted to restore order to his empire: he banned Christian worship, and ordered their churches destroyed, and all Christian books burned! In a second edict, he ordered all Christian priests arrested. Eusebius records that he,

> saw with my own eyes the houses of worship demolished to their foundations, the inspired and sacred Scriptures committed to flames in the middle of the public squares, and pastors of the churches hiding shamefully in one place or another, or arrested and held up to ridicule by their enemies.

> Countless numbers of men women and children, disdaining this passing life to endure a variety of deaths for the sake of our Savior's teaching. Some of them were scrapped, racked, ruthlessly whipped, and tortured in ways too terrible to describe, and finally given to the flames or tossed in the sea.

The Diocletian Persecutions, or the Great Persecutions, were the most difficult for Christianity. Eusebius may have reported seeing things with his own eyes, but the Roman history books show something different. Churches and books were certainly burned, property was taken, priests were arrested, people were punished and imprisoned. But the records show the number of executions were minimal. In the Balkans, there are records of just 42 executions, while in Palestine there were just seven.[547] In the western part of the empire, the edict was simply not enforced.[548]

---

[546] *When Jesus Became God: The Struggle to Define Christianity during the Last Days of Rome,* Richard E. Rubenstein (Harcourt, 1999) p. 32 In the footnote for this section Rubenstein provides several sources for this story.

[547] *Constantine the Emperor*, David Potter (Oxford University Press, 2013) p. 94 In the notes for this conclusions Potter gives detailed evidence for this conclusion.

[548] *A New History of Early Christianity*, Charles Freeman (Yale University Press 2009) p. 221

Banishment was the most common punishment.[549] In eight years of the Diocletian persecution, "only" 1,500 in total were estimated to have faced death in the arena.[550] Less than 200 per year, far from the perception of widespread genocidal killings. Today, 500 shooting murders per year in Chicago alone elicits barely a shrug.[551]

Most bishops and deacons simply did as commanded and handed over their chalices and books, while Christian laypeople decided to go back to the "Roman Church," as it was just too dangerous to keep going to the "Jesus Church." Then "an ill-fated disease attacked the foremost of the emperors [Diocletian] which deranged his mind so he returned to ordinary private life along with the one who was in second place after him [Maximian]."[552] By 305 AD, there was a general amnesty[553] as Rome looked to celebrate its 1000th Anniversary. A perfect time for retirement, "In 305 AD, in impressive ceremonies in Nicomedia and Milan, Diocletian and Maximian abdicated power."[554]

Diocletian and Maximian had set up a new ruling system: two equal augusti or emperors, each ruling half the Roman Empire, each with an assisting caesar. Diocletian and Maximian would retire by promoting their caesars to augusti. The new augusti, in turn, would appoint their new assistants as caesars. And each caesar would marry the daughter of the other augusti. It was designed to avoid the bitter leadership fights and civil wars that had plagued the Roman Empire. It looked great on paper.

---

[549] *A New History of Early Christianity*, Charles Freeman (Yale University Press 2009) p. 213

[550] *Caesar and Christ (The Story of Civilization, vol. III)* Will and Ariel Durant, (MJF Books, 1944) p. 662

[551] http://crime.chicagotribune.com/chicago/homicides

[552] All of these quotes are from *Eusebius: The Church History,* translation by Paul L. Maier (Kregel, 1999) pp. 260, 266, and 273

[553] *Constantine the Emperor,* David Potter (Oxford University Press, 2013) p. 95

[554] *Caesar and Christ* (The Story of Civilization, vol. III) Will and Ariel Durant, (MJF Books, 1944) p. 644

# Chapter Twelve – Legalizing Christianity

The question of Jesus' divinity was still fragmenting his followers. If Jesus was God, were there not two Gods? For Christianity to be monotheistic, somehow the answer had to be no. If there were two Gods, it is just a hop, skip, and a jump and Christianity is just another version of polytheism, and no different than the religions of the broader Roman Empire. Tertullian, a Christian writer of the time, explained there was only one God in the same sense that, "the root puts forth the tree, and the fountain the river, and the sun the ray." Perhaps true, said the others, but the rays derive from the sun and are therefore lesser. Did not Jesus pray, *The Father is greater than I* (John 14:28)? Call the lawyers for a dense discussion of the definition of words like "begotten" and "substance."[555] As President Clinton famously stated in his Grand Jury testimony, everything "depends upon what the meaning of the word 'is' is."[556]

---

[555] *A History of Christian Theology: An Introduction,* William C. Placher (Westminster Press, 1983) p. 73

[556] https://www.youtube.com/watch?v=UEmjwR0Rs20 This is the video of the statement by President Clinton in his Grand Jury Testimony August 17, 1998

During Diocletian's reign, a priest named Arius began preaching his answers. Arius said that there was one supreme God, the Father, and that below him were other gods, including Jesus. Jesus was not of the same stuff as the Father and was created by the Father out of nothing at some time.[557] Or in Arius' own words, Jesus was "not from eternity, but was made out of nothing. Wherefore there was a time when he did not exist.… He is neither like the Father as it regards his essence…but indeed one of his works and creatures." Arius set his slogan to music and soon, all over Alexandria, Christians were singing that snappy song, "There was a time when the Son was not."[558]

That did not sit well with Arius' superior, Alexander, the bishop of Alexandria. But neither Alexander nor anyone else had a good answer to the thorny problem: Was Jesus God? And if so, when did he become God? When you don't have the answer, attack the person. And Alexander attacked the Arians: "Their immoral women folk…their younger women followers run around the street in an indecent fashion and discredit Christianity."[559] Where have we heard that sort of thing before?

Immoral women? In indecent clothes? Singing a snappy song? Arianism was about to become a big hit.

Diocletian and Maximian's plans to transfer power lasted three years. Civil war broke out in 308 AD with no less than six men claiming the title of emperor.[560] After the preliminary rounds of "Who Wants to be Emperor," only four contestants remained. The first of the semi-finals was fought on October 28th

---

[557] *A Dictionary of Christian Beliefs: A Reference Guide to More Than 700 Topics Discussed by the Early Church Fathers,* edited by David W. Bercott (Henrickson, 1998) p. 35 This is a simple summary of some of the key ideas.

[558] *A History of Christian Theology: An Introduction,* William C. Placher (Westminster Press, 1983) p. 73

[559] *A History of Christianity,* Paul Johnson (Simon & Schuster a Touchstone Book, 1995) p. 51

[560] *Caesar and Christ (The Story of Civilization, vol. III),* Will and Ariel Durant, (MJF Books, 1944) p. 655

of 312 AD between Constantine and Maxentius in the Battle of Milvian Bridge. It was an epic fight that produced myths and legends that changed history!

Shortly after the battle, Eusebius published a second edition of his book *Church History*. In it, he tells a straightforward story of Constantine's win at Milvian Bridge.[561] When Eusebius retold the story 25 years later in his book *The Life of Constantine*, the battle was highly dramatized, with God sending signs in the heavens, Constantine having dreams, and soldiers placing Christian crosses on shields.[562] Whether or not Constantine saw miraculous signs in the heavens the day before the battle and had a come-to-Jesus moment that gave him the victory has been argued ever since.

The evidence is on the Arch of Constantine, a sort of Roman "extra, extra, read all about it," built within three years of the battle. It still stands in Rome next to the Colosseum, showing the pagan goddesses Victory and Roma beckoning Constantine to cross the river over the fallen body of Maxentius,[563] testifying that the Sun god delivered the victory to Constantine.[564] Constantine will unquestionably propel Christianity towards the eventual domination of Western civilization, but on October 28, 312 AD, his Christian trappings were not to be seen. They would only become visible with the glasses of historical imagination.

The following year, Constantine and Licinius met in Milan. Licinius was about to fight Maximinus II in the other semi-finals of "Who Wants to be Emperor." These were not win-or-go-home shows but win-or-die battles. Constantine and Licinius agreed that, should Licinius win, they would be co-emperors just as Diocletian and Maximian had been a few years before.

---

[561] *Eusebius: The Church History,* translation by Paul L. Maier (Kregel, 1999) pp. 294-295

[562] *The Life of Constantine,* Eusebius (Heraklion Press 2004) Chapters 27 through 32

[563] *Constantine the Emperor*, David Potter (Oxford University Press, 2013) p. 144

[564] *A History of Christianity*, Paul Johnson (Simon & Schuster a Touchstone Book, 1995) p. 67

Constantine even gave his sister to Licinius as a wife to seal the deal!

They also agreed that, if Licinius won, they would issue one of the most important documents in world history: the "Edict of Milan."[565] Licinius defeated Maximinus II on 30th of April, and the edict was published on June 14th of 313 AD. The Edict was sent to all Roman governors and read in part:

> I, Constantine Augustus, and I, Licinius Augustus,…grant the Christians and all others the freedom to follow whatever form of worship they pleased, so that all the divine and heavenly powers that exist might be favorable to us and all those living under our authority….

> No one at all was to be denied the right to follow or chose the Christian form of worship or observance, and everyone was to be granted the right to give his mind to that form of worship that he thinks suitable to himself.

> The edict goes on to order the return of all Christian property taken in the recent persecutions and that the edict "should be announced by your order, published everywhere, and brought to the attention of all so that the enactment incorporating our generosity may escape the notice of no one."[566]

And it should escape no one's notice that the Edict of Milan is precisely the grant of religious freedom enshrined in the American Constitution. Everyone in the Roman Empire was now free to worship whatever god they wanted in the manner they wanted. Pagans, and all the various versions of Christianity that existed at that time—Apollinarians, Docetists, Manicheans,

---

[565] *A History of Christianity*, Paul Johnson (Simon & Schuster a Touchstone Book, 1995) p. 67

[566] *Eusebius: The Church History,* translation by Paul L. Maier (Kregel, 1999) pp. 322-324

Miaphysites, Monophysites, Valentinians, Basilides Ebionites Montanists, Adoptionists, Arians, Cerinthians, Chalcedonians, Eutyches, Gnostics, Marcions, Nestorians, Sabellians, and even the Carpocratians—now had the right to practice their religion, as they saw fit. (I wonder if they were obliged to bake cakes for everyone?) After three centuries, the many religions of Jesus were finally legal.

It looks great on paper, but total religious freedom wouldn't work for the ancient Romans and isn't exactly working for modern man today either. Words cannot diminish the power and emotions of people's beliefs in their God. When the banners all read, "My God is better than your God," each will kill for their God. Whether that banner is held high over Christians, or over the battles of the Sunni-Shiite divide, or if it's the Clash of Civilizations with the West, or at the Hindu-Islamic flashpoint along the Indus River Valley, or in the Protestant-Catholic Wars, or in hundreds of other religious wars of history, the "live and let live" motto does not have a peaceful track record in religion.[567]

The legal religions of Jesus were like cats of many different stripes, spots, and colors. We have looked at a handful of the religions of Jesus that had developed in the first centuries, just to glimpse at the vast differences in their theologies. Differences bigger than between, say, Mormons and Methodists today. Since there was no definition of Christianity, Constantine applied the Latin adjective "catholicus," to encompass all those different religions of Jesus. Catholic was an all-encompassing word that would be used in Constantine's pronouncements.[568] The Romans

---

[567] While outside the scope of this book, the freedom of religion is not the freedom from religion, and the separation of church and state is not the separation of religion and state. As DeTocqueville pointed out in "Democracy in America" protestant religion was hand in hand and indispensable to the State. This was exactly the case of Rome and Religion.

[568] *Early History of the Christian Church: From Its Foundation to the End of the Fifth Century (Vol. 1),* Louis Duchesne (Lex de Leon Publishing, 1909) Kindle Edition loc 23906

put all Christian theologies under one catholic tent, but in the coming decades all Christians would be put under one Roman Catholic theology.

The literature of Christianity portrays the Edict of Milan as the result of divine intervention of Abraham's God in converting Constantine to Christianity and guiding him to victory at the Battle of Milvian Bridge. Myths, often repeated, become fact, and the story of Constantine seeing a sign from Heaven, converting to Christianity, and becoming its savior has been repeated often. But Constantine's conversion "was a consummate stroke of political wisdom,"[569] and "not the result of a sudden momentous revelation, but a journey over time and in his own mind."[570]

Constantine did as much for paganism as he did for Christianity. He restored pagan temples, carried out the required pagan rituals, and used pagan magic to protect crops and cure diseases,[571] but he also gave the religions of Jesus the legal right to be practiced throughout the Roman Empire. Rome and the catholic Christianity's seemed off to a good start. Everything was looking up.

Constantine returned to Trier to continue the never-ending Roman fight with the barbarians. From there, in 313 AD, new coins were minted, celebrating Constantine. The coins were not engraved with any symbol of Jesus or Christianity, but with Constantine's pagan god, Sol Invictus.[572] "The devotion of Constantine was directed to the genius of the Sun, the Apollo of Greek and Roman mythology.... The Sun was universally

---

[569] *Caesar and Christ (The Story of Civilization, vol. III),* Will and Ariel Durant, (MJF Books, 1944) p. 653

[570] *Constantine the Emperor,* David Potter (Oxford University Press, 2013) p. 159

[571] *Caesar and Christ (The Story of Civilization, vol. III),* Will and Ariel Durant, (MJF Books, 1944) p. 656

[572] *Constantine the Emperor,* David Potter (Oxford University Press, 2013) p. 177

celebrated as the invincible guide and protector of Constantine,"[573] who never abandoned worship of the Sun god and kept the Sun on his coins. In March of 321 AD, Constantine officially declared "Sun" day as a day of rest for the people of the Roman empire.

Over the centuries, Constantine's decree was forgotten as Sunday became the day of rest embedded into the routines of almost all Christian leaning societies. In 1961, the Supreme Court case of McGowan v. Maryland (366 U.S. 420) overturned the practice of Sunday rest. In that decision, Justice William O. Douglas wrote, "No matter how much is written, no matter what is said, the parentage of these laws is the Fourth Commandment, and they serve and satisfy the religious predispositions of our Christian communities."[574] Little did Justice Douglas know that Sunday was a day of rest, a day of closings established to honor Constantine's pagan god of the Sun.

Although much debated, whether Constantine was really a Christian or not, is of fleeting importance. The most important factor was that the legalization of Christianity brought it under Roman rule. As an outlawed organization, Christianity had no rules, no structure, and its theology was scattered across dozens of doctrinal divides, each with their own rituals, rules, and rubrics. Being a legal religion within the Roman Empire required Christianity to be integrated into the Roman legal and institutional structure. Factions of its disparate beliefs could no longer be barroom brawls outside the system but would instead require a disciplined structure within the system. And the system was a

---

[573] *The History of the Decline and Fall of the Roman Empire, Volume 3,* Edward Gibbon, (Fred de Fau and Co., 1906) p. 237

[574] Prior to the 1961 decision, those seeking to repeal Sunday closing laws had looked to the U.S. Supreme Court to find such laws unconstitutional. The McGowan case found them Constitutional, and the opponents turned to the States where one by one Sunday closing laws were overturned or abandoned by the legislatures. In my State of Indiana Sunday Closing laws were only repealed by the State Legislature in 1977. Indiana Law Journal, Volume 55 Issue 1 Article 9 which can be found here: http://www.repository.law.indiana.edu/ilj

monolithic church/state establishment with Constantine as the Pontifex Maximus, the head of *all* the religions of the Roman world, now including Christianity. Christians may have had bishops, but as Constantine himself said, he was the bishop of bishops.[575] All those recalcitrant cantankerous cats were now on his stage: The Roman Empire. Some had already started a cat fight—scratching, screeching and making a horrible discordant sound. Christianity needed a maestro.

---

[575] *A History of Christian Theology: An Introduction*, William C. Placher (Westminster Press, 1983) p. 90

# Chapter Thirteen – The Continuing Crisis... Was Jesus a God?

The word "traitors" comes from the Latin *traditores*, meaning *to hand over*, which is exactly what many did with their Christian books during the Diocletian persecutions.[576] Some said that the traitors could no longer be priests and officiates, and all their actions—baptisms, the appointment of priests, etc.— were invalid. Donatus, a bishop at Carthage, said that those who were traitors could not be priests and officiants in churches. That faction became known as the Donatists. A minor civil war broke out. Excommunications, unsanctioned appointments, claims and counter claims abounded and divided. For the first time, Christians were now persecuting Christians.

And for the first time as head of the Christian Church, Constantine was called on to settle the matter. After considerable muddled complications, in 316 AD, Constantine decided against the Donatist and ruled they should lose their civil rights and have their property confiscated.[577] Freedom of religion, that great

---

[576] *The New History of Early Christianity,* Charles Freeman (Yale University Press 2009) p. 229

[577] *Caesar and Christ (The Story of Civilization, vol. III),* Will and Ariel Durant, (MJF Books, 1944) p. 658

principal on paper, had failed, and Constantine ordered in the Imperial troops to enforce his decision.[578] It was the first use of Roman force to settle internal Christian problems.[579] Constantine may have decided the issue, but that does not mean it was settled. Five years later, he softened his ruling, but Donatists' disputes would continue to disrupt Christianity in North Africa until the arrival of Islam.[580]

Constantine had a bigger problem. The Christian "diversity of religious belief was incompatible with the purely secular needs of imperial administration." In fact, "Over large parts of empire, Christian elements formed a multiplicity of troublesome groups, each trying to thrust its own levers into the cracks of the Imperial structure."[581] Constantine was dismayed that instead of unifying his empire, the disputes among Christians were disrupting it.[582]

But he also had to worry about the Barbarian invasions and his uneasy relationship with his co-emperor Licinius. As they say, "It's complicated," but the finals of the "Who Wants to be Emperor?" playoffs were held on July 3, 324 AD at the Battle of Adrianople.[583] Constantine won the title match and was now the sole ruler of the entire Roman Empire. But there was no letup in the problems. The Barbarians continued to invade, and the people of his Empire were divided and at each other's throats. Constantine needed to resolve the same problem Lincoln would face over 1500 years later. He needed to unite his quarrelling

---

[578] *Christianity: The First Three Thousand Years*, Diarmaid MacClulloch (Viking, 2010) p. 212

[579] *Christianity: The First Three Thousand Years*, Diarmaid MacClulloch (Viking, 2010) p. 212

[580] *Caesar and Christ (The Story of Civilization, vol. III),* Will and Ariel Durant, (MJF Books, 1944) p. 658

[581] *A History of Christianity*, Paul Johnson (Simon & Schuster a Touchstone Book, 1995) p. 86

[582] *Caesar and Christ* (The Story of Civilization, vol. III), Will and Ariel Durant, (MJF Books, 1944) p. 658

[583] *Caesar and Christ* (The Story of Civilization, vol. III) Will and Ariel Durant, (MJF Books, 1944) p. 655

people. On top of everything else, almost immediately after defeating Licinius, there was a crisis in Egypt.[584]

The girls of the Arian Five had sung their snappy song just once too often. Alexander, the bishop of Alexandria, was shocked at just how popular the ideas of Arius had become. To end it, Alexander called his bishops together and excommunicated Arius. Arius escaped and went to other bishops, including Eusebius, the bishop of Caesarea. This was a serious divide, just as Constantine was dealing with all the administrative issues of integrating his rule over the Eastern and Western Roman Empires. Constantine sent his closest Christian theological advisor, the bishop of Cordova, to Alexandria to investigate.[585] Hosius took with him a letter to both Arius and Alexander outlining Constantine's view. It read, in part:

> I had hoped to lead back to a single form the ideas which all people conceive of the Deity; for I feel strongly that if I could induce men to unite on that subject, the conduct of public affairs would be considerably eased. But alas! I hear that there are more disputes among you than recently in Africa [referring to the Donatist problem]. The cause seems to be quite trifling, and unworthy of such fierce contests. You Alexander wished to know what your priests were thinking on a point of law, even on a portion only of a question in itself entirely devoid of importance; and you Arius, if you had such thoughts should have kept silence .... There was no need to make these questions public...since they are problems that idleness alone raises, and whose only use is to sharpen men's wits.... These are silly actions

---

[584] *When Jesus Became God: The Struggle to Define Christianity during the Last Days of Rome,* Richard E. Rubenstein (Harcourt, 1999) p. 46
[585] *Eusebius: The Church History,* translation by Paul L. Maier (Kregel, 1999) p. 327 n. 20

worthy of inexperienced children, and not of priests or reasonable man.[586]

Questioning Jesus divinity may have been childish to the emperor, but it was not childish to the people. Hosius reported back to Constantine that, "Confusion everywhere prevailed, for we saw not only the prelates of the churches engaged in disputing, but the people also divided…to a disgraceful extent that this affair carried, that Christianity became a subject of popular ridicule, even in the very theaters."[587]

The bishops of Christianity were agitating the people over the familial relationships between the Creator of the Universe and his son? Great…just what Constantine needed—another divisive problem to add to the pile when trying to bring his divided empire together. The Donatists' issue was bad enough. Another Christian uproar could not be allowed to descend into chaos and violence. Constantine might naïvely think this was a silly question, but he could not ignore it. His goal of unity for his Empire required the unity of Christianity.

Constantine called for a council of bishops under Hosius to meet after Easter, 325 AD, in Ancyra. He would let his trusted advisor and the bishops work out their childish bickering. But then the bishop of Antioch died, and the political jockeying began. A council met in Antioch and appointed a new anti-Arian as bishop and excommunicated several Arian-leaning bishops, including Eusebius. Seeing events getting out of control, Constantine moved the location of his council to Nicaea, so that he could "be present as a spectator and participate in those things

---

[586] *Caesar and Christ* (The Story of Civilization, vol. III) Will and Ariel Durant, (MJF Books, 1944) p. 659 as quoted from the Life of Constantine by Eusebius.

[587] *The New History of Early Christianity* Charles Freeman (Yale University Press 2009) p. 231 Hosius as quoted by Socrates in "Ecclesiastical History" Book One Chapter Six

which will be done."[588] His goal was to resolve the Arian issue. If Jesus was the Son of God, just what kind of God was he? Most importantly, Constantine wanted to put in place a structure to resolve future disputes before they grew and further disrupted the Roman Empire.

With an offer of free food and travel expenses, well over 200 bishops and their entourages accepted the emperor's invitation.[589] Many came with lost eyes, severed Achilles heals, deformed backs, and scars from the Diocletian persecutions. Now that was all a bad dream. After the persecutions, this emperor had rebuilt their churches, given them back their jobs, restored their honor and legal rights, and paid them compensation.[590] And now, here they were, living in the Roman emperor's palace and sitting in his judgement hall waiting for Constantine's arrival. Constantine entered the hall wearing a magnificent purple robe and the royal diadem glittering with diamonds.[591] What did he want?

In his opening speech, Constantine made his point clear: "I mean to receive you all gathered together and to observe one unanimous opinion shared by all…. For me, internal division in the church of God is graver than any war or fierce battle, and these things cause more pain than any secular affair."[592] And to put an exclamation point on the matter, and show how compromise worked, there was the condemned Arian heretic Eusebius making the first speech of the Council. Roman emperors understood great political theater.

---

[588] *Christianity: The First Three Thousand Years*, Diarmaid MacClulloch (Viking, 2010) p. 214

[589] *Caesar and Christic* (The Story of Civilization, vol. III) Will and Ariel Durant, (MJF Books, 1944) p. 659 The actual number of attendees is unknown, with different sources reporting anywhere from 200 to 318.

[590] When Jesus Became God: The Struggle to Define Christianity during the Last Days of Rome, Richard E. Rubenstein (Harcourt, 1999) p. 72

[591] A New History of Early Christianity, Charles Freeman (Yale University Press 2009) p. 231

[592] *Constantine the Emperor,* David Potter (Oxford University Press, 2013) p. 234

But the question of Jesus' divinity was painful, perilous, and beyond political theater. In almost 300 years, Jesus' divinity had never been defined in any acceptable form.[593] For Christianity today, Jesus as its Godhead is a bedrock of belief, but it was a question for debate as Constantine made his speech. Christianity then was a collection of local churches, each with its own opinion of Jesus and his relationship with Abraham's God. Arius' central question of Jesus' divinity had to be decided before anything else could be considered. It had never been decided because it was insoluble.

Athanasius, the secretary to the bishop of Alexandria, understood things perfectly, "If Christ and the Holy Spirit were not of one substance with the Father, polytheism would triumph."[594] The bishop of Milan, Ambrose, argued the other side, saying something like this:

> Imagine! Some fools maintain that Jesus Christ, the Son of Man, and the omnipotent unknowable Creator are made out of the same essential stuff. Did God somehow divide his own substance to make a Son? And if so, how many more Gods might he produce by further division? No idea could be more absurd![595]

Either to say Jesus 'was God' or 'became God' took you to the anathema of polytheism. As if further complications were required, Jesus himself had said, *"I go unto the Father: for my Father is greater than I"* (John 14:28). Was Jesus then a lesser God? The deity of Jesus may have seemed trivial to Constantine,

---

[593] When Jesus Became God: The Struggle to Define Christianity during the Last Days of Rome, Richard E. Rubenstein (Harcourt, 1999) p. 53

[594] *Caesar and Christ* (The Story of Civilization, vol. III) Will and Ariel Durant, (MJF Books, 1944)   p. 660

[595] When Jesus Became God: The Struggle to Define Christianity during the Last Days of Rome, Richard E. Rubenstein (Harcourt, 1999) p. 80

but it was a Gordian knot. Was Constantine the equal of Alexander the Great?[596]

Perhaps Constantine could cut the Gordian knot of Jesus' divinity with a sword of semantics. The word for 'essential stuff' and 'substance' in Greek is *homoousios*. Adding one little *i* makes the word *homoiousios*, and the meaning becomes 'the same type of stuff.' It's the difference such as: two chairs made from the same tree are *homoousios*, while two chairs made of wood are *homoiousios*.[597] The fate of the Roman Empire and Christianity rested on the single letter 'i'—one iota.[598] Constantine seemed to be proven right; this was a silly thing indeed.

No minutes and official records of the Council were kept. Only fragments of writings, a few documents, and some recollections written years later would provide a glimpse of the proceedings.[599] Something like the following occurred. At some point in the discussions, the bishop of Nicomedia read from a document directly from Arius. Pandemonium ensued. When calm was restored, Eusebius introduced a creed, to which the emperor replied, "That is exactly what I believe, with one minor exception." He proposed to add that the Son was *homoousios*, of the same substance with the Father.[600] To which the Arians said they could agree, if the infamous *i* were added. The Council voted

---

[596] The Gordian knot was the famous myth of a knot that could not be untangled. When presented to Alexander the Great he simply took out his sword and cut it.

[597] This is a reasonable analogy; the original Greek seems to have had a much more precise distinction. In addition, the concept has elements from Plato and was not to be found in any scriptural writings.

[598] When Jesus Became God: The Struggle to Define Christianity during the Last Days of Rome, Richard E. Rubenstein (Harcourt, 1999) p. 197 Quoting Gibbons "The Decline and Fall of the Roman Empire" p. 670

[599] When Jesus Became God: The Struggle to Define Christianity during the Last Days of Rome, Richard E. Rubenstein (Harcourt, 1999) See footnote 73 from p. 76

[600] When Jesus Became God: The Struggle to Define Christianity during the Last Days of Rome, Richard E. Rubenstein (Harcourt, 1999) p. 78

that down, after which the emperor Constantine proposed the final wording of the Nicaean Creed.[601]

> We believe in one God, the Father almighty, maker of all things visible and invisible;
>
> And in one Lord, Jesus Christ, the Son of God, begotten from the Father, only begotten that is, from the substance of the Father, God from God, light from light, true God from true God, begotten not made, of one substance with the Father, through Whom all things came into being, things in heaven and things on earth, Who because of us men and because of our salvation came down, and became incarnate and became man, and suffered, and rose again on the third day, and ascended to the heavens; and will come to judge the living and dead,
>
> And in the Holy Spirit.[602]
>
> The vote was called, and Jesus was declared to be the God of all time by a count of 314-2.[603]

The Holy Spirit was left dangling, as well as a host of other questions. For example, now that Jesus was the God of all time, how was he also man? The question of Jesus' deity will haunt Christianity for centuries to come. From Muhammad to Isaac Newton,[604] from respected theologians to common people; the ideas of Arius will ring truer than those propounded by the

---

[601] *Caesar and Christ* (The Story of Civilization, vol. III) Will and Ariel Durant, (MJF Books, 1944) p. 660

[602] The actual wording of the Creed then concludes with criticisms of Arianism.

[603] Whether there were 316 who voted or some lower number no one really knows. The only agreement is that there were only two negative votes.

[604] Isaac Newton wrote more on theology than on science. He denied the Nicene Creed and divinity of Jesus. See A *History of Christian Theology: An Introduction,* William C. Placher (Westminster Press, 1983) p. 90

Roman emperor and adopted by vote in Nicaea in the year 325 AD.

The unity that Constantine sought had been denied by those two pesky votes. But that was an easy problem for a Roman emperor—just exile them. As the two who had voted against the Nicene Creed were being escorted out of the Hall, they bitterly denounced Eusebius. Eusebius may have believed as they did, but he knew how to vote.[605] Constantine and the Great Council in the coming weeks approved twenty ecclesiastical laws or canons. Any bets on what those votes were?

The new canons provided the basic structure of the emerging Christian church.[606] There could only be one bishop in a location (Canon 8). To be a cleric required a probationary period after membership (Canon 2). Roaming priests and bishops were outlawed, you must stay where you were ordained (Canon 15). You could not be ordained outside of the area where you were originally a church member unless the bishop of the original area concurred (Canon 16). The same rules of locality applied to those who were excommunicated (Canon 5). No one could become a bishop without a vote of the bishops of the province and the approval of the Metropolitan Bishop (Canon 4). The bishops of Alexandria, Antioch, and Rome were given wide area authority through veto over the appointment of bishops (Canon 6).

The rest of the canons were such things as a rule that eunuchs could be priests (Canon 1) the church could not make loans at interest (Canon 17) all must stand and not kneel when praying (Canon 20) and clerics could neither marry nor have concubines (Canon 3). There might have been a dissenting murmur or two on that one.

---

[605] *The New History of Early Christianity* Charles Freeman (Yale University Press 2009) p. 233 and When Jesus Became God: The Struggle to Define Christianity during the Last Days of Rome, Richard E. Rubenstein (Harcourt, 1999) p. 83

[606] *Christianity: The First Three Thousand Years*, Diarmaid MacClulloch (Viking, 2010) p. 347

Taken together, the requirements of allegiance to the Nicene Creed and following resolutions built the structure of the Christian Church. Dissent was curtailed by the imposition of rules that turned roaming clerics into Roman clerics. No longer could an Arius or Donatist roam the countryside preaching their understanding of Christianity.[607] There would be rules! And the power of the Roman Empire would enforce them. For starters, all books by Arius were ordered to be burned, and concealment of them was made punishable by death.[608] Constantine was the emperor of the Roman Empire; he imposed these beliefs and could enforce them with his army. Now, are there any questions? Meeting adjourned.

Constantine's decree stayed in force until the 20th century, when the infamous *i* was again resurrected. In 1959, Pope John XXIII called for another ecumenical council. Vatican II provided for the English Mass of the Nicene Creed to say that Jesus is "one in Being with the Father."[609] This is the *homoiousios* version acceptable to the Arians. But then the anti-Arians, such as the Society of St. Pius X, and others in the Church hierarchy, fought back. In 2007, Pope Benedict XVI sided with those wanting the words "consubstantial with the Father"—a theological difference that realigned the Church with Constantine's *homoousios* version.[610] And so the old battle raged once again, but this time without riots and fighting in the streets.

On September 3, 2017, Pope Francis attempted to end the fights and divisions by issuing "Magnum Principium" (The Great Principle). Pope Francis is a mere pope, and not an emperor. He

---

[607] Had James and the First Jewish Jesus Church of Jerusalem had such rules, Paul would have been prevented from preaching!

[608] *Caesar and Christ* (The Story of Civilization, vol. III) Will and Ariel Durant, (MJF Books, 1944) p. 660

[609] *Catechism of the Catholic Church* Part One Section Two The Credo which can be seen here: http://www.vatican.va/archive/ccc_css/archive/catechism/credo.htm

[610] *Jesus of Nazareth*, Joseph Ratzinger (Benedict XVI) (Ignatius, 2007) p. 355

no longer anoints kings and controls them with threats of excommunication and certain hell, and he has no army to enforce his position. So, Pope Francis did his best Rodney King impersonation, "Can't we all just get along?" Pope Francis effectively decreed that the Catholic Church now accepted *both* versions.[611] After centuries and centuries of constant struggle, the nature of Jesus' divinity is still not settled. Those two pesky votes!

Constantine thought he got what he wanted. "Constantine's great hope was to convene a conference that would end the bishops' bitter wrangling and begin an era of harmony in the Church."[612] Not just harmony, but a symphony on a grand scale.

At the beginning of the 4th century, the off-key voices of the choir of Christian teachers, preachers, and bishops were singing a discordant song. The Roman Empire needed everyone singing the same song. The emperor Constantine became the Maestro and only those who sang the song his way were allowed in the choir. Those who could not or would not sing in the emperor's key were outlawed.

Constantine wanted everyone singing from the same musical score. He ordered Eusebius to write that Nicaea Report and make 50 copies of the "sacred scriptures." Eusebius complied with the emperor's "request" by supplying a list of books: Mark, Matthew, Luke, John, Acts, 1 John and 1 Peter, the Epistles of Paul, and also some disputed books.[613] In 367 AD, Athanasius followed

---

[611] At the time of this writing it has been less than a month since news of this decree has been in the Press. Magnum principium can be read here https://en.wikipedia.org/wiki/Magnum_principium and reports of the background and effects can be found in many papers and periodicals, including the *New York Times* and *Wall Street Journal*'s September 9, 2017 editions.

[612] *When Jesus Became God: The Struggle to Define Christianity during the Last Days of Rome,* Richard E. Rubenstein (Harcourt, 1999) p. 69

[613] Eusebius: The Church History, translation by Paul L. Maier (Kregel, 1999) 3:25 The disputed books were James, Jude, 2 Peter, 2 and 3 John, and the 'spurious books' were Acts of Paul, the Shepard of Hamas, Barnabas, Didache, Revelations,

with his list and included some of those disputed books. In 405 AD, Jerome's Latin translation, the Vulgate, followed Athanasius' list and became the Bible of the Roman Catholic Church.

The Bible was the charter of Christianity. It established Christian legitimacy in antiquity, provided its history, narrative, mission, and rituals and was the definitive reference for Christian theology. The Vulgate was the score for the Christ the Messiah Symphony, a duet for Paul and Jesus. The harmonious melody the emperor was conducting was of the victorious theology written by Paul.[614] Paul, the man who never knew Jesus, became the greatest composer of all time, and perhaps the most influential person in human history.

And that symphony would be the only Christian music for over 1100 years.[615] It would be performed in Cathedrals, those soaring spiritual concert halls for kings, queens, and the nobility. It would be played in the humblest back-alley playhouses for the poor and the meek. The Christ the Messiah Symphony was a masterpiece and became the anthem of Western civilization. Everyone knew the melody by heart, repeating it infinitely, reciting it at every ceremonial event, and reading it daily and weekly in the church-theater. Christ the Messiah Symphony and its New Testament score would be the only music to which people listened and danced for centuries in Western civilization.

---

and Hebrews. He labels the Gospels of Peter, Thomas, Matthias, and the Acts of Andrew and John, as 'dissident from true orthodoxy.' The winners of course deciding orthodoxy.

[614] *A History of Christianity*, Paul Johnson (Simon & Schuster a Touchstone Book, 1995) p. 89

[615] There is some debate if the "final list" was approved at the Council in 397 or in 419, and it would only be at the Council of Trent in 1546 the "Bible" became officially and finally determined, at least for the Roman Catholic Church under Constantine. In 1603, the King James Version was released and became the standard of the Protestant faiths.

The wealth of the Roman Empire would power Christianity's growth, and the power of the Roman Empire would enforce the Christian rules. Constantine exempted the clergy from most public burdens, provided them with salaries from municipal and imperial treasuries, made significant contributions in money and grain, and granted the right of legacy so that the wealthy could convey their property to the Church. Within a few decades, the Church would own 10% of all the land in the Roman Empire! "The ecclesiastical revenue was vested to the bishops,"[616] as enormous treasures of money, silver and gold, as well as houses and property, entered the purse of the Church. Yes, some found its way to the poor, sick, widows, orphans, and elderly, but it also brought extravagance, luxury, sloth, and moral decay to those who ran the Christian Church. None of this happened overnight, but Constantine opened the gates, and the money just kept flowing in.

The standard Christian narrative tells of Constantine's miraculous come-to-Jesus conversion at Milvian Bridge, and forever after, he is the implement of God and champion of Christianity. Like the Assyrians in the book of Isaiah, Constantine is now the "rod of God's anger" as he presages anti-Semitism across the ages: "Let us then have nothing in common with the detestable Jewish crowd."[617]

Constantine was the godfather of Christianity, in both the religious and Hollywood sense, as he tended to both his pagan and Christian flocks. Constantine showered Christianity with money and favors, but only 15% of the Roman Empire was

---

[616] *History of the Christian Church (The Complete Eight Volumes in One)* Philip Schaff (2014) Kindle, beginning at loc 24833 Chapter III, "Alliance of the Church and State and Its Influence on Public Morals and Religion" details in depth the impact of Constantine's favors to the Church. In Chapter III, Section 14, "The Rights and Privileges of the Church, Secular Advantages" contains the specifics of this paragraph.

[617] *Eusebius: Life of Constantine (Clarendon Ancient History Series)* translated by Averil Cameron and Stuart G. Hall (Clarendon Press, 1999) Book 3, Chapter 18. This translation from http://www.newadvent.org/fathers/25023.htm

Christian at the beginning of his reign.[618] He was the classic politician talking out of both sides of mouth as he reveled Eusebius and others with tales of Christian piety one week and presided over a pagan ritual the next. Each side only recalled what was told to them. If he had any Christian charity, it seldom was shown. Here was a man who executed his wife and son. Constantine did things out of his selfish needs, personally and politically. Constantine solved his uppermost political need of unity in the Roman Empire by laying the cornerstone of the Christian Church, but he laid it in sands of soft theology.

---

[618] *The Rise of Christianity: How the Obscure, Marginal Jesus Movement Became the Dominant Religious Force in the Western World in a Few Centuries, Rodney Stark* (Harper Collins, 1997) p. 13

# Chapter Fourteen – The Three Amigos

The year after Nicaea, Constantine executed his wife and son in a swirl of sexual innuendo. Constantine's mother, Helena, needed to get out of town and headed to Palestine.[619] Paganism and idolatry had forever revolved around relics, and Helena was about to merge the pagan practice of relics into Christianity. Helena was one of the greatest sleuths of all times, even greater than Indiana Jones or Tom Hanks. Either that, or a sucker for con men and forgeries. On her trip, she located the supposed sites of Jesus' birth in Bethlehem, his death on Golgotha, the cave of his burial, and the spot of his ascension on the Mount of Olives! She consecrated the sites by building churches over each.[620]

Relics are items supposedly endowed with special power from the gods that perform miracles, or at least induce better outcomes. "In an age when everyone took all sorts of miraculous powers for granted," relics were believed to carry a hodgepodge of special powers.[621] But in Helena's case, the miracle was that,

---

[619] When Jesus Became God: The Struggle to Define Christianity during the Last Days of Rome, Richard E. Rubenstein (Harcourt, 1999) p. 92

[620] *A New History of Early Christianity*, Charles Freeman (Yale University Press 2009) pp. 235-236

[621] *A History of Christian Theology: An Introduction*, William C. Placher (Westminster Press, 1983) p. 129

after 300 years, she found the cross, the true cross on which Jesus had been hung, and on it still remained the paper, the very paper on which Pontius Pilate had proclaimed Jesus "King of the Jews." Amazing—just amazing! But that's not all. In the most exciting and unbelievable archeological find ever, Helena found the nails, the very nails that had pierced Jesus' body and pinned him on the cross! She kept them as souvenirs and had one made into a bit for her son's horse and the other a trinket for his diadem.[622] All to fulfill the scriptures: *In that day there shall be upon the bridle of every horse Holiness to the Lord Almighty* (Zec. 14:20, LXX). The saints be praised!

Over the next sixty years, many other relics miraculously appeared. The body of St. Stephen, the head of John the Baptist, the chair of St. Peter, the chains of St. Paul, the column to which Jesus was chained while being scourged.[623] There is no telling what might turn up when true piety, or lots of money, is involved.

Ambrose, the bishop of Milan, was a superstitious guy, and an innovative marketer of Christianity. He filled his daily services by dramatizing them with spectacular vestments, antiphonal singing, and professional choirs. He was quick to see the possibilities in relics, martyrs, and saints. He systemized the practice in his Basilica and the surrounding churches. The cult of relics would become one of the most influential practices in the history of Christianity.[624]

In the 4th and 5th centuries, the credulity of Christians is staggering. Things appeared from everywhere: the bones of the prophet Samuel and the Patriarch Jacob from dozens of centuries earlier, the very ax Noah had used to hew the Ark, the twelve

---

[622] *A History of Christianity*, Paul Johnson (Simon & Schuster a Touchstone Book, 1995) p. 106

[623] *A History of Christianity*, Paul Johnson (Simon & Schuster a Touchstone Book, 1995) p. 106

[624] *A New History of Early Christianity* Charles Freeman (Yale University Press 2009) p. 214

baskets used by the Apostles in the feeding of the 5000, the robe Jesus' mother Mary had worn when she was assumed into Heaven, the arm of Stephen the first martyr, and an icon of Mary herself, painted by the writer of the Gospel of Luke! [625] And the list is long. The gullibility of Christians was not just the acceptance of the reality of these items, but the further belief in their magical properties.

Not all were ready to accept even the idea of relics. Many railed against the practice including Basil the Bishop of Caesarea who wrote, "As the sun does not need the lamplight, so also the church of the congregation can do without the remains of the martyrs. It is sufficient to venerate the name of Christ."[626] But they could not overcome the support of relics by St. Augustine. In his *City of God,* Book XXII, Chapter 8, titled, "Of Miracles Which Were Wrought that the World Might Believe in Christ, and Which Have Not Ceased Since the World Believed," Augustine recounts miracle after miracle which he has witnessed, including the restoration of sight to a blind person with the relics of St. Stephen. The Roman Empire converted to Christianity but retained many of its polytheistic and pagan practices and beliefs.[627]

While relics have mostly faded as superstitious mumbo jumbo, medallions—their cousins in superstition—remain.[628] When growing up in Fort Wayne in the early 1960s, all of my Catholic friends had St. Christopher medallions hanging from the rearview mirrors of their cars. This was to protect them from car

---

[625] *Holy Bones, Holy Dust* Charles Freeman (Yale University Press 2011) These examples are from chapters 4 and 5.

[626] *Holy Bones, Holy Dust* Charles Freeman (Yale University Press 2011) Kindle Loc 736

[627] *Holy Bones, Holy Dust* Charles Freeman (Yale University Press 2011) Kindle Loc 723

[628] For a humorous take on relics see the first few minutes of the BBC sitcom Blackadder, here: https://www.youtube.com/watch?v=pt-VzpLNNHM&feature=youtu.be&t=20m24s

accidents or girls getting pregnant or something.[629] And they are still sold by the thousands on Amazon and eBay today.

Despite all that apparent unity with the Nicene Creed, the nagging question of Jesus' divinity and monotheism just would not go away. How could it with Saints and relics added to the mix? If you are going to have the One God, the Almighty Ruler of All, and you had a Father, a Son, Christ The Holy Spirit,[630] then all those Saints and the miracles of their relics— how did they all fit with the idea of One God? Monotheism, One God and One God only, was the unique and compelling claim of Judaism that was now attached to Christianity. But if Christianity now had multiple Gods, then how many gods and levels of gods might there be? There might be one "Very God of Very God," but then how many Demi God of Demi Gods were there?[631] Jesus, the Holy Ghost, Angels, saints, demons, etc.? If you allowed this, old fashion polytheistic paganism and Christianity were starting to look alike, just change the names of the gods, and the words of the prayers and who could tell the difference? No one wanted to accept that.

At Nicaea, the unity of the vote was not the unity of men's minds. In American Presidential elections, delegates of the party get together, argue, and fight over a platform. Compromises are made, the party proclaims unity, and they unanimously adopt the platform. Once the candidates get back home, they disregard the platform and do and say whatever they deem necessary to stay in office. It was the same for the Nicene Creed. Once the bishops got back home, they disregarded the platform of the Nicene Creed. It was a unifying document, only if the emperor was watching over everyone. And when he wasn't, the debate quickly

---

[629] At least this was the joke among my Catholic peers in the early 1960's.

[630] As a total aside, what if they had said the Holy Spirit was Asherah, Gods wife or consort in the Old Testament?

[631] A common translation of a section of the Nicene Creed is "Begotten of his Father before all worlds, God of God, Light of Light, Very God of Very God; "

started afresh. Even Constantine came to realize that the *homoousios* formula he foisted on the Council of Nicaea effectively blocked the path to Christian unity. In the last years of his reign, he attempted to correct this, going so far as to pardon Arius.[632] In essence, this is what Pope Francis did in September of 2017.

But a pardon still could not solve the unsolvable. Constantine died, unable to be the equal of Alexander the Great. The Gordian knot of Jesus' deity was still blocking the path to Christian unity.

Christianity would grow enormously in the following decades under the beneficence of Constantine's legacy, as his sons repeated the fights of the father in another season of "Who Wants to be Emperor?" The ultimate winner, Constantius II, tried to repeat his father's approach by holding Church councils. He ended up holding nine of them during his reign: Sirmium in 351, Arles in 353, Beziers in 353, Milan in 355, Sirmium again in 357 and 358, and the biggest, most widely attended council in Rimini-Seleucia in 359, and finally Constantinople in 360.[633] All of these were held to heal the rifts that now divided a Christianity supposedly unified by the Nicene Creed. Some of the councils produced modifications to prior creeds, but to no avail. They only succeeded in widening and hardening the divide and coalescing it along the lines of the eastern and western parts of the Roman Empire.[634]

Lots of discussions, lots of politics, and yes, riots ensued as the passions of the priests poured into the streets; "Those who were supposed to be pastors cast off the restraining influence of the fear of God and quarreled heatedly with each other engaged

---

[632] *Christianity: The First Three Thousand Years,* Diarmaid MacClulloch (Viking, 2010) p. 214

[633] When Jesus Became God: The Struggle to Define Christianity during the Last Days of Rome, Richard E. Rubenstein (Harcourt, 1999) p. 182

[634] *The Search for the Christian Doctrine of God* R.C.P. Hanson (Baker Academic 2005) p. 306

solely in the swelling disputes threats envy and mutual hostility and hate."[635] It is difficult to overstate the extremes of Christian absurdity from this time. Christians were the ISIS of the 4th century. Here is a minor example: A Christian group in North Africa called the Circumcellions, believed that scriptures prevented them from using a sword, so "they beat to death those who differed from their theological opinions with massive clubs."[636] In such an environment, neither politics nor theology could solve the central problem. Making Jesus a God was a very tough problem.

Flavius Julius Valens became emperor in 364. He was openly Arian, and a fanatical opponent of the Nicene crowd,[637] but he had a policy of toleration. He permitted debate but not disturbances. He was not about to have a repeat of the Donatist wars in North Africa. Valens, by enforcing civility, created the space for Arians and the Nicene believers to attempt to find a solution to their differences in how Jesus could be God.[638]

Just north of Tarsus, where Paul was born, is the area in Turkey called Cappadocia. It is the area where Paul had done much of his preaching, and appropriately, the area where the solution to the Jesus-and-God debate would originate. My friend Bruce Patterson and I had often debated matters of religion in high school, but nothing like the debates of Basil and Gregory of Nyssa and their friend Gregory of Nazianzus. Basil and the two Gregories were clearly a lot smarter.

The Cappadocian theory—three Gods in One, known as the Triune God—could resolve the bitter and convoluted debates that

---

[635] *Eusebius: The Church History,* translation by Paul L. Maier (Kregel, 1999) p. 260

[636] *History of European Morals from Augustus to Charlemagne* William Leckey (Longmen Green & Co 1913 Vol II) p. 4,1 which can be seen here: https://archive.org/stream/historyofeuropea0leckuoft#page/40/mode/2up/search/circumcelliones

[637] *The Search for the Christian Doctrine of God* R.C.P. Hanson (Baker Academic 2005) p. 582

[638] *When Jesus Became God: The Struggle to Define Christianity during the Last Days of Rome,* Richard E. Rubenstein (Harcourt, 1999) pp. 203-204

continued after Nicaea. If alive today, the Cappadocians would have been teaching law at Harvard. Their solution involved Plato, and the linguistic distinctions between Latin and Greek words such as *hypostasei, ousia, personae, hypostasis, substancia,* and, of course, the familiar *homoousios* and *homoiousios*. Indeed, the solution "depended so much on particular words that one could hardly express it in any language but Greek."[639] It may have all sounded like Greek, but Greek or not, Christianity and the Roman Empire needed a solution, and the Cappadocians provided one. Praise Father, Son, and Holy Ghost!

It's a great idea they came up with, but where is the biblical support? "Behind its own verbal smokescreen, the substantive judgment on which it rests is nowhere to be found."[640] That is actually a comment on Roe v. Wade but could be a comment on the Cappadocian explanation. Both provided widely accepted solutions to large, contentious debates, but neither have obvious support in their foundations: the U.S. Constitution and the Bible. In the case of the Triune God, there is no biblical support.[641] Wait, you might say, "What about, *For there are three that bear record in heaven, the Father, the Word, and the Holy Ghost: and these three are one?* (1 John 5:7). See, the Bible spells the Trinity out clearly!" Except this is a great example of how things were added to the Bible to support an accepted belief.

Known to scholars as the "Johannine Comma," the verse obviously justifies the doctrine of the Trinity and is the only direct reference to the Trinity in the Bible.[642] However the passage is not found in the very oldest known versions of

---

[639] *A History of Christian Theology: An Introduction,* William C. Placher (Westminster Press, 1983) pp. 74

[640] "The Supreme Court, 1972 Term–Foreword: Toward a Model of Roles in the Due Process of Life and Law," Laurence H. Tribe, 87 *Harvard Law Review* 1, 7 (1973).

[641] There are numerous references and allusions to the Father Son and Holy Ghost, such as Matthew 28:19, but only one direct reference to their being one God.

[642] There are several indirect passages such as Matthew 28:19, but 1 John 5:7-8 is the only direct support.

Vulgate, nor most Greek versions, leading to the conclusion that this passage was added to the Bible later. This important discrepancy was known centuries ago and has been argued over ever since. Such notaries as Isaac Newton and John Calvin were commenting on this important addition in their times. The overwhelming consensus of Bible scholars is that the 1 John 5:7 was added to the text. Therefore, it has been removed from many of the more recent Bible translations, including the 1979 Catholic Church's official Nova Vulgata (New Vulgate) while it remains in the New King James Version and other English versions.[643]

Without a Trinity, Christianity reverts to three Gods and is indistinguishable from polytheism. Without definitive biblical support for a Trinity, Christianity is not built on the rock of St. Peter, but on the malleable clay of the human mind. How did the Cappadocian theory of the Trinity become the bedrock of all Christian faith without solid biblical support?

The internal division and turmoil within Christianity came against the backdrop of the battles on the borders. "Barbarians" is the term used to include the Goths, Visigoths, Ostrogoths, Scots, Picts, Saxons, Vandals, Franks and others who were invading the Roman Empire. Which ones were attacking at any

---

[643] Note the difference between the New International Version, which represents the oldest manuscripts, and the New King James Version, which although a recent translation, retains this later insertion:

7 For there are three that testify: 8 the Spirit, the water and the blood; and the three are in agreement. (NIV)

7 For there are three that bear witness in heaven: The Father, the Word, and the Holy Spirit; and these three are one. 8 And there are three that bear witness on earth: [b] the Spirit, the water, and the blood; and these three agree as one. (NKJV) That footnote [b] has a disclaimer that major source texts "omit the words from in heaven (verse 7) through on earth (verse 8). Only four or five very late manuscripts contain these words in Greek." But how many people read the footnotes? My Thanks to Kristen Stieffel who pointed to the different translations in the NKJV and NIV versions. I was originally made aware of the Johannine Comma in *An Introduction to the New Testament*, Raymond E. Brown, First edition (Yale University Press, 2010) p. 388 n14. Here is a starting point for more information. https://en.wikipedia.org/wiki/Comma_Johanneum

moment is immaterial. They all followed Durant's formula and invaded as they themselves were pressured by the Huns from the plains beyond the steppes.[644] Emperors Julian, Jovian, Valentinian I, Valens, Gratian, and Valentinian II had limited successes at keeping them out. In August of 378, emperor Valens was killed while fighting the Visigoths in the worst defeat ever of the Roman army.[645] The Roman Empire was in need of new strong leadership.

By the age of 31, the Spanish General Theodosius had shown himself to be a brilliant general, fighting the invaders in Britain and what today is Bulgaria.[646] On January 19, 379, Theodosius replaced Valens as the emperor of the Eastern Empire, [647] and after a few sporadic civil wars, he became the last emperor of all the Roman Empire.

Theodosius was a tested, battle-hardened military commander. Now, he would be tested ruling Roman civilians, and dealing with the Christian divide. He spoke Latin and likely had little appreciation for the problem of the deity of Jesus in Greek.[648] Or perhaps he thought, like Constantine, that this was a silly question for childish minds. We know little of his religious background or how he eventually came to his decisions but decide he did. Theodosius seized the Cappadocian sledgehammer and pounded the Gordian knot of the Father, Son, and Holy Ghost into the unity of the Trinity. Like a banner in battle, he thrusted the Trinity high and commanded its belief. The Edict

---

[644] *When Jesus Became God: The Struggle to Define Christianity during the Last Days of Rome*, Richard E. Rubenstein (Harcourt, 1999) p. 213

[645] *When Jesus Became God: The Struggle to Define Christianity during the Last Days of Rome,* Richard E. Rubenstein (Harcourt, 1999) p. 217

[646] The Age of Faith (The Story of Civilization, Volume 4) Will Durant (MJF Books, 1980) p. 25

[647] *The Search for the Christian Doctrine of God* R.C.P. Hanson (Baker Academic 2005) p. 804

[648] *A New History of Early Christianity* Charles Freeman (Yale University Press 2009) p. 219

Cunctos Populus was signed into law on February 27, 380:[649] It stated:

> It is our desire that all the various nations...believe in the one deity of the Father, the Son and the Holy Spirit, in equal majesty and in a holy Trinity.

It went on to officially define the Catholic Church: "We authorize the followers of this law to assume the title of Catholic Christians."

And for those who did not accept this belief, "They are foolish madmen...with the ignominious name of heretics" who will suffer "divine condemnation and...the punishment of our authority which...we shall decide to inflict."[650]

Believe this or else! Theodosius, then went off to fight the Goths.

Successful in battle again, Theodosius returned to his capital on November 24, 380. He immediately went to the bishop of Constantinople and asked if he accepted the Triune God. No, replied Bishop Demophilus. "Then you're fired," said Theodosius. He then installed none other than Gregory of Nazianzus, one of the Cappadocian authors of the Triune God, as the new bishop of Constantinople. In short order, he did the same in Antioch and Alexandria, putting bishops in those cities who would support his policy: his theology of the Trinity. To make sure everything was clear, 45 days later, on January 10th of 381, Theodosius sent out the decree "Nullis haereticis" (No Heretics) which prohibited anyone not accepting the Triune God from worshipping in any church or living inside any city walls.[651]

---

[649] *The Search for the Christian Doctrine of God* R.C.P. Hanson (Baker Academic 2005) p. 804

[650] *Documents of the Christian Church* Henry Bettenson (Oxford University Press 1967) p22

[651] *The Search for the Christian Doctrine of God* R.C.P. Hanson (Baker Academic 2005) p. 306 p. 804

Now that everyone had read the memo, Theodosius called a council so that the Church could bless what he had already done. The Council of Constantinople was held in May, June, and July of 381 AD. Theodosius welcomed the bishops in his throne room of the Imperial Palace but did not participate in any of the meetings. The entire town was following the debates. "If you ask for change, the man launches into a theological discussion about *begotten* and *unbegotten*; if you inquire about the price of bread, the answer is given that the Father is greater and the Son subordinate; if you remark that the bath is nice, the man pronounces that the Son is from non-existence." [652]

The bakers, bankers, and bath attendants may have had a better discussion than the bishops inside. The head of the Council, the recently installed bishop of Constantinople, Gregory of Nazianzus, reported that the pious bishops of the Catholic Church,

"squawked in every direction, a flock of jackdaws combining together a rabble of adolescents, a gang of youths, a whirlwind raising dust under the pressure of air currents, people to whom nobody who was mature, either in the fear of God or in years, would pay any attention, they sputter confused stuff or like wasps rush directly at whatever is in front of their faces."

He became so frustrated that he resigned, both from the council and as the bishop. [653]

The bishops then picked a man by the name of Nektarios to replace Gregory. It was the equivalent of the College of Cardinals

---

[652] *The Search for the Christian Doctrine of God* R.C.P. Hanson (Baker Academic 2005) p. 806

[653] *The Search for the Christian Doctrine of God* R.C.P. Hanson (Baker Academic 2005) p. 809

picking the mayor of Rome as a Pope, "Few people can have been less qualified for greatness."[654] But didn't Jesus say, *"The last shall be first"* (Matt. 20:16)? The council did little; they ousted some specific bishops and passed a canon giving the bishop of Constantinople precedence over the bishops of Antioch and Alexandria. They reaffirmed the Nicene Creed in general terms. Decades later, it will be said that the Council of Constantinople modified the Nicene Creed, but there is no copy, nor did any writers make mention of a modified Nicene Creed for the next seventy years.[655] They did affirm the new laws of Theodosius. In July of 381, at the end of the council, Theodosius did the heavy work by issuing "Episcopis tradi." [656] The edict opened with:

> We now order that all churches be handed over to the bishops who profess Father, Son, and Holy Spirit of a single majesty, of the same glory, of one splendor who established no difference by sacrilegious separation, but who affirm the order of the Trinity by recognizing the Persons and uniting the Godhead.[657]

Christians had been ordered to believe in the Triune God, and now Theodosius' law codified the Triune God—the Father, Son, and Holy Ghost—as the only belief of the Christian Church.

For 350 years, the followers of Jesus had told stories, written, argued, fought, and died attempting to make sense of Jesus' existence. A myriad of explanations had been offered, blending elements of the ancient beliefs of Plato, Judaism, and Zoroastrianism. Others merged voices from dreams, while others added pure

---

[654]*The Search for the Christian Doctrine of God* R.C.P. Hanson (Baker Academic 2005) p. 811

[655]*The Search for the Christian Doctrine of God* R.C.P. Hanson (Baker Academic 2005) p. 812

[656] *The Search for the Christian Doctrine of God* R.C.P. Hanson (Baker Academic 2005) p. 820

[657] When Jesus Became God: The Struggle to Define Christianity during the Last Days of Rome, Richard E. Rubenstein (Harcourt, 1999) p. 223

and violent passions. Religious politics, red in tooth and claw had evolved the contradicting species of beliefs until only a handful survived. The written texts, including the Bible, were at best convoluted guides which added conflict instead of clarity. The Roman emperors had cried out in frustration to the churches of Jesus, "Tell us what your religion is." But the priests, bishops, theologians, and the people themselves had no answer; they could only offer a chaotic growl.

Finally, a Roman emperor, a Spanish military general, did what generals do: he made the decisions! In less than 18 months, he ordered belief in the Trinity, defined the Catholic Church as believers in the Trinity, declared all others as heretics, and enacted laws allowing only believers in the Trinity to be priests, bishops, and clerics. He even required clerics to have a certificate of Triune orthodoxy before they could preach![658] The Roman emperor Theodosius created the Christianity of Western civilization that the world would know until this day! Every Sunday, around the world, Christians act in accordance with the commands of the Roman Emperor Theodosius when they proclaim the Trinity—Father, Son, and Holy Ghost. Amen![659]

The movie *Monty Python and the Holy Grail* parodies this moment when the monk offers instructions for the Holy Hand Grenade:

> First, thou shalt take out the Holy Pin, then shalt thou count to three—no more, no less. Three shalt be the number thou shalt count, and the number of the counting

---

[658] *A New History of Early Christianity* Charles Freeman (Yale University Press 2009) pp 251-252

[659] Among large mainstream denominations in the United States, only Latter-day Saints (Mormons) and Jehovah's Witnesses and Christian Scientists reject the doctrine of the Trinity.
https://en.wikipedia.org/wiki/Nontrinitarianism#Christian_groups_with_nontrinitarian_positions

shalt be three. Four shalt thou not count nor either count thou two, excepting that thou then proceed to three. Five is right out.[660]

I have painted this picture of the deification of Jesus as simple and straightforward. It was not. The twists and turns of theology and politics, of riots and war, conjecture and speculation, are immensely complex. What is considered by many as the definitive book on the issue, is the 1988 book *The Search for the Christian Doctrine of God* by Richard Hanson. Cited frequently in this section, Hanson takes 900 pages to cover every twist and turn of the search for the role of Jesus and his becoming a God. Hanson tells of a bishop who accuses the emperor Constantius, of violating Church canon. Constantius replies, "But what I wish, that must be regarded as the canon." Hanson concludes, "The will of the Emperor was the final authority."[661] Ironic; one might think that the will of God was the final authority. But God remained absent and silent.

Now, some of you, I am sure, are saying, "Yes, thank God for Constantine and Theodosius, for getting to the truth and for the miracle of God sending it to them." The doxology, *"In the name of the Father and of the Son and of the Holy Spirit,"* is said several times at almost every Christian church service. But like the Johannine Comma, the words were added to Matthew 28:19 centuries later to confirm the Trinity and were not said by Jesus.[662] The next time you hear the Doxology, instead of adding

---

[660] *Jesus Wars: How Four Patriarchs, Three Queens, and Two Emperors Decided What Christians Would Believe for the Next 1,500 Years*, John Philip Jenkins (Harper One, 2010) p. 64

[661] *The Search for the Christian Doctrine of God* R.C.P. Hanson (Baker Academic 2005) p. 849

[662] The issue has been widely debated. The original words were '*Go ye and make disciples of all nations in my name.* as found in Eusebius Church History, Book 3, Chapter 5, Section 2, and Oration of Eusebius, Chapter 16, Section 8. While a discussion of this is beyond the scope of this book Pope Benedict the XVI summed

your "Amen," ask yourself why the almighty ruler of the universe needed 350 years and a Roman sheriff to define and enforce the message of the Trinity. Or, more profoundly, ask yourself if a Triune God is the right complex theological answer to all existence. Yes, yes, I know, "It's a mystery!" When Jesus said, *"Unto you it is given to know the mystery of the kingdom of God"* (Mark 4:11) he should have said "Unto Theodosius it will be given to know the mystery of the kingdom of God!"

For 350 years, Christian attempts to deify Jesus collapsed at the anathema of polytheism. Three hundred and fifty years of Christian prayers for Heavenly certainty only brought three hundred and fifty years of earthly calamity. The Roman emperor Theodosius, like a sheriff from a Western movie, fired his pistol in the air and shouted, "Stop the fighting, the Trinity is what Christianity will believe!" And Christianity has believed it ever since.

---

up the conclusion of most Bible scholars "The basic form of our (Matthew 28:19 Trinitarian) profession of faith took shape during the course of the second and third centuries in connection with the ceremony of baptism. So far as its place of origin is concerned, the text (Matt. 28:19) came from the city of Rome." "Introduction to Christianity" Ignatius Press 2004 Kindle 928 and This has been the position of Bible scholars for a long time the International Standard Bible Encyclopedia says "Matthew 28:19 in particular only canonizes a later ecclesiastical situation, that its universalism is contrary to the facts of early Christian history, and its Trinitarian formula (is) foreign to the mouth of Jesus." Howard Severance 1915 Vol. 4, page 2637

# Chapter Fifteen – The Control of Bodies and Souls

A fter the fights over the basic theology for the next life were settled, Christianity could now fight over the theology for living in this life. By late in the 4<sup>th</sup> century Christianity had become the majority and official religion of the Romans, but substantial percentages were still Pagans, and large numbers of Jews remained within the Empire. And with their newly developed political power and organization Christians could now deal with Jews, Pagans and the daily lives of Christians. Christian minds that had focused their creative energies on solutions for entrance into the next life, could now focus their minds on solutions for bodies and souls in this life. Would that prove as messy as the last four centuries?

In 390 CE, a popular race car driver, a charioteer, was arrested for homosexual rape in Thessalonica. Then, as now, celebrities are judged by a different set of standards. Riots ensued for his release. The imperial governor, Botheric, refused, and a mob tore his body apart and paraded his limbs through the streets. No Roman emperor could tolerate such insurrection. Theodosius sent a ruthless commander, Flavius Rufinus, to punish the people of Thessalonica. Rufinus rounded up 7,000 men, women, and children and slaughtered them in the arena.[663] For this deed, the Bishop of Milan Ambrose excommunicated Theodosius until he did penance. Eventually, Theodosius relented. In a public display of humility, stripped of his royal attire, Theodosius entered the Cathedral and begged forgiveness.[664] Less than 10 years after the Roman emperor commanded Christian beliefs, a Christian bishop was commanding the Roman emperor.

Nothing could now stop the previously persecuted Christians from unleashing their pent-up aggression and persecuting the pagans. And persecute them they did! Just as ISIS and Al-Qaeda destroyed ancient buildings and statues in our times, Christian monks destroyed everything pagan as they were cheered on by St. Augustine. "That all superstition of pagans and heathens should be annihilated is what God wants, God commands, God proclaims!"[665] "The black-robed tribe who hasten to attack the (pagan) temples with sticks and stone and bars of iron . . . utter desolation follows, with the stripping of the roofs, demolition of the walls, the tearing down of statues."[666] The amount of Christian violence in this period though has been ignored by historians. [667] No loving image of Jesus would preside over the ruthless violent vengeful end of Paganism. A century earlier Christians reverted to paganism for fear of property and life, now pagan opted for Christianity out of the same fear. Paganism was near its end.

---

[663] The Age of Faith (The Story of Civilization, Volume 4) Will Durant (MJF Books, 1980) pp. 25-26

[664] *A New History of Early Christianity* Charles Freeman (Yale University Press 2009) p. 256

[665] *The Darkening Age: The Christian Destruction of the Classical World* Catherine Nixey (Pan MacMillan 2017) Kindle location 139 The entire book covers in detail the massive and savage Christian destruction of books, art, temples and people.

[666] *A New History of Early Christianity* Charles Freeman (Yale University Press 2009) p. 255

[667] *A.D. 381: Heretics, Pagans, and the Christian State* Charles Freeman (Overlook Press, Peter Maier Publishers, Inc. 2009) Kindle edition loc 1387

Over the next few decades Christians would kill or force conversion on any remaining pagans and destroy a thousand years of pagan art and culture. [668] Christianity saw this as an heroic act of righteousness.

"… if good and holy men never inflict persecution upon any one, but only suffer it, whose words they think that those are in the psalm where we read, "I have pursued mine enemies, and overtaken them; neither did I turn again till they were consumed?" If, therefore, we wish either to declare or to recognize the truth, there is a persecution of unrighteousness, which the impious inflict upon the Church of Christ; and there is a righteous persecution, which the Church of Christ inflicts upon the impious." [669]All this was done "in the spirit of love." [670] [671]

Christianity exhibited no spirit of love towards the Jews. Relations with the Jews had been souring ever since the end of the Jewish–Roman War. And while there was little biblical support for the new theology of the Trinity, there was much biblical support for dealing with the Jews. The Gospel of John is well understood for its anti-Jewish tone. In the Gospel Jesus' claims of the Jews:

*Ye are of your father the devil, and the lusts of your father ye will do. He was a murderer from the beginning, and abode not in the truth, because there is no truth in him.*

---

[668] Dozens of stories relating the wanton cruelty visited by Christians on pagans and the destruction of pagan culture can be found *The Darkening Age: The Christian Destruction of the Classical World* by Catherine Nixey (Pan MacMillan, 2017) and *A.D. 381: Heretics, Pagans, and the Christian State* Charles Freeman (Overlook Press, Peter Maier Publishers, Inc. 2009)

[669] St. Augustine's words echo today in the Islamic politics as directed towards "the impious West".

[670] St. Augustine Letter 185 1:11 St. Augustine to Boniface

[671] This was not the real damage Christianity did to civilization, destroying irreplaceable centuries of art architecture and literature, the real damage was done with the destruction of thought and learning by the closing of all the study of the Greek and Latin classics.

*When he speaketh a lie, he speaketh of his own: for he is*
*a liar, and the father of it.* (John 8:44)

Many Christians agreed with this, and antisemitism became the Church policy in Christianity.[672]

Many Christians followed the anti-Jewish preaching of the Gospels and often took action. In the city of Callinicum in 388 AD. a mob destroyed a Jewish synagogue. Theodosius, from his capital in Milan, ordered the Christian bishop of the Callinicum to rebuild it. Ambrose, the bishop of Milan, berated the emperor, saying that there should be no building where Christ is denied, and the bishop there should not have to go against his conscious by rebuilding the synagogue.[673,674] The emperor backed down, sending a bad signal that violence against Jews would now be tolerated. The message was received and began a long wave of attacks on Jewish synagogues around the Empire [675] as antisemitism became the creed of Christianity across the centuries.

Bishop John Chrysostom, at the time of Theodosius, preached shocking tasteless polemics against the Jews in Antioch.[676] Martin Luther would write his "The Jews & Their Lies" [677]in 1543 as well as preach many other hateful sermons

---

[672] *The Jews in the Time of Jesus: An Introduction*, Stephen M. Wylen (Paulist Press, 1996) pp. 195-196

[673] *When Jesus Became God: The Struggle to Define Christianity during the Last Days of Rome*, Richard E. Rubenstein (Harcourt, 1999) p. 225 and *A New History of Early Christianity*, Charles Freeman (Yale University Press 2009) p. 255

[674] Just as a baker in our time should not have to go against his conscience in baking cakes, or a company being forced to provide birth control?

[675] When Jesus Became God: The Struggle to Define Christianity during the Last Days of Rome, Richard E. Rubenstein (Harcourt, 1999) p. 226

[676] *A New History of Early Christianity*, Charles Freeman (Yale University Press 2009) p. 265

[677] "From Luther's Works", Volume 47: The Christian in Society IV (Fortress Press 1971) pp 268-293.

against the Jews.[678] Antisemitism was the church policy in Christianity that carried into the 20th century.[679] Adolf Hitler was unquestionably following centuries of Christian beliefs about Jews. "Hence today I believe that I am acting in accordance with the will of the Almighty Creator: by defending myself against the Jew, I am fighting for the work of the Lord." [680] Only after seeing Hitler's handiworks in Christian theology, have Christians shirked from the anti-Semitism of their Gospels.

The Roman pagan religion "did not provide a moral handbook for everyday life. They issued no commandments or catechisms or creeds to guide the souls of the uncertain between birth and death."[681] Over centuries though, the routine of life in the Roman Empire had settled around the rules and practices of the pagan gods. It was one thing for Christians to replace pagan statues with Christian relics, or to destroy pagan temples and replace them with Christian churches. It was another to evolve and adapt a new way of life under Jesus, and the newly instituted God of the Trinity. The premise of Christianity had been that Jesus was returning to rule on Earth; tomorrow, next week, next year, or certainly before the death of the apostles and Paul, hence rules for daily life were of little consequence. That premise had proven false; no Jesus had returned, and Christianity needed to tell believers how to live their lives while the wait for Jesus dragged on.

---

[678] In 1991 after the fall of the Berlin Wall my wife and I traveled to Wittenberg which at the time was exhibiting Luther's teachings on anti-Semitism in the Stadtkirche (Town Church). Posted were many of the hateful anti-Jewish sermons Luther delivered in that church. On the church's stone façade is a Judensau, a caricature of a Rabbi examining the pig's ass.

[679] *The Jews in the Time of Jesus: An Introduction*, Stephen M. Wylen (Paulist Press, 1996) pp. 195-196

[680] *Mein Kampf*. Ralph Manheim, ed. (Houghton Mifflin. 1998) p. 65 And today while Islam has adopted the Christian position of centuries past, Christianity in the late 20th century abrogated its anti-Semitism and adopted a policy of friendship, even solidarity with the Jews.

[681] *The Darkening Age: The Christian Destruction of the Classical World* Catherine Nixey (Pan MacMillan, 2017) Kindle location 522

Jerome and Augustine living at the time of Theodosius responded to that need. Their writings and correspondence would now tell Christians how to live their daily lives. "They were the greatest pair in a remarkable age."[682]

Jerome was the secretary to the bishop of Rome, Damasus. The Church, made nouveau riche by Roman law, displayed an opulence that dismayed Jerome. He recorded that; "Parchment is died purple, gold is melted into lettering and manuscripts are dressed up in jewels, while Christ lies at the door naked and dying."[683] While some followed the words of Jesus and donated their wealth to the Church, charity, convents, and hospitals, etc., most joined their pagan friends at the parties, theater, games, or races. Jerome was shocked by the lascivious lives led by Christians.

Jerome's outlook on life darkened, and he left Rome and holed up in a cave near Bethlehem for the remaining 34 years of his life. From there, he created the Vulgate, the Latin official Bible of the Catholic Church. But his real influence on Christianity was his correspondence with many of the bishops.

Jerome placed sex at the center of human sin. He spoke of concubines and women who cut their hair short and wore men's clothes; of breasts in "strips of linen" and clothes that "hastily hide what was intentionally revealed"; of priests who, at dawn, visited women for sex before prayers, and he told of his dreams among a bevy of naked women as the fires of lust raged. For Jerome, sex, and the desire for it, were dirty and sinful. "When lust tickles the senses and the soft fire of sensual pleasure sheds over us it pleasing glow, let us immediately break forth and cry, 'The Lord is on my side, I will not fear what the flesh can do to

---

[682] *The Age of Faith* (The Story of Civilization, Volume 4) Will Durant (MJF Books, 1980) p. 55

[683] *A New History of Early Christianity*, Charles Freeman (Yale University Press 2009) p. 276

me.'"[684] But he had a doubt as he rhetorically asked, "Why should I refrain from the food which God made for my enjoyment?"[685] A question Catholic priests have been thinking about ever since.

Augustine was the bishop of Hippo, a city on the Mediterranean about 100 miles west of Tunis, Algeria, and due south of Sardinia. He unquestionably was the most influential theologian in early Christianity.[686] Augustine had no problem with sex while he was young. He spoke passionately of the sweetness of enjoying the body of his lover. He had a mistress and a son. He changed his mind after becoming entranced with the writings of Paul. *For the good that I will to do, I do not do; but the evil I will not to do, that I practice. Now if I do what I will not to do, it is no longer I who do it, but sin that dwells in me* (Rom. 7:19-20, NKJV).[687] Based on this, Augustine saw human souls as pure and good, just trapped in evil bodies.[688] Augustine, like Jerome, concluded that our sexual desire was the origin of our evil[689] and Sex was the Original Sin.[690]

Augustine was clear: Man is motivated by lust "which is in his members"[691] and is incapable of control. Ever since Adam

---

[684] *A New History of Early Christianity*, Charles Freeman (Yale University Press 2009) p. 278

[685] *The Age of Faith (The Story of Civilization, Volume 4)* Will Durant (MJF Books, 1980) pp. 52-53

[686] *A History of Christian Theology: An Introduction,* William C. Placher (Westminster Press, 1983) p. 108

[687] "This concept will come to the fore front of modern society in our times and will be discussed later.

[688] *A History of Christian Theology: An Introduction,* William C. Placher (Westminster Press, 1983) p. 111

[689] *The Age of Faith (The Story of Civilization, Volume 4)* Will Durant (MJF Books, 1980) p. 69

[690] *A New History of Early Christianity*, Charles Freeman (Yale University Press 2009) Charles Freeman Yale University Press 2009 pp. 288-289

[691] From Augustine's "City of God" 14:13 which can be found here http://biblehub.com/library/augustine/anti-pelagian_writings/chapter_11_ix_an_objection_of.htm#1

and Eve, generations have been created through the lust of human bodies.[692] We are all "so incapable of virtue that in the very womb of their mothers they are filled with bygone sins." Sex was bad enough in Augustine's Christianity, but he went even further, saying that "married couples (should) restrain that evil" and not "jump into bed whenever they like, whenever they felt stirred by desire."[693] Augustine would be aghast at Cialis commercials.

Not all Christians agreed with the concept of Original Sin. Julian, a bishop from Italy led the opposition, with a group called Pelagians.[694]  Julian retorted,

> 'Tiny babies,' you say, 'are not weighed down by their own sin, but they are burdened with the sin of another.' Tell me then, tell me who is this person who inflicts punishment on an innocent creature? You answer God, God you say…you have come so far from religious feeling, from civilized thinking, so far indeed from mere common sense, in that you think the Lord God is capable of committing a crime against justice; such is hardly conceivable among Barbarians."[695]

But there was no common sense in the Christian Church and the case became a football. First, two different synods declared Pelagians orthodox, and heretic. So, the case was appealed to Pope Innocent I, who found the Pelagians heretics. When he died, the new bishop of Rome, Zosimus, reversed the decision of Innocent I, and the matter was sent to the Pontiff Maximus,

---

[692] *Adam and Eve and the Serpent: Sex and Politics in Early Christianity* Elaine Pagels (First Vintage Books 1989) Chapter V provides a full description of how Augustine's lust became the original sin and the theology of the Catholic Church.

[693] *A History of Christianity*, Paul Johnson (Simon & Schuster a Touchstone Book, 1995) p. 121

[694] *A New History of Early Christianity*, Charles Freeman (Yale, University Press 2009) p. 295

[695] *A History of Christian Theology: An Introduction, William* C. Placher (Westminster Press, 1983) p. 117

Roman Emperor Honorius, who reversed the nascent Pope. Finally, after 20 years of wrangling, the Council of Ephesus embedded Augustine's concept of Original Sin into Christianity by condemning Pelagians as heretics.[696] The Christian Church had declared little babies as evil, requiring infant baptism as a form of exorcism to remove them from the state of sin. Being baptized "is to wash away sin and expel the evil spirits." That is the belief and practice of most Christians even today.[697] After the year 431 AD the official doctrine of Christianity is that all people are born in a state of sin. And if you were born in the year 430? Church lawyers are still working on that one.

Jerome and Augustine inculcated Christianity with a deeply anti-sexual attitude. Jerome implored virginity and imparted chastity and celibacy on the clergy. Augustine's *Marriage and Concupiscence* dictated Christian Catholic rules against sexual pleasure. Pope Leo III, summarized the position the Christian Church thusly:

> Man has been formed of dust, clay, ashes and a thing far more vile, of filthy sperm. Man has been conceived in the desire of the flesh, in the heat of sensual lust, in the foul stench of wantonness. His evil doings offend God, offend his neighbors, offend himself.... Accordingly, he is destined to become the fuel of everlasting, eternally

---

[696] *The Age of Faith (The Story of Civilization, Volume 4)* Will Durant (MJF Books, 1980) pp. 69-70

[697] In reading the baptismal rites of several Christian Churches, it is a personal observation that until the last half of the 20th century baptismal rites were clearly intended to exorcise evil spirits and forgive sins while by the 21st century the Baptismal rites seem much more focused on forgiving sins often omitting the concept of exorcism of evil spirits.

painful hellfire; the food of the voracious consuming worms.[698]

For Augustine, intercourse for pleasure, even in marriage, was sinful.[699] Hence, birth control itself was sinful, as it implies having intercourse for sinful pleasure. At the advent of the birth control pill in 1965, Pope Paul VI stated that "it is absolutely necessary that the methods and instruments of rendering conception ineffectual...be openly rejected...for in this matter admitting doubt can bring about the gravest danger to the general opinion."[700] Instead, doubt in Christianity's aversion to sex became the gravest danger to the general opinion of Christianity. Paul VI's encyclical "Humanae Vitae," of July 1968, reaffirmed Jerome and Augustine, but was the turning point to the downward spiral of allegiance to Catholicism and Christianity.[701] With every infant baptism, Christianity simply reconfirms the demented concepts of Jerome and Augustine. Oh, make that St. Jerome and St. Augustine.

That sex equals evil was preached from pulpits and permeated the consciousness and guilt in Western civilization for over 1500 years. The toll of torment and pain inflicted on humanity, from Bishops to the laity, by the Christian Church adopting and enforcing the sexual concepts of Jerome and Augustine cannot be imagined. Infant baptism should be a remembrance of this dark aspect of Christian beliefs.

---

[698] *A New History of Early Christianity*, Charles Freeman (Yale University Press 2009) p. 297

[699] "For intercourse of marriage for the sake of having children has no fault; but for the satisfying of sexual passion, even with one's husband or wife by reason of marital fidelity, it has venial fault;" On *Marriage* St. Augustine Chapter 6

[700] November 24th, 1965 message of Paul VI instructing Second Vatican Council from *A History of Christianity*, Paul Johnson (Simon & Schuster a Touchstone Book, 1995) pp. 511

[701] *A History of Christianity*, Paul Johnson (Simon & Schuster a Touchstone Book, 1995) pp. 513

Even in our 21$^{st}$ century, the consequences remain in our almost daily headlines. Like those being tortured for refusing to eat pork in centuries earlier, should we now torture those whose faith alone accepts Christianity's long-held belief that sex is evil? Go to jail or pay for birth control, go to jail or bake cakes for queer marriages.[702] Both of those questions were before the Supreme Court and are directly linked to Christian beliefs on sex originated by Jerome and Augustine.[703] The message that sex is evil was abandoned in the 20$^{th}$ century for sexual abandon in the 21$^{st}$. Jerome and Augustine may have brought tortuous sexual repression to humanity, but will sexual abandon bring tortuous results to humanity? It will be the 22$^{nd}$ century before the preliminary results are in.

Augustine's thought on sex was not his only idea that would have far reaching consequences. He argued, as did Paul, that people had a duty to obey the powers that be. He supported the use of force by the government, and of some forms of torture to bring heretics into line. "What does brotherly love do? Does it, because it fears the short-lived fires of the furnace for the few, abandon all to the eternal fires of hell?" That question was used for centuries to justify violently purging heretics from the Church and was the centerpiece of theology in the Inquisition.[704]

Augustine also used his argument of sexual sin to support Jesus as God. If sex were the sin, then for Jesus to be God he had

---

[702] NPR in "WUSSY Mag Wants Queer Voices Heard Around the World" Miranda Hawkins June 13, 2018 reports that "Queer" is now the preferred word rather than "Gay" in the LGBT community.

[703] Burwell v. Hobby Lobby, 573 U.S. (2014) said that closely held companies can hold Christian beliefs and do not have to pay for employee's birth control, Masterpiece Cakeshop, Ltd. v. Colorado Civil Rights Commission 584 U.S. (2018) remanded back to lower courts in essence whether the meaning of Paul in 1 Cor. 6:9, that men who have sex with men will not inherit the kingdom of God is a religious belief exempt from threats of government torture.

[704] *A New History of Early Christianity*, Charles Freeman (Yale University Press 2009) p. 314

to be free from sin and must have had a virgin birth, untainted by filthy sperm. Augustine then fully embraced the Trinitarian God because it was the only way for Jesus to come sinless from Heaven. Yes, I know it is a circular argument. The Arians believed that Jesus was born a man, hence was sinful, and elevated to his position of God. But how could you have a sinful God?

Jesus, though, was not the first virgin birth. There are several such stories or myths of history, including Buddha.[705] One virgin birth was just 50 years before the birth of Jesus. The future emperor, Caesar Augustus Octavius, was born to Atia in a virgin birth. His father was the Roman god Apollo.[706] One has to wonder how that story influenced the virgin birth of Jesus coming into the Christian narrative.

Time out. Before going ahead into the 5th century, I can see some of you thinking, "Okay, okay, we are all sinners, we get that; but we get some water sprinkled on us, say the magic words of the Nicene Creed, and we get to go to Heaven. Right?" Is it really that simple? Many at the end of the 4th century were asking the same question.

Theodosius died on January 17, 395 AD, and the Roman Empire was separated into two parts, never again to be united. The East was ruled by Theodosius' 18-year-old son Arcadius, and the West by his 11-year-old brother, Honorius. One of Theodosius' key generals, Stilicho, was made regent.[707] Over the next 12 years, Stilicho skillfully held the Barbarians at bay until he was murdered in court intrigue. Alaric, the king of the Visigoths, saw his opening and attacked. In 408 AD, he agreed not to pillage Rome in return for a huge ransom. In 409 AD, the

---

[705] *The Book of Miracles* Kenneth L Woodward (Touchstone 2001) pp. 202-203

[706] *The Birth of Christianity: Discovering What Happened in the Years Immediately After the Execution of Jesus*, John Dominic Crossan (Harper San Francisco, 1999) p. 28

[707] *The Age of Faith (The Story of Civilization, Volume 4)* Will Durant (MJF Books, 1980) p. 26

Roman Senate allowed Alaric to name a puppet emperor and made Alaric head of the Roman armies. Honorius sued for peace but attacked Alaric during the negotiations. Feeling betrayed, Alaric in 410 AD pillaged Rome for the first time in 800 years.[708] The Rome of the Roman Empire was almost over.

While Alaric was sacking Rome, the Vandals were pouring over the Rhine into Northern France and sweeping south across the Seine and the Loire. They reached the Pyrenees at the end of 408 AD, leaving Gaul pillaged and devastated. In 409 AD, they crossed into Spain and, within two years, were looking out across the straits at Africa.[709]

For many decades, the Vandals and Goths had been slowly infiltrating Italy, France, and Spain. Many Vandals and Visigoths had become slaves captured by the Romans in battles or had come freely as skilled craftsman. They were Arian Christians, converted by missionaries, such as Ulfilas, in the mid-4th century. Accordingly, the Goths and Vandals mostly left the churches and clergy unmolested as they ravished the Western Empire. By default, the Church became the surviving organizing force and, in many cases, the bishops became the central magistrates of the cities. The Church was in control of almost everything as the Dark Ages approached.[710]

Jesus was now officially God. And as Jesus' mother, Mary, was clearly the Mother of God. Devotion to Mary became prominent throughout Christianity. So prominent that the bishop Nestorius was concerned that the pagan worship of a mother-goddess was being revived.[711]

---

[708] *The Age of Faith (The Story of Civilization, Volume 4)* Will Durant (MJF Books, 1980) p. 36

[709] *The Age of Faith (The Story of Civilization, Volume 4) Will Durant (MJF Books, 1980)* p. 37

[710] *A History of Christianity*, Paul Johnson (Simon & Schuster a Touchstone Book, 1995) p. 127-130

[711] *Christianity: The First Three Thousand Years,* Diarmaid MacClulloch (Viking, 2010) p. 225

Whether pagan or Christian, Virgin Mother of God or not, Christians had a commonsense rationale for prayer and devotion to Mary, "When we have offended Christ, we should first go to the Queen of heaven and offer her...prayers, fasting, vigils, and alms; then she, like any mother, will come between us and Christ, the father who wished to beat us, and she will throw the cloak of mercy between the rod of punishment and us." Or so said a Franciscan monk some years later.[712] Jesus had said, *"I am the way, the truth, and the life: no man cometh unto the Father, but by me"* (John 14:6). I guess others thought no man cometh unto Jesus but by Mary.

Nestorius disagreed. "Let no one call Mary the Mother of God, for Mary was but a woman and it is impossible that God should be born of a woman!" proclaimed the Nestorians. How could a teenage country girl from a remote village be the mother of the God who created the sun, stars, and earth? Mary "did not bear the Creator but bore a man," preached Nestorius.[713] His mistake may have been preaching this at Christmas time.

If the Jesus/God "Two Natures" issue had been proclaimed dead and buried by Theodosius, it was resurrected with the Mary debate. The bishop of Alexandria, and Nestorius, the bishop of Constantinople, were the leading spokesmen for each side. Here is a letter from Cyril to Nestorius to show just how inane the issue was:

> Besides what the Gospels say our Savior said of himself, we do not divide between two hypostases or persons. For neither he, the one and only Christ, to be thought of as double, although of two and they diverse, yet he has joined

---

[712] *A History of Christian Theology: An Introduction,* William C. Placher (Westminster Press, 1983) pp. 131

[713] *Jesus Wars: How Four Patriarchs, Three Queens, and Two Emperors Decided What Christians Would Believe for the Next 1,500 Years,* John Philip Jenkins (Harper One, 2010) pp. 34-35

them in an indivisible union, just as everyone knows a man is not double although made up of soul and body, but is of one both…. Therefore, all words which are read in the Gospels are to be applied to One Person, to One hypostasis of the Word Incarnate.[714]

In other words, was Jesus man-and-God like a bottle of water and wine, inseparable? Or rather like water and oil, mingled but not mixed?[715] It all again came down to a single letter, the difference between *ek duo* and *en duo*. A silly argument to some, but deadly serious to others. Did the man on the street, or even the clergy, really grasp this stuff? "Church debates became a matter of dueling slogans, phrases shouted at councils and synods, or recited antiphonally in a precursor of modern rap."[716] Yes, people were actually rioting over this.[717] In North Africa, Augustine had done his best to resolve the divide, but the argument would not die. It needed to be killed.

In the middle of this dividing debate, the Vandals had figured out that North Africa was the breadbasket of the Roman Empire. In the 420s, they crossed into Africa and began their conquest. The Moors and the Donatist, who had suffered under the Church and the Roman rule, ran to join the invading Vandals. In 431 AD, they killed Augustine and banished the Catholic hierarchy, seizing their property:[718] The Donatists had won and, with their

---

[714] *Jesus Wars: How Four Patriarchs, Three Queens, and Two Emperors Decided What Christians Would Believe for the Next 1,500 Years, John Philip Jenkins (Harper One, 2010)* p. 63

[715] *Christianity: The First Three Thousand Years*, Diarmaid MacClulloch (Viking, 2010) p. 223

[716] *Jesus Wars: How Four Patriarchs, Three Queens, and Two Emperors Decided What Christians Would Believe for the Next 1,500 Years, John Philip Jenkins (Harper One, 2010)* p. 66

[717] *Jesus Wars: How Four Patriarchs, Three Queens, and Two Emperors Decided What Christians Would Believe for the Next 1,500 Years, John Philip Jenkins (Harper One, 2010)* p. 62

[718] *The Age of Faith (The Story of Civilization, Volume 4) Will Durant (MJF Books, 1980)* p. 38

Vandal allies, soon controlled all of North Africa. The Vandal Commander, General Gaiseric was an Arian Christian who was shocked to find brothels on every street.[719] Jerome and Augustine's ideas on sex didn't seem to have reached past the church doors.

The issue of Mary and Original Sin needed to be settled, and to do so Theodosius II called for another Ecumenical Council, this time at Ephesus. The Emperor did not attend, but sent Candidian, his captain of the imperial guard, to open the meetings on June 7, 431.[720] He went with firm instructions, "to take care that no member of the Synod should attempt, before the close of the transactions, to go home, or to the court, or elsewhere." The captain was also ordered "not to allow that any other matter of controversy should be taken into consideration before the settlement of the principal point of doctrine before the Council."[721] You are going into that room and you are going to stay there until Mary and Original Sin are decided. Get this thing fixed! Understand?

Celestius had taken up the banner of free will and that humans were not intrinsically evil, in opposition to Augustine's position on Original Sin—that humans were born intrinsically evil. Nestorian was representing that Mary was the mother of Jesus but could not be the Mother of God, and that Jesus had "two natures." To head the council, the emperor appointed Cyril, who opposed both Celestius and Nestorian.[722]

After some messy debate, Celestius and Nestorius lost. Henceforth, to be a member of the Christian Church, you would

---

[719] *The Age of Faith (The Story of Civilization, Volume 4) Will Durant (MJF Books, 1980)* p. 30

[720] *Jesus Wars: How Four Patriarchs, Three Queens, and Two Emperors Decided What Christians Would Believe for the Next 1,500 Years, John Philip Jenkins (Harper One, 2010)* p. 148

[721] *The Seven Ecumenical Councils,* Henry Robert Percival (Veritas Splendor Publications, 2013) p. 285

[722] *The Penguin History of the Church: The Early Church,* Henry Chadwick (Penguin Books, 1993) Kindle loc. 4670

revere Mary as the Mother of God and believe that lust and sex in the Garden of Eden was the downfall of all humanity. The pleasure of sex was evil, and now outlawed by the Christian Church. Canon IV made sure no one would follow in their footsteps, "If any of the clergy should fall away, and publicly or privately presume to maintain the doctrines of Nestorius or Celestius, it is declared just by the holy Synod that these also should be deposed."[723]

The world that Jesus had preached—of little children, forgiveness, turning the other cheek, loving your neighbor as yourself, the kingdom of God was at hand—had been debauched by the Church. But then again, Jesus had failed to return as the conquering Messiah.

From the beginning of human existence, polytheistic paganism had carried the baton defining the roles of god and man. The baton had now been passed to Christianity and Paul's narrative of Jesus. Christian attempts to now carry that baton had plunged the Church and Empire into a "bewildering welter of intrigue and complication" that had ripped the Christian Church apart.[724] After the Council of Ephesus the Church was again professing unity, while the Empire itself was being ripped apart.

---

[723] *The Seven Ecumenical Councils,* Henry Robert Percival (Veritas Splendor Publications, 2013) pp. 320-323

[724] *Christianity: The First Three Thousand Years,* Diarmaid MacClulloch (Viking, 2010) p. 225

# Chapter Sixteen – The End of Roman Empire in the West

For decades, the Romans had been battling invaders from the North and East. For the Empire to survive, it needed unity in the Empire which meant unity in the Christian Church. That unity was now to be tested by the Huns.[725] Following the Vandal and Visigoth conquest, the "barbarians" continued to flow into the Western Roman Empire, as they were pushed out of their native homelands by "a vulgar herd of barbaric conquers."[726] The Huns had crossed the Volga river from central Russia decades before and had pushed west into central Europe. Attila and his brother, Bleda, became rulers of the Huns in 433, and by 441, had reached

---

[725] The following account is from *Twenty Decisive Battles of the World,* Lt. Col. Joseph B. Mitchell and Sir Edward Creasy (Konecky & Konecky, 1964) Chapter 6 and The Age of Faith (The Story of Civilization, Volume 4) Will Durant (MJF Books, 1980) pp. 38-41

[726] One of the books I read in my journey for answers, was Will Durant's *The Age of Faith*, published in 1950. I was struck by the prescience of a passage: "The higher birthrate outside of the Empire and the higher standard of living within it, made immigration or invasion the manifest destiny of the Roman Empire then, as for North America today." This was in the late 1940s, folks! The biggest political problem faced by the United States today not only was presaged by Rome over 1600 years ago, but Durant observes a lesson in history and stated our future fate as a matter of fact. *The Age of Faith (The Story of Civilization, Volume 4) Will Durant* (MJF Books, 1980) pp. 22-23

the Danube and set up their capital in Buda, as in Budapest, Hungary. By 447 AD, Bleda was dead, and Attila and the Huns invaded Greece, conquering everything until they reached Constantinople. Theodosius II bought peace with a huge tribute.

Ataulf was Alaric's brother-in-law, the Visigoth King who sacked Rome in 410. Ataulf had married Placidia, the daughter of Theodosius and sister of the emperor Honorius. When Ataulf died, Placidia married Constantius III, and they had a daughter they named Honoria, who was named after her uncle.[727] Got that? Anyway, she was a royal princess, who got caught doing what good Christian princesses aren't supposed to do and was sent to the tower. Instead of staying in her room as she was told, she sent a message to Atilla, along with her ring. Attila took it for a marriage proposal and agreed, providing he got France and Germany and a couple of other countries as her dowry. [728]

When the Romans said no in 451 AD, Attila's Hun army headed from Budapest across Slovakia, Austria, and southern Germany, and crossed the Rhine into northern France. Atilla left few alive in his wake. He sacked and burned Trier and Metz, massacring all the inhabitants. Attila the Hun was earning his reputation. Attila was no civilized warrior, as were the Caesars, Alaric, or even Gaiseric. They were the horrible, hideous Huns come to punish whoever stood in their way. And everyone in their way was stunned.

In order to stop Attila, the Visigoths, the Vandals, and the Romans joined forces with Aetius at the head of the joint army. On June 20, 451 AD, the Huns and the Visigoth/Vandal/Roman armies engaged on the Catalaunian Plains in Northeast France. One hundred sixty-two thousand men lost their lives fighting for a draw in one of the bloodiest and most decisive battles of world

---

[727] *The Age of Faith (The Story of Civilization, Volume 4) Will* Durant (MJF Books, 1980) pp. 36-37
[728] *The History of the Medieval World* Susan Wise Bauer (W.W. Norton 2010) pp 112-113

history. Attila retreated, and the Visigoth/Vandal/Roman Empire was saved.[729]

Only one year later Attila tried again, this time attacking Italy, ravaging and looting the cites north of the Po River, including Verona, Milan, and Pavia. Nothing remained to stop the Huns from conquering Italy, except an army of three. Leo I, bishop of Rome, and two Roman Senators, met with Attila to negotiate a settlement. There is no record or writings of their meeting. History only records that Attila took his army back across the Alps. Leo may have said some magic words to Attila, or perhaps he left Italy because a plague had infected his army.[730]

On his return to Buda, Attila consoled himself with a new young bride, Ildico. On their wedding night, Attila died of an aneurism, drowning in his own blood.[731] After that, the Huns broke up in disorder and disappeared into that dust bin of history.[732] The remnants of the flag of Rome still fluttered, but the patrons Romulus and Remus had been replaced by Peter, Paul, and Mary.[733] The Church was now the rock on which Rome was built.

Marcian, a tough-minded Roman soldier, became emperor just when Attila was launching his attack.[734] Like Constantine and Theodosius, Marcian faced disunity in the Church when confronted by foreign aggressions. And the disunity was the same basic problem faced by Constantine and Theodosius: the

---

[729] *Twenty Decisive Battles of the World*, Lt. Col. Joseph B. Mitchell and Sir Edward Creasy (Konecky & Konecky, 1964) pp 94-105

[730] *The Age of Faith (The Story of Civilization, Volume 4)* Will Durant (MJF Books, 1980) p. 40

[731] *The Age of Faith (The Story of Civilization, Volume 4) Will* Durant (MJF Books, 1980) p. 41

[732] *Twenty Decisive Battles of the World*, Lt. Col. Joseph B. Mitchell and Sir Edward Creasy (Konecky & Konecky, 1964) p. 103

[733] *A History of Christianity*, Paul Johnson (Simon & Schuster a Touchstone Book, 1995) p. 1. 66

[734] How he got to this position is again a story of mothers, daughters, sons and stepsons, murders and political intrigue -- far more complicated that the story of Ataulf, Placidia, Honoria, and Valentius, etc. A good summary of Marcian's rise to power can be found *The Age of Faith (The Story of Civilization, Volume 4)* Will Durant (MJF Books, 1980) pp. 40-41

persistent problem of the deity of Jesus. Constantine at Nicaea had made Jesus God. The debate between Constantine's rule and Theodosius' rulings was "How can Jesus and the Holy Ghost be God, when there is only one God?" Theodosius then ruled Jesus was a part of the Triune God. After Theodosius, the debate became, "How can Jesus be both God and man?" Nestorius had argued that Jesus was oil and water, two separable natures, Human and God, adding more difficulty to the Triune God theory. Ephesus had ruled Nestorius wrong. Would passing another law resolve anything?

In the mid-1960s, the United States passed laws declaring the equality of the races. Yet, over 50 years later, the arguments over racial equality continue to rage. Law, even when reasonable does not trump passion and emotion. There are polemics, riots, and murders because the word *equality* means very different things to different people. Laws never change the minds of men.

It was the same then. The first Council of Ephesus made laws; yet passion and emotion continued to swirl as the Arian Goths overran the Western Empire. The "Two Natures" debate raged on in one form or another. If Jesus was of one substance with the Father and the Triune God, what was the substance of Jesus who was born, laughed and learned, cried and died? God or Man? Could Mary really be the mother of God? The questions divided the Empire as Attila was attempting to carve it up.

Theodosius II had tried to resolve the issue by calling the Second Council of Ephesus in 449, even before Attila attacked. It had been a disaster, only confusing the issues and inciting further emotions. They were still churning when the emperor was thrown from his horse and died in 450. The new emperor, Marcian, then called for yet another council. Pope Leo I objected, wanting to avoid another angry and divisive debate. The invading Huns made transportation and safety a difficulty, and the venue was moved to Chalcedon near Constantinople, closer to the security of the emperor himself.

Attila was marching back to Buda on October 8, 451, when the meetings opened. The urgency, passions, and interlude during the Huns' retreat produced a huge turnout of bishops. The venue was sealed off; no mere monks or laymen were allowed in the area with their mobs to influence this council.

In the prior century, Damasus, the bishop of Rome from 366 to 384, had made Rome a place of pilgrimage for Christians. "The bodies of the apostles Peter and Paul glitter with such great miracles and awe," and guidebooks and hostels were established to help those seeking miraculous cures from the martyrs of the catacombs. People came and lowered trinkets on string into Peter's tomb believing they had been transformed into holy relics and powerful amulets. A visit to Peter's tomb was not simply a symbolic ritual; people believed that Peter was physically present and was taking an active role in the affairs of the Church.[735] Pope Leo I now saw how to use the power of these relics.

Leo I had written a letter to the prior Ephesus Council called Leo's Tome, and now used that same letter to his political advantage at the Council of Chalcedon. Leo I believed that he was the successor of St. Peter and that when he preached or wrote a letter, St. Peter himself was speaking or writing.[736] Some even believed that Peter himself had miraculously edited the Tome.[737] Whether Peter or Leo, the Tome itself was artfully drafted to bring as many bishops as possible to his view.[738] While the proceedings were reported as a wild and rowdy affair, Peter, as speaking through Leo I, was eventually approved, "We believe, as Leo: Peter hath spoken by Leo: we have all subscribed the letter: what has been set forth is sufficient for the Faith: no other

---

[735] *A History of Christianity*, Paul Johnson (Simon & Schuster a Touchstone Book, 1995) p. 168

[736] *The Penguin History of the Church: The Early Church*, Henry Chadwick (Penguin Books, 1993) Kindle loc. 3662

[737] *A History of Christianity*, Paul Johnson (Simon & Schuster a Touchstone Book, 1995) p. 169

[738] *Christianity: The First Three Thousand Years*, Diarmaid MacClulloch (Viking, 2010) p. 226

exposition may be made."[739] The formula adopted was a play on the Triune God. Now, it was three Gods in One, and Two Natures in One of those Gods.

Marcian, like Theodosius and Constantine before him, used the power of an emperor to shape the Church. The Council gave the emperor's bishop of Constantinople, the power of sanction over the bishops of the Eastern Empire, making him second only to the bishop of Rome. It is only from this point forward that the bishop of Rome can be thought of as the Pope in our modern sense.[740] All monks were now put under the authority of the local bishop. The reforms were made into canon law, some verbatim from the emperor himself.[741] Most importantly, Marcian and Valentinian III issued a joint edict on February 7, 452 declaring:

> At last that which we wished, with earnest desire, has come to pass. Controversy about the orthodox religion of Christians has been put away.... Unholy strife must now cease.... It is the mark of utter madness to search, in the full light of day, for counterfeit illumination.... No one, therefore, be he cleric, or official, or of any other estate, shall henceforth collect a crowd for an audience and publicly discuss the Christian faith.... Wherefore if any cleric venture to deal with religion in public, he shall be removed from the list of the clergy; if any official does so, he shall lose his appointment; while others guilty of this offence shall be banished from the Imperial city; and all shall be rendered liable to the appropriate penalties by the bench of judges. For it is agreed that public disputations and debates are the source and stuff of heretical madness. All, therefore,

[739] The Seven Ecumenical Councils, Henry Robert Percival (Veritas Splendor Publications, 2013) p. 340

[740] *A New History of Early Christianity,* Charles Freeman (Yale University Press 2009) p. 316

[741] *The Seven Ecumenical Councils,* Henry Robert Percival (Veritas Splendor Publications, 2013) p. 369

shall be bound to hold to the decisions of the sacred Council of Chalcedon, and to indulge no further doubts. Take heed, therefore, to this edict of our Serenity; abstain from profane words and cease all further discussion of religion. It is wrong…it will also be restrained by the authority of the laws and the judges.[742]

The theology of Christian Orthodoxy was now complete and no longer to be questioned. There would be no more debate as to the nature of Jesus' divinity, or the role of Mary, or all of the other questions that for centuries had plagued Christianity. All of the religions of Jesus that had formed over the centuries—that had morphed, evolved, and reformed—had become one: The Roman Catholic Church. The Roman emperors had decreed it. "You will believe what we tell you!" Further debate was illegal. And now the Emperors put in place the disciplinary structure to enforce it.

Easy enough for Marcian to decree. But this debate was no different than the earlier ones at Nicaea and Ephesus. And so it was after the Council at Chalcedon. The argument simply would not be resolved, and the opinions continued to fuel dissention. In the areas under control of the bishop of Rome, Western Europe, Leo's Tome and the Declaration of Faith from Chalcedon found support. In the east and across North Africa, Palestine, Syria, and Asia Minor, there were uproars. The biggest uproar was in Alexandria, where the debates turned to riots, forcing Marcian to send 2000 imperial troops to attempt to bring order.[743]

To have multiple Gods, as the Trinity implied, or Gods with multiple natures, as Chalcedon stated, was simply another form of polytheism. Add to that the relics and rituals and you had

---

[742] http://www.ccjr.us/dialogika-resources/primary-texts-from-the-history-of-the-relationship/249-roman-laws

[743] *Jesus Wars: How Four Patriarchs, Three Queens, and Two Emperors Decided What Christians Would Believe for the Next 1,500 Years*, John Philip Jenkins *(Harper One, 2010)* p. 221

paganism, with spirits and demons that brought evil and disasters to man. The separate forms of Christianity that we think of today as Coptic, Syrian, Ethiopian, and Armenian, all stem from these questions of a Jesus with two natures, which was decreed at Chalcedon, or one nature, which was deemed heretical.[744]

In the West, the bishops had accepted the two natures of Jesus as promulgated by Leo I. But the West had another problem that would make a great TV series: "Mothers, Daughters and Murderers of Rome." In the end, another princess, Eudocia, asked another Barbarian king, Gaiseric, for help. Gaiseric was the king of the Vandals, who had overtaken North Africa and killed Augustine, among other dastardly deeds. Again, Pope Leo I and his army of three were called upon to stop the advancing Barbarians. Leo met Gaiseric and offered more magic words on why Rome should not be sacked. But, in 455, there was no magic left. Pope Leo I could only beg Gaiseric to just take whatever he wanted, but please not massacre the people or burn Rome. Gaiseric and the Vandals had a two-week holiday "vandalizing" Rome (yes, that is where the word comes from). The Vandals took every ounce of gold and silver and stripped the lead and bronze from every building, taking with them shiploads of furniture and people for slaves. Included on their ships as they sailed home were the spoils Rome had taken from the Temple in Jerusalem 400 years prior. Princess Eudocia became a souvenir Gaiseric was taking home for his son, Huneric. And, just like Barbarian soldiers everywhere, the Vandals, I am certain, were polite to all the good-looking ladies of Rome.[745]

Like Isaiah a thousand years earlier, and the Gospels a few centuries prior, had sought to explain the fall of Jerusalem, Augustine now attempted to explain the fall of Rome. A chorus

---

[744] *A New History of Early Christianity,* Charles Freeman (Yale University Press 2009) p. 306

[745] *The Age of Faith (The Story of Civilization, Volume 4)* Will Durant (MJF Books, 1980) p. 41

of pagans declared Christianity as the cause of the calamity and shook the faith of many. It took Augustine over a decade to write and publish his famous "The City of God" to attempt to refute the pagan claim and deflect blame to the moral and political corruption of Rome.[746]

During the next 21 years, nine men would fight over who would turn out the lights on the "Glory that was Greece and the Grandeur that was Rome."[747] Neither glory nor grandeur was left in Rome. Less than a century before, Rome had been the largest known city in the world, with a population of 1,500,000. Now it was probably less than 300,000. The villas of the rich and famous were now but ghost towns. Much of Europe was the same, ravaged through decades of invasion and conquest. Thousands of farms were in ruins, and grounds were left fallow. The invaders were herders and hunters, not farmers and traders. The Roman system of life, with its order, culture, and law, now had neither the authority nor the power to protect. Those who were left had to live on the courage and strength they alone could provide for themselves.[748]

By the beginning of the 6th century, the Roman Empire was no longer declining—it was in free fall. The invasion of the western part of the Roman Empire by the barbarians is the simplified common perception. But Rome did not need to be invaded by foreigners to fall; it had already fallen to the internal intruders.

When Constantine had held the Council of Nicaea, he had been attempting to unify the discord among the 15% of his empire that was Christian. By the time Gaiseric and the Vandals sacked Rome, only 15% were *not* Christian. This was a massive change in little more than a century. While Christians might

---

[746] The entire book can be found within the *Catholic Encyclopedia* with a summary of the 22 books found here: http://www.newadvent.org/fathers/1201.htm

[747] "To Helena" Edgar Allen Poe

[748] *The Age of Faith (The Story of Civilization, Volume 4) Will* Durant (MJF Books, 1980) p. 42

believe that their newly approved Trinitarian God had opened the hearts and minds of the Romans, it was also the work of Christians inflicting pain on the pagans.[749]

When Gaiseric and his Vandals left Italy, the Catholic Church was the only thing left standing in the West on which people could lean. The tribes that had swept through the land had brought new DNA, new blood that, over the next 50 generations, would be separated into the ethnicities of the Spanish, Italian, French, German, and English. Those same tribes had eliminated all remaining vestiges of order and control of the Roman Empire in the West. The Church and its structure remained, and the power of the Church would now oversee the affairs of those lands and control the lives and souls of their people. The Christian Church would now preside over the Dark Ages.

The thorny questions of Christianity were now settled in the orthodoxy of the Roman Catholic Church. Western Civilization would indoctrinate that orthodoxy with repetition, ritual, and often violence for the next 1000 years. But the questions of the Deity of Jesus within the Trinity, of his human and divine natures, of the nature of human sin and sex, and the role of Mary and the saints would remain fertile ground for questions and doubt.

In the 7th century, the Middle East and North Africa would hear the echoes of centuries of Christian wrangling, as a new religion of Abraham's God appeared in Arabia. Islam would offer its own answers to Christian questions and doubts.

---

[749] This will be discussed in *Abraham's Devil*. For an in-depth look at Christianity's wanton destruction of the pagan temples, literature, art and people see *The Darkening Age: The Christian Destruction of the Classic World,* Catherine Nixey (Pan MacMillan, 2017).

# Islam

# Introduction

In the 1950s, Islam was an obscure religion, and Muslims were a miniscule portion of the U.S. population.[750] Perhaps there was a mention of Islam in a history class, but there were certainly no Muslims either in my home town of Fort Wayne, nor in almost every city in the United States. The Nationality Act of 1940 provided that "the right to become a naturalized citizen under the provisions of this chapter shall extend only to white persons, and descendants of races indigenous to the Western Hemisphere."[751] It was only in 1944 that a Muslim immigrant was granted US citizenship.[752]

That changed with the passage of the "Immigration and Naturalization Act of 1965," which allowed Muslims to legally immigrate to the US. At the signing ceremony, President Johnson said the act would "not affect the lives of millions. It will not

---

[750] "Muslim Population in the Americas: 1950 –2020" Houssain Kettani *International Journal of Environmental Science and Development,* Vol. 1, No. 2, June 2010 pp. 128-129

[751] The Nationality Act of 1940, 8 U.S.C.A. § 703

[752] 54 F. Supp. 941 (1944) Ex parte MOHRIEZ. No. 1500. District Court, D. Massachusetts. April 13, 1944.

reshape the structure of our daily lives."[753] How wrong he was. By the beginning of the 21st century, communities across the US were fighting against the muezzin singing the call to prayer on loudspeakers, and school districts struggled with Muslim girls wearing the hijab to class.[754] Today, Fort Wayne Indiana has six mosques.[755]

My very first recollection of Islam was in 1964, when Cassius Clay changed his name to Muhammad Ali and announced his conversion to Islam. That sparked a great deal of interest. Islam was mostly a curious oddity to Americans as Malcolm X and Elijah Muhammad's Nation of Islam occasionally entered the news cycle with their message of racial separation.[756]

The American consciousness of Islam was raised with the Six Day War of 1967, even as it was often cast as a war between Israel and its Arab neighbors, not between Jews and Muslims. Islam continued to grow in the public conscious until 1979, when Iran was declared an Islamic Republic, with the American Embassy being seized, while Iran's Islamic leader, Ayatollah Khomeini, declared the United States as the "Great Satan."[757] To complete the wake-up call, twenty years later, Islamic martyrs

---

[753] Public Papers of the Presidents of the United States: Lyndon B. Johnson, 1965. Volume II, entry 546, p. 1037

[754] For example "Tension in a Michigan City Over Muslims' Call to Prayer" John Leland New York Times May 5, 2004 and IN THE UNITED STATES DISTRICT COURT FOR THE EASTERN DISTRICT OF OKLAHOMA EYVINE HEARN and NASHALA HEARN, a minor, suing through her next friend, EYVINE HEARN, Plaintiffs, UNITED STATES OF AMERICA, Plaintiff-Intervenor,v. MUSKOGEE PUBLIC SCHOOL DISTRICT 020; et al., Defendants. C.A. No.: CIV 03-598-S

[755] https://www.salatomatic.com/sub/United-States/Indiana/North Indiana/Lv9hETT 8bH

[756] Malcolm X, "Racial Separation" in *Civil Rights: Great Speeches in History,* Jill Karson, ed. (Greenhaven Press, 2003 p. 50

[757] "An Anthology of Imam Khomeini's Speeches, Messages, Interviews, Decrees, Religious Permissions, and Letters" Volume 10 September 17, 1979 – November 7, 1979 *The Institute for Compilation and Publication of Imam Khomeini's Works* p. 344

flew planes into the World Trade Center in New York. Osama bin Laden planned the attack and said that, under Islam, the attacks were "legal religiously and logically."[758] Fifty years after Islam was just an obscure religion, its most vocal leader declared war on America. Islam has remained in daily news ever since.

Islam is the world's second largest and the fastest growing religion, with 1.8 billion adherents. Almost one of every four humans in the world today is a Muslim, and over 1% of Americans are now Muslims. Most Westerners at least have the words *Islam, Muslim, Muhammad, Qur'an (*probably spelled *Koran) mosque, Mecca,* and certainly *jihad* in their vocabularies. Missing is an understanding of Islam and its theological entanglement with Judaism and Christianity. Very few understand that they are fundamentally the same religion, all worshipping the same God of Abraham, all holding the same theological tenets. Even fewer know anything about Muhammad, the founder of Islam.

Western core values of individual liberty, of an open society, and democracy clash with Islamic values of theocratic, closed societies that deny individual liberty and oppress women. Given the growth of Islam within the United States, and its often-violent interactions with Western culture around the world, understanding the history and origins of Islamic belief is more important than ever.

Fourteen hundred years ago, Islam joined Christianity and Judaism in the worship of Abraham's God. Siblings sharing anything is a problem for parents; Jews, Christians, and Muslims sharing God has been a dominant problem for humanity. Islam exploded out of Arabia into the Middle East and across North Africa in the 7th century and was stopped at the Pyrenees by Christian Europe in the 8th century. In the 11th century, Christians

---

[758] "British cite videotape tying bin Laden to terror attacks" Liz Sly *Chicago Tribune* November 15, 2001

took back Palestine but were thrown out in 1244 AD. The fight continued sporadically, and by 1529, Islam was labeled the "present terror of the world"[759] as they first laid siege to Vienna. In 1551, Muslims began a strategy to attack Europe through Malta and were eventually defeated in the sea battle of Lepanto. In 1683, Islam made its final attempt to enter Europe through Vienna. Failing, they retreated, and over the next 250 years, European powers led by the British and the French took control of Islamic lands across North Africa, the Middle East, and as far as Indonesia and Southeast Asia. By the end of World War II, the Western powers had subjugated virtually all the Islamic lands.

The West attempted to include Islamic countries into their economic and political culture, while those same Islamic countries struggled to throw off the mantle of colonialism. Success and independence brought the resurgence of Islamic pride and power in the late 20th century. Elements of Islam then again became the "terror of the world." The resulting enmity between the Judeo-Christian West and Islam now transcends the historical geographic divide. Shia, Sunni, martyrs, mosques, and Muhammad now disrupt the Western world, just as the Western world disrupted the Islamic world in centuries prior. The culture of Western civilization is in peril internally and threatened along the geopolitical fault lines, as Huntington's *Clash of Civilizations* has become a clear reality.[760] Only the willfully blind refuse to see it.

---

[759] The phrase has been recorded in numerous books, but was first used by Richard Knolles an English Historian, this is from *"The Muslim Discovery of Europe"* Bernard Lewis (WW Norton 2001) p. 32

[760] Samuel P. Huntington first posited in a 1992 lecture at the American Enterprise Institute, the idea that peoples cultural and religious identities were insuperable, which was then developed in a 1993 *Foreign Affairs* article titled "The Clash of Civilizations?" Huntington later expanded his thesis in a 1997 book *"The Clash of Civilizations and the Remaking of World Order."* (Simon and Schuster a Touchstone Book 1997) In it all he predicted the current situation between Islam and the West and expounded on the rationale for its inevitability.

Western and particularly American historical ignorance of Islam as well as Muslim ignorance of historical Islam must be overcome. This section begins with a primer on the history of Muhammad, Islam, and Islamic theology, as presented by the standard Islamic narrative—something like the Luke and Matthew versions of Jesus' birth and life. Islam's rise to the status of an empire can only be understood in the context of the funeral pyre of the Roman and Persian empires. The beliefs of Islam in the Noble Qur'an will be covered before a discussion on the writing of the Qur'an, as well as critiques of Islam. The story of the Qur'an itself, and the formation of Islam as told by Islam has raised questions. Those will be explored, and a plausible alternative to the standard Islamic narrative and its rise will be presented. The beginnings of the Sunni-Shia divide are presented because of their extreme importance in today's world. The goal is to provide the basics of Islamic history and development, to explore its beliefs and narrative, while explaining its essential bond with Christianity and Judaism.

"My God is the right God; your God is the wrong God" is a historic catastrophe, made tragic by Abraham's God being the one God of Jews, Christians, and Muslims. Where Christians see a Triune God, perhaps Abraham's God sees a Triune religion.

# Chapter One – The Scriptural Beginnings of Islam

The story of Islam begins in the Old Testament book of Genesis, when Abraham and his maid, Hagar, have a son named Ishmael. Shortly thereafter, Abraham has a second son, Isaac, by his wife, Sarah. A jealous conflict ensues as Sarah tells Abraham, *Get rid of that slave woman and her son. He is not going to share the inheritance with my son, Isaac. I won't have it!* (Gen. 21:10, NLT).

But God tells Abraham not to worry about sending Hagar and Ishmael away: *I will surely bless him; I will make him fruitful and will greatly increase his numbers. He will be the father of twelve rulers, and I will make him into a great nation* (Gen. 17:20). Moreover, *Early the next morning Abraham took some food and a skin of water and gave them to Hagar. He set them on her shoulders and then sent her off with the boy. She went on her way and wandered in the Desert of Beersheba* (Gen. 21:14).

When the water ran out, she, *put the boy under one of the bushes. Then she went off and sat down about a bowshot away, for she thought, "I cannot watch the boy die." And as she sat there, she began to sob* (Gen. 21:16). *Then God opened her eyes and she saw a well of water. So she went and filled the skin with water and gave the boy a drink. God was with the boy as he grew up. He lived in the desert and became an archer* (Gen. 21:19-20).

The Arab tradition continues the story as Ishmael and Hagar wander until they end up in the Becca Valley. Just as in Genesis, Hagar sat and sobbed, then paced seven times back and forth between two hills until the well, known as Zamzam, appeared and saved them. Years later, Abraham travelled hundreds of miles to visit his son. Together, they built a sanctuary using a heavenly stone brought to Abraham by an angel. It was a white stone that was turned pure black by the sins of the sons of Adam.[761] Today, we know Becca as Mecca, and the stone and the sanctuary is known as the Ka'bah.

An allusion to the Ka'bah is found in Psalm 118:22-23, which was quoted by Jesus: *Did ye never read in the scriptures, The stone which the builders rejected, the same is become the head of the corner: this is the Lord's doing, and it is marvelous in our eyes?* Just as Christians use allusions to say Jesus was prophesized in the Old Testament, *Islam* uses an allusion to the stone to say that Jesus foretold the coming of Islam:

> *Therefore, I say unto you, the kingdom of God shall be taken from you, and given to a nation bringing forth the fruits thereof. And whosoever shall fall on this stone shall be broken: but on whomsoever it shall fall, it will grind him to powder.* (Matt. 21:43-44)

The Bible mentions Ishmael again only at Abraham's funeral when, *His sons Isaac and Ishmael buried him in the cave of Machpelah* (Gen. 25:9). In the Qur'an, Abraham had offered a prayer before dying.

---

[761] Muhammad: His Life Based on the Earliest Sources, Martin Lings (Inner Traditions, 2006) pp. 2-3

*Our Lord, I have settled some of my descendants in an uncultivated valley near Your sacred House, our Lord, that they may establish prayer. So make hearts among the people incline toward them and provide for them from the fruits that they might be grateful.* (Qur'an 14:37)

Ishmael was fruitful and had twelve sons, *Nebaioth the firstborn of Ishmael, Kedar, Adbeel, Mibsam, Mishma, Dumah, Massa, Hadad, Tema, Jetur, Naphish and Kedemah,* and, *lived a hundred and thirty-seven years.* Their tribes, *settled in the area from Havilah to Shur, near the eastern border of Egypt, as you go toward Ashur* (Gen. 25:13-18).

Back in Canaan, Isaac's son, Esau, had lost his birthright through the swindle of Rebecca[762] and, *went to Abraham's son Ishmael and married Ishmael's daughter Mahalath* (Gen. 28:9). Sorry, biblical genealogy can be confusing. What difference does this make, you say? Because the Bible tells us the story that the Arabs are the descendants of Abraham through Ishmael and Esau. This is exactly as the narrative of Islam contends.

Now, there are a couple of small problems with this story. Genesis has the "Arab," descendants of Ishmael and Esau living from Havilah to Shur. That is the arc of the Arabian Peninsula. Hence, the idea that Ishmael and Esau are the fathers of the Arabs is quite plausible lore. But Mecca is 800 miles, a 40-day camel ride, across the desert from where Abraham lived.[763] The idea that Hagar and Ishmael wandered down to Mecca in ancient times is even less probable than an 8-month pregnant Mary making a 100-mile donkey ride over mountainous terrain! And Abraham just popping down for a visit with his son is just as improbable, as is Ishmael getting a Qur'anic telegram one day

---

[762] The complete story is told in Genesis 27:1-40 of Rebecca deceiving Isaac so that his inheritance went to the second son Jacob, and not Esau.

[763] *In the Shadow of the Sword: The Birth of Islam and the Rise of Global Arab Empire,* Tom Holland (Doubleday, 2012) p. 50

that his dad had died and making it home before the funeral. But it made a good story for Islam, just as Luke had written a good story for Christianity.

Just as Christians have come to believe Luke's story of Jesus, Islam's adherents have come to fervently believe the Genesis story of their connection with Abraham and his God.

# Chapter Two – Muhammad before His Visions

Water from the well of Zamzam made Mecca into a prosperous trading city. Hundreds of idols to the gods and demons of every Arab tribe made the Ka'bah[764] a point of pilgrimage.[765] Not all Arabs were idol-worshipping pagans; many belonged to Jewish or Christian[766] tribes[767] found scattered around the peninsula. "Christianity, mainly Nazarene, was well established in the Arabian Peninsula before the birth of Muhammad."[768] Two areas had large concentrations of Jews: Yathrib, eleven camel-days from Mecca,[769] and Himyar, a Jewish kingdom with Jewish kings located in the general area of what is

---

[764] *In the Shadow of the Sword: The Birth of Islam and the Rise of Global Arab Empire,* Tom Holland (Doubleday, 2012) p. 17

[765] *Islam: A Short History,* Karen Armstrong (Modern Library, 2000) p. 3

[766] As will be discussed later the term *Christian* is used here to denote "followers of Jesus" and not the legalized Orthodox Christianity found in the Roman Empire.

[767] *John of Damascus, First Apologist to the Muslims: The Trinity and Christian Apologetics in the Early Islamic Period,* Daniel J. Janosik (Pickwick Publications, 2016) p 195

[768] *What are the Sacred Roots of Islam?* Jamil Effarah (Authorhouse, 2016) Kindle loc. 1586

[769] *Muhammad: His Life Based on the Earliest Sources,* Martin Lings (Inner Traditions, 2006) p. 7

today north Yemen. This is confirmed by a stone dating from 440 AD marking the dedication of a dam to the God of Israel.[770]

Pagans, Jews, and Christians on the Arabian Peninsula were a divided lot. "Throughout Arabia, one tribe fought another in a murderous cycle."[771] However, the Quraysh tribe of Mecca welcomed all Christians, Jews, and pagans. The Quraysh were the protectors of the Ka'bah and enforced in Mecca a no-violence agreement. Something like checking your guns with the sheriff while in Tombstone in the American Wild West. In the 6th century, the Quraysh sheriff of Mecca was Abd al-Muttalib. He was "nearer the religion of Abraham" while others "maintained the full purity of Abrahamic worship."[772]

Sometime in the 500s, the Christian ruler of Yemen, Abraha, built a great Cathedral in Sana'a. Supposedly built with marble from the palace of the Queen of Sheba, it was a beautiful structure, with ivory and ebony pulpits adorned with crosses of gold and silver. Abraha intended its magnificence to divert the Arabs from their pagan pilgrimages to Mecca.[773]

It wasn't working as planned, so in the year 570 AD, Abraha set out with his troops and an elephant to destroy the Ka'bah and thereby force pilgrimages to his cathedral of Sana. Two miles short of Mecca, Abraha met with Abd al-Muttalib and told him he only wanted to destroy the Ka'bah. Muttalib was greatly outnumbered and withdrew his forces from the city but warned Abraha that the Lord would protect the Ka'bah. With his elephant in the lead, Abraha marched forward, but as the Ka'bah came into view, the elephant kneeled. Nothing would make the elephant move forward. So, Abraha and his men turned and began to

---

[770] *In the Shadow of the Sword: The Birth of Islam and the Rise of Global Arab Empire*, Tom Holland (Doubleday, 2012)   pp. 246-247

[771] *Islam: A Short History,* Karen Armstrong (Modern Library, 2000) p. 3

[772] *Muhammad: His Life Based on the Earliest Sources,* Martin Lings (Inner Traditions, 2006) p. 16

[773] *Muhammad: His Life Based on the Earliest Sources,* Martin Lings (Inner Traditions, 2006) p. 19

march in retreat, and the elephant rose and followed. Encouraged, Abraha again turned towards Mecca, and the elephant again knelt down. Suddenly, the sky was darkened with swallows, each carrying three pebbles. The birds bombed Abraha and his army, killing many and sending them in retreat back to Sana'a.[774] History tells a slightly different story—nothing about the birds, but rather Abraha retreated because the Persians had invaded Yemen.[775,776]

While this was going on, Abd al-Muttalib's son was dying in Yathrib, and his daughter-in-law was pregnant in Mecca. While she was watching the miracle of the birds, she had a vision: "Thou carriest in thy womb, the lord of this people; and when he is born say: I place him beneath the protection of the One, from the evil of every envier; then name him Muhammed."[777]

No wise men on or angels appeared at the time of Muhammad's birth, but when he was three years old, two angels performed open-heart surgery on little Muhammad. They removed the touch of Satan, Augustine's Original Sin, found in every son of Adam, excepting "only Mary and her son."[778]

Muhammad, like all other "city" Arab children of that time, was sent out to be raised by nomadic tribes. This social custom bound together urban and nomadic families, taught children the way of the desert, and protected them from diseases and epidemics that were more prevalent in the towns and villages.

---

[774] *Muhammad: His Life Based on the Earliest Sources,* Martin Lings (Inner Traditions, 2006) pp. 19-22

[775] *God's Crucible: Islam and the Making of Europe, 570-1215,* David Levering (Lewis Norton, 2008) p. 25

[776] There is some historical irony in that Yemen in the past years has been again invaded by the Iranian Persians to fight the Arabs in Saudi Arabia.

[777] *Muhammad: His Life Based on the Earliest Sources,* Martin Lings (Inner Traditions, 2006) pp. 21-22

[778] This entire story known as the" Year of the Elephant," is from *Muhammad: His Life Based on the Earliest Sources,* Martin Lings (Inner Traditions, 2006) pp. 19-22 in which the quote is from page 102 of Wustenfeld's edition of *Sirat Rasul Allah* by Muhammad ibn Ishaq.

Muhammad's destiny was foretold, as his foster parents' herds were miraculously more productive than all the others.[779]

When Muhammad was six, his mother died, and he became the ward of his grandfather, Abd al-Muttalib. For two years, Muhammad sat at his grandfather's side while the elders in the Assembly of Mecca discussed community issues and met with visiting dignitaries. When Muhammad was eight years old, Muttalib died, and he was entrusted to his uncle, Abu Talib.[780]

Muhammad joined Uncle Talib on a trading caravan to Syria, where they met the Christian monk Sergius, also is known in Islam as Bahira. After seeing the mark from angelic surgery on Muhammad's back, Sergius saw a "cloud" over Muhammad and proclaimed him for greatness. Then, an angel told Uncle Talib, "Take thy brother's son back to his country, and guard him against the Jews, for by God, if they see him and know that which I know, they will contrive evil against him."[781]

Over the next years, Muhammad traveled on caravans learning the trading business. By the time he was 20, he was trading for himself on commission, buying and selling goods for others. In Mecca, a twice-widowed, wealthy woman named Khadijah hired Muhammad to trade her goods in Syria. To keep an eye on things, she sent one of her servants with the caravan. Wouldn't you know it, but on the way, they ran into another Christian monk, this one named Nestor. Nestor pointed to Muhammad and told the servant, "None other than a Prophet is sitting beneath that tree."[782]

---

[779] *Muhammad: His Life Based on the Earliest Sources,* Martin Lings (Inner Traditions, 2006) pp. 23-26

[780] *Muhammad: His Life Based on the Earliest Sources,* Martin Lings (Inner Traditions, 2006) pp. 27-28

[781] *Muhammad: His Life Based on the Earliest Sources,* Martin Lings (Inner Traditions, 2006) pp. 29-30 in which the quote is from page 117 of Wustenfeld's edition of *Sirat Rasul Allah* A life of the Prophet Muhammad, by Muhammad ibn Ishaq written in approximately 750.

[782] *Muhammad: His Life Based on the Earliest Sources,* Martin Lings (Inner Traditions, 2006) p. 34. The Islamic tradition is found on p. 83 of The Leyden Addition of

On their return from this profitable business trip, the servant told the story to Khadijah, who then proposed to Muhammad. Khadijah was 15 years older than Muhammad, but, for 20 camels, Muhammad accepted. At the wedding, there were slaves given as gifts, and everyone, including the slaves, were happy. One slave, Zayd, was offered his freedom to return to his father and uncle, but he refused to leave. Muhammad was honored and adopted the boy as his son. Within a few years, Khadijah and Muhammad had six children, two sons and four daughters.[783]

By the year 605 AD, the Ka'bah was getting a little run down. After all, it had been built by Abraham and Ishmael over 2000 years before.[784] Muhammad laid the cornerstone to the re-built Ka'bah using that rock,[785] from Abraham.[786] He was also the first to enter the rebuilt sanctuary, the home of some 360 idols[787] and a painting of Jesus and Mary.[788]

The stories told above are the standard Islamic narrative of Muhammad's early years. The books of Matthew and Luke telling the story of Jesus' birth and early life were written 75 to 90 years after his birth. The stories of Muhammad's life are contained in biographies written over two hundred years after his birth. Martin Lings' book, *Muhammad: His Life Based on the Earliest Sources* is a compilation of those biographies and is the main source used in this chapter. But as we will see later, there are other versions of Muhammad's early life.

---

Kitah al Maghazi a chronicle of the Prophets campaigns by Muhammad ibn Sa'd written in the late 800s.

[783] *Muhammad: His Life Based on the Earliest Sources,* Martin Lings (Inner Traditions, 2006) p. 37

[784] That would have been 1400 BC and Abraham is dated much earlier.

[785] That rock is thought to be a meteorite.

[786] *Muhammad: His Life Based on the Earliest Sources,* Martin Lings (Inner Traditions, 2006) pp. 42-43

[787] *Islam: A Short History,* Karen Armstrong (Modern Library, 2000) p. 3

[788] *The Evolution of God,* Robert Wright (Little Brown and Company, 2009) p. 336

# Chapter Three – Dreams from Mecca

ummers in the Mecca area are hot. The average daytime temperature is 109° F in August, with an average low of 96° F.[789] The ninth lunar month of the Arab calendar is Ramadan, which appropriately means "Scorching."[790] Even before Islam, the Arabians had created a festival month of daytime rest, reflection, and fasting. What else could one do in the scorching heat? Muhammad sought respite from the heat during Ramadan in a cave on Mt. Hira, just a few miles from Mecca.[791] For several years, during his hike to his cave, he had been hearing a voice that said, "Peace be on thee, O Messenger of God."[792] But he was simply hearing things; he did not see anyone.

Sleeping in the cave one night in the year 610 AD, Muhammad saw the Angel Gabriel. The Angel commanded him to read what appeared before him. The scene was similar to Rembrandt's

---

[789] http://jrcc.sa/climate_data_observatory_sa.php

[790] *The Qur'an and Its Interpreters,* Mahmoud M. Ayoub (State University of New York Press, 1984) p. 191

[791] This pagan tradition, fasting in the month of Ramadan was carried over into Islam by Muhammad and became the Fourth Pillar of Islam called the Sawm..

[792] *Muhammad: His Life Based on the Earliest Sources,* Martin Lings (Inner Traditions, 2006) p. 43

famous painting, "Belshazzar's Feast,"[793] where writing appeared on the wall. In Muhammad's cave, the writing appears on brocaded material.[794] Muhammad said he could not read and, after he and Gabriel went back and forth, Muhammad recited:

> *Read with the name of your Lord who created* (everything) *He created man from a clot of blood. Read, and your Lord is Most Gracious, Who imparted knowledge by means of the pen. He taught man what he did not know.*[795] (Qur'an 96:1-5)

Muhammad was a little shook up by his dreams and hallucinations. One might speculate that even in the 7th century, hallucinations were looked at with some suspicion. Muhammad's wife decided to consult her cousin, Waraka ibn Nawfal, who confirmed Muhammad was God's messenger. Muhammad's revelations continued for the next 22 years. As Muhammad tells it:

> Sometimes it cometh unto me like the reverberations of a bell, and that is the hardest upon me; the reverberations abate when I am aware of their message. And sometimes the Angel taketh the form of a man and speaketh unto me, and I am aware of what he saith.[796]

---

[793] It is the story from Daniel 5:30–31 If you are not familiar with the painting it is in the National Gallery in London and can be seen here: http://www.nationalgallery.org.uk/paintings/rembrandt-belshazzars-feast

[794] *In the Shadow of the Sword: The Birth of Islam and the Rise of Global Arab Empire,* Tom Holland (Doubleday, 2012) pp. 16-17

[795] This quotes from the Qur'an are from the Mufti Taqi Usman translation that can be found online at http://www.Qur'anexplorer.com/Qur'an/ This translation has associated comment.

[796] As quoted from" Muhammad ibn Ismail al-Bukhari, Collections of Sayings of the Prophet" in *Muhammad: His Life Based on the Earliest Sources,* Martin Lings (Inner Traditions, 2006) p. 46

Muhammad and Paul tell the same story of their hallucinations, voices, and visions. Both attribute their experiences to messages from God. As mentioned earlier, it is another example of theophany, and no different than the experiences reported by Joseph Smith,[797] Jim Jones,[798] David Koresh,[799] Rachael Armstrong, [800] many others throughout history, and others found on the streets of every major city in the United States. [801]

All of them admit to having trances or hallucinations, hearing voices, seeing visions, or floating out of their bodies. Depending on your religion, either Paul, Jim Jones, Joseph Smith, or Muhammad is a true messenger from God, while the others are simply psychotic. Is faith alone how you are to distinguish between the psychotic and the messenger from God? Whomever you pick, be certain that the one of your faith is certainly a true messenger from God.

From his dreams and visions, Muhammad preached an all-powerful God who created everything. He preached a resurrection, a last judgement, eternal life in Heaven or Hell, and greater equality in society. Sounds an awful lot like Zoroastrianism and Christianity, doesn't it? However, Muhammad did provide a few more details. The one relevant today is that dying in jihad immediately takes you to Heaven (Surah 3:169).

For Christians, the final Jeopardy question at the Last Judgement is, "Were you baptized?" For Islam, the final

---

[797] *The History of Religion,* Karen Farrington (Barnes and Noble, 2001) p. 164
[798] *Cults, Religion & Violence,* David Bromley and J. Gordon Melton (Cambridge University Press, 2002) pp. 149 - 151
[799] *Cults, Religion & Violence,* David Bromley and J. Gordon Melton (Cambridge University Press, 2002) pp. 149 - 151
[800] "Rachel Armstrong Accused of Beating Grandmother Angela Armstrong Whom She Thought Was Possessed" David Moye, *The Huffington Post* 12/05/2012 http://www.huffingtonpost.com/2012/12/05/rachel-armstrong-beat-angela-armstrong_n_2246505.html
[801] "Spirituality and Hearing Voices" Simon McCarthy Jones, Amanda Waegeli and John Watkins; *Psychosis* October 5, 2013 Published online 2013 Oct 23. doi: 10.1080/17522439.2013.831945

Jeopardy question is, "Have you performed the Shahada?" The Shahada is simply a ceremonial recitation of the Islamic faith. The time when this began is uncertain, but in 621, Usayd bin Hudayr testified, "There is no god but God and Muhammad is the Messenger of God."[802] This is the first pillar of Islam. What about those before Muhammad? Or those that never heard of him? Did God just write them off? Why not be baptized *and* do the Shahada?

The Salat, or prayer, is the second pillar of Islamic faith. Prayers were to be performed kneeling on the ground five times each day while facing towards Jerusalem.[803] The idea of prostrating oneself on the ground rubbed many as servile. The idea was unacceptable to the tribe that ruled Mecca—Muhammad's own tribe, the Quraysh. Muhammad's followers retired to ravines outside Mecca where they could pray in secret.[804] The ritual would later be changed.

One night, Muhammad was sleeping at the Ka'bah, when an angel brought him a magic horse: Buraq. Off they rode, faster than the wind, all the 800 miles to the Temple Mount in Jerusalem where Moses, Abraham, Jesus, and others were waiting for him. From where the Dome of the Rock now stands, and the Jewish Temple once stood, he again mounted Buraq and flew to Heaven. After a tour, he was shown to the "Lote Tree of the Uttermost End," where God instructed him to command the people to pray 50 times a day. On leaving, Muhammad saw Moses, who told him to go back to God and negotiate for fewer prayers. So, Muhammad did and was able to reduce it to 40 times a day. And passing Moses again on the way out, Moses told him to go try again. This time it was 30, and Moses chastised him for

---

[802] *Muhammad: His Life Based on the Earliest Sources,* Martin Lings (Inner Traditions, 2006) p. 112

[803] *Islam: A Short History,* Karen Armstrong (Modern Library, 2000) p. 6

[804] *A History of God: The 4,000-Year Quest of Judaism, Christianity and Islam,* Karen Armstrong (Alfred A. Knopf, 1994) p. 142

being a bad negotiator. Well, this went on a few times and eventually the number got down to just five prayers a day. When Moses again told Muhammad to try for fewer, Muhammad said he was ashamed and five was good enough. And that is the rest of the story on why Muslims pray five times a day.[805]

Like Jesus, Muhammad also preached justice, equity, and compassion. Muslims, though, were required to build a community on those principals and give alms for the poor. This almsgiving was called the Zakat. This was the third pillar of Islam. Based on these principles, Muhammad built a following of some 70 families[806]—the same number of disciples that followed Jesus.

Jews and Christians living in Arabia had exposed the Arabs to monotheism: one God. The Ka'bah was, at that time, the polytheistic home of 360 gods.[807] One of those gods was al-Lah, the tribal god of Muhammad's own clan, the Quraysh.[808] The Quraysh were expected to protect all of the gods, and Muhammad's insistence on there being but one God insulted believers in the other gods. This insult jeopardized the trade brought to Mecca.[809] Muhammad was preaching against Mecca's goose that laid the golden egg.

Very few Meccan's accepted Muhammad's message, and some became hostile. It didn't help that Muhammad had proclaimed that his grandfather, the Quraysh leader, Abd al Muttalib, had gone to hell for not converting to Islam.[810] This was

[805] *Muhammad: His Life Based on the Earliest Sources,* Martin Lings (Inner Traditions, 2006) pp. 104-106

[806] *Islam: A Short History,* Karen Armstrong (Modern Library, 2000) p. 12

[807] *Muhammad: His Life Based on the Earliest Sources,* Martin Lings (Inner Traditions, 2006) p. 16

[808] *A History of God: The 4,000-Year Quest of Judaism, Christianity and Islam,* Karen Armstrong (Alfred A. Knopf, 1994) p. 135

[809] *Islam: A Short History,* Karen Armstrong (Modern Library, 2000) p. 11

[810] *God's Crucible: Islam and the Making of Europe, 570-1215,* David Levering (Lewis Norton, 2008) p. 38

something like Jesus commanding that his followers must hate their *father and mother, and wife and children, and brethren and sisters* (Luke 14:26) to be a disciple of Jesus.

All of this upset the elite clans of the Quraysh who decided to act against Muhammad. A boycott was imposed—no marriage or trade with Muhammad's Muslims. That and other pressures made life so difficult that some Muslims left Mecca and migrated to the Christian area of Abyssinia,[811] now Ethiopia. Muhammad could remain safely in Mecca because he was under the protection of a venerated leader of Mecca, his uncle, Abu Talib.

Some 250 miles north of Mecca was the town of Yathrib. It was a community of Jewish and pagan tribes that had only recently abandoned the nomadic way of life. They were trapped in a cycle of deadly tribal feuds. In 620, the leaders of Yathrib converted to Islam, and asked Muhammad to come to Yathrib to resolve the feudal killings. Around the same time, Muhammad's protector, Uncle Abu Talib, died, exposing Muhammad and his Muslims to the threat of death from other tribes in Mecca.[812]

Over the next two years, the Muslim families fled to Yathrib, until only Muhammad and his sidekick, Abu Bakr, remained in Mecca. The Angel Gabriel appeared and warned Muhammad that he must flee because the Quraysh were about to assassinate him.[813]

The story of Muhammad's escape reads something like an Old Western movie: surrounding the house, climbing out of windows onto camels, tracking the hoof prints in the sand, hiding in a darkened cave with the searchers just feet away. To throw

---

[811] *Muhammad: His Life Based on the Earliest Sources,* Martin Lings (Inner Traditions, 2006) p. 83

[812] The points of this paragraph are discussed both in *Islam: A Short History* by Karen Armstrong p. 13, and *Muhammad: His Life Based on the Earliest Sources* by Martin Lings pp. 54-55.

[813] *In the Shadow of the Sword: The Birth of Islam and the Rise of Global Arab Empire,* Tom Holland (Doubleday, 2012) pp. 16-17 p. 19

his pursuers off the trail, the pair first circled south and west of Mecca before heading north and east towards Yathrib. The New Moon of Ramadan in 622 AD was rising as Muhammad and Abu Bakr ambled along the Red Sea towards Yathrib.[814] One can almost imagine Abu Bakr turning to Muhammad and saying, "Plenty close call, Kemosabe."[815] The event is called the Hijra and marks the starting point for the Islamic calendar.[816] Muhammad's destination of Yathrib was soon to be known as "the City," al-Madinah, or as we know it today, Medina. They reached it on September 27, 622.[817] Over the next ten years, Muhammad would convert most of the Arabian tribes to his new evolving religion, Islam. Along the way, he would return to Mecca and define the rituals and practices of Islam. He would wrangle and fight with Jews and Christians and would have numerous wars with Arabian tribes. At the end of those years, Muhammad had united Arabia into his Islamic Ummah,[818] that was poised to conquer much of the world in the following century. The words he recited would guide and inflame much of the world for many centuries to follow.

---

[814] *Muhammad: His Life Based on the Earliest Sources,* Martin Lings (Inner Traditions, 2006) pp. 119-123.

[815] This was the tag line used by the Lone Ranger's sidekick Tonto when they escaped from danger. The Lone Ranger (1956).

[816] *In the Shadow of the Sword: The Birth of Islam and the Rise of Global Arab Empire,* Tom Holland (Doubleday, 2012) p. 53

[817] *Muhammad: His Life Based on the Earliest Sources,* Martin Lings (Inner Traditions, 2006) pp. 124-126

[818] The religious nation of Islam which transcends ethnic or political definitions. *The New Encyclopedia of Islam 4th Edition,* Cyril Glasse (Rowman & Littlefield, 2013) p. 543

# Chapter Four – From Dreams to Islam

In the harsh deserts of Arabia, one's allegiance was first to your blood family, your tribe. Living on the edge of existence, the tribe came above the individual, and all depended on each other for survival.[819] As trade became more predominate, the old ways had become less certain. Muhammad saw that the new ways had created new competitions, which led to greater inequity in the tribal communities. To overcome this, Muhammad created the *Ummah*, a new tribe based on his new religion of Islam. Muslims as members of the tribe or Ummah of Islam would supersede the ancestral tribes of old. The old tribes were either pagans, Jews, or Christians. For Muhammad, all Arabs now belonged to the super tribe of Islam.[820]

Almost 600 years earlier, Paul had preached a similar philosophy in his religion, *There is neither Jew nor Greek, there is neither bond nor free, there is neither male nor female: for ye are all one in Christ Jesus. And if ye be Christ's, then are ye Abraham's seed, and heirs according to the promise* (Gal. 3:28-29). Paul preached the imminent return of Jesus the Messiah,

---

[819] *A History of God: The 4,000-Year Quest of Judaism, Christianity and Islam,* Karen Armstrong (Alfred A. Knopf, 1994) p. 133

[820] *The Evolution of God,* Robert Wright (Little Brown and Company, 2009) p. 357

therefore his preaching had little emphasis on the material issues of his adherents. But Muhammad preached a distant return and Last Judgement and his preaching emphasized compassion and a fairer distribution of wealth in this life. Where Jesus had said that people should give to the poor, Muhammad required and annual payment going to the poor and the needy called the Zagat. [821]

While Paul had preached 'neither Jew nor Gentile', Muhammad preached 'neither Muslim nor Jew'. Jews and Muslims were to have equal status and must mutually assist one another. But the pureness of that concept took hold for neither Paul nor Muhammad. The Jews expressed doubts as to the divinity of Muhammad's revelations and were not prepared to accept a descendent of Ishmael as God's Messenger.[822] And of course, Muhammad had a new revelation to explain the situation, *Many of the People of the Book* (Jews) *long to bring you back to disbelief through envy which is in their souls* (Qur'an 2:109).

In Medina, Muhammad's tribe of Muslims was formed from people who had broken their allegiance and blood ties with their ancestral families. "Helpers" were those from Medina, and "emigrants" were those who came from tribes outside the area. The new religion was breaking apart old tribes, and their families. Jesus had said, *For I am come to set a man at variance against his father, and the daughter against her mother, and the daughter in law against her mother in law. And a man's foes shall be they of his own household* (Matt. 10:35-36) and now Muhammad followed, *O you who believe! Indeed, amongst your wives and your children are your enemies [since they make you turn away from treading the Divine Path]. Therefore, beware of them!*

---

[821] Qur'an 9:60

[822] *Muhammad: His Life Based on the Earliest Sources,* Martin Lings (Inner Traditions, 2006) pp. 129-130

(Qur'an 64:14).[823] This could not be allowed to stand. For Arabs, the idea of leaving your ancestral tribe was blasphemy.[824]

The antagonisms between the Quraysh in Mecca and the Muslims who had made the Hijra to Medina turned into battles of war fueled by family blood. The life blood of the Arabian tribes coursed in the veins of the trade routes between Arabia and Syria, and that was where the Islamic–Arab wars were fought. The first was the Battle at Badr, where Muhammad attacked a lucrative Meccan caravan. The Muslims defeated an overwhelming Meccan force with a unified command and a better field position.[825] The Meccans vowed revenge and, a year later, sent their forces to attack Medina. The Battle of Uhud was basically a draw after the Meccans withdrew, prematurely thinking that they had killed Muhammad.[826]

But the Meccans were not the only antagonists; Jews and Muslims were quarreling as well. In one of the marketplaces, a Jewish goldsmith had insulted a Muslim woman. A Muslim man accompanying her killed the Jewish goldsmith, and then the Jews killed him. An eye for and eye had been satisfied, if the Jews had been willing to accept the intervention of Muhammad. Instead, the Jews of the Bani Qaynuqa tribe withdrew into a fortified place and solicited help from other Jewish tribes. While the Jews mounted a formidable force, they were soon surrounded by a larger Islamic force that demanded surrender. After a two-week siege, they did just that. Muhammad, of course, had a revelation handy, *If thou overcomes them in war, then make of them an example, to strike fear into those that are behind them, that they make take heed* (Qur'an 8:57). Muhammad let his Jewish

---

[823] *The Evolution of God,* Robert Wright (Little Brown and Company, 2009) p. 356
[824] *Islam: A Short History,* Karen Armstrong (Modern Library, 2000) p. 14
[825] *Islam: A Short History,* Karen Armstrong (Modern Library, 2000) p. 19
[826] *Muhammad: His Life Based on the Earliest Sources,* Martin Lings (Inner Traditions, 2006) p. 191

captives live but exiled the tribe without their possessions, which were distributed as booty. Muhammad took 20% for his cut.[827]

Another time, the Angel Gabriel warned Muhammad in an apparition: The Banu Nadir, a Jewish tribe a short distance from Medina, was planning to assassinate him. Muhammad quickly rounded up an army and surrounded the Jewish village. He first cut down the palm trees, which were the pride and economic support of the community. Then he demanded that the Jews leave, but only with the possessions their camels could carry. Muhammad gave the Jewish land, homes, and remaining property to the Muslim emigrants, who had come from Mecca and elsewhere.[828] Pretty much what Israel did 1425 years later with the Muslims, after WWII.

Muhammad's position in the community and the customs of the time obliged him to establish at least a small harem. When a family friend suggested that Muhammad should marry either A'isha, a 6-year-old daughter of Abu Bakr, or Sawdah, a 30-year-old widowed cousin, Muhammad thought a moment and said, how about both.[829] When A'isha was 9, the wedding took place. Here is her description: "I was playing on a seesaw and my long streaming hair was disheveled. They came and took me from my play and made me ready."[830] Although estimates vary, Muhammad had 16 wives and 3 concubines in total. One of them was Zaynab bint Jahsh, who was his daughter-in-law. Now, marrying 9-year-olds was not a problem, but marrying your daughter-in-law was. So, Muhammad whipped up a special

---

[827] *Muhammad: His Life Based on the Earliest Sources,* Martin Lings (Inner Traditions, 2006) p. 166

[828] *Muhammad: His Life Based on the Earliest Sources,* Martin Lings (Inner Traditions, 2006) p. 209-211

[829] *Muhammad: His Life Based on the Earliest Sources,* Martin Lings (Inner Traditions, 2006) p. 109

[830] As quoted from the Leydon edition of "Kitab at-Tabaqau al-Kabir" by Muhammad ibn Sa'd in *Muhammad His Life Based on the Earliest Sources,* Martin Lings (Inner Traditions, 2006) p. 136.

dream from God that gave him a dispensation that daughters-in-law of adopted sons didn't count.[831] Sounds like something David Koresh might have come up with.

The Jews and the Quraysh of Mecca were by then the sworn enemies of Muhammad and Islam. They made a pact to take Medina with a force of 10,000 men. To strengthen the defense of Medina, Muhammad ordered a trench to be dug in the open areas around the city to make the Meccan cavalry ineffective. Everyone went out to dig, but there was not enough food to feed everyone. So, just like Jesus multiplying the fishes and loaves for four or five thousand, Muhammad arranged a lamb and date dinner for hundreds, out of a single lamb and a handful of dates.[832]

Muhammad's defensive trenches were effective in thwarting the Meccans. But if the Meccans could persuade the remaining tribe of Jews, the Banu Qurayzah, to break their truce with Muhammad and join forces, perhaps the trenches could be overcome. The Qurayzah broke their truce but, through double dealing, there arose mistrust in the alliance, and the Meccans withdrew, leaving the Jews of Qurayzah abandoned. The Angel Gabriel was Johnny-on-the-spot, telling Muhammad, "Verily God in his might and his Majesty commandeth thee, O Muhammad, that thou shouldst go against the sons of Qurayzah."[833] After a month, the Jews surrendered. Muhammad showed no mercy and had 700 Jewish men beheaded. The women were given out to the Muslim men. Muhammad took the prettiest one, Rayhana, for himself, of course.[834]

---

[831] *Muhammad: His Life Based on the Earliest Sources,* Martin Lings (Inner Traditions, 2006) pp. 219- 221

[832] *Muhammad: His Life Based on the Earliest Sources,* Martin Lings (Inner Traditions, 2006) p. 226

[833] *Muhammad: His Life Based on the Earliest Sources,* Martin Lings (Inner Traditions, 2006) pp. 237-241

[834] *Muhammad: His Life Based on the Earliest Sources,* Martin Lings (Inner Traditions, 2006) pp. 241

Even before the slaughter of the Jews of Qurayzah, Muhammad had made a change to the Salat. No longer would they pray in the direction of Jerusalem, but in the direction of Mecca. Jerusalem was the fountain of faith for Christians and Judaism. By bowing and praying towards Mecca, Muhammad symbolically was returning to the God of Abraham, who had built the Ka'bah in Mecca and was rejecting the Jews and Christians who had rejected his religion.[835] Muslims were now psychologically being set to take Mecca.

Muhammad and his followers set off for Mecca, unarmed, to make the Hajj. (The Hajj is the fifth pillar of Islam, which requires every able-bodied Muslim to make the pilgrimage to Mecca at least once in their life.) This put the pagan Quraysh in a bind. As the sacred keepers of the Ka'bah, it would have been a blot on their tribe to block the peaceful pilgrims yet allowing Muhammad and his Muslims into Mecca would have been a huge moral victory for Islam.

The Quraysh first tried to prevent the Muslims from reaching Meccan territory. Muhammad took an extended detour and the Muslims ran out of water. When the Israelites were without water in the desert, *Moses lifted up his hand, and with his rod he smote the rock twice: and the water came out abundantly, and the congregation drank, and their beasts also* (Num. 20:11). Now Muhammad performed the same miracle to save his pilgrims by stirring a small pool of water with his arrow turning it into a flowing spring. After a while, the Quraysh and Muhammad negotiated a deal that would allow his Muslim followers into Mecca, but only the following year and for several years thereafter.[836]

---

[835] *Islam: A Short History,* Karen Armstrong (Modern Library, 2000) p. 18

[836] *Muhammad: His Life Based on the Earliest Sources,* Martin Lings (Inner Traditions, 2006) pp. 256-257

The following year, the Hajj went off without incident, but thereafter the relations between the Muslims of Medina and the pagans of Mecca broke down. Muhammad put together a large force and marched on Mecca. He issued a general amnesty to those who stayed in their homes and locked their doors. Everyone did, and Mecca fell without a fight.

Muhammad entered Mecca and rode around the Ka'bah. As he pointed his staff, each of the 360 idols fell on its face. He ordered all who had idols in their homes to bring them to the Ka'bah where he had all of them broken and burned. There is no record of what happened to the picture of Jesus and Mary. Most of the Meccans then pledged their allegiance to Muhammad and converted to Islam on that day.[837]

Other battles would follow as Muhammad unified Arabia, from Yemen to Syria, building the Ummah of Islam. During that process, he delivered another one of his timely dreams to bolster his authority in a form of a "divine right of kings."

> *The Arabs of the desert say: We have faith. Say thou: Faith ye have not, but say 'we submit,' for faith hath not entered your hearts. And if ye obey God and his Messenger, He will no wise withhold from you your need for what ye do.*
> (Qur'an 49:14)

But there would no longer be a Muhammad to obey. He died unexpectedly from some form of fever on June 8, 632.[838]

Vastly more than Jesus, Muhammad had made a difference during his lifetime.[839] When Jesus was born, the Jews were a collection Sadducees, Pharisees, Essenes, and Zealots ineffectively opposing their Roman masters. When Jesus died, nothing had

---

[837] *Muhammad: His Life Based on the Earliest Sources,* Martin Lings (Inner Traditions, 2006) pp. 310-316

[838] *Muhammad: His Life Based on the Earliest Sources,* Martin Lings (Inner Traditions, 2006) p. 341

[839] *The Evolution of God,* Robert Wright (Little Brown and Company, 2009) p. 374

changed except another sect was added to the divide. When Muhammad was born, the Arabs were a collection of pagans, Jewish, and Christian tribes fighting each other for survival and pride. Within two years of Muhammad's death, the Arabs were an Islamic super-tribe, united in religion and politics.[840]

Muhammad had supplanted the pagan gods of the nomadic Arab tribes with the God of Abraham, the monotheistic transcendent God of the Jews, Zoroastrians, and Christians. Through his trances and visions, Muhammad had attached the name al-Lah of Mecca to the God of Judaism and Christianity.[841] Muhammad gave the Arab people simple, understandable, and easy-to-follow rituals: the Shadaha, the confession of faith; the Salat, the prayers to be said five times a day; the Zakat, the giving of alms and compassion for the needy; the Shawn, fasting for the month of Ramadan; and the Hajj, the trip to the holy site in Mecca. For that, there was a promise that God would reward you with Paradise. For 7th-century Arabs, this was something they all could understand, and they all could believe. And they did. And still do.

Christianity had been divided by a confusing debate over the deity of Jesus. Islam was united in a simpler theology of monotheism. Christianity had never been resolved by the finest minds of the Empire. Islam was resolved in all the minds of Arabia. The rituals of Christianity supported its aura of mystery. The rituals of Islam could be clearly seen and understood. In the coming decades, a choice of Islamic certainty or Paul's mysterium would be offered to most of the Roman and Persian empires. Most chose Muhammad's Allah over Paul's Christ.

Muhammad was now dead, and there was no one who claimed a phone line to God, and no revelation had said what to

[840] *The Middle East: A Brief History of the Last 2,000 Years,* Bernard Lewis, (Scribner, 1995) p. 53
[841] *A History of God: The 4,000-Year Quest of Judaism, Christianity and Islam,* Karen Armstrong (Alfred A. Knopf, 1994) p. 138-141

do next. Abu Bakr, Muhammad's long-time sidekick, was elected to succeed Muhammad as the caliph. However, not all of the tribes of Arabia were in agreement. Some had joined for political reasons and now wanted to leave the Ummah, while others in the Persian Gulf area had never joined. For two years, Bakr fought against new "prophets" who arose and tribes that wanted to leave the Islamic Ummah. Over 1800 years earlier, Joshua had tried to conquer Canaan in the name of Abraham's God and built a Jewish nation; now Bakr conquered Arabia in the name of Abraham's God and built the Islamic Ummah. By the time of his death in 634 AD, all the tribes of the Arabian Peninsula were members of a unified Ummah of Islam.[842]

As the Arab Islamic Ummah united and gained strength, the Roman and Persian empires were weakening, gasping for their last breath. Within a century, the Ummah would become an enduring empire, "in what was surely one of the swiftest and most dramatic changes in the whole of human history."[843]

---

[842] *Islam: A Short History,* Karen Armstrong (Modern Library, 2000) pp. 25-28
[843] *The Middle East: A Brief History of the Last 2,000 Years,* Bernard Lewis, (Scribner, 1995) p. 55

# Chapter Five – Islam Ends the Roman and Persian Empires

For almost a thousand years, since before the days of Alexander the Great, Greece and then Rome had been at war with the empires of Persian Mesopotamia. Both were exhausted and barely standing in the 6$^{th}$ century. During Muhammad's lifetime, the Persians (Sassanids) and the eastern remnant of the Roman Empire (Byzantium)[844] had been locked in the final years of their death thrall. Death in battle, death from plague.

Alexandria was the grain capital of the Roman world. Barges brought grain from the floodplains of the Nile to Alexandria, where it was loaded onto ships bound for Rome, Constantinople, and all the ports of the Mediterranean. In the summer of 541 AD, a plague came to Alexandria. "So putrid were the streets with

---

[844] The Roman Empire of common understanding had been moved to Constantinople by Constantine around the year 300. The Italian peninsula and the Western portion of the realm was then conquered by numerous Northern invaders and the Eastern remnant of the Empire became known as the Byzantium Empire although its lineage is the "Roman" Empire. I will use that term for the remainder of the section to avoid needless confusions to the wifebook. There is a similar potential terminology confusion using the term the "Sassanid's" and I will simply use Persian.

piles of the dead, so slippery underfoot with blood and melted flesh."[845] We no longer can conceive such scenes of real hell. And the hell in Alexandria was spread by rats on the grain ships to the corners of the realm. The plague plowed through people: pagans, Jews, and Christians of every sect. The plague knew no God.[846]

Within four years, a quarter of the empire had died. The shortage of labor increased its price, and with that the cost of all production went up. Besides, who was left to pay the taxes, much less to collect them? Justinian thought he could solve the problem with a law fixing prices but learned the hard way this was a fool's errand. Justinian learned he could only manage the economics, not prohibit its natural laws.[847] Like politicians to the present day, Justinian found out the hard way that there were laws of economics, like the laws of nature, which will not bend for human masters.

But the plague did not disappear; rather, it returned here and there for decades. Whole towns, villages, and stretches of the empire were now empty,[848] waiting for conquerors. The Barbarian army again crossed the Danube from Bulgaria as the Lombards invaded and captured northern Italy.[849] In the East, the Persian emperor attempted to isolate and quarantine the plague, but the attempt only delayed it and perhaps even made things worse.[850]

---

[845] *In the Shadow of the Sword: The Birth of Islam and the Rise of Global Arab Empire,* Tom Holland (Doubleday, 2012) p. 270

[846] Intriguingly, scientists have just unlocked the foundation of this plaque. A cold wave from 536 to 543 AD created the conditions for the plaque that killed one out of every four people, millions. http://www.nature.com/articles/s41598-018-19760-w

[847] *In the Shadow of the Sword: The Birth of Islam and the Rise of Global Arab Empire,* Tom Holland (Doubleday, 2012) p. 275

[848] *In the Shadow of the Sword: The Birth of Islam and the Rise of Global Arab Empire,* Tom Holland (Doubleday, 2012) pp. 278-279

[849] Only on March 17th in 1861, would Italy again be re-united as a single nation.

[850] *In the Shadow of the Sword: The Birth of Islam and the Rise of Global Arab Empire,* Tom Holland (Doubleday, 2012) p. 272-273

The Ghassanids were a tribe of Arab Christians. They were the shield of the Christian Empire as they stood between Palestine and the Persians. By 600 AD, the plague had virtually wiped them out. Along the entire border with the Persians, the plague had weakened the Roman defenses.[851]

In 610 AD, while Muhammad was dreaming in his cave near Mecca, Heraclius was being crowned the Roman emperor, and the Persians were attacking in Syria, taking advantage of infighting between the Trinitarian and Monophysite sects of Christianity.[852] In 611 AD, the Persians took Antioch and in 613 AD, seized Damascus.

In early May of 614 AD, 20,000 Jews joined the Persians in a siege of Jerusalem.[853] Rather than negotiate a surrender, the Christian Archbishop Zacharias decided to rely on the protection of God just as the Jews had relied on the protection of the same God 500 years earlier. Same location, same result. The Persians, with the help of the Jews, slaughtered the Roman Christians,[854] just as the Romans had slaughtered the Jews.

Fifty thousand Christians were killed, and 35,000 taken in slavery, including Zacharias. The surviving Christians were expelled, and control of Jerusalem returned to the Jews.[855] In revenge, the Jews destroyed the Christian churches, including the

---

[851] *In the Shadow of the Sword: The Birth of Islam and the Rise of Global Arab Empire,* Tom Holland (Doubleday, 2012) p. 280-288

[852] *Jesus Wars: How Four Patriarchs, Three Queens, and Two Emperors Decided What Christians Would Believe for the Next 1,500 Years,* John Philip Jenkins (Harper One, 2010) pp. 229-262. Chapter 8 goes into considerable detail in the all of the Christian disputes between the Nestorians and Monophysites from Chalcedon to the rise of Islam.

[853] *Jerusalem: The Biography,* Simon Sebag Montefiore (Knopf, 2011) pp 170-171

[854] *God's Crucible: Islam and the Making of Europe, 570-1215,* David Levering (Lewis Norton, 2008) p. 61

[855] *Jerusalem: The Biography,* Simon Sebag Montefiore (Knopf, 2011) p. 170

Church of the Holy Sepulcher, and massacred the remaining 4500 Christians who had somehow survived.[856]

The Persians carried off the True Cross on which Jesus had been crucified, the Holy Lance that had been thrust into his side, and the very sponge by which he had been given vinegar as he hung on the cross. No, really, it's true! Three hundred years earlier Constantine's mother, Helena, had bought them and many more purported relics of Jesus.[857] For centuries, people had paid to see them. An enterprising con man would have also sold her futures on the Brooklyn Bridge. By 619 AD, the Persians had pushed on to conquer Egypt and Chalcedon.

Back in Mecca, Muhammad had another dream that included one of the few historical references in the entire Qur'an. *The Romans have been defeated. In a land close by; but they will soon be victorious-Within a few years. Allah's is the command before and after; and on that day the believers shall rejoice* (Qur'an 30:2-4).

In 622 AD, Heraclius counterattacked and, in a stunning set of victories, defeated the Persians and retook Jerusalem. It was the same year that Muhammad and Abu Bakr made their escape from Mecca.

By 629 AD, Heraclius had defeated the Persians and agreed to a peace with their ruler, Kavadh II. On March 21, 630, Heraclius entered the Golden Gate of Jerusalem to return the True Cross and the other relics he had recaptured from the Persians.[858] On this journey, he stopped in Tiberius, where he met a Jew who had persecuted the Christians under the Persian rule. Why had the Jews done this, asked the emperor? "Because they

---

[856] *In the Shadow of the Sword: The Birth of Islam and the Rise of Global Arab Empire,* Tom Holland (Doubleday, 2012) pp. 290-291

[857] *In the Shadow of the Sword: The Birth of Islam and the Rise of Global Arab Empire,* Tom Holland (Doubleday, 2012) pp. 205-209

[858] *Jerusalem: The Biography,* Simon Sebag Montefiore (Knopf, 2011) p. 173

are the enemies of my faith," came the reply. Heraclius resolved that issue with a law requiring all people of the Roman Empire to be baptized. Christianity was now not just the official religion; it was the *only* religion in the remains of the Roman Empire.[859]

After the plague and eight years of war, the Roman and Persian Empires were totally exhausted. The Arabs had been fighting among themselves as well, but on a much smaller scale. Muhammad had united most of Arabia, and on his death, Abu Bakr finalized the unification of the Arabs. Violence within the Islamic Ummah was then forbidden.[860] So who could the Arabs fight?

Umar ibn al Khattab, Muhammad's father-in-law, became caliph when Bakr died in 634 AD. Umar had the brilliant answer of turning "the Bedouin's combative energies away from one another and conquering the settled lands to the North."[861] The exhausted empires of Rome and Persia were dead men standing, and just as Muhammad had destroyed the powerless idols of Mecca, Umar knocked over the hollow Empires of Rome and Persia. The Jews who had previously been faced with forced conversion to Christianity by Heraclius were there to help.[862]

The Arabs did not begin a religious war. "There was nothing religious about these campaigns, and Umar did not believe that he had a divine mandate to conquer the world. The objective of Umar and his warriors was entirely pragmatic, they wanted plunder,"[863] and the booty was there for the pickings.

In 636 AD, the Arabs attacked Syria. Heraclius was shocked and ordered his best battle-hardened troops to expel the Arabs

---

[859] *In the Shadow of the Sword: The Birth of Islam and the Rise of Global Arab Empire,* Tom Holland (Doubleday, 2012) p. 296

[860] *Islam: A Short History,* Karen Armstrong (Modern Library, 2000) p. 27

[861] *A Concise History of the Middle East,* Arthur Goldschmidt Jr. (Westview Press, 7th Edition, 2001) p. 53

[862] *In the Shadow of the Sword: The Birth of Islam and the Rise of Global Arab Empire,* Tom Holland (Doubleday, 2012) p. 352

[863] *Islam: A Short History,* Karen Armstrong (Modern Library, 2000) pp. 29-30

from Roman territory. In August, the Romans had 30,000 troops positioned just east of the Sea of Galilee. They had built a bridge across a large gully near the Yarmuk River for resupply and retreat. In the battle, greatly outnumbered Arabs feigned retreat, and when the Romans advanced, the Arabs took the bridge with hidden troops, trapping the Romans who panicked and were then slaughtered.[864] Or, in another account, God delivered a dust storm that blinded the Christians, making them ripe for the slaughter. Whether dust storm, or military guile, it was one of the decisive battles of history.[865]

By April of 637 AD, Jerusalem gave up without a fight and the Muslims and their Jewish allies were welcomed into the city. For Jews, the ancient Roman ban on living in Jerusalem was revoked and 70 Jewish families were invited to settle near the Temple Mount.[866] Jews were joyous to hear that their great prophet Moses was shared with Islam and that they agreed that their common God gave the Holy Land to the Jews:

> *Remember when Moses said to his people: 'My people, remember Allah's favour upon you when He raised Prophets amongst you and appointed you rulers, and granted to you what He had not granted to anyone else in the world. My people! Enter the holy land which Allah has ordained for you.* (Qur'an 5:20-21)

Palestinians today, and Muslims in general seem to have forgotten this passage in the Qur'an.

Both Jews and Christians saw the coming of Islam as a sign of the end times. "People are saying that the Prophet has

---

[864] *God's Crucible: Islam and the Making of Europe, 570-1215,* David Levering (Lewis Norton, 2008) p. 73

[865] *Jerusalem: The Biography,* Simon Sebag Montefiore (Knopf, 2011) p. 181

[866] *Jerusalem: The Biography,* Simon Sebag Montefiore (Knopf, 2011) p. 185

appeared, coming with the Saracens. They are saying he is proclaiming the advent of the Anointed One – the Christ who is to come."[867] Theodosius had decreed a singular Trinitarian definition of Christianity, but now, the Muslims, "extended the same legally defined tolerance to all forms of Christianity."[868] Henceforth, belief in the Trinity and Chalcedon definitions of Jesus were no longer required. "Christians viewed the Muslim Arabs as liberators…and often welcomed them."[869] Christians in Egypt virtually surrendered to the Islamic Arabs. Almost everyone was happy. Even the taxes were lower!

The Arabs moved on and defeated the Persians at al-Qadisiyya, in November of 636 AD, and in the following years, overtook all of Iran and the former Persian Empire. The events were later put into verse, "Damn this world, Damn this time, Damn this fate. Uncivilized Arabs have come to make me a Muslim"[870] (I understand it rhymes far better in Persian).

While the Arab Army fought for plunder, Umar demanded discipline. Soldiers were not allowed to acquire property outside of Arabia and were forced to live in newly built garrison towns outside the cities they conquered. Only personal goods were considered booty, and one fifth of that had to be sent to Umar. [871]

Twelve years after Muhammad died, Umar was assassinated in 644 AD. By then, the Arabs controlled what today is Saudi Arabia, Kuwait, the Emirates, Yemen, Egypt, Syria, Jordon,

---

[867] "The Teachings of Jacob" 5:16 as quoted in *In the Shadow of the Sword: The Birth of Islam and the Rise of Global Arab Empire,* Tom Holland (Doubleday, 2012) p. 352

[868] *The Middle East: A Brief History of the Last 2,000 Years,* Bernard Lewis, (Scribner, 1995) p. 56

[869] *A Concise History of the Middle East,* Arthur Goldschmidt Jr. (Westview Press, 7th Edition, 2001) p. 54

[870] From the Persian National Epic, the" Shah-nameh", written about the year 1000 by Ferdowsi as quoted in *God's Crucible: Islam and the Making of Europe, 570-1215,* David Levering (Lewis Norton, 2008) p. 76

[871] *A Concise History of the Middle East,* Arthur Goldschmidt Jr. (Westview Press, 7th Edition, 2001) p. 56

Israel, eastern Turkey, Iraq, and parts of eastern and southern Iran.[872] Still, his successor wanted more.

Uthman ibn Affan was a member of the powerful Umayyad family and had married Ruqayyah, the daughter of Muhammad.[873] He was elected third caliph by the companions of Muhammad. Under him, Islamic control expanded west with the taking of Libya. The first Islamic navy was formed in 655 and used to conquer Cypress.[874] To the east, they took Armenia, the Caucasus, going as far as the Oxus River in Iran, Herat in Afghanistan, and what is today Pakistan.[875]

"The Arab conquests…restored to circulation vast accumulated riches frozen in private, public, and Church possessions." The conquering Islamic Arabs possessed fabulous wealth, which they spent with abandon,[876] "The influx of money and treasure enriched Medina and Mecca beyond anything Muhammad could have anticipated, and eventually beyond what his associates could assimilate. Greed and vice proliferated, especially among the young."[877] But there was discontent and division in the garrison towns.

Uthman had continued Umar's policies forbidding the establishment of private estates in foreign land. He gave the most lucrative posts to his favorites and was spectacularly greedy in keeping the loot for himself and his family.[878] There were "fierce

---

[872] *Islam: A Short History,* Karen Armstrong (Modern Library, 2000) See map on p. 28

[873] *Muhammad: His Life Based on the Earliest Sources,* Martin Lings (Inner Traditions, 2006) p. 72

[874] *A Concise History of the Middle East,* Arthur Goldschmidt Jr. (Westview Press, 7th Edition, 2001) p. 57

[875] *Islam: A Short History,* Karen Armstrong (Modern Library, 2000) pp. 31-32

[876] *The Middle East: A Brief History of the Last 2,000 Years,* Bernard Lewis, (Scribner, 1995) p. 60

[877] *A Concise History of the Middle East,* Arthur Goldschmidt Jr. (Westview Press, 7th Edition, 2001) p. 58

[878] *In the Shadow of the Sword: The Birth of Islam and the Rise of Global Arab Empire,* Tom Holland (Doubleday, 2012) p. 360

dissensions and (Muhammad's) state foundered amid rebellion and civil war."[879] To a Christian Armenian bishop writing at the time, it appeared that God had sent a "disturbance among the armies of Ishmael so that their unity was split."[880]

Surprise, surprise! The disturbance was over money. Uthman practiced nepotism, giving his family, the Umayyads, the most prestigious posts and allowing them to grow rich off the work of the soldiers. In addition, the Army was incensed when Uthman banned many favorite variations of the revelations of Muhammad.[881] It all came to a head when, "Soldiers from al-Fustat garrison rode into Medina from Egypt, furious about the tinkering of the sacred and the niggardly spread of the spoils of war and office. Uthman died shouting at the man who struck him down to let go of his beard."[882] You may not know the name, but Uthman is the man who gave Islam the Qur'an.

---

[879] *The Middle East: A Brief History of the Last 2,000 Years,* Bernard Lewis, (Scribner, 1995) p. 62

[880] *In the Shadow of the Sword: The Birth of Islam and the Rise of Global Arab Empire,* Tom Holland (Doubleday, 2012) pp. 360-361

[881] *Islam: A Short History,* Karen Armstrong (Modern Library, 2000) p. 31-32

[882] *God's Crucible: Islam and the Making of Europe, 570-1215,* David Levering (Lewis Norton, 2008) pp. 87-88

# Chapter Six – The Noble Qur'an: The Islamic Beliefs

*I*n the name of Allah, the Entirely Merciful, the Especially Merciful* (Qur'an 1:1). And thus, begins the Qur'an. After the introduction, we are told, *This is the Book about which there is no doubt, a guidance for those conscious of Allah.... Who believe in the unseen.... And who believe in what has been revealed to you, O Muhammad* (Qur'an 2:1-4). Either those are Words from God or all the words that follow are the ultimate pseudepigraphal document.

The Qur'an is the single scriptural book of Islam. It contains 114 named chapters,[883] over 6000 versus and about 78,000 words. The Bible is a compendium of books that is ten times longer, with about 780,000 words divided into 1200 chapters and 31,000 verses. Length and arrangement aside, the Bible is a historical narrative document from which theologies have been derived, while the Qur'an is mostly a theological document which also contains historical narratives. This explains a very critical difference. Because the Bible is not a definitive theological document, Judaism—and especially Christianity—

---

[883] For simplicity, only the numbers will be used, unless required for a specific purpose.

have evolved theologies across numerous diverse sects. The Qur'an, however, provides Islam with a consistent theology that only evolved through the Hadiths, which are a separate set of stories and sayings of Muhammad.

The Qur'an retells Old Testament stories, as well as several Jesus stories from the New Testament. In doing so, it attempts to rectify the history of Judaism and Christianity within the theology of Islam. Beyond theology and its retold biblical stories, the Qur'an contains both practical and ethical lessons for life. For example, the Qur'an offers clear business advice; *when you contract a debt for a specified term, write it down. And let a scribe write [it] between you...and let the one who has the obligation dictate...not leave anything out of it* (Qur'an 2:282) and a clear instruction on dealing with your parents: *Be good to your parents; and should both or any one of them attain old age with you...speak to them with respect, and be humble and tender to them* (Qur'an 17:23-24).

The Qur'an is meant to be recited, read aloud in Arabic.[884] Its spiritual beauty comes from the poetry of the sounds in its reading, its intrinsic rhythm and rhyme. "It is not enough to say that the sound of the recitation is in harmony with the meaning of the words, but that the sound itself conveys meaning."[885] It is that rhythm and rhyme that acts as a mnemonic for its memorization, but only in Arabic,[886] *And if We had made it a non-Arabic Qur'an, they would have said, "Why are its verses not explained in detail [in our language]? Is it a foreign [recitation] and an Arab [messenger]?"* (Qur'an 41:44). The Arabs had no scriptures in Arabic until Muhammad provided one.

---

[884] *The Story of the Qur'an: Its History and Place in Muslim Life,* Ingrid Mattson (Wiley Blackwell, 2nd Edition, 2013) p. 27

[885] *The Story of the Qur'an: Its History and Place in Muslim Life,* Ingrid Mattson (Wiley Blackwell, 2nd Edition, 2013) p. 34

[886] *The Story of the Qur'an: Its History and Place in Muslim Life,* Ingrid Mattson (Wiley Blackwell, 2nd Edition, 2013) p. 88

The spiritual beauty of Christianity is not intrinsic in the words of its scriptures. Christians receive spiritual emotion from the hymns of Beethoven, the artistry of stained glass, the beauty and majesty of the churches, listening to a Bach choral, viewing the ceiling of the Sistine Chapel, or absorbing any of the millions of Christian artistic works. All of that is inherent in the Arabic recitation of the Qur'an.

Beyond its poetic beauty, the Qur'an is a very different book than the Bible. The Bible is a history, with names and dates of people in the geopolitical arena and nominal references to the divine. The Qur'an makes very little mention of geopolitical events or people but makes constant reference to the divine. The Bible was selected and compiled to fit a religious and political outcome from a large pool of documents, each written at a different time and place with different religious and political purposes. The Qur'an is a single work written within a narrow time frame to fit a religious and political purpose. The Old Testament is an anthology of many redacted documents compiled across the breadth of many centuries. The Qur'an is one document that presents a uniform theology. The New Testament was selected from many tracts to attempt to unify multiple theological understandings of Jesus. The Bible is the product of several languages: Aramaic, Hebrew, and Greek. The Qur'an is of one language: Arabic.

Perhaps the most significant difference is that the Bible was written over the course of many centuries by numerous unknown authors while the Qur'an was developed over decades by one known man. Jesus had preached for as little as one year and at most three. Muhammad preached his Islam for 22 years. Jesus did not live long enough to hone his theology, nor document it, nor build a political movement around it. Muhammad had the time to hone his message and build a political movement around it.

This can be seen, for example, in Muhammad's changes in praying while facing Mecca rather than Jerusalem, his attitude towards the Jews, his marriage to his daughter-in-law, and in his building political power. Muhammad admits the evolution of his message, *We do not abrogate a verse or cause it to be forgotten except that We bring forth [one] better than it or similar to it* (Qur'an 2:106). But there is no way of understanding all the ways his message and the theology of Islam may have evolved.

While Christianity claims that the Bible is the Word of God, it contains very few words from God. Islam makes a much more audacious claim about the Qur'an: All the words of the Qur'an are believed by Muslims to be words from God.[887] Therefore, the Qur'an must be perfect and unchanging. The bedrock of Islamic faith is that Muhammad recited the words *from* God, and that his words were written down and compiled into the Qur'an, which has remained the perfect Words *from* God down to every last letter and punctuation mark!

That point cannot be over emphasized; it is the a priori of Islam. "The Qur'an is the only scripture which has been preserved in its exact original form, in its entire content, as it was revealed to the Prophet fourteen centuries ago, not a word added or removed. This is a historical fact beyond dispute."[888] At least by Muslims.

The Qur'an does retell some of the Old Testament Bible stories. A rough analogy might be the retelling of Jane Austen's *Emma* and *Pride and Prejudice* in the movies *Clueless* and *Bridgett Jones' Diary*. The plots are the same, told in different words with different emphasis. It is much the same in the Qur'an; this time the Bibles stories are actually told by God. Which is

---

[887] *The Story of the Qur'an: Its History and Place in Muslim Life,* Ingrid Mattson (Wiley Blackwell, 2nd Edition, 2013) p. 85

[888] This and other quotations regarding Islamic literature and the Qur'an's textual accuracy is in the opening of: THE PRESERVATION OF THE QUR'AN by Samuel Green, which can be found here: http://www.answering-islam.org/Green/uthman.htm

how most Hollywood producers probably feel, when converting a book into film.

The famous story of Noah and the flood is told in a very long passage in the Qur'an. Since many people have a reasonable recollection of that Bible story, I have included the entire story from the Qur'an to show how very different the style of Qur'an is from the Bible.

*And We had certainly sent Noah to his people, [saying], "Indeed, I am to you a clear warner That you not worship except Allah. Indeed, I fear for you the punishment of a painful day." So the eminent among those who disbelieved from his people said, "We do not see you but as a man like ourselves, and we do not see you followed except by those who are the lowest of us [and] at first suggestion. And we do not see in you over us any merit; rather, we think you are liars." He said, "O my people have you considered: if I should be upon clear evidence from my Lord while He has given me mercy from Himself but it has been made unapparent to you, should we force it upon you while you are averse to it? And O my people, I ask not of you for it any wealth. My reward is not but from Allah. And I am not one to drive away those who have believed. Indeed, they will meet their Lord, but I see that you are a people behaving ignorantly. And O my people, who would protect me from Allah if I drove them away? Then will you not be reminded? And I do not tell you that I have the depositories [containing the provision] of Allah or that I know the unseen, nor do I tell you that I am an angel, nor do I say of those upon whom your eyes look down that Allah will never grant them any good. Allah is most knowing of what is within their souls. Indeed, I would then be among the wrongdoers." They said, "O Noah, you have disputed us and been frequent in dispute of us. So bring us what you threaten us, if you should be of the truthful." He said, "Allah will only bring it to you if He wills, and you will not cause [Him] failure. And my advice will not benefit you - although I wished to advise you - If Allah should intend to put you in error. He is your Lord, and to Him you will be returned." Or do they say [about Prophet Muhammad], "He invented it"? Say, "If I have invented it, then upon me is [the consequence of] my crime; but I am innocent of what [crimes] you commit." And it was revealed to Noah that, "No one will believe from your people except those who have already believed, so do not be distressed by what they have been doing. And construct the ship under Our observation and Our inspiration and do not address Me concerning those who have wronged; indeed, they are [to be] drowned." And he constructed the ship, and whenever an assembly of the eminent of his people passed by him, they ridiculed him. He said, "If you ridicule us, then we will ridicule you just as you ridicule. And you are going to know who will get a punishment that will disgrace him [on earth] and upon whom will descend an enduring punishment [in the Hereafter]." [So it was], until when Our command came and the oven overflowed, We said, "Load upon the ship of each [creature] two mates and your family, except those about whom the word has preceded, and [include] whoever has believed." But none had believed with him, except a few. And [Noah] said, "Embark therein; in the name of Allah is its course and its anchorage. Indeed, my Lord is Forgiving and Merciful." And it sailed with them through waves like mountains, and Noah called to his son who was apart [from them], "O my son, come aboard with us and be not with the disbelievers." [But] he said, "I will take refuge on a mountain to protect me from the water." [Noah] said,*

*"There is no protector today from the decree of Allah, except for whom He gives mercy." And the waves came between them, and he was among the drowned. And Noah called to his Lord and said, "My Lord, indeed my son is of my family; and indeed, Your promise is true; and You are the most just of judges!" He said, "O Noah, indeed he is not of your family; indeed, he is [one whose] work was other than righteous, so ask Me not for that about which you have no knowledge. Indeed, I advise you, lest you be among the ignorant." [Noah] said, "My Lord, I seek refuge in You from asking that of which I have no knowledge. And unless You forgive me and have mercy upon me, I will be among the losers." It was said, "O Noah, disembark in security from Us and blessings upon you and upon nations [descending] from those with you. But other nations [of them] We will grant enjoyment; then there will touch them from Us a painful punishment." That is from the news of the unseen which We reveal to you, [O Muhammad]. You knew it not, neither you nor your people, before this. So be patient; indeed, the [best] outcome is for the righteous. And to 'Aad [We sent] their brother Hud. He said, "O my people, worship Allah; you have no deity other than Him. You are not but inventors [of falsehood]. O my people, I do not ask you for it any reward. My reward is only from the one who created me. Then will you not reason? And O my people, ask forgiveness of your Lord and then repent to Him. He will send [rain from] the sky upon you in showers and increase you in strength [added] to your strength. And do not turn away, [being] criminals."* (Qur'an 11:25-49, SAHIH INTERNATIONAL)

I'll bet you did not read that all the way through and just skipped to the end! That's okay, it makes the point that while the words are English and formed into sentences, the language of the Qur'an is deeply difficult to follow. The basic story is the same as that told in Genesis; God was unhappy with the evils of people and sent a flood that killed everyone, except Noah and his family, who survived because God told Noah to build an ark. But this Qur'anic version repeatedly stresses believing in God, and the punishment for not believing, with very little of the mechanics, the size of the ark, its construction, the release of the doves, etc. which are found in the Genesis version.

The Qur'an retells all the main Old Testament Bible stories in this fashion: The Creation story, Adam and Eve, Abraham and Isaac and Ishmael as told earlier, [889] Sodom and Gomorrah, the Tower of Babel, Moses, the Exodus from Egypt, David and Solomon, Jonah, Elijah, Job and others. They are all told in the language sampled above, and mostly stricken of the details usually thought of as critical to the Old Testament story. For example, the Qur'an tells the story of the Exodus, but without the ten plagues of Egypt. And all the retellings are very difficult for Western minds to read and follow. Well, at least it is difficult for me.

The Qur'an acknowledges the Old Testament, saying, *And We sent...the Torah as guidance and instruction for the righteous* (Qur'an 5:46). However, according to the Qur'an, the Torah was corrupted: *Among the Jews are those who distort words from their [proper] usages* (Qur'an 4:46) and *there is among them a party who alter the Scripture* (Qur'an 3:78). The Qur'an was given to Muhammad to correct the errors. *And We have revealed to you, [O Muhammad], the Book in truth, confirming that which preceded it of the Scripture and as a criterion over it* (Qur'an 5:48). While there are other passages, these are succinct in conveying the Islamic belief that the Qur'an is the correct version of biblical stories.

---

[889] In the Qur'an, Abraham sacrifices Ishmael, not Isaac.

The Qur'an says that the book of Psalms was also given by God to King David (Qur'an 4:163) and that a gospel was given to Jesus (Qur'an 3:3; 5:46). This is not necessarily referring to the Gospels Christians had decided to put into the New Testament, but the gospel which Jesus taught.

In the Qur'an, Jesus has a virgin birth by Mary: *"How, O Lord, shall I have a son, when no man has ever touched me?"* *"Thus shall it be,"* was the answer. *God creates whatever He wills. When He decrees a thing, He only says, "Be" and it is* (Qur'an 3:47).

And Jesus will be born on the road from Jerusalem to Bethlehem:

*And the pains of childbirth drove her to the trunk of a palm tree. She said, 'I wish I had died before this, and had been long forgotten [Mary was worried that people would think badly of her as she was not married.]. Then (baby Jesus) called her from below her, saying, 'Don't be sad. Your Lord has provided a stream under you.' Shake the trunk of the palm tree towards you, and it will drop on you fresh ripe dates. So, eat and drink and be happy.* (Qur'an 19:23-26)

The Qur'an says that Jesus was not crucified. *And they did not kill him, nor did they crucify him; but [another] was made to resemble him to them. And indeed, those who differ over it are in doubt about it. They have no knowledge of it except the following of assumption. And they did not kill him, for certain* (Qur'an 4:157). Instead, God took Jesus back to heaven. *"O Jesus, now I will recall you and raise you up to Myself and cleanse you of (the uncongenial company and the filthy environment of) those who have rejected you and will set up those who follow you above those who have rejected you till the Day of Resurrection* (Qur'an 3:55).

In the Qur'an, Jesus is not God or part of the Trinity or the Son of God. Jesus is a prophet, a messenger from God.

*The Messiah, Jesus, the son of Mary, was but a messenger of Allah and His word which He directed to Mary and a soul [created at a command] from Him. So, believe in Allah and His messengers. And do not say, "Three"; desist - it is better for you. Indeed, Allah is but one God. Exalted is He above having a son.* (Qur'an 4:171)

The Nicene Creed is pointedly denied: *Praise be to Allah, who begets no son, and has no partner* (Qur'an 17:111, Yusif Ali).

Jews, Christians, and Muslims all believe in a messiah who will return at the end of times, but both Christians and Muslims believe that the returning Messiah will be Jesus: *And indeed, Jesus will be [a sign for] knowledge of the Hour, so be not in doubt of it, and follow Me. This is a straight path* (Qur'an 43:61). *And there is none of the people of the Scripture (Jews and Christians) but must believe in him (Jesus son of Mary as a Messenger of Allah and a human being) before his death. And on the Day of Resurrection, he will be a witness against them* (Qur'an 4:159).

Other than the retelling of biblical stories, the rest of the Qur'an varies "from short ecstatic utterances to theological and ethical discourses on the importance of monotheism and moral behavior."[890]

Or perhaps what many might think of as immoral behavior, martyrdom:

*And never think of those who have been killed in the cause of Allah as dead. Rather, they are alive with their Lord, receiving provision, Rejoicing in what Allah has bestowed upon them of His bounty, and they receive good tidings*

---

[890] *Life After Death: A History of the Afterlife in Western Religion,* Alan F. Segal (Doubleday, 2004) p 641

*about those [to be martyred] after them who have not yet joined them.* (Qur'an 3:169-170)

*And those who leave their home for the cause of Allah and then were killed or died - Allah will surely provide for them a good provision. And indeed, it is Allah who is the best of providers.* (Qur'an 22:58-59)

Then this somewhat peculiar passage:

*Allah hath purchased of the believers their persons and their goods; for theirs (in return) is the garden (of Paradise): they fight in His cause, and slay and are slain: a promise binding on Him in truth, through the Law, the Gospel, and the Qur'an: and who is more faithful to his covenant than Allah?* (Qur'an 9:111)

This implies that not just Muslims, but also Christians and Jews fighting for Abraham's God will receive a bountiful reward. And what if they are fighting each other?

These examples show how, in general, Muhammad attempted to unify Judaism and Christianity in the theology of Islam—a theology that is presented much more clearly in the Qur'an than in the Bible. Humans possess a soul, separate from the body, which on death will be returned to God. *Allah takes the souls at the time of their death* (Qur'an 39:42). However, Islam is vague on what happens to the soul prior to the resurrection (Qur'an 6:60-61; 32:10-11; 39:42). Except if you are a martyr, in which case you with your body go directly to paradise (Qur'an 56:1-26). Islam absolutely believes in a resurrection. *Allah - there is no deity except Him. He will surely assemble you for [account on] the Day of Resurrection, about which there is no doubt* (Qur'an 4:87). And while sometimes debated, it is a bodily resurrection (Qur'an 7:24-25; 19:66-68; 22:7).

The apocalypse or end times, called "the Hour" in Islam, is very much like that of its sibling religions of Abraham's God. The Qur'an has nothing like the Book of Revelations, but the Hadiths offer detailed descriptions and mysterious signs of the Hour. The general understanding runs something like this: Humanity will be full of a variety of sins, injustice, and corruption. Muslims will be divided and will have lost their faith. Someone called the Mahdi will arise and lead the Muslims back to their faith and unite them against their enemies, led by a false Messiah or antichrist for a final confrontation between good and evil. But Mahdi will not be successful, and Jesus will descend to earth and win the battle, after which there will be the Last Judgement and the consignment to Heaven or Hell.[891]

Like in Revelations, there will be signs of the coming end times: Some are very ominous:

> *The last hour would not come unless the Muslims will fight against the Jews and the Muslims would kill them until the Jews would hide themselves behind a stone or a tree and a stone or a tree would say: Muslim, or the servant of Allah, there is a Jew behind me; come and kill him.* (Sahih Muslim 4:6985)[892]

And some, while stating specifics, are quite vague:

> *"It will never begin until you see ten signs before it." He mentioned the smoke, the Dajjaal, the Beast, the rising of the sun from its place of setting, the descent of Jesus son of Mary (peace and blessings of Allah be upon him)*

---

[891] *The Islamic Jesus: How the King of the Jews became a prophet of the Muslims,* Mustafa Akyol (St. Martin's Press, 2017) pp. 187-188

[892] These verses cannot be dismissed as hyperbole. The public statements by many leaders of the Islamic community all reflect exactly the tone of this passage. One example is "Erdogan's Vision: Uniting an 'Army of Islam' to Destroy Israel in 10 Days" from the Turkish daily *Yeni Şafak,* as translated and published in the *Middle East Media Research,* March 7, 2018.

*Ya'jooj and Ma'jooj, and three landslides, one in the east, one in the west and one in the Arabian Peninsula, and the last of that is a fire which will emerge from Yemen and drive the people to their place of gathering.* (Sahih Muslim, Book 041:6931)

Such vague and mysterious things give rise to different interpretations among the various Islamic sects, but while the Hadiths attempt to forecast the events of the final days, the Qur'an provides the ultimate ending: *And those who believed and those who were Jews or Christians or Sabeans [before Prophet Muhammad] - those [among them] who believed in Allah and the Last Day and did righteousness - will have their reward with their Lord* (Qur'an 2:62). Note that only Jews, Christians, or Sabeans (Zoroastrians) who came *before* Muhammad will be saved. *Those [believers in the former revelations] believe in the Qur'an. But whoever disbelieves in it from the [various] factions - the Fire is his promised destination* (Qur'an 11-17). And to make the point, the Qur'an is filled with descriptions of Hell— lots of fire and boiling water, and the same nasty stuff usually associated with Hell.[893]

One God created all: humans with a soul, a path of righteousness for redemption, an end of time with the return of Jesus, the resurrection of the dead, a final judgement with an afterlife in paradise for the believers, and a fiery hell for the non-believers. That is Islam! Yet all of Islam—all the instructions, theology, wisdom, and advice, and all of the Qur'an—is based on the presumed reality of Muhammad visiting with God and seeing and hearing from God's agents. Or was it really just a dream?

---

[893] The chapter 'Islam and the Afterlife' *Life After Death: A History of the Afterlife in Western Religion,* Alan F. Segal (Doubleday, 2004) pp. 639-676 provides a more in-depth view of Islamic eschatology including some of the differences between the sects.

# Chapter Seven – Islam: The Qur'an & Hadiths

There was no written Qur'an when Muhammad died; hence, Muhammad did not write the Qur'an. Now, that is a historical fact that even Muslims do not dispute.[894] Muslims do believe that Muhammad authored the Qur'an, which is the written collection of what people remembered Mohammad saying, or the memory of what people had been told Mohammad said, and the shorthand notes of what people thought they heard Muhammad say. That collection of sayings was then gathered, written, and became the Qur'an.

For two years, Muhammad told only his family and friends about his dreams and visions.[895] In 612 AD, Muhammad began performing his recitations to larger public audiences and continued doing so until his death in 632 AD.[896] Unlike Paul, who wrote to tell of his own dreams, Muhammad was *unlettered*

---

[894] Actually, a few do think that Muhammad ordered and edited at least a portion of the Qur'an in written form before he died.

[895] *The Story of the Qur'an: Its History and Place in Muslim Life,* Ingrid Mattson (Wiley Blackwell, 2nd Edition, 2013) explains on pp. 18-22 how Muhammad's dreams would occur and how they were reported by Muhammad's biographers 200 years later.

[896] *Islam: A Short History,* Karen Armstrong (Modern Library, 2000) p. 4

(Qur'an 7:157)[897] or *can neither read nor write* (Qur'an 7:157 Pickthall) or is usually considered illiterate.[898] An illiterate Muhammad could only verbally tell of his dreams and visions, leaving his audiences to tell others what they heard or take some notes on pieces of stone, bone, paper, or palm stems.

At first, this was made easy by Muhammad; he was reciting only 3 to 4 Surahs, or Books a year, averaging about 5 verses a month, and then between the years 618 and 620, the number exploded to over a book a month, averaging over 3 verses a day. After moving to Medina, the pace returned to an average of 3 to 4 books per year for the last ten years of his life.[899]

Muhammad repeated his recitations at different times and different places. That cannot be argued; whether he said them in different order, in different words, with different themes is extensively argued. This could help explain why the Qur'an is divided into chapters without regard to theme or chronology. For example, his first revelation is in the 96th book, called "The Pen," while his last revelation is in the 48th book, called, "The Victory." There has always been a debate over the timing and process of the compiling and writing of the Qur'an.

The Bible was wrapped in a cocoon of protection until "Divino afflante Spiritu" approved the process to unwind it in the 20th century. Through that process, we now know the Bible was written many decades after the events it reports, by people having

---

[897] The Sahih International translation of the Qur'ān will be used except as otherwise noted.

[898] The claim of Muhammad being illiterate is based on Surah 7:157-158. While Sahih al-Bukhari, Volume 1, Book 3, Number 65 and 114 claims that he could write. There is no claim that he ever wrote down any part of the Qur'an.

[899] Using the Standard Egyptian Chronology.

| Period | Books | Verses |
|---|---|---|
| 610-618 | 30 | 504 |
| 618-620 | 30 | 2648 |
| 620-622 | 26 | 1461 |
| Total Mecca 86 | 4613 | |
| 622-632 | 28 | 1623 |
| Total Medina 28 | 1623 | |

little or no connection with those events, after which there was further editing and redaction. Islam stands resolutely against critical scholarship, hence strongly against any unwinding of the protective cocoon of the Qur'an. That cocoon is made of strong thread.

Islam is based not just on the Qur'an but also on the life and actions of Muhammad. Hadiths are the sayings, actions, and habits of Muhammad, which collectively are referred to as the Sunna. The terms Sunna and Hadiths are often used interchangeably. Hadiths are the basis of Islamic law and ethics, which are more important to the daily lives of Muslims than is the Qur'an.[900] The cocoon that surrounds the Sunna was made of weak thread.

Almost everything we know about Muhammad, Islam, and the Qur'an comes from just ten books, all of which were written 200 years *after* Muhammad.[901]

1. The Sira of Ibn Hisham (d. 834)[902]
2. A History of Military Campaigns by al-Waqidi (d. 822)
3. "Classes" or "Generations" by Ibn Sa'd (d. 845)
4. Annals by al-Tabari (d. 922)

Hadiths by

5. Al-Bukhari (d. 870)
6. Muslim (d. 875)
7. Abu Dawud (d. 888)
8. Al-Tirmidhi (d. 892)
9. Al-Nasa'I (d. 915)
10. Ibn Maja (d. 886)

---

[900] *Hadith: Muhammad's Legacy in the Medieval and Modern World (Foundations of Islam) Jonathan* A. C. Brown (One World, 2009) p. 3
[901] As listed in *The Hidden Origins of Islam: New Research into Its Early History,* edited by Karl-Heinz Ohlig and Gerd-R. Puin, (Prometheus Books, 2010) p. 8.
[902] The exact dates of writings are unknown, but the dates of death of the authors are given.

The first book is the biography of Muhammad, and the next three are the political and war history of the Arabs in their age of conquest. The last six are Hadiths, as collected and edited by several writers. They were all written to validate Islam and the Qur'an as the identity and purpose of the Arab Empire after the Arab/Islamic civil wars.[903] This is the same process that Christianity underwent after the Jewish–Roman War. An identity had to be defined, explained and asserted; a raison d'être was required.

The Hadiths were almost entirely verbal for the first centuries after Muhammad. This led to a major problem:

> Hadith forgery emerged as a blatant problem when the generation of Muslims who had known the prophet well died off…. From that point onward, the forgery of hadiths would be a consistent problem in Islamic civilization. The heyday of hadith forgery was in the first four hundred years of Islamic history when major hadith collections were first compiled.[904]

Those collections first appeared under the Abbasids in the late 8th and early 9th century, when Islamic writers began collecting and writing the Hadiths of Muhammad. Ever since the first collection of the Hadiths, Islam has been sorting fact from fiction. An impossible task.

Imam Muhammad al-Bukhari, number five above, was writing between 840-870 AD: "His collection is recognized by the overwhelming majority of the Muslim world to be the most

---

[903] *The Hidden Origins of Islam: New Research into Its Early History,* edited by Karl-Heinz Ohlig and Gerd-R. Puin, (Prometheus Books, 2010) This concept is presented in the forward to this book, pp. 7-12 and the case is presented in detail throughout the entire book.

[904] *Hadith: Muhammad's Legacy in the Medieval and Modern World (Foundations of Islam)* Jonathan A. C. Brown (One World, 2009) p. 21

authentic collection of reports of the Sunnah (the history and teachings) of the Prophet Muhammad."[905] Bukhari traveled the length and breadth of the Arab/Islamic Empire, collecting and collating the stories of Muhammad. He collected over 600,000 stories, of which he thought only 4000 were authentic.[906] (Can there be any doubt that there were also thousands of stories of Jesus that existed in the 2nd century?) As stories passed orally from one to the next, "The floodgates of error, exaggeration, and fiction were thrown open."[907] In the course of three civil wars and many sectarian struggles, Hadiths were "forged by different parties trying to manipulate the authority of the Sunna."[908] If *forgery* sounds too strong, remember the many Christian forgeries: from the "Donation of Constantine" to Helena's nails from Jesus' hands to at least several passages in the Gospels. And if you still don't like that term, okay, we'll say that many Hadiths were simply made up. It sounds better.

Whereas Christians judged books based on their presumed authorship, Islam judged every story or verse. Hence, as covered earlier, we now know the Bible contains pseudonymous books whose authors' names were forged and verses that are likely false. As for Islam, who made the decisions to throw out 596,000 sayings and stories of Muhammad and keep just 4000? Maybe they should have thrown out 592,000 and kept 8000 or kept 2000 and thrown out 598,000. Or even 599,990 and 10; certainly, some were true. No matter how many, the stories in the Bible and the Hadiths are infected with the same virus that occurs when stories

---

[905] http://sunnah.com/bukhari

[906] As quoted by Ibn Warraq in *The Hidden Origins of Islam: New Research into Its Early History,* edited by Karl-Heinz Ohlig and Gerd-R. Puin, (Prometheus Books, 2010) p. 226

[907] *The Life of Mahomet,* William Muir, 3rd Edition (Indian reprint, 1992) as quoted in *The Hidden Origins of Islam: New Research into Its Early History,* edited by Karl-Heinz Ohlig and Gerd-R. Puin, (Prometheus Books, 2010) [907]p. 226

[908] *Hadith: Muhammad's Legacy in the Medieval and Modern World (Foundations of Islam) Jonathan* A. C. Brown (One World, 2009) p. 3

are passed around and around orally. And the Qur'an may have caught a cold as well.

Beginning in 1985, the West Star Institute gathered a group of about 50 Bible scholars together in 'The Jesus Seminar' to study all the sayings of Jesus, not just from the New Testament, but in all the gospels known to have been written in the first couple of centuries. The Jesus Seminar spent 14 years studying and debating to try and determine which things Jesus almost certainly said, probably said, and almost certainly did not say, thus repeating the process that Islam likely attempted with the Hadiths thirteen centuries ago.[909]

"Muhammad said X" became the common way of defending one's position on virtually any topic. In the late 7th century during the Second Arab/Islamic civil war, there were so many Hadiths that people began to respond with, "Who told you that?" Muhammad and his companions were long dead, and responding in the name of one of Muhammad's disciples lent authority to the process, which developed into the Islamic tradition of the Isnad.[910] An Isnad is like keeping track of the telephone game: Billy told Mary, who told Joan, who told Jack, who told Ali that.... But that is simple. Here is an example of an actual Isnad:

"I, Muhammad ali al Battah of the Ahdal clan heard from my teacher Ahmad son of Dawud al Battah who heard from his teacher the Mufti Sulayman son of Muhammad al-Ahdal, from Muhammad son of Abd al-Rahman al-Ahdal, from the Mufti...." This continues for 19 more people until reaching, "...from the

---

[909] The results of their work and a more detailed discussion of their process can be found in *The Five Gospels: What Did Jesus Really Say? The Search for the Authentic Words of Jesus,* Robert W. Funk, Roy W. Hoover, and the Jesus Seminar (Harper San Francisco, 1998).

[910] *Hadith: Muhammad's Legacy in the Medieval and Modern World (Foundations of Islam)* Jonathan A. C. Brown (One World, 2009) p. 79

Messenger of God, who said...."[911] Not all Isnads are this complex, but every saying of Muhammad requires an Isnad.

In his book, *Hadith*, Johnathon A.C. Brown[912] explains in detail the terminology of Hadiths, the methodology of Isnads, and the numerous problems over the centuries with the collection and publishing of Islamic Hadiths. But then, how many Isnads were like the underling Hadiths, simply made up?

But even if either Jesus or Muhammad positively said something, what does it mean? The Constitution of the United States is a well-known document of which there is no doubt about its written text. Yet lawyers, politicians, and citizens have passionately argued its meaning for over two hundred years. In dealing with the Bible or the Hadiths, Christians and Muslims must first deal with the uncertainty of what was said and then what it means.

Islam resolves half that issue by claiming that the Qur'an is the perfect Word of God, so like the US Constitution, there is no doubt as to what it says. But then, back to the questions as to how the Qur'an was compiled and written. And for that, we must start with one of the Hadiths. Here is one of the 4000 stories that made the cut. It is contained in Sahih al-Bukhari's book and is Islam's accepted story of the *compiling* of the Qur'an as recorded by Al-Bukhari over 200 years after Muhammad died; don't worry it is much easier to read than the Qur'anic passage on Noah from the last chapter:

> Abu Bakr As-Siddiq sent for me when the people of Yamama had been killed (i.e., a number of the Prophet's Companions who fought against Musailama). (I went to him) and found `Umar bin Al-Khattab sitting with him.

---

[911] *Hadith: Muhammad's Legacy in the Medieval and Modern World (Foundations of Islam)* Jonathan A. C. Brown (One World, 2009) p. 3

[912] *Hadith: Muhammad's Legacy in the Medieval and Modern World (Foundations of Islam)* Jonathan A. C. Brown (One World, 2009)

Abu Bakr then said (to me) "'Umar has come to me and said: "Casualties were heavy among the Qurra' of the! Qur'an (i.e. those who knew the Qur'an by heart) on the day of the Battle of Yalmama, and I am afraid that more heavy casualties may take place among the Qurra' on other battlefields, whereby a large part of the Qur'an may be lost. Therefore, I suggest, you (Abu Bakr) order that the Qur'an be collected." I said to 'Umar, "How can you do something which Allah's Apostle did not do?" 'Umar said, "By Allah, that is a good project. "'Umar kept on urging me to accept his proposal till Allah opened my chest for it and I began to realize the good in the idea which 'Umar had realized." Then Abu Bakr said (to me). 'You are a wise young man and we do not have any suspicion about you, and you used to write the Divine Inspiration for Allah's Messenger (.(🕌 So you should search for (the fragmentary scripts of) the Qur'an and collect it in one book." By Allah if they had ordered me to shift one of the mountains, it would not have been heavier for me than this ordering me to collect the Qur'an. 'Umar. So I started looking for the Qur'an and collecting it from (what was written on) palmed stalks, thin white stones and also from the men who knew it by heart, till I found the last Verse of Surat at-Tauba (Repentance) with Abi Khuza'ima Al-Ansari, and I did not find it with anybody other than him. The Verse is: 'Verily there has come unto you an Apostle (Muhammad) from amongst yourselves. It grieves him that you should receive any injury or difficulty (till the end of Surat-Baraa' (at-Tauba) (9.128-129). Then the complete manuscripts of the Qur'an remained with Abu Bakr till he died, then with `Umar till the end of his life, and then with Hafsa, the daughter of `Umar.[913]

Hafsa, one of Muhammad's many wives, ended up with a pile of bits and pieces of paper, bone, and stones with scribbling on them, all of which was transcribed, and she put it away in the cupboard. That was the Qur'an. Unfortunately, a hungry goat ate some of it. More on that later.

The Qur'an continued to be passed from one person to another for several decades, leading to alterations as the recitations were passed around and around in bits and pieces. Eventually, some thought that, "reports about the Prophet were being fabricated" by those "who wanted to justify their political position."[914] In order to correct this, Islam began to keep records of the chain of the oral transmission sometime between 657 AD and 732 AD.[915]

Today, learning to recite the Qur'an is an arduous process of studying and testing. The certification process to qualify to recite the Qur'an and pass it down through the generations is, like Hadiths, called the Isnad. The genealogy of the Qur'an now has 28 generations between God and those who are currently certified to recite.[916] In the 7th century though, there was no Isnad, no training process, and no certification to recite, much less no collected written text, no single written master Qur'an from which to recite.

This led to differences in the Qur'an as it was recited by different people around the expanding Arab Empire. Caliph

---

[913] Sahih al-Bukhari 4986: Book 66, Hadith 8 USC-MSA web (English) reference: Vol. 6, Book 61, Hadith 509 http://sunnah.com/bukhari/66/8

[914] *The Story of the Qur'an: Its History and Place in Muslim Life,* Ingrid Mattson (Wiley Blackwell, 2nd Edition, 2013) p. 29

[915] "The Role of Isnad in the Preservation of the Islamic Civilization" Kamal Abu Zahra TUESDAY, JUNE 12, 2007. http://islamicsystem.blogspot.com/2007/06/role-of-isnad-in-preservation-of.html

[916] *The Story of the Qur'an: Its History and Place in Muslim Life,* Ingrid Mattson (Wiley Blackwell, 2nd Edition, 2013) pp. 79-85

Uthman decided to correct the problem. Here is the official Islamic narrative on the *writing* of the Qur'an recorded about 850 AD by Bukhari, 200 years after the events of the story.

> Hudhaifa bin Al-Yaman came to `Uthman at the time when the people of Sham and the people of Iraq were Waging war to conquer Arminya and Adharbijan. Hudhaifa was afraid of their (the people of Sham and Iraq) differences in the recitation of the Qur'an, so he said to `Uthman, "O chief of the Believers! Save this nation before they differ about the Book (Qur'an) as Jews and the Christians did before." So `Uthman sent a message to Hafsa saying, "Send us the manuscripts of the Qur'an so that we may compile the Qur'anic materials in perfect copies and return the manuscripts to you." Hafsa sent it to `Uthman. `Uthman then ordered Zaid bin Thabit, `Abdullah bin AzZubair, Sa`id bin Al-As and `Abdur Rahman bin Harith bin Hisham to rewrite the manuscripts in perfect copies. `Uthman said to the three Quraishi men, "In case you disagree with Zaid bin Thabit on any point in the Qur'an, then write it in the dialect of Quraish, the Qur'an was revealed in their tongue." They did so, and when they had written many copies, `Uthman returned the original manuscripts to Hafsa. `Uthman sent to every Muslim province one copy of what they had copied, and ordered that all the other Qur'anic materials, whether written in fragmentary manuscripts or whole copies, be burnt.[917]

Just so you have the official Islamic story straight: Muhammad was seeing and hearing things. One night, he rode his magic horse to Jerusalem, saw Jesus, Moses, and Abraham, then went to Heaven and met with God. God, speaking in Arabic, told

---

[917] Sahih al-Bukhari 4987 In-book reference: Book 66, Hadith 9 USC-MSA web (English) reference: Vol. 6, Book 61, Hadith 510. http://sunnah.com/bukhari/66/9

Muhammad the "real corrected story." Muhammad returned to earth and recited his story together in bits and pieces as the Angel Gabriel for many years dropped by from time to time to fill in the details. Some people took notes of Muhammad's recitals on bits of paper, fig leaves, pieces of bone, and stones. Sometime after Muhammad died, Caliph Umar had these bits and pieces rounded up and the oral memories of others transcribed and given to Hafsa, who kept them somewhere, unprotected from wandering goats. Twenty years later, Caliph Uthman had those things sent to him and appointed a committee to collate, translate the dialect, write things down and have copies made and sent out. All other versions of the Qur'an were to be burned and replaced with the Uthman version.

The reviews of Uthman's new Qur'an were not all favorable. "Reciters were appalled when cherished versions of the Qur'an went up in smoke."[918] And in all, despite this, Islam contends there was never a change made to a single word or punctuation mark. Hallelujah! God's Words, just as he planned it. Sacred and forever.

Fourteen centuries later, believers of that story fly airplanes into buildings, bomb events and hotels, and fire machine guns into music halls and dance clubs in Paris, San Bernardino, and Orlando; in Syria they decapitate, immolate, and otherwise torture people to death. God, if you are really out there somewhere, could you please leave your message a little more clearly? Ten lines on some stones no one can find—not a single sentence from you on your own son! Only dreams and hallucinations from Paul, Muhammad, and numerous others? Heck of a way to run a universe!

The *Satanic Verses* by Salman Rushdie was a contemporary novel first published in 1988. It was a fanciful story that alluded

---

[918] *A Concise History of the Middle East,* Arthur Goldschmidt Jr. (Westview Press, 7th Edition, 2001) p. 57

to the "Satanic verses" in the Qur'an. Briefly and simplified, Muhammad had a revelation that three Meccan pagan goddesses, al'Lat, al-Uzza, and Manat, were valid and authentic intersessionaires with God. This would have conflicted with the "no God but Allah" belief. So, of course, Muhammad had handy another revelation, saying that the devil made him do it, *And We did not send before you any messenger or prophet except that when he spoke [or recited], Satan threw into it [some misunderstanding]* (Qur'an 22:52). Problem solved for Islam.

But now, you have to ask, which other revelations did the devil *throw into* the Qur'an? Not to worry, it's all okay, because Muhammad says that Allah is the great editor in the sky and catches all the errors, *But Allah abolishes that which Satan throws in; then Allah makes precise His verses. And Allah is Knowing and Wise* (Qur'an 22:52). Then how did the Satanic verses get into the Qur'an, and how did they remain in the Qur'an?

Even though *Satanic Verses* was written as a novel, every Muslim knew what the story was about. Islam did not want this can of worms opened and, in 1989, a well-publicized death warrant was issued on Rushdie. Writing papers not supporting the standard narratives of global warming will keep you from getting a cushy post-doc position these days. Writing papers not supporting the standard narrative of Islam might get you killed.

The Qur'an may have been written on hundreds of sticky notes made of stone, bone, paper, and palm stems, but even raising a question about the Qur'an is forbidden: *do not ask about things which, if they are shown to you, will distress you"* (Qur'an 5:101). Looking behind the curtain of the Qur'an is not allowed. Let's not get too distressed—take a chill pill, let's at least take a little peek.

# Chapter Eight – The Qur'an: Another Look

"Muhammad heard from God...." "No, he didn't!" "Yes, he did!" "No, he didn't!" "Yes he did...." You can keep that up until a large voice from the heavens says clearly to everyone, "Yes, he did." In the silence thus far, whether God talked to Muhammad is strictly a matter of opinion, of faith. It is also a matter of faith that the words Muhammad said he heard from God are the words in the Qur'an. We only have what others said that Muhammad said that God said to him. Or like in the case of the Isnad mentioned earlier, we have what others said that others said that, etc. That is just a different version of "Yes, he did," "No, he didn't" that cannot be settled. That is also a matter of opinion—of faith.

What is not a matter of faith is whether what people heard Muhammad say is what ended up in the Qur'an. The answer might not be as certain as the Earth orbiting the Sun, but perhaps to a level causing doubt for those tempted to fly planes into buildings, or bomb trains, shoot up clubs, or behead others. The improbability of some aspects of the Qur'an has already been alluded to earlier. In this chapter, we will take a closer look at a couple of those improbable ideas. Keep in mind that being improbable does not mean being impossible.

Muhammad recited for 23 years. On average, that is about 260 verses a year. How many times did he repeat the same verse? Did he repeat them the same way every time? Even Muhammad and the Qur'an says he did not. *Nothing of our revelation (even a single verse) do we abrogate or cause be forgotten, but we bring (in place) one better or the like thereof* (Qur'an 2:106). According to this, if Muhammad changed a verse when he repeated it, the second one was the new and improved version. That is understandable if these were the words of Muhammad, but since these are supposed to be the Perfect Words of God, does that mean the original was not so perfect?

Earlier, from the Infancy Gospel of Thomas, I told the story of Jesus as a young boy making clay birds, then making them come alive and fly away. This story is told twice in the Qur'an which came from God. Yet the origin of that story is also told in a Hadith where Muhammad claims he heard it from Christians.[919] Did Muhammad hear it from God, or did he hear it from someone who had read Thomas? And these types of discrepancies can go on and on.

That flood story you might have read in an earlier chapter is told twice in the Qur'an, once in Chapter 11 and again in Chapter 71, and it is mentioned by example in several other chapters. In Qur'an 11:42-43, Noah's son is drowned, but not in the version in Chapter 71. Did God also tell the story twice, or just once, and Muhammad repeated it, reciting it differently? Over the course of 23 years, which "sermons" did Muhammad repeat from his memory and which version did people remember, or take notes on?

When all those "sermons" were consolidated into the Qur'an, are we sure they did not change and have not changed even by a single word, ever since then? Islam contends that the Qur'an was

---

[919] *The Life of Muhammad: A Translation of Ishaq's Sirat Rasul Allah,* (Oxford University Press, 1955) p 271-272.

compiled and written by 656 AD from the notes and memories of Muhammad's contemporaries. If it was compiled and written after that, then the direct connection to Muhammad's telling of his dreams is lost. And if the Qur'an has changed over time, then it was the words of men and not the Perfect Words of God and this would call into question other elements of Islam.

But things are not so clear-cut. If the Qur'an were compiled and written in, say, 756 AD, it might only mean that the Hadith telling of its writing was wrong, like the other 596,000 Hadiths. If changes or variations were made after the Qur'an was written, it might only mean that *one* Qur'an was the Perfect Words of God and the rest possessed human flaws. But then no one would know which *one* Qur'an was the Perfect Words of God. Those uncertainties would make Islam damaged human knowledge and not the Perfect Words of Allah. Muslims shouting "Allah Akbar" while flying planes into buildings or other such abdominal actions could no longer cling to the certainty of divine origination. Hopefully their certainty might then only be eternal hellfire.

The very idea of gathering hundreds or thousands of sticky notes made of stone, bone, paper, and palm stems, as well as the memory of hundreds or more people, and assembling it all into a complete perfect polished document, recording the precise words that Muhammad told strains even faith. Muhammad himself forgot things: "May Allah bestow his mercy on him as he reminded me of such and such verses from such and such Surah which I was caused to forget."[920] The son of the second Caliph Umar and brother-in-law of Muhammad, summarized the issue: "Let none of you say, 'I have got the whole of the Koran' How

---

[920] Bukhari, al-Sahih hadiths 1720 and 1721 as quoted in *Which Koran? Variants, Manuscripts and Linguistics,* Ibn Warraq (Prometheus Books, 2011) p. 26

does he know what all of it is? Much of the Koran has gone. Let him say instead, 'I have got what has survived.'"[921]

Even if those first Muslims got all the sticky notes, and people remembered everything correctly, it could not have been written down accurately in Arabic. Why? Because Arabic writing was very new at that time and was simply not capable of producing the elegant structure of the Qur'an. Arabic writing, until the late 700s and early 800s, was the "inarticulate handmaiden of the oral language."[922] The sophisticated and polished Arabic of the Qur'an came about only in the 9th century.

Aramaic writing had been widespread in the ancient Middle East and evolved into Nabataean script around 200 BC, and eventually evolved later into Arabic script.[923] The earliest example of Arabic writing was discovered in 2015 in southern Saudi Arabia and dates to 470 AD. It was on a stone ironically written by Christians.[924] Even then, there were ten different alphabets being used in Arabia, with diverse styles of Arabic script.[925] At the time of Muhammad, and for some time thereafter, Arabic script was "quite rudimentary compared to its later development."[926] Besides Muhammad's Muslims learned to write only after moving to Medina and attending its Jewish

---

[921] "The Collection of the Koran," p. 117, as quoted in *Which Koran? Variants, Manuscripts and Linguistics*, Ibn Warraq (Prometheus Books, 2011) p. 24

[922] *The History of the Qur'an,* Ingrid Mattson (Wiley Blackwell, 2nd Edition, 2013) p. 102

[923] http://www.ancient-origins.net/news-general/oldest-arabic-inscription-provides-missing-link-between-nabatean-and-arabic-writing also http://www.medinaproject-epigraphy.eu/was-the-nabatean-script-the-root-of-the-modern-arabic-script/

[924] http://www.journal.com.ph/editorial/mysteries/archaeologists-discover-that-earliest-known-arabic-writing-was-penned-by-a-christian

[925] *New Researches on the Quran: Why and How Two Versions of Islam Entered the History of Mankind,* Seyed Mostafa Azmayesh (Mehraby Publishing, 2015) p. 18

[926] *The Story of the Qur'an: Its History and Place in Muslim Life,* Ingrid Mattson (Wiley Blackwell, 2nd Edition, 2013) explains on p. 92.

schools.[927] By then, 86 of the Qur'an's 114 books had already been recited! How does that work?

Arabic writing started as a "shorthand" that only used consonants; it had no vowels. Something like texting shorthand IMHO, IIRC, POV, or MMW. Or the first sentence in this paragraph might have been written something like this: RBC WRTNG STRTD SSH THT NL CNSNNTS THDNVWLS. The problem was further compounded by different dialects and a lack of spelling rules. Sometime after Muhammad, dots and marks called "diacritical marks" were added to signify vowels. The very first example of rudimentary diacritical marks is in a document known as PERF558, dating to 643 AD,[928] a decade after Mohammad died. This was a decade after the Qur'an was supposedly first gathered. At most, the Qur'an at that time was a shorthand "consonantal skeleton" without vowels.

Nicolai Sinai's 2014 paper, "When did the consonantal skeleton of the Qur'an reach closure?"[929] marshals considerable evidence in his "emergent canon" model to suggest that a Qur'an "achieved a recognizable form by 660" but "continued to be reworked and revised until c. 700"[930] Reworked and revised? Sounds like it changed to me. Even after the consonantal skeleton was settled, diacritical marks—those very subtle marks—implied judgement and changes often modifying the meaning of the original text.

---

[927] *New Researches on the Quran: Why and How Two Versions of Islam Entered the History of Mankind,* Seyed Mostafa Azmayesh (Mehraby Publishing, 2015) p. 20, see note 12.

[928] " The Dotting of a Script and the Dating of an Era: The Strange Neglect of PERF 558", Alan Jones, *Islamic Culture,* 1998, Volume LXXII, No. 4, pp. 95-103. It may be viewed here: http://www.islamic-awareness.org/History/Islam/Papyri/jones.html

[929] My thanks to Johnathon A. C. Brown for pointing me to this article by Nicolai Sinai: "When did the consonantal skeleton of the Qur'an reach closure?" Part II. *Bulletin of the School of Oriental and African Studies,* May 2014 Available on CJO 2014 doi:10.1017/S0041977X14000111

[930] "When did the consonantal skeleton of the Qur'an reach closure? Part II". *Bulletin of the School of Oriental and African Studies* May 2014, p. 4.

An exaggerated version of these types of errors can be found in the very first printing of the Qur'an. Paganino and Alessandro accomplished this task in 1538. An original copy was found only in 1987 by Angela Nuovo in the Franciscan library in Venice. That Qur'an has a huge number of errors—in fact there is not a word without an error because the "similar forms of the Arabic language is completely ignored."[931] If converting Arabic script to a printable form using the diacritical marks demonstrates the difficulty of getting the meaning right, then think of the errors and changes in meaning in adding the diacritical marks in the first place. The lack of a developed Arabic script is a strong indication that even if the Qur'an was finalized by Uthman in 656, it was not the final Qur'an.

There is also a lack of corroborating evidence. Uthman's successor was Muawiyah ibn 'Abī Ṣufyān I, who was caliph from 661–680 AD. The writings from the Muawiyah period mention nothing of Muhammad, the Qur'an, or Islam.[932] "Apart from the Qur'an" the Arabs, "did not leave behind any literary evidence in the first two centuries," following the Hajj.[933] Until 822 AD, "There is an almost total lack of any contemporary sources from the Islamic side until the late 8th century almost 150 years after the death of Muhammad."[934] For 200 years, the Arabs said nothing about their miraculous new Islamic religion, its prophet Muhammad, and its Qur'an.

---

[931] *Bound in Venice: The Serene Republic and the Dawn of the Book,* Alessandro Marzo Magno (Europa Editions, 2013) p 15

[932] *John of Damascus, First Apologist to the Muslims: The Trinity and Christian Apologetics in the Early Islamic Period,* Daniel J. Janosik (Pickwick Publications, 2016) p. 75

[933] *Early Islam: A Critical Reconstruction Based on Contemporary Sources,* Edited by Karl-Heinz Ohlig (Prometheus, 2013) p. 176

[934] *John of Damascus, First Apologist to the Muslims: The Trinity and Christian Apologetics in the Early Islamic Period,* Daniel J. Janosik (Pickwick Publications, 2016) 2016 p. 52

The Christians, however, were doing a great deal of writing. They had a "flourishing intellectual life" and left behind "an abundance of literature."[935] In the areas the Arabs had conquered, the Christian bishops were writing about everything having to do with Christianity, but barely a word on Islam?[936]

One early writer named John of Damascus was not only a Christian monk but the chief administrator for the caliph of the Islamic Empire, Abd al-Malik, who had succeeded Muawiyah. (Imagine a Christian becoming a high-ranking official today in Iran.) John used his position and knowledge to write several books defending Christianity and questioning Islam. In them, John shows a "clear, though limited knowledge of the writings" of Islam and Muhammad. He quoted parts of a Qur'an, including a chapter known as the She Camel. This chapter, although well-known to Muslims, never made it into the final version of the Qur'an.[937] John makes other references to the Qur'an show a "later mental labor aimed at the redaction, selection, and stylistic reorganization of the text and carried out during the final composition" of the Qur'an.[938] In other words, the Qur'an available to John of Damascus, the man who was at the very center of the Islamic Empire, was different than the final version of the Qur'an.[939] That is solid evidence that there was no final Qur'an in the court of the caliph of Islam in the first decades of the 8th century.

---

[935] *Early Islam: A Critical Reconstruction Based on Contemporary Sources,* Edited by Karl-Heinz Ohlig (Prometheus, 2013) p. 176

[936] *Early Islam: A Critical Reconstruction Based on Contemporary Sources,* Edited by Karl-Heinz Ohlig (Prometheus, 2013) p. 176

[937] *John of Damascus, First Apologist to the Muslims: The Trinity and Christian Apologetics in the Early Islamic Period,* Daniel J. Janosik (Pickwick Publications, 2016) 2016 p. 251

[938] *The Hidden Origins of Islam: New Research into Its Early History,* edited by Karl-Heinz Ohlig and Gerd-R. Puin, (Prometheus Books, 2010) p. 200

[939] Some have argued that John did not write these critical books, or that he wrote them later at a time; he did not have a Qur'an in hand.

Alfred-Louis de Premare lays out several more examples that contradict the Islamic narrative in the section 'Abd al-Malik ibn Marwan and the process of the Qur'an's Composition' in Part I of "The Hidden Origins of Islam." [940]All these point to a Qur'an continuing to evolve after Islam says it was completed in 656 AD.

When asked to compile the Qur'an, Abu Bakr told Umar, "How can you do something which Allah's Apostle (Muhammad) did not do?"[941] If God's Prophet Muhammad felt so strongly that his revelations were from the One True God, Creator and Ruler of the Entire Universe, why on God's green earth would he not have inscribed those words on every stone from Arabia to China? Would not his joy of going to Heaven, and meeting Jesus and Moses and the others, have spurred him to record these events on monuments bigger than the pyramids? If not Muhammad, then his followers? Our guy just went to Heaven and met THE Big Man! The total absence of such things is another contraindication of the Islamic narrative on the writing of the Qur'an.

At the time when Islam says the Qur'an was written, the Arab Empire was not an Islamic Empire; indeed, many of the conquered lands remained Christian and Jewish.[942] Like the case of John of Damascus, much of the empire's bureaucracy, the tax base, and even much of the army were not Islamic at the time.[943] And one even questions the beliefs of the early Islamic leaders. When Muawiya ascended to the position of caliph in Jerusalem, he followed the path of Jesus, ending on Golgotha, where he prayed.[944] It does not seem that Muawiya was aware of the

---

[940] *The Hidden Origins of Islam: New Research into Its Early History,* edited by Karl-Heinz Ohlig and Gerd-R. Puin, (Prometheus Books, 2010),

[941] Bukhari Sahih al-Bukhari, 6:60:201

[942] *In the Shadow of the Sword: The Birth of Islam and the Rise of Global Arab Empire,* Tom Holland (Doubleday, 2012) p. 365

[943] *A Concise History of the Middle East,* Arthur Goldschmidt Jr. (Westview Press, 7th Edition, 2001) p. 61

[944] *In the Shadow of the Sword: The Birth of Islam and the Rise of Global Arab Empire,* Tom Holland (Doubleday, 2012) p. 365

Qur'an and Islamic belief that the crucifixion of Jesus was a myth, *But they killed him not, nor crucified him, but so it was made to appear to them* (Qur'an 4.157). Maybe it just appeared that Muawiya went to Golgotha? Or maybe the Qur'an wasn't written yet?

Several books have been written detailing the reasons why the Qur'an was not finalized until the late 8th or early 9th century. I will not attempt to summarize all their arguments, but I will tell an interesting side story about two of them: *The Origins of the Koran: Classic Essays on Islam's Holy Book* by Ibn Warraq was published in 1998, and *The Syro-Aramaic Reading of the Koran: A Contribution to the Decoding of the Language of the Koran*, written by Christoph Luxenberg, was first published in Germany in 2000.

Both Ibn Warraq and Christoph Luxenberg are pseudonyms because writing about Islam is deadly and dangerous. I previously mentioned the death threats to Salman Rushdie. In 1991, Suliman Bashear, a professor of Islamic History at the University of Nablus in Palestine, was thrown from his window for even suggesting that Islam developed differently from its historical narrative.[945] Geert Wilders is a member of the Dutch House of Representatives and has written a very chilling book, *Marked for Death: Islam's War Against the West and Me*, which describes the Islamic attempts through death and intimidation to silence critics of Islam, including the academic scholars of Islam and the Qur'an. An American scholar, afraid to be named, said that "Between fear and political correctness, it's not possible to say anything other than sugary nonsense about Islam."[946] And that is from 2002, before Theo van Gogh, the Dutch filmmaker

---

[945] "Scholars Are Quietly Offering New Theories of the Koran" Alexander Stille, *The New York Times* March 2, 2002

[946] "Scholars Are Quietly Offering New Theories of the Koran" Alexander Stille, *The New York Times* March 2, 2002

was killed,[947] before Kurt Westergaard, the Danish cartoonist, was attacked with an ax[948] and, of course, before the Charlie Hebdo murders in Paris.[949] Writing anything negative about Islam is very dangerous, indeed.

If the central question in Christianity was the deity of Jesus, then the central question of Islam is the writing of the Qur'an. Islam claims the Qur'an is the Perfect Words of God—every word. The errors in the Bible can and are overlooked or glossed over by its Jewish and Christian believers. Islam considers any challenge to the veracity of the Qur'an as an existential question that Islam will defend at all costs.

While there is evidence that the compilation of the Qur'an was later than the Islamic narrative, the other contention of Islam is that it has never changed since then. Not even by a single word. *Which Koran? Variants, Manuscripts and Linguistics,*"[950] edited by Ibn Warraq, offers scholarly articles showing differing verses among Qur'ans from different parts of the Islamic World that concludes that the Qur'an has changed. However, most of the examples would only be understandable to those who speak Arabic, which I certainly do not.

But the evidence is not all stacked against the Islamic narrative. Recent discoveries of copies of the Qur'an written very close to the time of Muhammad and Uthman are providing Islam evidence to rally around. Remember the story told earlier of

---

[947] Leo Von Gogh was murdered in 2004 by a Muslim for the production of a film on Islam's abuse of women. On his chest was pinned the death threat against Geert Wilders. http://www.washingtontimes.com/news/2012/jun/13/how-free-speech-led-to-jihad/

[948] "The Danish cartoonist who survived an axe attack" Marie Louise Sjølie, January 4, 2010. https://www.theguardian.com/world/2010/jan/04/danish-cartoonist-axe-attack

[949] Twelve people were murdered by on January 7, 2015 at the Paris offices of the French magazine *Charlie Hebdo* in response to the satirical illustrations and commentary on Muhammad and Islam. The killers proclaimed, "We have avenged the Prophet Muhammad" and "God is Great" during their killing spree. "Deadly attack on office of French magazine *Charlie Hebdo*". BBC News. 7 January 2015.

[950] *Which Koran?: Variants, Manuscripts and Linguistics,* Ibn Warraq (Prometheus Books, 2011)

Josiah when he was 26, embarking on a program to repair the temple in Jerusalem? Remember during the work how the High Priest Hilkiah and his scribe Shaphan discovered the books of Moses? Remember the story of the Christian ruler of Yemen, Abraha, who sent his troops and an elephant to destroy the Ka'bah and divert pilgrimage to the Cathedral of Sana'a? Well, those stories came together in 1972. This time the Cathedral of Sana'a, now known as the Mosque of Sana'a, needed the repairs, and in between the rafters of the roof they found some very old documents, including a Qur'an.

In the last 40 years, there have been three major discoveries of old Qur'ans. The first was the Sana'a document; the second at the University of Tübingen in Germany in 2014, where a partial Qur'an was found and dated to 649-675 AD; and at the University of Birmingham in England where in 2015 a partial Qur'an dating to 568-645 AD was found, possibly within the life time of Muhammad!

In 1981, the document found in Sana was identified as a palimpsest copy of the Qur'an dating from 646-671 AD. A palimpsest is a document with two different layers of writing. Writing material at the time was very expensive, and about 5% of the documents from this time frame were erased and used a second time. For complex chemical reasons, both layers are easily readable today. Both layers of the Sana'a document were Qur'ans, with the top layer being written in the late 7th or early 8th century in the Uthmanic textual tradition of 656 AD. "The lower Qur'an is of enormous interest because it is so far the only manuscript that is known to be non-'Uthmānic, that is, from a textual tradition other than the standard one."[951]

---

[951] All information in this section concerning the Sana Qur'an, unless otherwise noted can be found in the article "Ṣan'ā' 1 and the Origins of the Qur'ān" Der Islam: *Journal of the History and Culture of the Middle East* by Behnam Sadeghi Mohsen Goudarzt, De Gruyter, March 2, 2012.

Political events in Yemen, and scholarly rivalries, have not allowed the analysis of the documents to proceed as thoroughly and rapidly as would be hoped. The initial academic work on the Sana'a Qur'an was done in Germany at the Inârah Institute for Research of Early Islamic History, and the Koran at the Religious Studies Department of the University of Saarlandes. Most of that work is only in German, but books have been translated into English and published: *Early Islam: A Critical Reconstruction based on Contemporary Sources* and *The Hidden Origins of Islam*, both edited by Karl-Heinz Ohig and Gerd. R. Puin and published by Prometheus Books in 2010 and 2013. Both are compendiums of academic papers and studies on various aspects of the history of early Islam, including evidence from the Sana'a Qur'an. Both cast substantial doubt on the standard narrative of the Qur'an and Islam.

In 2012, *Ṣan'ā' 1 and the Origins of the Qur'ān*, by Behnam Sadeghi of Stanford University and Mohsen Goudarzt of Harvard, was published in *Der Islam: Journal of the History and Culture of the Middle East – De Gruyter* March 2, 2012. Their discussion is similar to the discussions of the synoptic Gospels of the New Testament, showing Luke and Matthew copied Mark and had a third source. The wording this time is the "Uthmānic text agrees with one of the others against the third. This is compatible with…the 'Uthmānic text may be a hybrid formed on the basis of a number [of texts] in which preference was usually given to the majority reading." Which is what you would expect from a committee trying to standardize a text from numerous versions. Which is what the Hadith on Uthman's writing of the Qur'an says!

Much more work needs to be done to complete the story of Islam, but the headwinds against such work are very strong. Many might proclaim, "Je suis Charlie" (We are Charlie) but the fact is that the slaughter of the staff of Charlie Hebdo by radical

Muslims unconstrained by the broader Islamic community, intimidates and greatly dampens the needed work in Islamic research. Beyond these very real dangers, Islamic resources and research are often controlled or greatly influenced by Muslims themselves, limiting the scope of critical access. It may be several decades before the foundations of Islam are understood beyond the repetition of Islamic Hadiths, whether the 4000 or the 596,000.

Christians today tolerate irreverent jokes and even laugh at plays like *Monty Python and the Holy Grail*, or *The Book of Mormon*. Not only does Islam have zero tolerance for such satire, Islam considers even fundamental research and questioning of its foundation as blasphemies. Radical Islam follows that revered Saint of Medieval Christianity, Thomas Aquinas, who said blasphemers "can be put to death and despoiled of their possessions...even if they do not corrupt others, for they are blasphemies against God."[952] Until Islam can effectively sanction and control such deadly beliefs, the truth of Islam will not be known, and the West must be wary.

The Qur'an is one source stating the words of Muhammad, which is vastly superior to multiple sources stating the words of Jesus. Christians jump through two hoops: what did Jesus say and what does it mean? Muslims jump through one hoop: what do Muhammad's words mean? And Muhammad might have meant something far different than many Christians and Muslims think.

---

[952] As quoted in *Blasphemy: Verbal Offense Against the Sacred, from Moses to Salman Rushdie,* Leonard Williams Levy (UNC Press, 1993) p. 52

# Chapter Nine – If Muhammad….

In the 6th century before Muhammad's birth, the world around the Mediterranean was a mess. The Christian Roman and Zoroastrian Persian Empires were collapsing, and the lands between them were "a kind of Jurassic Park"[953] of Judaism, paganism, and numerous versions of Christianity. Into that religious and political chaos, Muhammad was born. Within that chaos, Muhammad formed Islam, and out of that chaos, Islam swiftly conquered all the Persian and much of the Roman Empire. The divine revelation of God's message to Muhammad explains all of that for Muslims. Islamic faith is all that is needed—no further explanation is required, nor sought.

To reject the idea of Muhammad's divine revelation, another explanation of events is required. You can believe that the magician on the stage really made the tiger appear out of nowhere, or you can look for how it was done. Muslims believe Muhammad made Islam appear out of the ether of divine dreams. We can look for a plausible explanation of where Muhammad got

---

[953] *The Islamic Jesus: How the King of the Jews Became a Prophet of the Muslims* Mustafa Akylol (St. Martin Press 2017) p. 89 Akylol credits Jack Tannous in "Syria between Byzantium and Islam: Making Incommensurables Speak" (PhD dissertation, Princeton University, 2010) p. 396.

his theology and knowledge of Jewish history, Jesus, and Christianity.

In Christianity, Paul's Jewish background and association with Jesus' apostles provides the plausible basis for his preachings, without accepting his claim to divine revelation. In Islam, Muhammad's lack of Jewish/Christian background is often cited as proof of his divine revelation. How else could he know the Jewish and Christian stories that he recited? Perhaps a deeper look at the Hadiths and the Qur'an might reveal where Muhammad received his education in Judaism and Christianity.

As the year of Muhammad's birth was approaching, Arabia was being affected by the other tumultuous events of the 6th century. The lines dividing Rome and Persia were shifting like the desert sands. The religions of paganism, Judaism, Zoroastrianism, and various versions of Christianity were shifting as well. In Mecca, the religious forces began to collide.

The town of Mecca sits in a valley that lacks natural resources. The Quraysh tribe that controlled the area dependent on trade and pilgrimages to support their existence. Good relationships with all the tribes that pilgrimaged and traded through Mecca was an essential part of Quraysh existence. "Of crucial importance for a proper understanding of the role of Mecca in trans-Arabian commerce, are the special status enjoyed by the Quraysh...and the protection granted by them to any merchant asking for it on Meccan territory."[954] Caravans had alternative routes. "After aṭ-Ṭā'if the road split into two branches: one to Mecca and one leading directly to Medina."[955]

---

[954] "Mecca on the Caravan Routes in Pre-Islamic Antiquity" Mikhail D. Bukharin from *The Qur'an in Context: Historical and Literary Investigations into the Qur'anic Milieu* Edited by Angelika Neuwirth Nicolai Sinai Michael Marx Leiden ( Boston 2010) pp. 116-117

[955] "Mecca on the Caravan Routes in Pre-Islamic Antiquity" Mikhail D. Bukharin *The Qur'an in Context: Historical and Literary Investigations into the Qur'anic Milieu* Edited by Angelika Neuwirth Nicolai Sinai Michael Marx Leiden • (Boston 2010) p. 122

To maintain themselves, the Quraysh needed to be like the Swiss: neutral and accommodating. Nothing could be allowed to jeopardize this profitable position for the Quraysh of Mecca.

Not all the residents of Mecca found satisfaction in the valueless nature of multiculturalism. In the center of Mecca was the Ka'bah. Over the centuries, it had become the place of worship to Abraham's God and many other pagan gods. At a religious feast around the time of Muhammad's birth, four men concluded:

> That their people had corrupted the religion of their father Abraham, and that the stone they went round was of no account; it could neither hear, nor see, nor hurt, nor help. 'Find for yourselves a religion,' they said; 'for by God you have none.' So they went their several ways in the land, seeking the Hanifiya, the true religion of Abraham.[956]

Hanif and those teachings might be explained by the story of Zayd, one of the four who went searching to find a religion. Zayd traveled about Arabia, Iraq, and Syria, asking about Judaism and Christianity. "Now Zayd had sampled Judaism and Christianity and was not satisfied with either of them."[957] He decided to ask about another religion.

> "Will you tell me of some other religion?" The Jewish scholar replied, "I do not know any other religion except the Hanif." Zayd enquired, "What is Hanif?" He said, "Hanif is the religion of (the prophet) Abraham who was neither a Jew nor a Christian, and he used to worship None but Allah (Alone)" After not getting satisfactory answers about Christianity, Zayd asked a Christian monk at Balqa

---

[956] *The Life of Muhammad: A Translation of Ishaq's Sirat Rasul Allah,* (Oxford University Press, 1955). P 99

[957] *The Life of Muhammad: A Translation of Ishaq's Sirat Rasul Allah,* (Oxford University Press, 1955). P 103.

"Will you tell me of some other religion?" He replied, "I do not know any other religion except Hanif." Zayd enquired, "What is Hanif?" He replied, "Hanif is the religion of (the prophet) Abraham who was neither a Jew nor a Christian and he used to worship None but Allah (Alone)." When Zayd heard their statement about (the religion of) Abraham, he left that place, and when he came out, he raised both his hands and said, "O Allah! I make You my Witness that I am of the religion of Abraham."[958]

Zayd returned to Mecca, where his thoughts were not popular. "He accepted neither Judaism nor Christianity...worshipped the God of Abraham, and he publicly rebuked his people for their practices."[959] Zayd met with strong opposition, was thrown out of Mecca, and went to live on Mt. Hira.

When Muhammad was a small child, he did what every small child has done at one time or another: darted out of sight at the mall, or in a crowd, thus panicking the parents. Likewise, Muhammad: "His foster-mother brought him to Mecca, he escaped her among the crowd while she was taking him to his people. She sought him and could not find him...." Waraqa ibn Nawfal found young Muhammad roaming in the street and returned him to his Grandfather,[960] Abd al-Muttalib II "who was a Hanif (A Nazarene)."[961]

---

[958] The entire story including the quotes is found in Sahih Bukhari Volume 5 Book 58 Hadith 169 Translator: M. Muhsin Khan

[959] *The Life of Muhammad: A Translation of Ishaq's Sirat Rasul Allah,* (Oxford University Press, 1955). P 99

[960] *The Life of Muhammad: A Translation of Ishaq's Sirat Rasul Allah,* (Oxford University Press, 1955). p 73

[961] *What are the Sacred Roots of Islam* Jamil Effarah (AuthorHouse 2016) Kindle loc 2093 It is beyond the scope of this book to delve into the differences between the terms "Nazarene" "Hanif" and "Muslim" which are often used interchangeably as this quote demonstrates. English translations of the Qur'an then interchange the term Hanif and Muslim. See Qur'an 2:125-127; 3:67, 22:26, 2:135, 3:95, 4:125, 10:104, 16:120, 16:123,

Waraqa was Muhammad's 3rd cousin and was a first cousin to Khadji, Muhammad's future wife. But more importantly, Waraqa was one of the four men, who like Zayd had gone searching for religion. Waraqa had "attached himself to Christianity and studied its scriptures until he had thoroughly mastered them."[962]

When Muhammad was a young man working the trading caravans in the desert, "at the height of noon when the heat was intense as he rode his beast," there were "two angels shading the apostle (Muhammad) from the sun's rays." Khadji told this story to Waraqa, who replied, "verily Muhammad is the prophet of this people. I knew that a prophet of this people was to be expected. His time has come. Or words to that effect."[963] At the time of Muhammad, the Arab world was expecting a prophet, just as at the time of Jesus the Jewish world was expecting a messiah.

Muhammad tells us himself that when he was "a young lad" he was up on Mt. Hira and saw Zayd, who had been banished for his Hanif rebuke of pagan practices in Mecca. Muhammad reports that he "went and sat with him. I had with me a bag of meat from our sacrifices to our idols...and I offered it to him." Zayd replied,

> "I never eat of these sacrifices and I want nothing to do with them." Then he blamed me and those who worship idols and sacrifice to them saying, "They are futile: they can do neither good nor harm," or words to that effect." The apostle (Muhammad) added, "After that, with that knowledge I never stroked an idol of theirs nor did I

---

[962]*The Life of Muhammad: A Translation of Ishaq's Sirat Rasul Allah,* (Oxford University Press, 1955). p 99

[963] *The Life of Muhammad: A Translation of Ishaq's Sirat Rasul Allah,* (Oxford University Press, 1955) p 83

sacrifice to them until God honored me with His apostleship."

Muhammad was in his late 30s when he reported his first visions. Muhammad had been seeking solitude in a cave on Mt. Hira, contemplating issues that troubled him. Was it problems with his wives? Business plans for the upcoming camel caravans? Or seeking some answer to the Jurassic Park of religion in which he lived?

When he had his first vision and told his wife Khadija, she said "I have hope that thou wilt be the prophet of this people." Khadija then went to her cousin "Waraqa...who had become a Christian and read the scriptures and learned from those that follow the Torah and the Gospel. And when she related to him what the apostle (Muhammad) of God told her...Waraqa cried '...If thou hast spoken to me the truth, O Khadija...he is the prophet of this people.'"[964]

Muhammad's visions were not simple dreams one remembers on waking. His wife reported he was suicidal: "he intended several times to throw himself from the tops of high mountains and every time he went up the top of a mountain in order to throw himself down."[965] He trembled and had convulsions: "his eyes turned misty with a liquid before the Qur'an has fallen on him.... Following such revelations, he suffered from the same physical reactions."[966] [967]

---

[964] *The Life of Muhammad: A Translation of Ishaq's Sirat Rasul Allah,* (Oxford University Press, 1955). P 107

[965] "Sahih Bukhari" Volume 9, Book 87, Number 111 Translator: M. Muhsin Khan

[966] "Sirah al-Halabiyyah" p 275-276 as quoted in "The Priest and the Prophet" Joseph Azzi (Pen Publishers 2005) pp 34-35

[967] There is speculation that Muhammad suffered from a condition known as temporal lobe epilepsy "Although an unequivocal decision is not possible from existing knowledge, psychomotor or complex partial seizures of temporal lobe epilepsy would be the most tenable diagnosis;" "A Differential Diagnosis of the Inspirational Spells of Muhammad the Prophet of Islam," F. R. Freemon *Epilepsia 17, 1976* p. 426

Muhammad sought relief for his troubles with Waraqa, who confirmed Muhammad as the expected prophet, which "added to his confidence and lightened his anxiety."[968] One, two, or three years later Muhammad began his public preaching. Preaching his visions of God. Clearly his preaching's could have come from his intimate contact Waraqa and Zayd, Hanif people of the God of Abraham who had considerable knowledge of Judaism and Christianity.

As mentioned earlier, the Qur'an, like the New Testament, is not arranged in chronological order. Both become different documents when arranged and read in the order in which they were written. Within a century of the Qur'an being written, Islam adopted a traditional chronology, which scholars over the years have refined into the widely accepted Egyptian Standard order, and later the Nöldeke Chronology.[969]

The chapters are first sorted into those that Muhammad recited in Mecca between 610 and 622 AD, and then in Medina between 623 AD until his death in 632 AD. Those from Mecca are then sorted into three-time buckets: Early (610-618 AD) Middle (619-620 AD) and Late (621-622 AD).[970]

Chapter 96 is from 610 AD and is the first chronological book of the Qur'an. Called "The Clot," it tells the story of Muhammad's first vision in the beginning five verses, then says:

---

[968] *The Life of Muhammad: A Translation of Ishaq's Sirat Rasul Allah,* (Oxford University Press, 1955). P 107

[969] There is very little difference in the chronological order of the Chapters of the Qur'an between the traditional approach and that of modern scholarship. For the former see "History of the Qur'an" Allamah Abu 'abd Allah al-Zanjani trans Mahliqa Qara'I *Part 3 X:The Order of Revelation of the Surahs of the Qur'an at Makkah and Madinah* and for a discussion of the later *"The Qur'an in Context: Historical and Literary Investigations into the Qur'ānic Milieu"* Edited by Angelika Neuwirth Nicolai Sinai Michael Marx Leiden • Boston 2010 The Qur'an as Process Nicolai Sinai pp. 407-440.

[970] The exact dates of these Meccan periods vary with no definitive agreement. For the purposes of this chapter the Early Meccan Surahs will be those believed to have occurred prior to the death of his wife Khadija and Abu Talib in 619 AD, and in particular 96, 68, 73, 74, 1, 111, 81, 87, 92, 89, 93, 94, 103, 100, 108, 102, 107, 109, 113, 114, 112,53, 80, 97, 91, 85, 95, 106, 101.

*Have you seen the one who forbids? A servant when he prays? Have you seen if he is upon guidance or enjoins righteousness? Have you seen if he denies and turns away - Does he not know that Allah sees? No! If he does not desist, We will surely drag him by the forelock - A lying, sinning forelock. Then let him call his associates; We will call the angels of Hell.* (Qur'an 96:9-18)

Here is "the rest of the story." Muhammad had been teaching servants to pray in the typical Islamic fashion: on your knees prostrated forward with your face on the ground. Abu Jahl, the head of the Quraysh tribe, noticed some of his slaves praying in this manner and dragged them in the street by their forelock.

Abu Jahl then asked the people of Quraysh: 'Does Muhammad set his face on the ground before you?' When they replied in the affirmative, he said: 'By Lat and Uzza [the names of Arab pagan gods], if I ever catch him in that act of worship, I would set my foot on his neck and rub his face in the dust.'[971]

This very first revelation in the Qur'an is an early rendition of Clint Eastwood: "Hey, Abu Jahl. Go ahead, Punk. Make my day!" Muhammad had the Angels of Hell on his side; Clint only had a .44 Magnum.

This is universally accepted as the very first story of the Qur'an, yet it is not about creation or God, but is a political statement on the rejection of Muhammad's prior preaching. Preaching that greatly upset his fellow Meccans who thought, "*He is crazy*" (Qur'an 68:51).[972] Isn't the story supposed to be that Muhammad was an illiterate Arab trader who had revelations

[971] Tafhim al-Qur'an - The Meaning of the Qur'an Sayyid Abul Ala Maududi downloaded from https://www.Qur'an411.com Chapter 96 Occasion of Revelation of verses 6-19 p. 3472
[972] Just as Jesus was thought to be crazy by his family [Mark 3:21].

and *then* preached those revelations? Something seems backward here, but the Qur'an is clear, Muhammad was preaching *before* he had claimed any revelations! And preaching something that was causing an uproar.

In the first five chronological chapters (96, 68, 73, 74, 1) Muhammad references all the basics of Islam: there is but one God (Qur'an 73:9); God created man (Qur'an 96:2); there will be a Resurrection (Qur'an 68:39); and a Last Judgement (Qur'an 1:4).[973] Also, there is a hell in the hereafter for the unbelievers (Qur'an 68:33) and a Heaven for believers (Qur'an 68:34). If you want to go to Heaven, say your prayers and give to charity (Qur'an 73:20).

Muhammad was preaching what Jesus preached: there is but one God (Mark 12:29); God created man (Mark 10:6); there will be a Resurrection (John 5:21-29) and a Last Judgement (Matt. 25:31-46). There is a hell in the hereafter for the unbelievers (Matt. 13:24-43) and a Heaven for believers (John 14:1-3). If you want to go to Heaven, say your prayers (Matt. 6:5-15) and give to charity (Matt. 19:21).

The Qur'an clearly shows that *before* his first revelation, Muhammad was preaching what Jesus had preached, not the Pauline Trinitarian Christianity imposed by the Roman emperors, but the gospel of the First Jewish Jesus Church of Jerusalem. Was he preaching Hanif?

That is not a new idea. In his book *Islamic Jesus*, Mustafa Akyol opens Chapter 4 entitled "The Missing Link" with the following quotation: "Here is a paradox of world-historical proportions: Jewish Christianity indeed disappeared within the Christian church but was preserved in Islam."[974]

---

[973] Although Muhammads "Judgement Day was pure Zarathustra" God's Crucible: Islam and the Making of Europe, 570-1215, David Levering (Lewis Norton, 2008) p. 36

[974] Hans-Joachim Schoeps, religious historian and philosopher "*The Islamic Jesus: How the King of the Jews Became a Prophet of the Muslims*" Mustafa Akylol (St. Martin Press 2017) p. 83

Akyol then goes on to argue that Muhammad must have received divine revelation because there is no connection between Muhammad and Jesus in Arabia.

> Various scholars have been tempted to hypothesize the existence of Jewish Christianity in the time and milieu of the Prophet Muhammad, by simply looking at the doctrinal connection between Jewish Christianity and Islam and then assuming there must be a historical connection between them.[975]

Akyol then discusses at length the doctrinal relations between Islam and Christianity, and the failed attempts by many to historically link them. He ends the chapter with this conclusion:

> After all the search for a historical connection between Jewish Christianity and Islam, we still are left with the observation that Guillaume Dye, one of the experts on the topic, shared in late 2015: "We have no evidence of Jewish Christian groups in Arabia in the early 7th century, and no evidence either that other putative Jewish Christian groups elsewhere in the Near East played a role in the emergence of early Islam."[976]

Ergo, Muhammad had divine revelation. But divine revelation is not required to explain Muhammad's knowledge of the Jewish and Christian scriptures and traditions. Unless you ignore his upbringing. Are we to believe that he learned nothing when he was in the care of his Grandfather, Abd al-Muttalib II "who was

---

[975] *The Islamic Jesus: How the King of the Jews Became a Prophet of the Muslims* Mustafa Akylol (St. Martin Press 2017) p. 89

[976] *The Islamic Jesus* Mustafa Akylol (St. Martin Press 2017) p. 99 quoting Guillaume Dye, "Jewish Christianity, the Qur'ān, and Early Islam: Some Methodological Caveats," paper presented at the Eighth Annual ASMEA Conference Washington, October 29–31, 2015, at the workshop "Jewish Christianity and the Origins of Islam."

a Hanif"? And are we to believe that Waraqa taught Muhammad none of the Christian scriptures that he learned from the Torah and the Gospel? At the very least from the story known to Muslims as the "Sack of Meat," Zayd clearly taught Muhammad monotheism, and perhaps much more of the Hanif beliefs. Muhammad then went out and preached these very beliefs. He was proclaiming one God and insulting the people of Mecca who worshipped the other gods in the Ka'bah. Zayd and Muhammad preached the one God of Abraham and both received harsh treatment from the Quraysh of Mecca.

Muhammad was to the established religions of Mecca, what early Christians were to the established religions of Rome. Christianity rejected the pagan Roman gods, and Muhammad was rejecting the pagan gods of Mecca. Polytheism demanded respect for all gods, and neither Christianity nor Muhammad's new Islam showed that respect. Islam and Christianity demanded exclusive monotheistic belief in Abraham's God and demeaned and rejected any other gods.[977] It was the rejection of those religions that caused the uproar. Christianity upset the multicultural balance of the Romans and Muhammad was upsetting the multicultural balance of the Meccans. And Muhammad, like Zayd before him, was shunned and rejected for his preaching the Hanif, Jewish, and Christian monotheism of Abraham's God. And all this was *before* Muhammad had any revelations, just as the Qur'an reports in its opening chapter. The evidence is that Muhammad learned the Jewish and Christian scriptures and traditions from his grandfather, his cousin Waraqa, and Zayd, and then had his visions of the divine.

---

[977] While Judaism and Christianity rejected those gods as well, the reported fact that a picture of Jesus and Mary was in the Ka'bah seems to show that they did not openly reject those other gods that Muhammad was preaching.

The Hanifiyya[978] is not a religion you hear much about because it no longer exists, at least not under that name. It is neither Jewish nor Christian but a religion of Abraham's God, which "retained some or all of the true tenets of Abraham's religion."[979] Before Muhammad, "in the pre-Islamic period, other people called Hanif had access to the written teachings related to Abraham and propagated calmly and softly his religion in the peninsula of Arabia."[980] The Hanif strongly adhered to monotheism, followed the ritual of circumcision, and believed the Ka'bah in Mecca was originally built by Abraham and Ishmael. The Hanif were in Arabia before Muhammad.

The Qur'an tells us three times that Abraham was the first Hanif: *"Who can be better in religion than one who submits his whole self to Allah, does good and follows the way of Abraham the true in faith [Hanifan]?"* (Qur'an 4:125) Abraham *was indeed a model devoutly obedient to Allah (and) true in faith [Hanifan]* (Qur'an 16:120) and *"Follow the ways of Abraham the true in faith [Hanifan] he joined not gods with Allah"* (Qur'an 16:123). Belief in the way of Abraham's God makes you a Hanif.

The Qur'an itself uses the Arabic word for Hanif twelve times,[981] but you seldom see that word in English translations of the Qur'an. For example, the version I mainly used in this book is Sahih International. It provides this translation: *Abraham was neither a Jew nor a Christian, but he was one inclining toward truth, a Muslim [submitting to Allah]. And he was not of the*

---

[978] Hanifiyya refers to the religion, its adherents are known as Hanif.

[979] "Concepts of Monotheism in Islam and Christianity" edited by Hans Kochler Braumueller, 1982. From *The Arabian Background of Monotheism in Islam.* Sheikh Ibramhim al-Qattan/Mahmud A. Ghul p. 29

[980] *New Researches on the Qur'an: Why and How Two Versions of Islam Entered the History of Mankind* Dr. Seyed Mostafa Azmayesh Mehraby (Publishing House 2015) p. 38

[981] *The Priest and the Prophet* Joseph Azzi (Pen Publishers 2005) p. 71 Nine of the twelve verses that I have found using the term in English are 2:135, 3:67, 3:95, 4:125, 6:161 30:30 10:104, 16:120, 16:123 not being able to read Arabic, I cannot find an English translation that uses the term Haniff because of the translation issue described.

*polytheists* (Qur'an 3:67). But a translation known as Shakir translates the verse this way: *And they say: Be Jews or Christians, you will be on the right course. Say: Nay! (we follow) the religion of Ibrahim, the Hanif, and he was not one of the polytheists* (Qur'an 2:135, Shakir).

Most English translations use the term Muslim to translate the Arabic word for Hanif. "The Arabic word *hanif* stands for *a person who chooses to follow one particular way after rejecting all other ways*. We have conveyed this meaning by saying, "a Muslim, sound in the Faith."[982]

But this confuses an important point. In Arabia, *before* there were Muslim followers of Muhammad, there were followers of Hanifiyya—Zayd, the mentor of Muhammad, being one of them. By implication, Muhammad did not found Islam, he only continued its beliefs.

Waraqa was a relative, confidant, and supporter of Muhammad who had a unique skill. One of Muhammad's wives, A'isha, said, "Waraqa...was a Christian convert and used to read the Gospels in Arabic...." Waraqa said, "Should I live till you receive the Divine Message, I will support you strongly."[983] A different Hadith says that Waraqa "during the pre-Islamic Period became a Christian and used to write the writing with Hebrew letters. He would write from the Gospel in Hebrew as much as Allah wished him to write."[984]

Waraqa's death greatly disturbed Muhammad. His visions "stopped for a time so that the apostle of God was distressed and

---

[982] "Tafhim al-Qur'an - The Meaning of the Qur'an" Sayyid Abul Ala Maududi 3. Al i Imran (The Family of Imran) footnote 59 A copy can be found at https://www.Qur'an411.com/

[983] Sahih Bukhari Volume 4 Book 55 Hadith 605 Translator: M. Muhsin Khan

[984] Sahih Bukhari Volume 1 Book 1 Hadith 3 Translator: M. Muhsin Khan The entire pdf file can be found here:
https://d1.islamhouse.com/data/en/ih_books/single/en_Sahih_Al-Bukhari.pdf

grieved."[985] Sometime later, perhaps three years later,[986] his visions "started coming strongly frequently and regularly."[987] For those three years, what had happened to Waraqa's writings and books? Is it too much to imagine that Waraqa's writings and Gospel had passed to Muhammad? Waraqa said he would support Muhammad strongly. No one can know what those writings were and what books he possessed, but we do know that the theology of Islam, Christianity, and Judaism are the same and that Christian stories were grafted into the Qur'an.

Two early Christian books that did not make it into the Bible are the Infancy Gospel of Matthew[988] and the Protoevangelium of James.[989] They contain a very different story of Jesus' birth than Luke and Matthew. The James version has Mary and Joseph on their way to Bethlehem from Jerusalem: *and they came to the midst of the way, and Mary said unto him: Take me down from the ass, for that which is within me presseth me, to come forth* (Infancy Gospel of James 17:8) and Jesus was born in a nearby cave.[990]

The Infancy Gospel of Matthew reports,

*Then the child Jesus, with a joyful countenance, reposing in the bosom of His mother, said to the palm: 'O tree, bend your branches, and refresh my mother with your fruit.' And immediately at these words the palm bent its top down*

---

[985] *The Life of Muhammad: A Translation of Ishaq's Sirat Rasul Allah,* (Oxford University Press, 1955p 111

[986] "The Life of Muhammad" Rev. Canon Sell (Christian Literature Society 1913) p. 40

[987] "Sahih Bukhari" Volume 1 Book 1 Hadith 3 Translator: M. Muhsin Khan which can be seen here
https://d1.islamhouse.com/data/en/ih_books/single/en_Sahih_Muslim.pdf

[988] Written between 600 and 625AD which is frequently cited to J Gijsel & R Beyers Libri de Nativitate Marie, Turnhout:Brepols 1997

[989] Written around 150 AD by someone other than James Lost Scriptures: *Books that Did Not Make It into the New Testament* Bart D Ehrman (Oxford University Press 2003) p. 63

[990] Even at the Church of the Nativity in Bethlehem the place of Jesus birth is in a cave.

*to the very feet of the blessed Mary; and they gathered from it fruit, with which they were all refreshed…. Then Jesus said to it: …and open from your roots a vein of water which has been hid in the earth, and let the waters flow, so that we may be satisfied from you.* (Gospel of Pseudo-Matthew 20)

These stories were written long before Muhammad, but they are the same story the Qur'an tells of Jesus' birth!

*And the pains of childbirth drove her to the trunk of a palm tree. She said, 'I wish I had died before this, and had been long forgotten [Mary was worried that people would think badly of her as she was not married.]. Then (baby Jesus) called her from below her, saying, 'Don't be sad. Your Lord has provided a stream under you.' Shake the trunk of the palm tree towards you, and it will drop on you fresh ripe dates. So eat and drink and be happy. And if you see any human, then say, 'Indeed I have vowed a fast to the Most Merciful so I will not speak to any human today.' Then she carried him and brought him to her people.* (Qur'an 19:23-27)

I know what you are thinking, "Okay, they were all just stories, but Luke and Matthew have the right stories." Well, maybe.

In 1992, archeologists working on a road between Jerusalem and Bethlehem discovered the remains of a very old church. Research showed that it was the remains of the Kathisma of the Theotokos, built around 451 AD, long before Islam. The Kathisma commemorates the place where Mary, according to these gospels, had stopped to give birth to Jesus.[991] On the floor

---

[991] ttp://www.israel.org/MFA/IsraelExperience/History/Pages/TheChurchofthe SeatofMary-Kathisma-.aspx

of this ancient church was a mosaic showing three palm trees full of dates![992] The church and these Gospels demonstrate that some early Christians believed a different version of Jesus' birth and, more importantly, that the narrative of Jesus' birth was available in Arabia and ended up in Muhammad's Qur'an.

Waraqa had mastered Christianity and studied its scriptures and translated at least some into Arabic. Which version of Christianity Waraqa had mastered, and the books he mastered it from are unknown. We do know that Muhammad's message was not the message of Paul, nor that of the Cappadocian brothers, nor of Constantine nor Theodosius. The weighty baggage Christianity acquired over the centuries had been scuttled, either by Waraqa or Muhammad. The deification of Jesus as part of a Triune God was gone. What remained was the long-dead Gospel of Jesus, resurrected by Muhammad and given new life. *"And let the People of the Gospel judge by what Allah has revealed therein"* (Qur'an 5:47).

---

[992] "Away in a Manger. . . or Under a Palm Tree?" Mustafa Akyol *New York Times* 12/21/2017 Opinion Section

# Chapter Ten – The Acceptance of Islam

B elieve only in the God of Abraham, worship only him with your prayers, and lead a life respectful of others—especially the poor, the widows, and the orphans—and Allah will provide you an eternal afterlife in paradise. Anything else and expect to find yourself in eternal torment and suffering. This was the message of the God of Abraham, the ultimate patriarch of the Jews and Arabs. It was the message that Jesus had preached, stripped of centuries of theological bickering. Muhammad expected his message to resonate among the Jews and the Christians. It was their message: a tolerant, inclusive message directly from their God. Preach it, and they will come. He preached, but few came.

In the first years, there were only a few who accepted his Islam. The Bible says that Jesus had 12 apostles and 72 followers.[993] After a few years of preaching, Muhammad probably had less than 100 followers as well.[994] While few

---

[993] Luke 10:1 and 10:17

[994] By my count, those directly listed in *The Life of Muhammad: A Translation of Ishaq's Sirat Rasul Allah,* (Oxford University Press, 1955 p 115, is nine and on p 116 thirty-eight with the implication that this was the total after three years of preaching.

followed Muhammad, many more became his enemy. For the people of Mecca, Muhammad had "cursed our gods, insulted our religion, mocked our way of life and accused our forefathers of error."[995] Muhammad's biographies tell of a lengthy set of discussions and negotiations between Muhammad and the Meccans during the Middle Meccan period.

Perhaps the problem was the Meccans had not understood Muhammad's message. Perhaps the Meccans "had never heard the Qur'an distinctly read and a Muslim by the name Abdullah ibn Mas'ud agreed to read it clearly to them." Abdullah, "turned towards them as he read so that they noticed him." As he read, the Meccans understood that "he was reading some of what Muhammad prayed" and "he continued to read so far as God willed that he should read." (Now what was it that he was reading, since the standard narrative of Islam says there was no Qur'an to be read at this time?) After a while, the Meccans had heard enough and beat him up.[996]

Times were so tough for the Muslims in Mecca that Muhammad suggested that those unprotected should go to Abyssinia, which is in today's Ethiopia. But then Ishaq reports that it was not a suggestion, but rather that some Muslims were expelled from Mecca. Whether they were expelled, or they left at Muhammad's suggestion, eighty-three men and their families fled to Ethiopia.[997]

For the Muslims who remained, times got even tougher. Khadija's death had saddened Muhammad, but the death of his uncle, Abu Talib, had exposed him and the remaining Muslims to mortal danger. Muhammad went to seek help in another

---

[995] *The Life of Muhammad: A Translation of Ishaq's Sirat Rasul Allah,* (Oxford University Press, 1955 Pp 119

[996] *The Life of Muhammad: A Translation of Ishaq's Sirat Rasul Allah,* (Oxford University Press, 1955) Pp 139-140

[997] *The Life of Muhammad: A Translation of Ishaq's Sirat Rasul Allah,* (Oxford University Press, 1955) Pp 146-150. The expelled reference is on p 149

trading town, Ta'if. None was given. "When the apostle returned to Mecca his people opposed him more bitterly than ever, apart from the few lower-class people who believed in him."[998]

It was about this time that Muhammad took the midnight horse to Heaven. In his hallucination, Muhammad rode Buraq to Jerusalem, then ascended to Heaven, where he met God and then returned. All in one night! Muhammad's telling of this story only made matters worse in Mecca. Most of them said, "By God, this is a plain absurdity! A caravan takes a month to go to Syria and a month to return." Even Muhammad's followers found the story ridiculous. "Many Muslims gave up their faith; some went to Abu Bakr and said, 'What do you think of your friend now?'"[999]

Sometime thereafter, an Arab tribe named Abdul-Ashhal came to Mecca seeking an alliance with the Quraysh. The Ashhal were enemies of another tribe, the Khazraj. Muhammad told the members of the Ashhal tribe that "he was God's apostle sent to humanity" and God "had revealed a book to him; then he told them about Islam and read to them some of the Qur'an." The leader of the Ashhal "took a handful of dirt from the valley and threw it in his face, saying, 'Shut up! we didn't come here for this.'"[1000] The outlook for Muhammad and his Islam was growing dimmer.

(Beyond telling us that Muhammad's Islam was quite small and in mortal danger, these Islamic stories say repeatedly that there was a physical document of beliefs which Muhammad was capable of reading. At that time, 619 AD, only half of the Qur'an[1001] had been spoken by Muhammad, and supposedly

---

[998] *The Life of Muhammad: A Translation of Ishaq's Sirat Rasul Allah,* (Oxford University Press, 1955) p. 194.

[999] *The Life of Muhammad: A Translation of Ishaq's Sirat Rasul Allah,* (Oxford University Press, 1955) p. 183

[1000] *The Life of Muhammad: A Translation of Ishaq's Sirat Rasul Allah,* (Oxford University Press, 1955). p. 197

[1001] Chapters 96,68,73,74,1,111,81,87,92,89,93,94,103,100,108,102,107,109,105,113,

none of it was written and supposedly Muhammad couldn't read?)

Things were about to change quickly. The most important event in the formation of Islam has only the barest of reports in Islamic documents. Six members of the Khazraj, the enemies of the tribe whose leader threw dirt in Muhammad's face, came to Mecca. The Khazraj of Medina were aligned with the Jews, who had spoken of a coming messiah or prophet. When the six heard Muhammad speak, they said, "Yeah, he's the guy the Jews have been talking about!"[1002] and returned to Medina and told their friends and neighbors, setting a favorable environment for Muhammad and Islam.

The following year, twelve leaders from the tribes of Medina came to Mecca and met with Muhammad. "There were twelve of us and we pledged ourselves to the prophet after the manner of women" (meaning they would protect the prophet as they protect their women) with the understanding that "we should associate nothing with God; we should not steal; we should not commit fornication; nor kill our offspring; we should not slander our neighbours; we should not disobey him in what was right; if we fulfilled this [then] paradise would be ours; if we committed any of those sins [then] it was for God to punish or forgive as He pleased."[1003] Interestingly, this pledge, called the First Pledge of Al-Aqaba, will be recited a few years later as Qur'an 60:12.

---

114,112,53,80,97,91,85,106,10175,77,50,90,86,54,38,7,72,36,25,35,19,20, 56,26,27,28,17,10,11,12,15,6,37,31,34,39,40 are through the Middle Meccan period and contain 3152 verses, versus 3084 verses spoken later by Muhammad

[1002] They actually said "This is the very prophet of whom the Jews warned us. *The Life of Muhammad: A Translation of Ishaq's Sirat Rasul Allah,* (Oxford University Press, 1955p. 199

[1003] *The Life of Muhammad: A Translation of Ishaq's Sirat Rasul Allah,* (Oxford University Press, 1955) . p. 199

In June of 620, these twelve returned to Medina with Muhammad's associate, Umayr.[1004] Umayr took with him a written copy of the Qur'an because he was told by Muhammad to "read the Qur'an to them and to teach them Islam."[1005] But is impossible, Islam says that the Qur'an wasn't written yet, and for sure at least half of it had yet to come into Muhammad's head. But whatever Umayr read, it convinced many in Medina to become Muslims.

The narrative of Islam is that Muhammad was invited to Medina to be their leader and settle their disputes. The authoritative biographer of Muhammad, Ishaq, tells the story a little differently. Somehow the Meccans, sympathetic to Muhammad:

Agreed to meet the apostle at al-Abaqa [and had] concealed our business from those of our people who were polytheists.... When a third of the night had passed, we went stealing softly like sandgrouse to our appointment.... We gathered together in the gully waiting for the apostle until he came with his uncle al-'Abbas, [who said] "O people of al-Khazraj You know what position Muhammad holds among us. We have protected him from our own people...but he will turn to you and join you. If you think that you can be faithful to what you have promised him and protect him from his opponents, then assume the burden you have undertaken. But if you think that you will betray and abandon him after he has gone out with you, then leave him now. For he is safe where he is." We replied, "We have heard what you say. You speak, O

---

[1004] "*The New Encyclopedia of Islam 4ᵗʰ Edition*" Cyril Glasse (Rowman & Littlefield 2013) p. 56

[1005] *The Life of Muhammad: A Translation of Ishaq's Sirat Rasul Allah,* (Oxford University Press, 1955). p 202

apostle, and choose for yourself and for your Lord what you wish."[1006]

The Muslims were in deep trouble in Mecca and were seeking safety somewhere. A deal had been offered whereby Muhammad and the Muslims could go to Medina, but would they be protected there? Those that offered to protect the Muslims did so behind the back their chief. Your choice, Muhammad. Different people at this meeting reported different things, ranging from Muhammad invoking Jesus, to the Devil shouting from the tops of the hills.[1007] In the end, Muhammad accepted the security offered by some of the Khazraj. It was now 621 AD.

But it was a secret meeting that had been concealed from the chief of the Khazraj and most of its leadership. When the Quraysh heard of the agreement, they went to the chief of the Khazraj and asked for a confirmation. The Khazraj "swore that nothing of the kind had happened and they knew nothing of it. And here they were speaking the truth, for they were in ignorance of what had happened." Those who had made the deal with Muhammad snuck out the back door and fled. One was caught and beaten, but eventually released. Nothing more is reported on the agreement for the Muslims to move to Medina, but they began leaving Mecca and moving there.[1008]

Muhammad and his Muslims were pacifists in the face of the persecutions and violence of the Meccans. Muhammad "had simply been ordered to call men to God and to endure insult and forgive the ignorant."[1009] Muhammad thought he could persuade

---

[1006] *The Life of Muhammad: A Translation of Ishaq's Sirat Rasul Allah,* (Oxford University Press, 1955). p. 203

[1007] *The Life of Muhammad: A Translation of Ishaq's Sirat Rasul Allah,* (Oxford University Press, 1955). p. 205

[1008] *The Life of Muhammad: A Translation of Ishaq's Sirat Rasul Allah,* (Oxford University Press, 1955) Pp 201-207 tell the entire story including the names of those present.

[1009] *The Life of Muhammad: A Translation of Ishaq's Sirat Rasul Allah,* (Oxford University Press, 1955) p. 212

the pagans and bring the Jews and Christians of many stripes into his big tent. *Do not debate with the people of the Book unless it is in the best manner.... And say, "We believe in what is sent down to us and sent down to you, and our God and your God is One, and to Him we submit"* (Qur'an 29:45-46). We have the same God, you accept your messenger, and we accept ours. Live and let live. Let's join hands and sing Kumbaya. Oh, that it could be so. Muhammad was about to learn that it could not be so.

When Umayr left with the people of Medina, they had only sworn to protect Muhammad as they protected their women folk. This did not go down well with the leader of the Khazraj. "This is a serious matter; my people are not in the habit of deciding a question without consulting me...." We do not know what, but everything changed sometime in the Fall of 621 AD and Spring of 622 AD. By the summer of 622 AD, the idea of sitting around the campfire and singing Kumbaya had blown away on the desert wind. That campfire now became a council of war.

*Permission is given to those who fight because they have been wronged. God is well able to help them—those who have been driven out of their houses without right, only because they said God is our Lord* (Qur'an 22:39).[1010] That summer, those who the year before pledged to protect Muhammad as women now pledged fealty in war, in jihad. "Now they bound themselves to war against all and sundry for God and his apostle, while he promised them for faithful service thus the reward of paradise."[1011] "Death in war, for peace in paradise" was Muhammad's motto

---

[1010] This quote is "the first verse that was sent down on this subject" from "Ishaq's Sirat Rasul Allah" Guillaume p. 212. The Qur'anic version is slightly different at Qur'an 22:39-40. *Permission [to fight] has been given to those who are being fought, because they were wronged. And indeed, Allah is competent to give them victory.* The sequence in Ishaq has this before the move to Medina, but the Qur'anic version is dated after the move to Medina. Part of what may have happened in this period is that things were "remembered" out of the factual sequence.

[1011] *The Life of Muhammad: A Translation of Ishaq's Sirat Rasul Allah,* (Oxford University Press, 1955) p. 208

for Islam. For twelve years, Muhammad failed as the peaceful prophet of Mecca; now he would succeed as the warlord of Medina. And his shadow as a warlord would stretch across time.

Between May 1 and May 15, 2018, about 60 Palestinians died and several hundred were wounded in rioting along the border of Israel and Gaza. CNN showed a video of Palestinian children "happily stating that they are finally going home and that dying at the border will guarantee them a place in paradise."[1012]

Abraham's God would authorize Muhammad to kill and conquer, just as Joshua was authorized to kill and conquer many centuries before. And Muhammad's dreams from God would grow from peaceful pronouncements in Mecca to violent and warlike cries in Medina; *"fight and slay the Pagans wherever ye find them, and seize them, beleaguer them, and lie in wait for them in every stratagem (of war)"* (Qur'an 9:5). *"And slay them wherever ye catch them and turn them out from where they have Turned you out; for tumult and oppression are worse than slaughter"* (Qur'an 2:191). *"And fight them on until there is no more tumult or oppression, and there prevail justice and faith in Allah altogether and everywhere"* (Qur'an 8:39). Fight until you have conquered the world!

Many believers in the Qur'an follow that command today. The Iranian Constitution commands that Iran's Army and Revolutionary Guard "will be responsible not only for guarding and preserving the frontiers of the country, but also for fulfilling the ideological mission of jihad in God's way; that is, extending the sovereignty of God's law throughout the world."[1013] Some should have read the Iranian Constitution before agreeing to giving Iran billions of dollars to arm the mission of jihad in Gaza,

---

[1012] "Why Gaza is no Selma" Thane Rosenbaum Updated 8:27 PM ET, Wed May 16, 2018 http//www.cnn.com or "Hamas tells its Gazan subjects that, if they get killed trying to murder Israelis, "they will be rewarded with a place in paradise." "Gaza deaths are fault of Hamas" *NEW YORK DAILY NEWS* Thursday, May 17, 2018

[1013] Preamble to the Iranian Constitution und the section "An Ideological Army" a copy can be found here : http://www.wipo.int/edocs/lexdocs/laws/en/ir/ir001en.pdf

Lebanon, Syria, and elsewhere in return for a dubious time-out on atomic weapons.

Despite this, the spectacular spread of Islam over the 7th century was not faith by the sword alone. The swirling winds of religious conflict and uncertainty had left Jews, Christians of all stripes, Zoroastrians, and even pagans receptive to the simple and historically appealing message of Muhammad.

Most Arabs believed they were the descendants of Abraham and Hagar. "Generally speaking, the pre-Islamic Arabs seem to have been well aware of their genealogical descent from Abraham and Ishmael."[1014] And there was a general acceptance that the Ka'bah was built by Ishmael and Abraham. "Traditions about Abraham relating him to Mecca and its sanctuary were current in the peninsula well before the rise of Islam."[1015] The Arabs understood that Abraham's God was indigenous and somehow important to them.

A rich and lengthy history of the Jewish presence on the Arabian Peninsula is a partial explanation. Arabian Jews may have originated from the Queen of Sheba visiting Solomon,[1016] or were the tribes that escaped during the Assyrian and Babylonian captivity. Or perhaps they were exiles from the Jewish–Roman wars or expelled by Christians from Jerusalem. Arabia had many Jewish tribes at the time of Muhammad.

Monotheism was also close by in its Zoroastrian form, which was restored as the state religion of Persia by King Kavadh I in 528 AD. Kavadh persecuted and purged the opposing sects from

---

[1014] "Hannifiyya and Ka'ba An inquiry into the Arabian pre-Islamic background of din Ibrahim" Uri Rubin *Jerusalem Studies in Arabic and Islam* N 13 1990 p 107

[1015] "The House of Abraham and the House of Amram: Genealogy, Patriarchal Authority, and Exegetical Professionalism" Angelika Neuwirth in *The Qur'an in Context: Historical and Literary Investigations into the Qur'anic Milieu* Edited by Angelika Neuwirth Nicolai Sinai Michael Marx (Leiden • Boston 2010) pp. 500-501

[1016] The Qur'an records that she converted to Judaism after her visit with Solomon [Qur'an 27:30-45].

his empire. The Mazdakites, a variant of Christianity/ Zoroastrian-ism/Manicheanism was practiced by a prominent Arab tribe who fled to Yemen, where they proselytized their religion in southern Arabia.[1017] This only complicated the century-old fight in Yemen between Christianity and Judaism.[1018]

Christianity in Arabia was not your mother's Methodist Church. All over the Arabian Peninsula, the Christian schisms added to the religious conflicts. While Trinitarian Christianity had the force of empire behind it, other versions became prevalent at the intersection of Arabia and the Empire "and were a constant theological threat to Chalcedonian (Roman) Christianity."[1019] Varying forms of Christianity acted as independent churches and "prevailed in great portions of Najran (South West Saudi Arabia) and others parts" as Christian "tenets were known far and wide."[1020] The "deep division within the Christian Church along both theological and geographical lines...to the coming of the Islamic community cannot be emphasized enough."[1021]

The Roman emperor Justinian was "determined to restore the unity to his kingdom where the split between his own (Trinitarian) Christianity and the Nestorian and Monophysite alternatives remained."[1022] Those not accepting the indecipherable theologies of the Trinity had disbursed from the centers of power and punishment into the hinterlands of the Empire and beyond.

---

[1017] *New Researches on the Qur'an: Why and How Two Versions of Islam Entered the History of Mankind*, Dr. Seyed Mostafa Azmayesh (Mehraby Publishing House 2015) pp. 27-28

[1018] *What are the Sacred Roots of Islam* Jamil Effarah (AuthorHouse 2016) Kindle loc 1555-1580

[1019] John of Damascus, First Apologist to the Muslims: The Trinity and Christian Apologetics in the Early Islamic Period, Daniel J. Janosik (Pickwick Publications, 2016) p 195

[1020] *Mohammed and Mohammedanism* S.W. Koelle (Rivingtons 1889) p. 23

[1021] *A History of Christian Muslim Relations* Hugh Goddard (Rowan & Littlefield 2000) p. 23

[1022] *A New History of Early Christianity*, Charles Freeman (Yale University Press 2009) p 309

The Arians, Nestorians, Gnostics, Jacobites, Nazarenes, Ebionites, Manicheans, Monophysites, and zebras of many stripes were scattered throughout the eastern empire. But it was far too late to agree on one formula of Christianity that would have "any stable basis for theology."[1023]

The Council of Chalcedon thought it had solved all the problems with statements such as this: Jesus was one person who had "two natures without confusion, without change, without division, without separation; the distinction of nature's being in no way abolished because of the union, but rather the characteristic property of each nature being preserved and coming together to form one person and subsistence."[1024] Paul's mysterium had become an impenetrable fog, and not one likely to be understood by wandering Arab tribes without a written language.

Justinian and Pope Vigilius held the Second Council of Constantinople in 553 AD attempting to bring unity by solving Christianity's complex puzzle of polytheism: of the Gods, Father, Son, and Holy Ghost. Amen. Councils and laws may have proclaimed Jesus as an eternal God of the Trinity, but that was neither fully understood nor accepted. The Second Council of Pope and emperor at Constantinople failed and was "bitterly opposed" throughout most of the Christian world.[1025] That muddle of Christian thought from the Atlantic to Syria would be "swept away in a few decades by the Arab tribes and their clear Muslim doctrine of One God."[1026]

---

[1023] A New History of Early Christianity, Charles Freeman (Yale University Press 2009) p 310

[1024] The Catechism of the Catholic Church Part 1, Section 2, Chapter 2 Article 3 Number 467

[1025] The Seven Ecumenical Councils, Henry Robert Percival (Veritas Splendor Publications, 2013) p. 426

[1026] A History of Christianity, Paul Johnson (Simon & Schuster a Touchstone Book, 1995) pp. 93

Muhammad had cleared the underbrush of Christian arguments on Jesus' divinity, reconciling the Judaism of Abraham into a powerful understandable theology that resonated with many Christian sects. Islam's easily understood narrative of Jesus and God played a significant role in the swift conversion of Christians to Islam in the Middle East and North Africa.[1027] Islam was the Second Jewish Jesus Church of Jerusalem.

The Dome of the Rock, one of the Four Wonders of the Islamic World, was built on the very spot of the First Jewish Jesus Church of Jerusalem Church.[1028] The Dome of the Rock exemplifies the message that Islam was sending to confused Christians.

A few years ago, my son and I sat on a patio overlooking Jerusalem and the Dome of the Rock. We had spent the day on Temple Mount and seen firsthand the exceptional beauty of this building and its mosaics of large Arabic script. Now at night, in the heart of Jerusalem, the Gold Dome shimmered its mystical aura, evoking the spiritual power of Judaism, Christianity, and Islam while its silhouette stood out as the iconic symbol of strife between the religions of Abraham's God.

Caliph Abd al-Malik built the Dome, deriving its architecture from two nearby Christian Churches: Church of the Anastasis[1029] and the Church of Kathisma (yes the same church as Mary and the dates).[1030] Finished in 691 AD, the Dome is located where Abraham prepared to sacrifice Isaac; this is also the site of

---

[1027] This is fully discussed in *When Jesus Became God* Richard E. Rubenstein (Harcourt 1999) pp. 230-231 and in *A History of Christianity*, Paul Johnson (Simon & Schuster a Touchstone Book, 1995) pp. 92-93

[1028] There was no building by this name, Jesus and his apostles worshipped at the Jewish temple in Jerusalem, the very location where the Dome of the Rock was built.

[1029] Better known as the Church of the Holy Sepulcher

[1030] *The Dome of the Rock in Light of the Development of Concentric Martyria in Jerusalem: Architecture and Architectural Iconography* Rina Avner Muquarnas (Brill Publishers 2010) Vol. 27 p 44

Solomon's Temple, where the Ark of the Covenant rested. It is very near to where Jesus was crucified and is the spot where Muhammad met Jesus, Moses, and Elijah and ascended to Heaven. It is a monument to those events, not a mosque.

The Dome may have been built in part to compete with the Ka'bah in Mecca and the mosques in Medina and Damascus, which together are the Four Wonders of the Islamic World.[1031] More importantly, it was built to engage Christians.[1032] A clear message in large Arabic script surrounds the outside of the octagonal dome and is repeated on the inside. It reads, in part:

O People of the Book, do not go to extremes in your religion. Do not say anything about God except what is true. Verily the Messiah Jesus the Son of Mary is the Messenger from God and God's word that He cast into Mary, and spirit from Him. So Believe in God and in his Messengers and do not say "Three" it is better for you to desist. Rather God is one God. He is too exalted to have a son, and everything in the heavens and on earth belongs to Him. It is enough to have God as the disposer of affairs. The Messiah does not scorn being a servant of God nor do the favored angels. Those who scorn servitude to Him and are arrogant will be gathered back to Him all together. Such is Jesus the son of Mary, it is a statement of truth about which they dispute. It is not befitting of God that he should take a son, He is exalted above that. When he decides a matter, He only says "Be" and it is. Verily God

---

[1031] *The Age of Faith (The Story of Civilization, Volume 4)* Will Durant (MJF Books, 1980) p. 229

[1032] *The Story of the Qur'an: Its History and Place in Muslim Life, Ingrid Mattson* (Wiley Blackwell, 2nd Edition, 2013) p. 153

is my Lord and your Lord so worship Him, this is the straight path.[1033]

The Dome of the Rock proclaims Jesus as the Messiah, a prophet, a messenger from God, a human born of Mary—the exact points argued among the Jesus sects during the evolution of Christianity! It is a "pre-Nicene Creed" of Jewish Christianity, a version of a Jesus religion, "Syrian-Arabian Christianity"[1034] that had percolated the meaning of Jesus' life for centuries. "Jewish Christianity...suddenly reemerge(d) as an attractive version of the Christian faith."[1035] Here in the very heart of Christianity, on the very spot where Jesus had taught and where James, Peter, and the apostles had prayed stood the Dome of the Rock, an Islamic billboard loudly proclaiming to Christians: *Come back to the true religion of Jesus. Reject the Christianity of Paul and the Roman emperors. Come home to Islam.* Perhaps the most effective advertising copy in the history of the world.

A century after Muhammad, virtually all the peoples from the Indus River to the Atlantic Ocean had dropped their banners of faith to raise the banner of Islam. Many who converted to Islam saw it as truth piercing the fog of Christian theology. Others converted to avoid the pierce of an Arab sword, just as their forbearers converted to Catholic Christianity to avoid the pierce of a Roman sword. How many of each will never be known. Does it matter if four or four million angels fit on the head of a pin?

Muhammad saw his message as a new inclusive tent under which Zoroastrians, Jews, and Christians could gather to worship

---

[1033] *The Story of the Qur'an: Its History and Place in Muslim Life,* Ingrid Mattson (Wiley Blackwell, 2nd Edition, 2013) pp. 152-153

[1034] *The Hidden Origins of Islam: New Research into Its Early History,* edited by Karl-Heinz Ohlig and Gerd-R. Puin, (Prometheus Books, 2010) p. 200

[1035] *Islam, Judeo-Christianity and Byzantine Iconoclasm* Patricia Crone (Ashgate Variorum 1980) p. 89. The complete text can be found here: https://www.hs.ias.edu/files/Crone_Articles/Crone_Islam_Judeo-Christianity_and_Byzantine_Iconoclasm.pdf

one God. The God of Abraham was already the God of the Jews, of the Hanif, of Jesus, and now of the Muslims. Muhammad preached that message with peace and inclusion for eight years, but his tent remained empty. In Mecca, Muhammad included Jews and Christians and was rejected with derision and disdain. In Medina, Muhammad excluded Jews and Christians and his message was finally accepted.

The catholic Christianity decreed by Constantine and the Trinitarian Christianity commanded by Theodosius were accepted by the masses and enforced on the rest by the swords of the Roman army. That is how Christianity spread and dominated the Roman Empire, until the Second Jewish Jesus Church of Jerusalem came with its Arab Army. Islam's army challenged Roman and Persian political power, while Islam's message challenged Christian and Zoroastrian religious power. Islam's message resonated with the masses.[1036] And that is how Islam spread.

---

[1036] *Islam, Judeo-Christianity and Byzantine Iconoclasm* Patricia Crone (Ashgate Variorum 1980) The army reference is on p. 60. The entire essay is a fascinating review of Jewish Christianity in Syria and a review of the convoluted relationships in Judeo-Christian and Orthodox Christianity occurring with the rise of Islam. This is exemplified on page 89 with this: "The exact relationship between Jewish Christians and Christian Jews is a hazy one." Within that haze Islam made sense!
https://www.hs.ias.edu/files/Crone_Articles/Crone_Islam_Judeo-Christianity_and_Byzantine_Iconoclasm.pdf

# Chapter Eleven – The Sunni-Shia Divide

When Muhamad died in 632 AD, Islam had become both a religion and a military/political entity. Ali-Talib was the natural successor to Muhammad; however, he was inexperienced and only 31. Abu Bakr, Muhammad's other long-time companion therefore became the caliph. Bakr used military force "with wisdom and clemency" to hold the Islamic political community together and "completed the unification of Arabia."[1037] Since Islam prohibited fighting among the Arab tribes of the Islamic Ummah, Abu Bakr initiated raids for treasure into the surrounding lands.

In August of 634 AD, Abu Bakr saw his imminent death, and appointed Umar ibn al-Khattab as the next caliph. Just as the raids into Syria were beginning, Bakr died and Ali was passed over again as caliph.

There is much debate over why Bakr appointed Umar over Ali, but Umar was a warrior who immediately became the "Commander of the Faithful."[1038] Umar did not set out to convert

---

[1037] *Islam: A Short History*, Karen Armstrong (Modern Library, 2000) p. 26
[1038] Several possibilities for Bakr's decision are covered in "No go but God the Origins Evolution and Future of Islam" Reza Aslan Random House 2011 pp. 121-126

the conquered citizens in the surrounding remnants of Rome and Persia. He only wanted their wealth.[1039] Umar was very successful but not greedy. He said that a king uses money as he pleases, while a caliph uses it for Islamic cause.[1040] He distributed the wealth equally among the citizenry of Medina. However, he required that his marauding Arab troops be garrisoned outside the towns they conquered, so that local cities could maintain their culture and organization.[1041]

For ten years, Umar was wildly successful in capturing and pillaging the surrounding lands of the former Roman and Persian empires and wisely used the funds for many civic projects and reforms. But one Persian was distraught over Umar's seizure of Persian heritage. In 644 AD, Umar was assassinated by a Persian slave. A committee of six was appointed to select the next caliph. Ali was again passed over for Uthman ibn Affan, one of the richest members of the Quraysh tribe. As the new caliph, he swore to continue the policies of Bakr and Umar.

Uthman expanded, building the empire east, conquering Iran and Afghanistan, and west, taking all of North Africa. "Uthman completed the conquest and continued those policies complicating everything with his greed and nepotism."[1042] Uthman's policies created so much dissension that members of the army went to Mecca to protest and ended up killing Uthman in a mutiny on June 17, 656 AD.

And thus begins the Shiite–Sunni split in Islam. The mutineers gave Ali Talib his opportunity as caliph. They thought he would "return to the old values of equality and doctrinal

---

[1039] *Islam: A Short History*, Karen Armstrong (Modern Library, 2000) p. 30

[1040] *The New Encyclopedia of Islam 4th Edition* Cyril Glasse (Rowman & Littlefield 2013) p. 541

[1041] *No god but God, The Origins Evolution and Future of Islam* Reza Aslan (Random House 2011) p. 125

[1042] *The Middle East: A Brief History of the Last 2,000 Years*, Bernard Lewis, (Scribner, 1995) p. 63

purity," or as a direct relation to the Prophet, he might bring a "return to the true original message of Islam."[1043] Ali Talib had the perfect pedigree: he was Muhammad's cousin, was a lifelong friend of Muhammad, and had married Muhammad's daughter, Fatima. His supporters were called Shi'atu Ali, which became Shia, or often today Shiites.[1044] They believe that only those descended from the Prophet should rule the caliphate and it should be a theocracy. It's an oversimplification, but everyone else is Sunni.[1045]

Muhammad's widow, A'isha, and others were against Ali Talib becoming the caliph. A'isha believed Talib had instigated a painful rumor of her sexual impropriety when she was 14. Uthman's relatives were also against Ali because he never punished Uthman's assassins. And then, there was the slight complication that A'isha's brother was the one who killed Uthman.[1046]

It was a great recipe for a family blood feud, something that all Arab tribes understood. It became a civil war known to Islam as the Fitnah. Uthman's relatives rallied around his cousin, Mu'awiyah ibn Abi Sufyan, who had been the governor of Syria. Five years of bitter fighting ensued. Ali's forces beat A'isha's at the Battle of the Camel, but he allowed her to return with an entourage to Mecca. Ali then battled Mu'awiyah and accepted his surrender. There are several versions of what happened next, and while the actual version is unknown, it is accurate to say that during negotiations of this surrender, Ali was assassinated. There

---

[1043] *God's Crucible: Islam and the Making of Europe, 570-1215*, David Levering (Lewis Norton, 2008) pp. 88

[1044] *The Middle East: A Brief History of the Last 2,000 Years*, Bernard Lewis, (Scribner, 1995) p. 64

[1045] The other sects are Sufi's, Baha'is, and Ahmadiyyas the latter two are considered heretics.

[1046] *A Concise History of the Middle East,* Arthur Goldschmidt Jr. (Westview Press, 7th Edition, 2001) p. 59

was no one left to challenge Mu'awiyah, who became the next caliph in 661 AD.[1047] He offered Fatima (who was Muhammad's daughter and Ali's wife) and Ali's sons deals they could not refuse, and they retired in wealth in Medina.[1048]

The followers of Ali saw him as the ideal Muslim, pointing the straight path to God. He was "the Proof of God on Earth." Mu'awiyah's caliphate was the foundation of the Sunnis, while all those who had supported Ali became the Shiites.[1049]

When Mu'awiyah died, in 680 CE, his son, Yazid I, was named caliph. Ali's son Husayn, the grandson of Muhammad, refused to swear allegiance. Another civil war, a Fitnah, broke out. But it was no contest, as all of Husayn's family was slaughtered at the Massacre at Karbala, which remains a major Shiite day of commemoration.

Over the following centuries, the Sunni and Shiites would drift apart, developing separate interpretations of Islam, often coalescing within different ethnic groups. In very general terms, Arabs are Sunni, but not all Sunni are Arabs, and Persians are Shiites, while not all Shiites are from Iran. The Ottoman Empire was mostly Sunni, and the Persian Empire under the Safavids was Shiite. Saudi Arabia is Sunni. Today about 85% of Muslims are Sunni. Today's fighting in Iraq and Syria basically devolves into the Sunni–Shia divide.

Think in terms of the Catholics and Protestants. Between 1618 and 1648, they fought the Thirty Years' War in Central Europe. Ferdinand II headed the Catholic faction, the Holy Roman Empire. He "saw his secular mission as carrying out the will of God" and could not deal with Protestants, "since they

---

[1047] *In the Shadow of the Sword: The Birth of Islam and the Rise of Global Arab Empire*, Tom Holland (Doubleday, 2012) p. 364

[1048] *A Concise History of the Middle East,* Arthur Goldschmidt Jr. (Westview Press, 7th Edition, 2001) p. 61

[1049] *God's Crucible: Islam and the Making of Europe, 570-1215*, David Levering (Lewis Norton, 2008) p. 93.

practice falsehood and misuse God and religion." It was the deadliest European religious war, resulting in eight million casualties and "one of the most brutal and destructive wars in the history of mankind."[1050] Protestants and Catholics, Shias and Sunnis, each believe they are following the true path of God. Fervent faith is a dangerous faith.

Still, the Shia and Sunni combined to forge Islam's rapid expansion into the Islamic Empire. In the east, the Arabs conquered the Persian Empire to the Oxus River and the borders of China. In the west, they conquered all of North Africa then crossed the straits of Gibraltar, conquered the Iberian Peninsula and began making forays into France. Charles Martel, King of the Franks, is accorded as the savior of Europe and Christendom for defeating the Islamic hordes at Tours in 732 AD,[1051] exactly 100 years after Muhammad's death.

Martel merely defeated a spent expeditionary force far from home.[1052] The path to Europe is shorter and easier through Constantinople than the long way around the Mediterranean through Spain and across the Pyrenees. Constantinople was besieged in the early 700s by the Arab armies and their new navy of a thousand ships.[1053] The city held, and the expansionary phase of Islam ended. For 500 years the demarcation between Islam and Christendom would be the Dardanelles, the Bosporus and the Pyrenees.

During those centuries, Islam and Christendom would fundamentally coexist, not as warring civilizations but as a quarrelsome couple, as a wary respect dominated Islamic and

---

[1050] *Diplomacy* Henry Kissinger (Simon and Shuster 1994) pp. 59-61
[1051] *A Concise History of the Middle East* Arthur Goldschmidt Jr. (Westview Press 7th Edition 2001) pp. 70-71
[1052] *The Muslim Discovery of Europe* Bernard Lewis (WW Norton 2001) p. 19
[1053] *A Concise History of the Middle East* Arthur Goldschmidt Jr. (Westview Press 7th Edition 2001) pp. 70-71

Christian relations.[1054] During the coming era, Islam and Christianity's beliefs would become deeply embedded into the institutions and cultures as the Dark Ages descended.

Oh, yes, I almost forgot. I said I would tell you about that hungry goat. A'isha, one of Muhammad's wives reported that, "The verse of the stoning and of suckling an adult ten times were revealed, and they were (written) on a paper and kept under my bed. When the messenger of Allah expired and we were preoccupied with his death, a goat entered and ate away the paper."[1055] How many goats and other quirks have altered the details of sacred religions?

---

[1054] *The Crusades the Authoritative History of the War for the Holy Land*" Thomas Asbridge (Harper Collins 2010) p 27

[1055] Multiple Islamic sources report the story. Musnad Ahmad bin Hanbal. vol. 6. p. 269; Sunan Ibn Majah, p. 626; Ibn Qutbah, Tawil Mukhtalafi 'l-Hadith (Cairo: Maktaba al-Kulliyat al-Azhariyya. 1966) p. 310; As-Suyuti, ad-Durru 'l-Manthur, vol. 2. p. 13 https://www.al-islam.org/Qur'an-its-protection-alteration-sayyid-saeed-akhtar-rizvi/sunni-attitude

# Abraham's God after Four Thousand Years

# Conclusion

From the first moment of thought, humans have beseeched the unseen for solace from the terrors of nature. The unseen roamed with human tribes and became their gods as man settled in the first cities. From that dawn of civilization, humans built temples and altars to the gods to bring reason and meaning to the events of life and death. In one of those first cities 4000 years ago, the voice of one man's God was heard. Abraham began a journey with his God across civilized existence as millions of humans joined in the caravan that has reached our 21st century. Abraham's God has been heard in the dreams and seen in the visions of many as Abraham's God became the God of the Jews, Christians, and Muslims.

*Abram was seventy and five years old* (Gen. 12:4) when he traveled to Palestine. His God had promised to *make of thee a great nation...and make thy name great.* Four thousand years later, those promises have been kept. Abraham has nations of descendants and His name is ever present as His religions fight to control the hearts and minds of humanity.

Abraham's God is the God of Christianity, once in total control of Western civilization. He is the God of Islam, now in control of North Africa across the Middle East and central Asia to the Indonesian Archipelago. He was always the God of Judaism, a people strewn across the lands of both Christianity and Islam.

The nebulous messages left with a few, brought to the masses comfort and direction, but also centuries of divide, hatred, and the horrors of war. Disputes of doctrinal discord within and between Judaism, Christianity, and Islam created conflict as human egos proclaimed, *We are right, and you are wrong!* When stripped of that ego, the beliefs of Jews, Christians, and Muslims are one, like their One God.

| | Judaism | Christianity | Islam |
|---|:---:|:---:|:---:|
| Abraham's God, Creator of all | ✓ | ✓ | ✓ |
| Sinful Humans with an everlasting soul | ✓ | ✓ | ✓ |
| Forgiveness of sins | ✓ | ✓ | ✓ |
| Emissary from God to End Time | ✓ | ✓ | ✓ |
| Last Judgement | ✓ | ✓ | ✓ |
| Heaven and Hell | ✓ | ✓ | ✓ |

Beyond these essentials of belief, each claims the absolute perfection of the details of fervent faith, while rejecting with hostility the faith of others. The disagreement on details has caused untold gruesome misery and become a barrier to the peaceful progress of humanity. Truly, it is the Devil that is in all those details. He just may have sent that goat!

Over ten thousand years ago, our human ancestors saw the sun and the stars, the storms and seasons, life and death. Like them, you wake up every morning and see the sun rise in the east and every evening watch it set in the west. What could be more obvious than the "fact" that the Sun revolves around the Earth? You see the that Sun going around you every day, yet you totally believe and accept that it is the Earth that revolves around the Sun. Why would you overrule the sights before your eyes?

Have you personally observed the stellar parallax or the phases of Venus or measured the angular size of the Moon and the Sun?[1056] No, I am sure you have not. But from the time you were a child, you heard others say countless times that the Earth revolves around the Sun. Everyone said that the Earth revolves around the sun. Despite the evidence of your eyes, you believe it. Almost all people come to their religious beliefs in that same way.

From the earliest childhood, people are told a belief. And it is repeated countless times as your family and community join in confirming that belief. And you read that belief from a what others told you was a holy book. Throughout life, you participate in the rituals and teachings of that belief and succumb to a lifetime of belief and participation in the religion of that belief. And if that religion is the only one in the society, those beliefs become a self-reinforcing cycle across generations.

We have no telescopes or stellar parallax or angular shift with which to confirm any of those beliefs. Our only telescope is one which can look backwards to examine the origins and history of those beliefs. Our telescope of history allows us to examine, to see, which of those details of faith are worthy of our continued belief. Or perhaps show us that everything is not exactly what we have been repeatedly told.

When Galileo took his telescope to the Catholic Christian Church in Rome, he was shocked to learn that they had no interest in his evidence that the Earth was the not the center of existence. Worse, he was forced to admit and recant the evidence of his telescope. Religion is faith that does not choose to be examined, much less confronted by evidence from the telescope of history.

Pastor Oldsen told me so many years ago, "Some things just have to be accepted on faith." Accept faiths that burn people at

---

[1056] These are all ways used by early astronomers to show the heliocentric model, prior to the modern telescopes and satellites.

the stake, or cut off heads, or fly into buildings, or detonate bombs, or pull triggers, or send innocent children to death at a fence in Gaza? Are those faiths worth accepting?

The bedrock of all faith in Judaism, Christianity, and Islam is that the God of the universe spoke to Abraham 4000 years ago. The details of those faiths are a matter of whether God also spoke to Moses, Paul, or Muhammad.

So far, our telescope has looked back into the religions of Abraham's God to see their history and the origins of their religious beliefs. Wherever our telescope pointed, we saw nothing of Abraham until around the time of King David— nothing whatsoever of the rich history of oral stories told to Abraham's descendants, which were written much later. We did see that even when the Israelite family came into view, they were pagan polytheists, accepting Abraham's God as one of many. Only at the time that the Israelite tribes are destroyed and taken to Babylon do we see the Israelite monotheism behind the opaque filter of their Zoroastrian masters. Our historical telescope still detects no signs of souls extending into another life. Only after 200 BC do we see that humans with a soul that survives death has been accepted by some in Judaism, and ideas of a last judgement and a heaven and hell are beginning to intermingle from the Zoroastrian and Greek beliefs found in the surrounding areas.

Things are becoming much clearer by the birth of Jesus. Some Jews certainly believe in an afterlife, a messiah, a last judgement, and an eternal heaven and hell. But not all, as the Jewish Sadducees cling to the ancient Jewish concept of one life, from dust to dust.

Our telescope has shown us clearly how, over the centuries, the theological fundamentals of the Abrahamic religions had finally come into place. That there is one God, who created Heaven and Earth, and humans with an eternal soul. That God will send an emissary to end time, resurrect the dead, and judge all by their deeds and beliefs before consigning each to an eternity of punishment or paradise. After this, it is all about the damming details.

Muhammad and Jesus both began religious movements, one in Galilee the other in Arabia. Jesus died before his movement was unified. Religions based on Jesus' life competed for three centuries, attempting to find a unified message. When that struggle affected the unity of the Roman Empire, it was resolved by a political process that imposed a unified religious message. Paul said God spoke to him, and it was essentially his set of details that won out for Christianity as Jesus was decreed God.

For Christians, this is hypercritical, and not a detail. Within the context of the Abrahamic theology, Jesus as a God is not an essential issue, but a detail within the process of redemption. All other theological elements are the same. As we have seen, Jesus as God creates multiple layers of complexity that tied Christianity in an unsolvable knot. Muhammad cut the Gordian knot that neither Constantine nor Theodosius had managed to untangle.

Jesus preached his message to humanity for only a couple of years. We cannot know how he would have refined his Gospel had he lived longer. Muhammad, however, lived to refine his religious message and intertwine it within a political movement that unified Arabia. While Jesus said, "Render under to Caesar the things that are Caesar's," laying the groundwork for the separation of Church and State, Muhammad integrated the Church and State in the theocracy of Islam. This alone is an irresolvable tension between the Western and Islamic systems that will fuel the clash of civilizations for at least another century.

By the 9th century, Islam and Christianity each had a strong set of spiritual beliefs universally proclaimed and embedded in the cultures of their realm. Each had deep institutional structures—of clergy, churches, mosques, monasteries, schools, and abbeys. Each had strong secular institutions that could enforce their beliefs. Each had powers to appoint emperors and caliphs, kings and dukes, emirs and sultans. Each had its own extremely profitable edifice of property and donations. And while skirmishes would continue, both Roman Catholic Western civilization and Islamic civilization no longer faced existential threats at their borders, from each other or from foreign invaders. Islam and Christianity would each be a hegemony for many centuries to come.

If Abraham had come back in 800 AD / 178AH, would he recognize the religions he started? Religions built on the fear of failure in this life would condemn your human soul to eternal torture in another life? Religions that used that fear to exert control and enforce obedience in this life for the promise of the reward of eternal ecstasy in another life? Would Abraham recognize his God in those religions? Or would he see Abraham's Devil?

That is the title of the next book. *Abraham's Devil: The History of Evil in Judaism, Christianity, and Islam and the Effects on the 21st Century.* It will tell the story of the religions of Abraham's God from the 9th through the 21st centuries. Having settled on man's relationship with God, the religions of Abraham's God, especially Christianity would focus on the relationship with evil, setting the stage for the cultural chaos of our times.

Hopefully some things of faith are clearer now, and they will be much clearer later.

# Sources

Burwell v. Hobby Lobby Stores, Inc. 573 U.S. ___. 2014.

The Nationality Act of 1940, 8 U.S.C.A. § 703

EYVINE HEARN and NASHALA HEARN, a minor, suing through her next friend, EYVINE HEARN, Plaintiffs, UNITED STATES OF AMERICA, Plaintiff-Intervenor, v. MUSKOGEE PUBLIC SCHOOL DISTRICT 020; et al., Defendants. C.A. No.: CIV 03-598-S

Ahmad bin Hanbal, Musnad. "The Sunni Attitude." *Al*, 29 Nov. 2013, www.al-islam.org/Qur'an-its-protection-alteration-sayyid-saeed-akhtar-rizvi/sunni-attitude.

"'I was tossed out of the tribe': climate scientist Judith Curry interviewed by David Rose The Spectator 28 November 2015

*1177 BC: The Year Civilization Collapsed*, Eric H Cline Princeton University Press 2014

*9-11 Commission Report,* National Commission on Terrorist Attacks upon the United States Government Printing Office 2004

*A Commentary on Daniel*, Leon J. Wood, Wipf and Stock 1998

*A Concise History of the Middle East,* Arthur Goldschmidt Jr. Westview Press 7th Edition 2001

"A Great United Monarchy? Archaeological and Historical Perspectives" Israel Finkelstein One *God - One Cult - One Nation, Archaeological and Biblical Perspectives* Ed. by Kratz, Reinhard G. / Spieckermann, Hermann De Gruyter Publishers 2010.

*A History of Christian Muslim Relations"* Hugh Goddard Rowan & Littlefield 2000

*A History of Christian Theology: An Introduction,* William C. Placher (Westminster Press, 1983)

*A History of Christianity*, Paul Johnson (Simon & Schuster a Touchstone Book, 1995)

*A History of God the 4,000 - Year Quest of Judaism, Christianity and Islam* Karen Armstrong Knopf 1994

*A History of the Jewish People in the Time of Jesus Christ*, Emil Schurer T& T Clark 1890

*A History of the Jews*, Paul Johnson Harper Perennial 1988

*A History of the World,* Hugh Thomas, (Harper and Row)

*A History of Zoroastrianism: Volume II: Under the Achaemenians* Mary Boyce (E.J. Brill 1982)

*A New History of Early Christianity*, Charles Freeman (Yale University Press, 2009) "A Sling and a Prayer" *New York Times Review of Books*, June 14th 2000 the review of "King David" Steven L. McKenzie Oxford University Press.

*A Study of History*, Arnold J. Toynbee (Oxford University Press, 1957)

*Adam and Eve and the Serpent: Sex and Politics in Early Christianity* Elaine Pagels First Vintage Books 1989

"An Anthology of Imam Khomeini's Speeches, Messages, Interviews, Decrees, Religious Permissions, and Letters" Volume

10 September 17, 1979 - November 7, 1979 *The Institute for Compilation and Publication of Imam Khomeini's Works*

*An Introduction to the New Testament*, Raymond E. Brown, First edition (Yale University Press, 2010)

*An Introduction to the New Testament and the Origins of Christianity* Delbert Burkett (Cambridge Press 2002)

*An Introduction to the New Testament: History, Literature, Theology* M. Eugene Boring (John Knox Press. 2012) p.587

"Archaeologists Discover that Earliest Known Arabic Writing Was Penned by a Christian" Sam Bostrom https://www.ancient-origins.net/news-history-archaeology/archaeologists-discover-earliest-known-arabic-writing-was-penned-christian-020778

"Artaxerxes II King of Persia" https://www.britannica.com/biography/Artaxerxes-II

"Away in a Manger . . . or Under a Palm Tree?" Mustafa Akyol *New York Times* 12/21/2017 Opinion Section

Babylon: Mesopotamia and the Birth of Civilization Paul Kriwaczek (Thomas Dunne Books 2012)

*Bible in the British Museum: Interpreting The Evidence* T.C. Mitchell (The British Museum Press 2014)

*Biblical Origins: An Adapted Legacy* Petros Koutoupis (Virtualbookworm Publishing Inc 2008)

*Blasphemy: Verbal Offense Against the Sacred, from Moses to Salman Rushdie* Leonard Williams Levy (UNC Press Books, 1995)

*Bound in Venice: The Serene Republic and the Dawn of the Book*, Alessandro Marzo Magno (Europa Editions, 2013)

*Caesar and Christ* (The Story of Civilization, vol. III) Will and Ariel Durant, (MJF Books, 1944)

Canaanite Myth and the Hebrew Epic Frank Moore Cross (Harvard University Press 1973)

"Catechism of the Catholic Church" Part One Section Two The Credo http://www.vatican.va/archive/ccc_css/archive/catechism/credo.htm

"Cathedral Age" Midsummer 2012 Edition

*Christianity: The First Three Thousand Years,* Diarmaid MacClulloch (Viking, 2010)

*Eusebius: The Church History*, translation by Paul L. Maier (Kregel, 1999)   translated by Rev. Arthur Cushman McGiffert

*City of God* Augustine http://biblehub.com/library/augustine/anti-Pelagian_writings/chapter_11_ix_an_objection_of.htm#1

*Civilizations: Culture, Ambition, and the Transformation of Nature* Felipe Fernandez-Armestopp (Free Press 2001)

*Concepts of Monotheism in Islam and Christianity* edited by Hans Kochler Braumueller, 1982. The Arabian Background of Monotheism in Islam. Sheikh Ibramhim al-Qattan/Mahmud A. Ghul

*Constantine the Emperor*, David Potter (Oxford University Press, 2013)

"Continuity and Admixture in the Last Five Millennia of Levantine History from Ancient Canaanite and Present-Day Lebanese Genome Sequences" Marc Haber, Claude Doumet-Serhal,et al 'The American Journal of Human Genetics', Volume 101, Issue 2, July 27, 2017

"Cosmos, Chaos and the World to Come" Norman Cohn (Yale University Press, 1993)

"Crime in Chicago" http://crime.chicagotribune.com/chicago/homicides

*Cults Religion and Violence* David Bromley J Gordon Melton (Cambridge University Press)

*Diplomacy* Henry Kissinger (Simon and Shuster 1994)

"Divino Afflante Spiritu" Encyclical of Pope Pius XII http://w2.vatican.va/content/pius-xii/en/encyclicals/documents/hf_p-xii_enc_30091943_divino-afflante-spiritu.html
*Documents of the Christian Church* Henry Bettenson *(Oxford University Press 1967*

*Early History of the Christian Church: From Its Foundation to the End of the Fifth Century (Vol. 1)* Louis Duchesne (Lex de Leon Publishing, 1909
*Early Islam: A Critical Reconstruction Based on Contemporary Sources*, Edited by Karl-Heinz Ohlig (Prometheus, 2013) Prometheus Books, 2013

*"Elijah"* Emil G. Hirsch, Eduard König, Solomon Schechter, Louis Ginzberg, M. Seligsohn, Kaufmann Kohler Jewish Encyclopedia 1906 http://www.jewishencyclopedia.com/articles/5634-elijah

"Erdogan's Vision: Uniting an 'Army of Islam' to Destroy Israel in 10 Days" Yeni Safak, The Turkish Daily as translated and published in the Middle East Media Research March 7th, 2018

"European Prehistory A Survey" Milisauskas, Sarunas editors, Springer Science & Business

Media 2011
*Eusebius: The Church History*, translation by Paul L. Maier (Kregel, 1999)

*Feet of Clay: Saints, Sinners and Madmen: A Study of Gurus*, Anthony Storr (The Free Press 1996)
*Food of the Gods* Terrence McKenna (Bantam New Age 1992)

*Forged: Writing in the Name of God - Why the Bibles Authors Are Not Who We Think* Bart D Ehrman (Harper Collins 2011)

*Giordano Bruno: Philosopher / Heretic* Ingrid D. Rowland (University of Chicago Press 2008)

"Gobekli Tepe: The World's First Temple" Andrew Curry *Smithsonian Magazine* November 2008 http://www.smithsonianmag.com/history/gobekli-tepe-the-worlds-first-temple-83613665/

*God's Crucible: Islam and the Making of Europe, 570-1215*, David Levering (Lewis Norton, 2008)

*Hadith: Muhammad's Legacy in the Medieval and Modern World* (Foundations of Islam) Jonathan A. C. Brown (One World, 2009)

"Hannifiyya and Ka'ba an inquiry into the Arabian pre-Islamic background of din Ibrahim" Uri

Rubin Jerusalem Studies in Arabic and Islam Jan 13, 1990

*History of European Morals* William Lecky (Longman Green & Co 1913) https://archive.org/stream/historyof europea0leckuoft#page/40/mode/2 up/search/circumcelliones
*History of the Christian Church Complete Eight Volumes in One* Philip Schaff Union Theological Seminary 1890

*History of the World* Hugh Thomas (Harper and Row 1979)

*Holy Bones, Holy Dust* Charles Freeman (Yale University Press 2011)

*How Jesus Became Christian* Barrie Wilson Phd, (St Martin Press 2008)

*How Jesus Became God: The Exaltation of a Jewish Preacher from Galilee*, Bart D. Ehrman, (Harper One, 2014)

*How the Mind Works* Steven Pinker (WW Norton and Company 1997)
"How Unique was Israelite Prophecy" by Jonathan Stokl in The Wiley-Blackwell *History of Jews and Judaism* Edited by Alan T. Levenson Wiley-Blackwell 1988

"Hymns of Martrydom" by Prudentius at

http://thegingerbeardman.blogspot. com/2012/08/sancte-laurentius-ora-pro-nobis.html

*In Search of Zarathustra, the First Prophet and the Ideas that Changed the World* Paul Kriwaczek (Alfred A Knopf 2003)

*In the Shadow of the Sword: The Birth of Islam and the Rise of Global Arab Empire,* Tom Holland (Doubleday, 2012)

*Interpretation A Bible Commentary for Teaching and Preaching First and Second Chronicles* Steven S Tuell (John Knox Press 2001)
*Islam: A Short History*, Karen Armstrong (Modern Library, 2000)

"Islam and the Afterlife' Life After Death: A History of the Afterlife in Western Religion, Alan F. Segal (Doubleday, 2004)

"Islam, Judeo-Christianity and Byzantine Iconoclasm" Patricia Crone Ashgate Variorum 1980 https://www.hs.ias.edu/files/Crone _Articles/Crone_Islam_Judeo-Christianity_and_Byzantine_Icono clasm.pdf
"Jerusalem a Biography" Simon Sebag Montefiorie Alfred A Knopf 2011
*Jesus: A Life*, A. N. Wilson (W. W. Norton & Company, 2004)

"Jesus a Revolutionary Biography" John Dominic Crossan (Harper Collins 1994)

*Jesus of Nazareth from the Baptism in the Jordan to the Transfiguration* Joseph Ratzinger Pope Benedict XVI (Ignatius Press 2007)

*Jesus of Nazareth* Pope Benedict XVI Translated by Philip J Whitmore (Ignatius Press 2011)

*Jesus Wars: How Four Patriarchs, Three Queens, and Two Emperors Decided What Christians Would Believe for the Next 1,500 Years,* John Philip Jenkins (Harper One, 2010)

*Jesus* A.N. Wilson (Random House 2003)

*Jewish History of Early Christianity* Juan Marcos Bejarano Qutierrez (Yaron Publishing 2017)

*Jews God and History* Max, I Dimont edited by Ethel Dimont 50th Anniversary, 2nd Edition Signet Classics 1994

*John of Damascus, First Apologist to the Muslims: The Trinity and Christian Apologetics in the Early Islamic Period,* Daniel J. Janosik (Pickwick Publications, 2016) 2016

*Josephus The Essential Writings* Paul L. Maier Kregel Publications 1988

"Last words of a terrorist" The *Guardian* 9/30/2011 https://www.theguardian.com/world/2001/sep/30/terrorism.september113

Life After Death - A History of the Afterlife in Western Religion Alan F Segal (Double Day 2004)

*Lives of the Popes: Illustrated Biographies of Every Pope From St Peter to the Present* Walsh, Michael J. Salamander (Books 1998)

*Lost Christianites the Battle for Scripture and Faiths We Never Knew* Bart D Ehrman Oxford University Press 2003

*Lost Scriptures: Books that Did Not Make It into the New Testament* Bart D Ehrman Oxford University Press 2003

"Mecca on the Caravan Routes in Pre-Islamic Antiquity" Mikhail D. Bukharin from *"The Qur'an in Context: Historical and Literary Investigations into the Qur'anic Milieu"* Edited by Angelika Neuwirth Nicolai Sinai Michael Marx Leiden Boston 2010

"Mike Wallace Interview of Drew Pearson" 12/7/57 http://www.hrc.utexas.edu/multimedia/video/2008/wallace/pearson_drew.html

*Milestones* Sayyid Qutb Edited by A.B. al-Mehri (Maktabah Book Sellers and Publishers 2006)

*Misquoting Jesus: The Story Behind Who Changed the Bible and Why* Bart D. Erdman (Harper One 2005)

*Mohammed and Mohammedanism* S.W. Koelle (Rivingtons 1889)
*Muhammad His Life Based on the Earliest Sources* Martin Lings (Inner Traditions 2006)
"Muslim Population in the Americas: 1950 -2020" Houssain Kettani International Journal of Environmental Science and Development, Vol. 1, No. 2, June 2010

*MythMaker Paul and the Invention of Christianity* Hyam Maccoby (Barnes and Noble 1998)

*Nag Hammadi Gnosticism and Early Christianity* Edited by Charles W. Hedrick and Robert Hodgson, Jr. (Hendrickson Publishing 1986)

*New Researches on the Qur'an: Why and How Two Versions of Islam Entered the History of Mankind,* Dr. Seyed Mostafa Azmayesh Mehraby Publishing House 2015

*No God but God; The Origins Evolution and Future of Islam* Reza Aslan (Random House 2011)

"Oldest Arabic inscription provides missing link between Nabatean and Arabic writing" April Holloway
http://www.ancient-origins.net/news-general/oldest-arabic-inscription-provides-missing-link-between-nabatean-and-arabic-writing

*Pagan Christs* J.M. Robertson (University Books Inc, 1966)

*Palestinian Identity: the construction of modern national consciousness* Rashid Khalidi (Columbia University Press 1998)

*Paul and Jesus: How the Apostle Transformed Christianity,* James T. Tabor *(*Simon and Schuster, 2012)

*Paul: The Mind of the Apostle* A. N. Wilson, (W. W. Norton & Co. 1997)

"Rachel Armstrong Accused Of Beating Grandmother Angela Armstrong Whom She Thought Was Possessed" David Moye *The Huffington Post* 12/05/2012
http://www.huffingtonpost.com/2012/12/05/rachel-armstrong-beat-angela-armstrong_n_2246505.html

*Racial Separation* Malcolm X, in "Civil Rights: Great Speeches in History" Jill Karson, ed. Greenhaven Press, 2003

"Sahih Ahih M Muslim" translated by Abd-al-Hamid Siddiqui edited by Mika'il al-Almany 2009
https://d1.islamhouse.com/data/en/ih_books/single/en_Sahih_Muslim.pdf

*Sahih al-Bukhari* translated by Dr. M. Muhsin Khan
http://sunnah.com/bukhari
"Saudi Time Bomb."
http://www.pbs.org/wgbh/pages/frontline/shows/saudi/
"Scholars Are Quietly Offering New Theories of the Koran" Alexander Stille *The New York Times* March 2, 2002
Sirah al-Halabiyyah p 275-276 as

quoted in *The Priest and the Prophet* Joseph Azzi (Pen Publishers 2005)

*Social History of Western Civilization Vol I* Third Edition by Richard M Golden (St, Martins 2003)

"Spirituality and Hearing Voices" Simon McCarthy Jones, Amanda Waegeli and John Watkins; *Psychosis* October 5th, 2013 Published on line 2013 Oct 23. doi: 10.1080/17522439.2013.831945

*St. Paul: The Apostle We Love to Hate*, Karen Armstrong (Icons Series) (New Harvest, 2015)

"Summers remarks on women draw fire" Marcella Bombardieri, January 17, 2005 *Boston Globe*

"Tafhim al-Qur'an - The Meaning of the Qur'an" Sayyid Abul Ala Maududi https://www.Qur'an411.com

*Teachings of Presidents of the Church:* Joseph Smith (The Church of Latter Day Saints of Jesus Christ 2007)

"Tension in a Michigan City Over Muslims' Call to Prayer" John Leland *New York Times* May 5, 2004
*The Age of Faith: The Story of Civilization, Volume IV* Will Durant (MJF Books 1949)
"The Ancient Roots of Disney's Blockbuster Film 'Frozen'" Stephanie Castellano June 1, 2014

https://antiquitynow.org/2014/06/03/the-ancient-roots-of-disneys-blockbuster-film-frozen/

"The Aniconic Tradition" Brian B Schmidt *The Triumph of Elohim From Yahwisms to Judahisms* edited by Diana V. Edelman (Kok Pharos Publishing 1995)

*The Antiquities of the Jews* Josephus Translated by William Whiston (Wilder Publications 2009)

"The Appearance of a Pantheon in Judah" Lowell K Handy *The Triumph of Elohim From Yahwisms to Judahisms* Diana V Edelman (ed) (Kok Pharos Publishing 1995)

*The Ascent of Man* J. Bronowski (Little Brown & Co 1973)

*The Bible in the British Museum* T.C. Mitchell (British Museum Press 1988)

*The Birth of Christianity: Discovering What Happened in the Years Immediately After the Execution of Jesus*, John Dominic Crossan (Harper San Francisco, 1999)

*The Birth of Writing* Robert Claiborne (Time Life Books1974)

*The Book of Miracles* Kenneth L Woodward (Touchstone 2001)

*The Brain* Richard M. Restak, MD (Warner Books 1980)

*The Brother of Jesus and the Lost Teachings of Christianity,* Jeff J. Butz, (Inner Traditions/Bear and Company, 2005)

"The Catechism of the Catholic Church" Part 1, Section 2, Chapter 2 Article 3 Number 467
"The Church of the Seat of Mary (Kathisma)" R. Avner on behalf of the Israel Antiquities Authority.
http://www.israel.org/MFA/IsraelExperience/History/Pages/TheChurchoftheSeatofMary-Kathisma-.aspx

*The Clash of Civilizations and the Remaking of World Order.* Samuel P Huntington (Simon & Shuster 1996)

"Which Koran? Variants, Manuscripts and Linguistics" Ibn Warraq from *The Collection of the Koran* (Prometheus Books 2011)

*The Crusades The Authoritative History of the War for the Holy Land* Thomas Asbridge (Harper Collins 2010)

"The Danish cartoonist who survived an axe attack" Marie Louise Sjølie The *Guardian* January 4 2010
https://www.theguardian.com/world/2010/jan/04/danish-cartoonist-axe-attack
*The Darkening Age: The Christian*

*Destruction of the Classic World,* Catherine Nixey (Pan MacMillan, 2017)
"The Digital Dead Sea Scrolls: The Great Isaiah Scroll"
http://dss.collections.imj.org.il/isaiah

*A Dictionary of Christian Beliefs: A Reference Guide to More Than 700 Topics Discussed by the Early Church Fathers*, edited by David W. Bercott (Henrickson, 1998)

"The Dome of the Rock in Light of the Development of Concentric Martyria in Jerusalem" Rina Avner Muquarnas *Architecture and Architectural Iconography Vol. 27*" (Brill Publishers 2010)

*The Dotting of A Script And The Dating Of An Era: The Strange Neglect Of PERF 558* Alan Jones *Islamic Culture, LXXII, No. 4 1998*

The End of History and the Last Man Francis Fukuyama (Free Press 1992)

The Evolution of God, Robert Wright (Little Brown and Company, 2009)

*The Final Philosophy: Or, System of Perfectible Knowledge Issuing from the Harmony of Science and Religion* Charles Woodruff Shields, DD, *Scribner, Armstrong & Co 1877* Republished by Arkose Press in 2015

*The First Cities* Dora Jane Hamblin (Time Life Books 1973)

*The First Paul: Reclaiming the Radical Visionary Behind the Church's Conservative Icon*, Marcus J. Borg and John Dominic Crossan, (Harper One, 2009)

*The Five Gospels, The Search for the Authentic Words of Jesus* Robert W. Funk, Roy W. Hoover, and the Jesus Seminar (Harper SanFrancisco 1998)

"The Future of World Religions: Population Growth Projections, 2010-2050" *The Pew Forum on Religion & Public Life*. Pew Research center. April 2, 2015

"The Gaza Protests" Rich Lowry *National Review* May 14th, 2018

*Gospels The Gnostic* Elaine Pagels (Vintage Press 1979)

The Golden Bough Sir James George Frazer (Simon and Schuster 1996)

*The Great Transformation: The Beginning of Our Religious Traditions* Karen Armstrong (Alfred A Knoff 2006)

*The Hellenistic Age* Peter Thonemann (Oxford University Press 2016)

*The Hidden Origins of Islam: New Research into Its Early History*, edited by Karl-Heinz Ohlig and Gerd-R. Puin, (Prometheus Books, 2010)

*The Historical Figure of Jesus*, E. P. Sanders (Penguin Books, 1993).

*The Historical Jesus life of a Mediterranean Jewish Peasant* John Dominic Crossan (Harper Collins 1992)

*The History of God: The 4,000-Year Quest of Judaism, Christianity and Islam* Karen Armstrong (Alfred A Knopf 1994)

*The History of Religion* Karen Farrington (Barnes and Noble 2001)

*The History of the Decline and Fall of the Roman Empire* Edward Gibbon, (Fred de Fau and Co. 1906)

*The History of the Devil* Dr. Paul Carus (Dover Edition, 2008 as originally published by The Open Court Publishing Company of Chicago in 1900)

*The History of the Medieval World* Susan Wise Bauer (W.W. Norton 2010)

*The History of the Qur'an* Ingrid Mattson (Wiley Blackwell, 2nd Edition 2013)

*The History of the World* Hugh Thomas (Harper and Row 1979)

"The House of Abraham and the House of Amram: Genealogy, Patriarchal Authority, and Exegetical Professionalism"

Angelika Neuwirth in "*The Qur'an in Context: Historical and Literary Investigations into the Qur'anic Milieu*" Edited by Angelika Neuwirth Nicolai Sinai Michael Marx (Leiden Boston Brill 2010)

*The Infancy Narratives of Jesus of Nazareth* Pope Benedict the XVI, Joseph Ratzinger (Image 2012)

*The Invention of God* Thomas Romer, translated by Raymond Geuss (Harvard University Press 2015)

*The Islamic Jesus: How the King of the Jews Became a Prophet of the Muslims* Mustafa Akylol (St. Martin Press 2017)

*The Jewish Encyclopedia* Emil G. Hirsch, Eduard König, Solomon Schechter, Louis Ginzberg, M. Seligsohn, (Kaufmann Kohler 1906 V:5)

*The Jewish People and Their Sacred Scriptures in the Christian Bible* Charles H Miller (Biblical Theology Bulletin 35 (2005): 34-39 http://www.ccjr.us/dialogika-resources/primary-texts-from-the-history-of-the-relationship/249-roman-laws

*The Jews in the Time of Jesus: An Introduction*, Stephen M. Wylen (Paulist Press, 1996)

*The Life of Constantine* Eusebius Tanslated by Averil Cameron and Stuart G. Hall (larendon Press 1999)

*The Life of Mahomet* William Muir 3rd Edition Indian reprint 1992, as quoted in "The Hidden Origins of Islam"

*The Life of Muhammad a translation of Ishaq's Sirat Rasul Allah* by A. Guillaume (Oxford University Press 1955)

*The Life of Muhammad* Rev. Canon Sell (Christian Literature Society 1913)

*The Lost Gospel: The Book of Q and Christian Origins*, Burton L. Mack, (Harper Collins, 1993)

*The Lost History of Christianity,* Philip Jenkins (Harper One, 2008)

*The Middle East a Brief History of the Last 2000 Years* Bernard Lewis (Scribner 1995)

"The most comprehensive guide to mosques and schools" Salatomatic https://www.salatomatic.com/sub/United-States/Indiana/North-Indiana/Lv9hETT8bH

*The Muslim Discovery of Europe* Bernard Lewis (WW Norton 2001)

*The Mysteries of Mithras: The Pagan Belief That Shaped the Christian World* Payam Nabarz (Inner Traditions 2005)

*The Mythmaker Paul and the Invention of Christianity* Hyman Maccoby (Barnes and Noble Books 1998)

*The New Encyclopedia of Islam*
*4th Edition* Cyril Glasse (Rowman
& Littlefield 2013)

*The New Jerome Biblical
Commentary* edited by Raymond
Brown, Joseph Fitzmyer, and
Roland Murphy (Prentice-Hall,
1990)

*The New Oxford Annotated Bible
with Apocrypha: New Revised
Standard Version* General editor:
Michael Coogan, Edited by Marc
Brettler, Carol Newsom, and
Pheme Perkins (Oxford University
Press. 2018)

"The Online Catholic
Encyclopedia"
http://www.newadvent.org/cathen/
05692b.htm
*The Origin of Satan: How
Christians Demonized Jews,
Pagans, and Heretics*, Elaine
Pagels (Vintage Books, 1996)

*The Penguin History of the Church*
Henry Chadwick (Penguin Books
1993)

"The Penn Law School Mob
Scores a Victory" Heather Mac
Donald *Wall Street Journal* March
18, 2018

*The Preservation of the Qur'an*
Samuel Green
http://www.answering-
islam.org/Green/uthman.htm

*The Priest and the Prophet* Joseph
Azzi (Pen Publishers, 2005)

The Quest: Revealing the Temple
Mount in Jerusalem Leen Ritmeyer
(Hendrikson Publishing 2006)

*The Qur'an as Process* Nicolai
Sinai (Leiden -Boston Brill 2010)

"The religion of the Magi was
fundamentally that of Zoroaster"
Catholic Encyclopedia
http://www.newadvent.org/cathen/
09527a.htm.

*The Rise of Christianity: How the
Obscure, Marginal Jesus
Movement Became the Dominant
Religious Force in the Western
World in a Few Centuries,* Rodney
Stark (Harper Collins, 1997)

"The Role of Isnad in the
Preservation of the Islamic
Civilisation" Kamal Abu Zahra
Tuesday, JUNE 12, 2007
http://islamicsystem.blogspot.com/
2007/06/role-of-isnad-in-
preservation-of.html

*The Search for the Christian
Doctrine of God* R.C.P. Hanson
(Baker Academic 2005)

*The Seven Ecumenical Councils*,
Henry Robert Percival (Veritas
Splendor Publications, 2013)

*The Social Conquest of Earth*
Edward O Wilson (Liveright 2012)

*The Story of the Jews: Finding the
Words 1000 BC to 1492 AD*,
Simon Schama (Harper Collins,
2013)

Sources

*The Story of the Qur'an: Its History and Place in Muslim Life*, Ingrid Mattson (Wiley Blackwell, 2nd Edition, 2013)

*The Story of Writing* Andrew Robinson (Thanmes and Hudson 2001)

"The Supreme Court, 1972 Term-Foreword: Toward a Model of Roles in the Due Process of Life and Law," Laurence H. Tribe, *Harvard Law Review 1, 7 (1973)*

*The Triumph of Elohim From Yahwisms to Judahisms* Diana V Edelman (ed) (Kok Pharos Publishing 1995)

The Wars of the Jews Josephus Translated by William Whiston (Wilder Publications 2019)

*World Religions: From Ancient History to the Present*, Geoffrey Parrinder, editor, (Facts on File Publications, 1984)

"To Helena" Edgar Allen Poe

*Twenty Decisive Battles of the World* Lt Col Joseph B Mitchell and Sir Edward Creasy (Konecky & Konecky 1964)

What are the Sacred Roots of Islam Jamil Effarah (AuthorHouse 2016)

"When did the consonantal skeleton of the Qur'an reach closure? Part II" Nicolai Sinai Bulletin *of the School of Oriental and African Studies* May 2014

*When Jesus Became God: The Struggle to Define Christianity during the Last Days of Rome*, Richard E. Rubenstein (Harcourt, 1999)

*Which Koran? Variants, Manuscripts and Linguistics* Ibn Warraq (Prometheus Books 2011)

*Who Wrote the Bible?* Richard Elliot Friedman (Perennial Library 1987)
*Who wrote the New Testament The Making of the Christian* Myth Burton L Mack (Harper Collins 1996)

*Why Did Europe Conquer the World?* Philip T. Hoffman (Princeton University Press 2015)

"Gaza deaths are fault of Hamas" *NEW YORK DAILY NEWS* Thursday, May 17, 2018

*World Religions from Ancient History to the Present* Geoffery Parrinder (Hamlyn Publishing Ltd 1971)

"WUSSY Mag Wants Queer Voices Heard Around The World" Miranda Hawkins June 13, 2018 NPR

*Zealot: The Life and Times of Jesus* of Nazareth Reza Aslan (Random House Paperback Edition 2014)

*Zoroastrians: Their Religious Beliefs and Practices* Mary Boyce, (Routledge 1979)

# Index